*Natives and Newcomers:*
*Canada's "Heroic Age" Reconsidered*

# Natives and Newcomers

## Canada's "Heroic Age" Reconsidered

BRUCE G. TRIGGER

McGill-Queen's University Press
Kingston and Montreal

© McGill-Queen's University Press 1985
ISBN 0-7735-0594-6

Legal deposit third quarter 1985
Bibliothèque nationale du Québec

Printed in Canada

This book has been published with the help of a
grant from the Social Science Federation of Canada,
using funds provided by the Social Sciences
and Humanities Research Council of Canada.

---

**Canadian Cataloguing in Publication Data**

Trigger, Bruce G.
    Natives and newcomers
    Includes bibliographical references and index.
    ISBN 0-7735-0594-6
    1. Indians of North America – Canada – History.
    2. Indians of North America – Canada – First
    contact with Occidental civilization. 3. Canada –
    History – To 1663 (New France). I. Title.
    E78.C2T75 1985      971'.00497      C85-098938-8

---

*To T.F. McIlwraith*
*1899–1964*
*In Memoriam*

# Contents

# Illustrations

# Preface

This book is intended not simply as another account of the "Heroic Age" of Canadian history (the period from European discovery to 1663, which is often wrongly stated to be overstudied and exhausted), but as a re-examination of the framework within which the whole of Canadian history must be considered. I will argue that the findings of archaeology and social anthropology must be taken fully into consideration to understand the role played by native people and also to achieve what has long been ethnocentrically regarded as the primary goal of Canadian historical scholarship: explaining how people of European origin have interacted with one another to shape the development of Canada. These arguments will be illustrated by a case study of relations between the French and the Iroquoian-speaking peoples of eastern North America.

The present work examines essentially the same period and subject matter as did *The Children of Aataentsic*, published in 1976. One of my hopes in writing this book has been to communicate the findings of that massive study to a wider audience. More pressing reasons, however, justify this undertaking. Since 1976 research on the early history of Canada and on native peoples generally has proceeded at an accelerating pace. New data have been discovered and unanticipated problems have been identified. These findings required a review of my previous conclusions. The present work presents the results of my research and rethinking of issues since 1976. I do not offer conclusions as final answers (as I did in my previous work), but instead evaluate current knowledge about Indian-White relations in the St Lawrence lowlands during the sixteenth and seventeenth centuries and try to determine what kinds of problems must be investigated and what techniques employed if further progress is to be made.

My interests have also expanded to include not only relations among native peoples and between them and the Europeans who came to North America but also the way in which these relations influenced the behaviour of Europeans towards one another and shaped the early development of the colony of New France. It has become increasingly apparent that relations among the Europeans who lived and worked in New France cannot be understood independently of those between native peoples and Europeans. The scope of my research and my general perspectives are thus considerably wider than they formerly were.

More attention is paid to tracing the history of Iroquoian archaeology in chapter 2 than is assigned to recording the development of other branches of anthropology elsewhere in this book. Outmoded archaeological interpretations still have widespread currency among historians and the general public; hence the best method for conveying an understanding of the current state of research on Iroquoian prehistory is to review that subject historically. The need throughout this book to make the assumptions, methods, and limitations of various disciplines comprehensible to specialists in other fields as well as to the general reader has required the inclusion of material that will seem all too familiar to some. This problem is inherent in all attempts to further interdisciplinary understanding.

The term *St Lawrence lowlands*, as used in this book, designates the territories located immediately to the north and south of Lakes Erie and Ontario as well as the St Lawrence Valley as far downstream as Quebec. It includes all of southern Ontario. In keeping with internationally accepted usage, *Iroquois* refers only to the confederated Five Nations of upper New York State: the Mohawks, Oneidas, Onondagas, Cayugas, and Senecas. They were joined in the eighteenth century by the Tuscaroras from North Carolina to become the Six Nations. The term *Iroquoian* embraces the broader linguistic grouping to which these tribes as well as the Hurons, Petuns, Neutrals, Eries, Cherokees, and some other groupings belonged. *Algonkin* refers specifically to a tribal unit made up of smaller bands that lived in the Ottawa Valley and adjacent regions early in the seventeenth century, while *Algonkian* designates the widespread linguistic grouping that embraced Algonkins, Montagnais, Micmacs, Mahicans, and many other peoples.

I wish to thank Professor William N. Fenton for his detailed comments on the manuscript; Professor James Axtell for stimulating discussions in person and by letter; Professor Denys Dêlage for lending me a copy of his doctoral dissertation; Professor Anne

Ramenofsky for sending me copies of sections of her doctoral dissertation dealing with the Iroquois; and Mr J.B. Jamieson for his work as a research assistant in the spring of 1983 and for drawing the maps. The manuscript has been carefully typed by Katharine Timmins. The significance of the illustrations on the map *Novae Franciae Accurata Delineatio* was first recognized by Professor C.E. Heidenreich. My work was generously supported by sabbatical leave from McGill University and a Leave Fellowship of the Social Sciences and Humanities Research Council of Canada, both for the calendar year 1983. I am grateful to Audrey Hlady for her painstaking and helpful editing of the manuscript.

I also wish to acknowledge the stimulation that I have received as a result of working over the past nine years with graduate students in the Department of Anthropology at McGill University who are investigating various aspects of the prehistory of eastern Canada: Brian Deller, David Denton, Pierre Desrosiers, William Fitzgerald, Bruce Jamieson, Moira McCaffrey, Robert Pearce, David Smith, Peter Timmins, Alexander von Gernet, Gary Warrick, and Ronald Williamson. Through research and publications, each of these students has made significant contributions to the understanding of Canada's past. Collectively they have been a powerful antidote against complacency. I have noted in the text when I have used their findings.

I dedicate this book to the memory of Professor Thomas Forsyth McIlwraith, a McGill undergraduate and later a talented ethnographer who founded the Department of Anthropology at the University of Toronto and was its Head until his death in 1964. He more than anyone else can lay claim to being the founder of academic anthropology in Canada. I wish to express my gratitude for his kindness and encouragement when I was an undergraduate at the University of Toronto. It was also through his good offices that my first paper on the Hurons was published in 1960, a work from which the present study has evolved. Finally, this dedication is my personal atonement for the failure of his colleagues and students to publish the festschrift that was promised him in 1964.

*Natives and Newcomers*

## CHAPTER ONE

# The Indian Image in Canadian History

Since the 1960s Canadians have been challenged to come to terms with a new and rapidly changing social reality. For almost three centuries White North Americans had assumed that native peoples were doomed to be culturally assimilated or to perish as a superior European civilization spread inexorably across the continent. In accordance with such expectations, historians asserted that native people had always been few in number and had had so little impact on their environment that North America remained a virgin land at the time of European occupation. The evolutionary gulf that separated natives and newcomers was also thought to make it difficult, if not impossible, for the former to adopt a civilized style of life. Hence native people were treated as part of a vanishing past. They were seen as more akin to the forests in which they lived and the animals they hunted than as competitors for control of North America. This view also seemed to justify ignoring the political and economic developments that explain why, for over 150 years, native peoples have suffered from impoverishment, social discrimination, and a White tutelage that was often simultaneously neglectful and oppressive.

Yet today's realities reveal the error of such views. Throughout Canada native people are increasing rapidly in numbers, renewing pride in their ancestral heritage, and playing an ever more visible role in the nation's political, economic, and cultural life. In opposition to the dominant White society, they have affirmed their lasting and important role as part of Canada's cultural mosaic; a development clearly noted by Pope John Paul II during his visit to this country in 1984. Such changes in the status of native people challenge traditional interpretations of the past and require a more objective understanding of the role played by native peoples in Canadian history.

Historians generally acknowledge that their studies reveal as much about historians and their circumstances as they do about former times (Collingwood 1946; Berger 1970). The past as an object of historical investigation also becomes a hostage that can be used to serve the needs of the present. When historians champion diverse regional or sectarian causes, their biases contribute to a lively and colourful debate that often results in an improved understanding of the past. The situation is quite different, however, when over long periods most historians ignore important aspects of the past or adhere uncritically to a single viewpoint that reinforces rather than challenges conventional stereotypes. The present work seeks to demonstrate that Canadian historical studies as a whole have suffered from the chronic failure of historians and anthropologists to regard native peoples as an integral part of Canadian society. By means of a case study dealing with New France and its Iroquoian neighbours, I wish also to consider what approaches must be employed if the roles played by native peoples are to be understood sufficiently to permit a more comprehensive and objective treatment of Canadian history. That, in turn, requires a reconsideration of the relationship between history and anthropology.

## HISTORY AND ANTHROPOLOGY

Although historians are becoming more interested in native history and culture, the history of Canada as it relates to people who have come to North America – largely from Europe – since the sixteenth century continues to be viewed as fundamentally different from that involving native peoples. In universities the study of Canadian prehistory and of contemporary native peoples has traditionally been the subject matter of anthropology, while history departments have concentrated on understanding the activities of Canadians of European origin within the broader context of European history. This situation has been alleviated only to a limited degree by the development of interdisciplinary native studies programs (Price 1978).

The relationship between anthropology and history has never been a particularly comfortable one. Anthropologists, with their diverse commitments to excavating archaeological sites, measuring bones, and recording the ways of life of living peoples, and historians, with their dedication to archival research, find it difficult to understand each other's work. More fundamentally, however, both in Canada and elsewhere, the split between these two disciplines reflects the long-standing refusal of scholars to accept native peoples, whose ways of life they have viewed as primitive, unchanging, and inferior to their own, as adequate subjects for historical research. Anthropology was created in the nineteenth century as a separate discipline charged with studying peoples who lacked their own history. As recently as 1966 Hugh Trevor-Roper, the Regius Professor of Modern History at Oxford University, echoed this distinction when he claimed that Africa had no history prior to the era of European colonialism: "Perhaps, in the future, there will be some African history to teach. But at present there is none, or very little: there is only the history of the Europeans in Africa. The rest is largely darkness ... and darkness is not a subject for history ... [which is] essentially a form of ... purposive movement" (p. 9).

The persistence of this dichotomy between history and anthropology reflects the chronic failure of most Canadians to accept native people as being Canadians in the same sense that they extend this recognition to people of French, English, Ukrainian, or Japanese ancestry. Anthropologists and historians must share part of the blame for a general lack of understanding of the role played by native people in Canada's history and developing ethnic mosaic. To overcome these shortcomings, it is necessary to know how widely accepted views about native people originated, to evaluate these views in terms of current research, and to consider how a more integrated and improved understanding of the role of native people can be achieved. I will attempt to do this specifically with reference to the Heroic Age.

## THE HEROIC AGE

Historians used to debate whether Canadian history began with the Viking voyages about the year 1000, John Cabot's reconnaissance of 1497, or Jacques Cartier's exploration of the Gulf of St Lawrence in 1534. Such discussions were bedevilled by the shifting borders of Canada, as well as by uncertainties about the routes followed by many early European visitors. The period from these explorations to the establishment of royal government in New France in 1663 has long been viewed as a "Heroic Age" during which French explorers, missionaries, and settlers performed noble deeds. Cartier, the "discoverer" of the St Lawrence Valley, was hailed as the prototype of a bold mariner; Champlain, the intrepid explorer and colonizer, was celebrated as a man who battled the greed of fur traders, the indifference of French officials, and the opposition of native peoples to become the Father of New France; the Jesuit missionaries, who were killed carrying the gospel to native peoples, became enshrined even in the hearts of staunch Protestants as heroic standard-bearers of civilization; while Dollard Des Ormeaux and his companions were lauded as stalwart men who sacrificed their lives to prevent New France from being over-run by savages. Larger than life, these individuals provided a model of heroic deeds in which later generations of Canadians, regardless of their ethnic origins, mother tongue, or religious creed, can take particular pride. Their disinterested efforts to implant civilization in the New World contrasted with the conflicting interests, ig-nominious factional quarrels, and human errors that all too ob-viously characterized later periods of Canadian history. Canadians derived additional satisfaction from knowing that leading histo-rians in the United States shared their admiration for these great men.

The Heroic Age played a prominent role in the nationalistic history-writing of the post-Confederation era. Many English-Canadian historians sought to promote national unity by urging their readers to honour the brave men and women of that period as the founders not only of New France but of modern Canada as well. Common ties were also promoted by asserting that a Norman heritage was shared by English and French Canadians (Berger 1970: 131–2), a claim to which even French-Canadian nationalists such as François-Xavier Garneau subscribed (1882–3, 1:viii). The fact that many of these heroic Frenchmen had been active in Ontario and the Maritimes as well as in Quebec made it all the easier to interest English readers in their exploits. The great deeds of the past were celebrated in true Victorian fashion, in voluminous pub-lications and in poems, paintings, and sculptures. Plaques, statues, and even shrines were erected to mark the places where these events had occurred. They were impressed on the minds of children by being recounted in history texts and readers. A primary school pupil in Ontario was urged to admire Cartier and Champlain no less than James Wolfe or Isaac Brock.

Few nineteenth-century historians would have admitted that Canadian history began prior to the arrival of the first Europeans. Prehistoric times were viewed only as a static prelude to real his-tory. Today, it is generally accepted, when the issue is pressed, that Canadian history began thousands of years before the arrival of the first European explorers, when native people first crossed the Bering Strait. Yet the study of native people prior to the arrival of the Europeans is still viewed, not as a part of Canadian history, but as the domain of prehistoric archaeology, a discipline which is alien to history in its data, methods, and modes of interpretation. While some historians, as well as anthropologists, now study native history since the arrival of Europeans, such research is still regarded as peripheral to the mainstream of Canadian history, just as in real life native people continue to be treated as marginal to Canadian society.

The shortcomings of such a view become strikingly evident in the study of the Heroic Age. Towards the end of the fifteenth century, a small number of European ships began to explore the northeastern extremity of North America. During the next 100 years increasing numbers of Europeans visited the east coast of Canada to fish, hunt whales, search for a sea route to the Orient, look for mineral wealth, and trade for furs. The first enduring European settlement within the present borders of Canada, however, was not established until 1608, and in 1663 there were still only 3,000 Europeans living in New France, no more people than constituted a small Iroquoian tribe. Moreover, these Europeans remained dependent on goods imported from France, many did not intend to remain in the colony, and those who did were only slowly learning to adapt to life in the New World. Yet, at that time, every part of Canada was settled by native peoples who possessed cultures that had evolved over thousands of years and that were adapted to a diversity of environments. In the first half of the seventeenth century, the French were in contact with native groups totalling more than 125,000 people. Not only their numerical superiority but also their knowledge and skills allowed native Canadians to play a far different role during the Heroic Period than history books have ascribed to them.

## VIEWS OF INDIANS IN THE EARLY NINETEENTH CENTURY

Early in the nineteenth century there was little interest in Canadian history or detailed awareness of native people. At that time most of the Indians who lived in the St Lawrence lowlands had come from elsewhere. The first native groups that Europeans had encountered were soon dispersed by illness and warfare. By the middle of the seventeenth century, the Hurons and their Iroquoian-speaking neighbours in southern Ontario had been driven from their homelands by the Iroquois. The Ojibwas, in turn, wrested southern Ontario from the Iroquois late in the seventeenth century

(Eid 1979), and continued to live on reserves there after its purchase by the British government. Meanwhile, beginning in the 1630s, Jesuit and Sulpician missions attracted other Indian groups, in particular Abenakis and Mohawks from the south. After the American Revolution many Iroquois refugees from New York State settled in Ontario at Grand River and Tyendinaga (Deseronto). A small number of Wyandots, descended from Hurons and Petuns whom the Iroquois had forced to flee to the upper Great Lakes, lived on a reserve near Windsor until 1880, while other Indian groups entered Ontario from the United States early in the nineteenth century. Yet, as the White population increased, individual contact with native people declined. Most White settlers no longer bothered to distinguish between one native group and another and they assumed that all Indians were much alike.

European settlers in Ontario in the early nineteenth century were too busy trying to establish their farms and settlements in what had been a wilderness to realize that there was a local past worth studying. Too few books, libraries, or translations of French historical records were available to remind them that Europeans had lived and worked in parts of Ontario in the seventeenth century. Limited awareness of the history of native movements made it difficult for White Canadians to know that most of the pottery and stone tools being ploughed out of the ground were not made by the ancestors of the native people who lived in their midst. Farmers knew only that these artifacts had been manufactured by native people and sometimes kept them as relics or curios. Beginning in the 1830s Iroquoian ossuaries, or communal graves, many of which contained European goods, were plundered by curiosity seekers. A few digs were inspired by genuine scientific interest but at that time there were no local scientific journals where findings could be recorded (Bawtree 1848). In 1852 the newly founded Canadian Institute in Toronto distributed throughout Ontario a circular drafted by the railroad builder Sandford Fleming, urging the recording of Indian sites and the donation of artifacts to the society's museum (*Canadian Journal* 1852). Nothing significant came of this initiative, which was inspired by E.G. Squier's *Aboriginal Monuments of the State of New York*, published in 1849. Only in a few areas, such as northern Simcoe County, where Huron sites yielded so many iron axes that scrap-metal dealers found it worthwhile to visit farms to purchase them, did the past become of greater interest (Jury and Jury 1954:53).

French-Canadian folklore kept alive the memory of Iroquois attacks against missionaries and European settlers in the seventeenth

The opening of a Huron ossuary. By Félix Martin, 1855. Reproduced from A.E. Jones *"8endake Ehen"* (1908).

century (D. Smith 1974:18–20). Yet it was not until 1845 that Garneau published the first widely read history of French Canada as a response to Lord Durham's assertion that the French Canadians were a people without history or culture. About the same time Jesuit priests began to pioneer the earliest Canadian archaeology with studies of their order's seventeenth-century mission to the Hurons. In 1844 Pierre Chazelle penned the first description of the visible remains of the mission centre of Sainte-Marie-among-the-Hurons, and in 1855 Félix Martin, the first scholar to devote his life to studying early Jesuit history in Canada, examined this and other sites associated with the Huron mission (Jury and Jury 1954:6–7). During the same decade Joseph-Charles Taché, who taught at Laval University, excavated sixteen Huron ossuaries and amassed a large collection of skulls and artifacts. Unfortunately, he published no account of his work (Martijn 1978:13).

### PARKMAN AND AMERICAN ANTHROPOLOGY

In the nineteenth century Boston produced two renowned historians who dealt substantially with native Americans. The first was William H. Prescott (1796–1859), whose *History of the Conquest of Mexico* appeared in 1843, to be followed four years later by a chronicle of the Spanish conquest of Peru. Prescott's powerful narrative style proved that epic history could achieve high literary standards (Levin 1959). While he was acknowledged to be a careful scholar, he was severely criticized for portraying the native civilizations of Mexico and Peru as kingdoms similar to those found in Europe. In fact Prescott stressed that the achievements of the civilizations of the New World fell far short of those of the Old and that the Aztecs had blighted progress and were destroying the accomplishments of their predecessors (1909, 1:131). On the whole, however, his books praised the advanced cultural development of the Aztecs and Incas. American readers were predisposed to admire the achievements of Mesoamerican peoples at that time as a result of John L. Stephens's (1805–52) lavishly illustrated accounts of his discoveries of prehistoric Mayan cities in the jungles of Central America (Stephens 1841). Some American scholars also accepted Prescott's views because they refuted galling claims made by certain eminent Europeans, such as Georges-Louis Leclerc, comte de Buffon; Cornelius de Pauw; Guillaume-Thomas Raynal; and William Robertson, that the Western Hemisphere was a less developed or more degenerate environment than the Old World, as evidenced by the inferiority of its plant, animal, and human life (Haven 1856:94).

Nevertheless, Lewis Henry Morgan (1818–81), a distinguished ethnologist and expert on the Iroquois, was adamant that Prescott was in error. He argued that the Spanish conquerors, on whose reports Prescott's work was based, had exaggerated the cultural sophistication of the Aztecs and Incas in order to glorify their own achievements and that they had been unable to understand New World cultures on their own terms. In his opinion the Aztecs were little different from the Iroquois; their alleged palaces were large communal dwellings and their kings and princes merely tribal chiefs (Resek 1960:133). Morgan's view that no indigenous people of the Western Hemisphere had evolved their own civilization was supported by many White Americans, who saw little to admire in the native peoples of their own country.

The popularity of Prescott's works influenced the writing style and heroic themes adopted by Francis Parkman (1823–93), the other eminent historian from Boston. Parkman's many books chronicling the struggle between England and France for control of North America had great influence in Canada. While French-Canadian historians debated their merits, through them many English Canadians became aware of their country's history for the first time. In Parkman's writings, the results of painstaking historical research were presented as a dramatic narrative, accompanied by exciting dialogue and fine character sketches. He had a talent for memorable phrases and for presenting even his more extravagant conclusions in such an authoritative manner that they were widely accepted as facts (Wade 1942; Doughty 1962).

Parkman viewed the contest for North America as one in which the most advanced society of the time had triumphed over more primitive ones. His New England loyalties and his pride in his Anglo-Saxon origins led him to view the struggle between England and France as one of democracy against feudalism and absolutism; free enterprise and individual initiative against state control; religious freedom against Roman Catholic tyranny; and peaceful commerce against militarism and a soldiers' ethic. It was a struggle in which Britain fought, often against heavy odds, to free North America from the fetters of military despotism. Yet, while Parkman despised the institutions of New France, he found himself admiring the loyalty, zeal, and bravery of many Frenchmen who risked their lives to defend its erroneous principles. As a romantic, he could not refrain from praising deeds that he believed were misguided and that ultimately would lead to ruin. Although they may have been on the right side of history, the sombre New Englanders paled in interest by comparison with their colourful French rivals.

Native people loomed large in Parkman's writings as another romantic but far less evolved collectivity over whom the Anglo-Saxons were to triumph. While a student at Harvard University, he had become preoccupied with Indians and early in his career had planned to write a history of the Iroquois and neighbouring tribes. He abandoned this project, however, after he concluded that such a work would not be of much interest to civilized readers (Doughty 1962:92). Howard Doughty (1962:133–8) believes that Parkman's romantic preconceptions were shattered when he spent three weeks living among the Oglala Sioux during his visit to the Great Plains in 1846. It is evident, however, that long before this encounter Parkman shared many of his countrymen's negative stereotypes of native peoples (Wade 1942:89, 178, 205).

Parkman was more careful than previous historians to consider the behaviour of each tribe separately and to study Indian leaders, such as Pontiac, as individuals. He assumed that each tribe possessed its own innate social, intellectual, and moral characteristics that could be used to explain why it behaved differently from other tribes, just as such characteristics were commonly used to account for the differing behaviour of European nations.

Pride of place was assigned by these tribal stereotypes to the Iroquois. Parkman described them as the boldest, fiercest, most politically astute, and most ambitious of all the native American peoples. Their success was attributed to their inherent energy, superior mental ability and moral capacity, and their ruthlessness. Though they remained "thorough savages," he believed that they were "finished and developed" to the highest level that could be reached without emerging from the "primitive condition." Yet he doubted that they could evolve a civilized way of life on their own initiative (1927:36–7).

Since they were all recognized to be descended from a single Iroquoian stock, Parkman believed that other Iroquoian tribes, such as the Hurons, possessed the same vitality, intelligence, drive, superior social organization, and commitment to agriculture that characterized the Iroquois. Their eventual domination by the Iroquois was attributed largely to the circumstances in which these groups lived rather than to inherent differences. This was not true of other tribes. Among the Algonkians, the Shawnees were described as bold, roving, and adventurous; the northern Algonkians as inferior in intellectual vigour and moral stability, slow learning, and incorrigible; the Ojibwas as a ferocious horde and likely to remain so; the Illinois as a corrupt and degenerate race; and the Montagnais as the lowest Algonkian type for whom even cannibalism was not abhorrent. These stereotypes echoed the biases of Parkman's sources and the prejudices of his own society. In particular, economic reliance upon hunting was felt to betoken a "visible descent in the scale of humanity" (Parkman 1927:7).

Parkman also maintained that certain characteristics were shared by all native peoples. Noting that all Indians were hunters to some degree, he concluded that their mentality was shaped by this common experience, an argument that ignored the variability in subsistence patterns that he himself had documented. As "tenants of the wilderness," Indians lacked the persistence, reason, and foresight of settled peoples. Their existence as hunter-gatherers encouraged a spirit of pride, independence, and fortitude but also made them mentally lethargic and content with a squalid and uncomfortable style of life (Parkman 1899,1:3–6). Indians were fiercely loyal to their own tribe, but the determination of each man to be his own master made it impossible for them to wage war effectively or to pursue any long-term political objectives. While he accepted that their sensory perception was developed to a high degree, he stigmatized this as an animal-like trait. He also argued that a White man could soon learn to be a better hunter and bush-fighter than any Indian (ibid., 166). He was inclined to believe that Indians were less sensitive to pain and less endowed with refined feelings than were the "higher races" (1927:21).

Parkman further asserted that ⌐ Indians' powers of reason and analysis were inferior to those of Europeans. Their religious beliefs were alleged to be vague and their power to understand complex situations limited. Like all primitive peoples, their character was full of contradictions. They were recklessly generous but at the same time morbidly suspicious; loving but capable of revolting cruelties; haughty but willing to beg; proud and independent but fearful of public opinion; self-restrained but given to fits of uncontrolled rage. The good order that generally prevailed in their communities was a thin, opaque veil covering their savage passions. The acquisition of guns speeded up, but did not otherwise modify, the meaningless slaughter of one tribe by another that had characterized North America throughout prehistoric times. Parkman concluded that Indians were basically childlike. Like badly disciplined children, they tended to be lying, treacherous, deceitful, capricious, jealous, refractory, and predisposed to violence. They also tended to confuse kindness with weakness and their courage was short-lived (Parkman 1927:31–81).

Indians were fixed and rigid in their attitudes, according to Parkman. They were unable to alter their ancient customs, in particular their ceremonies, fondness for gambling, and reverence for the dead. Their minds were closed to every improvement, and every change that civilized men had forced upon them had been for the worse. He noted that many of the greatest Indian leaders had opposed the spread of civilization and had championed their traditional barbarism (1899, 1:216). Their spirit of independence, however, made it impossible for them to be enslaved as the Africans had been; hence they were bound to become extinct as European civilization spread across North America. He saw "the savage prologue of the American drama" drawing to a close in his own lifetime (1927:8).

Parkman's vision of native North Americans was conveyed in the most colourful and derogatory terms. Indian women were not simply "squaws" but became "dusky mistresses" and "shrivelled hags," who bore "mongrel offspring" to White traders. Native people lived in "swarms" rather than communities and bore "barbaric appellatives" instead of "Christian names." He did not hesitate to describe chief Donnacona as a "greasy potentate." All of these literary devices reinforced Parkman's contemptuous portrayal of native people.

Scholars in his own time and since have criticized Parkman for his negative attitudes towards native peoples (Shulman 1971). Francis Jennings (1963) has demonstrated how in one instance Parkman seriously misrepresented his sources to avoid mentioning the important role that Indians had played in concluding a major peace treaty. Yet despite certain tendencies to romanticize native people that had become an established feature of American literature in the early nineteenth century, his portrayal of Indians was one that seemed fair to a wide audience. When James Fenimore Cooper, in *The Last of the Mohicans* (1826) and other works, romantically portrayed one Indian group being exterminated by another (Keiser 1933:101–43), he was essentially making the same point that Parkman was when he claimed that before they first encountered Europeans, the Iroquois had already embarked on a war of conquest that probably would have led them to obliterate every other tribe in eastern North America (Parkman 1927:4).

Closer examination reveals that Parkman was a careful student of American anthropology and, in particular, an admirer of the ethnologist Lewis Henry Morgan (Resek 1960). American anthropology had evolved in a society whose central experience for several centuries had been the competition between White settlers and native peoples for control of land and resources. A major grievance leading to the American Revolution had been the efforts of the British government to regulate White settlement west of the Appalachians. The American government used military force almost continuously during the nineteenth century to push Indians westward and to force them onto reservations. Colonizing powers have often claimed that native people are not making adequate use of land as an excuse for seizing it from them. Parkman's description of the Indians as "tenants of the wilderness" is one more example of the insistent charge that native people did not have a moral right to the land they occupied. While Puritan settlers in seventeenth-century New England observed their own legal forms in purchasing land from its native owners, their theologians religiously justified seizing Indian lands. They argued either that native peoples had manifestly earned God's disapproval by their failure to use his gifts or that their primitive cultural condition was evidence of his displeasure. The Puritans saw themselves as constituting a New Israel and the Indians as Canaanites whom they had a right to dispossess and enslave. Still later, Ezra Stiles, the president of Yale University, was to follow earlier French writers when he suggested that the Indians were probably literally descendants of Canaanites, who had fled from Palestine at the time of the Israelite conquest (Haven 1856:4).

Yet in the early days of European exploration and settlement, there was little evidence of racial prejudice against the Indians. They were often described as physically attractive, and their skin colour was not perceived to be notably different from that of Whites. It was widely maintained that they were born white and became sun-tanned or dyed themselves brown. Although their way of life was judged to be primitive or debased, it was hoped that they could quickly be taught to live as Christians and Europeans and would be grateful for such instruction (Vaughan 1982:927–9). Before conflicts developed, some English visitors, such as Thomas Harriot, praised their ingenuity and intelligence, notwithstanding their rudimentary technology (Orme 1981:3–4).

As disputes over land rights envenomed relations between English settlers and native peoples in the seventeenth century, it became fashionable for Whites to describe Indians as bloodthirsty monsters who were human only in shape. The chronic warfare of the eighteenth century encouraged the view that their refusal to accept the White man's way of life proved that they were vicious brutes who were innately incapable of being civilized. After most Indians, in an attempt to protect their own interests, sided with the British at the time of the American Revolution, it was widely agreed that all native Americans were savages who should be wiped from the face of the earth (Vaughan 1982:942). They were increasingly referred to as tawny pagans, swarthy Philistines, copper-coloured vermin, and by the end of the eighteenth century redskins. The notion that darker colour implied inferiority had a long history in European thinking and had been reinforced in the seventeenth and eighteenth centuries as a result of conscious and unconscious efforts to justify the African slave trade by dehumanizing its victims (Jordan 1968).

Physical differences among races were not generally regarded as immutable prior to the nineteenth century and no clear distinction was drawn between variations in physical, moral, and behavioural characteristics. Yet as the power of native people declined and they increasingly became the victims of White aggression, prejudices against them became more vocal and extreme. As they came to be viewed as inherently savage, it was argued that they could no more be civilized than an animal's nature could be changed. Even those who advocated assimilation now regarded it as a policy that would require centuries of persistent effort to bring to fruition. Hence nature itself decreed that Indians must give way to a superior order of human beings (Vaughan 1982:952–3). Europeans thus believed that they were biologically justified in their efforts to subjugate and replace native people.

During the nineteenth century there was a growing preference for biologically based explanations of human behaviour. Differences that had formerly been interpreted as reversible adaptations to specific climates or as insignificant historical accidents now tended to be viewed as immutable racial characteristics. This change had its beginnings in the nationalist reaction to the Napoleonic domination of Europe, which made it popular to view each European nationality as possessing its own biologically innate traits. The same reaction produced a widespread rejection of the rationalist art and literature of the Enlightenment in favour of that of romanticism (Kohn 1960).

In the 1840s George Gliddon, an amateur Egyptologist, and Josiah Nott, a physician from Alabama, espoused Isaac de la Peyrère's heretical doctrine of polygenesis. Observing that the earliest Egyptian paintings demonstrated that Whites and Africans had not changed noticeably over 5,000 years and believing that human beings had been created only 6,000 years ago, they argued that the major races of human beings must be distinct and immutable species, each fashioned to inhabit separate parts of the world. In this they received support from the distinguished anatomist Samuel Morton, who had already proclaimed the American Indian to be a separate species, the geologist Louis Agassiz, and many other leading American scientists. Nott and Gliddon believed that specific behavioural traits were innate to each human species and that the inferiority of the African justified his permanent enslavement. Indians were also viewed as inferior to Whites and untameable. Despite its obvious appeal as a justification for Negro slavery and Indian-fighting, polygenesis was rejected by the American public on religious grounds, even before it was rendered scientifically obsolete by Darwinian evolution (Stanton 1960).

Ironically, Darwinism provided a more broadly acceptable rationale for racist interpretations of human behaviour. Natural selection was seen as operating to adapt human beings intellectually and emotionally to their social environment; hence primitive groups lacked the selection to enable them to cope with civilized life. The gradient from most to least developed societies was thought to be paralleled by a biological gradient from most intelligent and morally sensitive to those who were only slightly different from the great apes. These ideas, as popularized by the Englishman John Lubbock (Lord Avebury) in *Pre-historic Times* (1865), offered a comfortable explanation for the primitive condition of the American Indian and his stubborn refusal to accept the benefits of civilization. White Americans could not be blamed for the tragic failure of natural selection over the course of millennia to produce native

North Americans who were biologically able to withstand the impact of Western civilization.

Like their European counterparts, American anthropologists such as Albert Gallatin (1761–1849), who has been called the Father of American ethnology, subscribed to the doctrines of cultural evolution that had been formulated by the philosophers of the Enlightenment and popularized by such works as William Robertson's *The History of America* (Hoebel 1960; Bieder 1975). They viewed European civilization as the product of an accelerating cultural development that promoted not only technological but also social, moral, and intellectual progress (Harris 1968:8–52). Native peoples, whose patterns of life had evolved more slowly, if at all, were interpreted as living examples of early stages in the evolution of European society. For that reason, their societies were regarded as being technologically, socially, and morally inferior to those of Europe. White Americans now had a persuasive scientific explanation for the Indians' failure to live up to their earlier expectations of rapid assimilation and to justify their own predatory expansion (Horsman 1975, 1981).

The ethnologist and Indian agent Henry Schoolcraft appeared to be closing the gap between history, which was concerned primarily with European civilization, and anthropology, concerned with native peoples, when he stated in 1846 that "Iroquois history is to some extent our history." Yet he quickly added that "it has been given to us [Whites] to carry out scenes of improvement, and of moral and intellectual progress, which providence in its profound workings, has deemed it best for the prosperity of man, that we, not they, should be entrusted with" (Hinsley 1981:10). Elsewhere he did not hesitate to describe the period prior to the arrival of the Whites as one in which the Indians maintained "their dark empire of powwows and jugglers undisturbed" (Stanton 1960:192).

The dichotomy between history as the study of rapidly evolving peoples and anthropology as the study of static ones explains the lines along which anthropology developed in North America and elsewhere during the nineteenth century. In the United States anthropology was identified with the study of the American Indian. Its four branches were ethnology, which sought to record the rapidly disappearing traditional cultures of the Indians; anthropological linguistics, which studied their languages; physical anthropology, which studied their physical types; and archaeology, which examined their prehistoric remains. These four branches began to constitute a single discipline in the 1840s, as an interest in amassing and classifying information about native languages and cultures that had begun in the eighteenth century became linked with a growing curiosity in prehistoric archaeology and a physical anthropology that sought to account for human behaviour in biological terms (Gruber 1967:5–9).

Only after 1875 did ethnologists conduct extensive fieldwork among living peoples. Even then, unlike today, they concentrated heavily on collecting reminiscences of traditional cultures from a few elderly native informants, who claimed to remember what life had been like in their youth. The result was a description of native cultures that focused on recording rules and ideal situations rather than observing how life was actually lived. Although ethnologists sought to portray native cultures as they had existed before European contact, many of them were so altered by the time they were studied that ethnologists were unable to verify what they were being told. Ethnologists also frowned on colleagues who identified too closely with the people they studied, ostensibly because this impeded objectivity but in reality because, from an evolutionary perspective, "going native" was viewed as a morally degrading experience (Hinsley 1981:196–7). This attitude hindered the study of surviving native cultures.

Archaeology, being concerned with the past, tends in most countries to have a historical orientation. From its beginnings European archaeology was viewed as an extension into prehistoric times of the study of the evolution of European society. The formal affiliations of European prehistoric archaeology drifted away from anthropology during the late nineteenth century and today it is generally recognized as being a historical discipline. The main role envisaged for American archaeology in the nineteenth century was to provide evidence that in prehistoric times native cultures had been as backward and sluggish as contemporary ones appeared to be. Since all historical cultures could be assigned to the Stone Age, evolutionary models suggested that there was little scope for development in prehistoric times (Willey and Sabloff 1980). A few archaeologists saw evidence of change in the archaeological record, but this was generally interpreted as indicating tribal movements rather than development within cultures (Trigger 1980:664).

Most significantly, nineteenth-century American anthropologists made no formal provision for studying cultural changes amongst native peoples since European contact, although there was abundant historical documentation for doing this. Such changes were viewed as a process of disintegration that would terminate with the physical extinction of most native people and the cultural assimilation into White society of any surviving remnants. Anthropologists treated such changes as impediments to the study of traditional cultures, and often ethnologists simply tried to ignore them, as Franz Boas did when he deleted sewing machines and other obviously modern devices from his descriptions of West Coast potlatches. Anthropologists ignored the fact that such changes transformed whole societies, instead of being confined to the loss and addition of specific traits. The most striking exception was James Mooney, who portrayed native societies as dynamic entities struggling to survive the trauma of acculturation and loss of power in his study of the Ghost Dance, an indigenous religious movement that late in the nineteenth century sought to restore the morale of the harassed Plains Indians. Curtis Hinsley (1981:207–8) has suggested that Mooney's Irish background and nationalist sympathies helped him to realize that native responses to White pressure should not automatically be interpreted as examples of cultural disintegration.

Ethnologists, especially those who had prolonged contact with native people, tended to view Indian life in a more rounded fashion than did the average White American. Their personal experiences revealed the falseness of many of the worst calumnies directed against Indians. Yet their opinions of the primitive state and the inevitable extinction of native cultures were generally in close agreement with popular White views on these subjects. Parkman's opinions concerning Indians cannot be condemned independently of those held by nineteenth-century anthropologists any more than the latter can be evaluated without considering the broader opinions of White society. As a good scholar, Parkman was aware of the anthropological thought of his time and his analysis of Indian life was shaped by it. He used his extraordinary talents as a writer to express contemporary scientific as well as popular views. Thus his books became the most enduring expression of America's consciousness of native peoples in the middle and late nineteenth century. As an author who is still widely read, Parkman continues to exert some direct influence, although changing social values now reveal his biases to many readers. Over the years, however, he influenced the manner in which native people were viewed both through his own works and through the influence he exerted on subsequent generations of historians.

## THE CHARLEVOIX TRADITION

Although Parkman's books did not quickly acquire a mass readership in the United States, by the 1870s they were having considerable impact north of the border. In Ontario they filled a widely felt need for a history of Canada that was written in a romantic, picturesque, and dramatic style. Many English Canadians also found his prejudices about their French-speaking compatriots as congenial as they found his style (Berger 1976:4). Parkman had close ties with historians in Quebec, whom he visited regularly between 1866 and 1879. He also made extensive direct use of the work of the historian Faillon (Jaenen 1982a:16). While conservative Roman Catholic historians were scandalized by his secular view of Canadian history, more liberal French-speaking scholars vacillated between admiration for his literary style and the enthusiasm with which he was revealing the epic of French Canada's glorious past to the English-speaking world and dismay at his portrayal of New France as a corrupt, semi-feudal society (Wade 1942:380–424). Mason Wade believed that both English and French Canadians still regarded him in 1942 "as the greatest and most eloquent historian of their country's early days" (ibid., 424).

Yet, important as Parkman's influence may have been in Canada during the late nineteenth century, Canadians had their own tradition of historical writing, which reflected their very different relations with native people. Settlement in Canada, unlike that in the United States, had not been dominated by violent clashes with native groups over rights to land. The St Lawrence lowlands had been largely stripped of their native inhabitants by epidemics and wars among the Indians themselves prior to European settlement. Contact between settlers and the Indians of the interior revolved around the fur trade, not land. Although the French and the Iroquois clashed violently as a result of rivalries over the fur trade, the French treated the Indians who lived within the present borders of Canada as producers of a valued asset. Even during the later European settlement of the West, enforcement of the policy established by the Royal Proclamation of 1763, which prevented the uncontrolled expansion of settlement, made overt conflict between Indians and Whites minimal (Tobias 1983). Finally, popular sentiment interpreted Indian leaders, such as Joseph Brant and Tecumseh, as national heroes who had fought alongside the British in their battles with the United States. In order to assess Parkman's impact on the portrayal of Indians in Canadian historical writing, we must consider not only the popular stereotypes about Indians that prevailed in Canada in the 1870s but also the treatment of native people within the Canadian tradition of historical writing.

Europeans never interpreted native American societies without preconceptions. Even the first European explorers sought to make sense of what they saw in terms of diverse and often contradictory medieval speculations about what the inhabitants of far-off regions of the world might be like. Most surprising to them was their failure to encounter the monsters with which the medieval imagination had populated such lands. Yet rumours persisted for a long time about tribes of people with one foot or with their heads fused to their chests living in the interior of the newly discovered continents. Europeans who were attracted by fleeting glimpses of native life described the Indians as the inhabitants of a terrestrial paradise, a surviving Golden Age, or as natural people uncorrupted by the vices and temptations of civilization (Dickason 1977a, 1984a). Some early visitors considered them as evidence of how all human beings had lived at the beginning of time. The Elizabethan artist John White, for example, did not hesitate to use his remarkable drawings of the Indians of Virginia as the basis for a later series of illustrations of ancient Britons (Kendrick 1950; Orme 1981:4–7). Yet other explorers described them as the thralls of a kingdom ruled by devils; lustful hairy men or brutal cannibals who had lost their original knowledge of God; or primitive peoples whose ignorance compelled them to live in terror of the elementary forces of nature. The debate whether native Americans represented the childhood of mankind or the products of degeneration was to continue into the nineteenth century.

A great variety of views about native people were expressed in the early French writings on North America, works which ever since have constituted the primary written sources of information about New France. The lawyer Marc Lescarbot (c. 1570–1642), influenced by Michel de Montaigne as well as by the classical authors Strabo and Tacitus, portrayed the Micmacs of Nova Scotia as noble savages, whose exemplary way of life was free from all the vices of civilized France. His and similar works written by Frenchmen who had detailed first-hand knowledge of native life reveal the error of the frequent suggestion that the noble savage was an image that could be sustained only in the salons of Europe. On the other hand, Champlain (1567?–1635), who also knew the region first hand, described these same people as rude and contemptible, while his conclusions about the Hurons echoed André Thevet's earlier description of the Tupinambas of South America as a "strange and savage people, without faith, without law, without religion, and without civility" (Gaffarel 1878:135).

The Recollet lay brother Gabriel Sagard (fl. 1614–36) also pictured the Indians as noble savages, although he did not fail to condemn their religious ignorance and stress the need for them to learn to live like Frenchmen. The writings of the Jesuits reveal individual variations and ambiguities that reflect their complex views of their missionary responsibilities as well as the contradictory influences of their religious zeal and secular learning. On the one hand, they viewed the Huron country as a remote stronghold of Satan where the devil sought to torment the Hurons and prevent them from acquiring a knowledge of Christianity; on the other, they sought to isolate the Hurons from Frenchmen who were not attached to their mission because they feared that those Frenchmen would debauch potential converts. Most Jesuits were prepared to adopt a liberal and relativistic view of customs that did not touch on religion. For example, they observed that standards of beauty varied immensely from one part of the world to another and doubted that there was any single standard by which such preferences could be evaluated. Their opinions of the Hurons ranged from strong praise for their intelligence and generosity to lurid descriptions of the "filth" and "immorality" of their domestic life and the "absurdity" and "depravity" of their religious practices, which were intended to elicit the reader's sympathy for the missionaries and their struggle.

The accounts of native people in the writings of early fur traders, such as Pierre Boucher (1622–1717), Pierre-Esprit Radisson (1636?–1710), and Nicolas Perrot (c. 1644–1717), while not without their biases, are less dominated by literary stereotypes than are the works of their more learned contemporaries. A remarkable exception was the curious memoirs, published in 1703, of the soldier Louis Armand de Lom d'Arce, baron de Lahontan (1666–1715), who had served in Denonville's campaign against the Senecas in 1687. Dialogues with a mythical Indian named Adario were used to express his dissatisfaction with the religious dogmas and social injustices of his time. The message of these dialogues, that Indians are truly free while Frenchmen are slaves, makes Adario a direct prototype of Jean-Jacques Rousseau's noble savage.

By contrast, in his *Moeurs des sauvages amériquains comparées aux moeurs des premiers temps*, Joseph-François Lafitau (1681–1746), a Jesuit who served as a missionary at Caughnawaga from 1712 to 1717, used an extraordinarily detailed description of Iroquois culture to argue in favour of divine revelation and against atheism and deism. He maintained that customs shared by native North Americans and the ancient Greeks, Romans, and Hebrews were survivals of the divinely ordered life of the Patriarchal period and attributed cultural differences to people's abandoning these precepts and hence losing sight of God's commands (Fenton and Moore 1974–7). Though often lauded as the father of comparative ethnology, Lafitau was the chief exponent of the doctrine of degeneration in the eighteenth century (Fenton 1969).

Lafitau's writing marked a reaction against the beginning of an intellectual movement that during the eighteenth century was to win widespread support for an evolutionary view of human development. Already in the seventeenth century the quickening pace of economic and cultural change had led scholars such as Francis Bacon to challenge the notion that the achievements of ancient Greece and Rome represented the apogee of human accomplishment. In the eighteenth century, the philosophers of the Enlightenment rejected the idea that a Golden Age had existed in the past. They championed a view of history that saw the exercise of reason leading mankind from a primitive state to ones characterized by increasing scientific knowledge, economic prosperity, and moral wisdom. Enlightenment philosophers believed that human nature was not basically altered by cultural change, although they were convinced that education improved human beings by eliminating primordial superstitions and refining gross passions (Toulmin and Goodfield 1966:123). At the same time many of them believed that if individuals were refined by learning, they were also corrupted by the vices of civilizations; hence they stressed the virtues of primitive man.

This view is reflected in Pierre-François-Xavier de Charlevoix's (1682–1761) *Histoire et description générale de la Nouvelle France,* published in 1744. For almost a century this book remained the chief source for the writing of early Canadian history, although it was not translated into English until 1866–72. A priest of the Society of Jesus, Charlevoix taught at the Quebec Seminary from 1705 to 1709, and between 1720 and 1722 he travelled on official business from Quebec to New Orleans by way of Michilimackinac and the Mississippi River. Hence, like Lafitau, his view of native peoples was based on first-hand experience as well as on extensive reading. From his travels, he had gained accurate knowledge of native peoples as a major presence in North America and a strong force in its recent history. Unlike previous works on New France, whether original accounts or digests of older ones, such as François

Du Creux's *Historiae Canadensis*, Charlevoix's history was equipped with an extensive scholarly apparatus that included chronological tables, annotated bibliographies, and footnotes. Despite an obvious pro-Jesuit bias, his careful evaluation of alternative sources of information marked a considerable advance in historiographic method.

Charlevoix's history popularized and transmitted to posterity a vast and often contradictory assortment of stereotypes about native peoples. Indians as a whole were decried as idolatrous, credulous, immoral (especially in the south), indolent, improvident, warlike, arrogant, given to slandering each other, and treacherous. He constantly reiterated the need for Europeans to keep the Indians in awe if they were not to be despised and taken advantage of (1866–72, 2:26, 38; 3:11; 6:72, 78). On the other hand, he praised Indians as brave, hardy, faithful, generous, gentle, intelligent, noble, and full of good sense. He also lauded the harmony of their domestic and community life. These positive qualities were even attributed to the Iroquois, although those who remained in New York State were often identified as enemies of New France and of Roman Catholicism. Charlevoix did not describe in lingering detail acts of torture, cannibalism, and atrocities committed against Europeans. The Lachine massacre, for example, was treated factually, and without flourishes intended to arouse the reader's indignation against the Iroquois.

Charlevoix shared the popular belief that nations, like individuals, have characters they can never lay aside and that in the course of their history they fall victim to the predominant faults of that character (1866–72, 5:23). These ideas were applied to Indian tribes as well as European nations. He described the Hurons as the ablest people in Canada, praising their industriousness, political acumen, eloquence, and bravery, but denounced their treachery and dissimulation, which made other tribes fear and mistrust them. He saw them as possessing the best and worst qualities of Indians in general. By comparison, the Ottawas were naturally dull; the Illinois cowardly, brutal, and lustful, yet faithful allies; and the Clamcoets of Louisiana treacherous, cruel, perverse, and habitually drunk. There are close resemblances between Charlevoix's tribal stereotypes and Parkman's. Charlevoix sought to explain some of these characteristics in environmental terms. He suggested that the Cayugas' rich agricultural land made them somewhat gentler than the other Iroquois tribes (ibid., 2:190). Such geographical explanations of differences in temperament were popular in the eighteenth century and had their roots in the ethnogeographical speculations of classical times (Briant 1982:12–34).

Above all, however, Charlevoix viewed Indians as rational people whose conduct, like that of other human beings, was determined mainly by considerations of personal honour and self-interest. He acknowledged that French presumptions and perfidy were major causes of conflict between themselves and the Iroquois. He denied that the French had a right to treat Indians without their consent as subjects of the French crown and denounced their enslavement as both immoral and politically inept (1866–72, 3:275–6). He observed that Indians had repeatedly been able to outwit Europeans and that the latter were never deceived more easily than when they underestimated the intelligence of native people. Even after Indians had become economically dependent on the Europeans, they were able to manipulate the political situation so that they remained in control of it. He also noted that, in order to balance the French and English against each other, the Iroquois had always stopped attacking the French at the point when they could have done them the most harm (ibid., 4:247–8). Chiefs such as the Huron Kondiaronk (Le Rat), who had duped the French, were praised for their courage and intelligence.

Charlevoix thought that the main difference between French and Indians was the latter's lack of education, which made them superstitious and violent. He also believed that nature can sometimes rise above culture; thus among native peoples individuals could be found whose innate intelligence, eloquence, and moral sense were equal to those of the most carefully educated Europeans (1866–72, 1:270; 2:136; 3:41). Such natives could exercise moral authority over Frenchmen as well as their own people and were entitled to the respect of the former. He maintained as well that members of even the most savage tribes could be mentally and morally improved by associating with more rational human beings (ibid., 3:30). The belief that reason and the ability to learn are common possessions of all human groups, which contrasts so sharply with the racist views of the nineteenth century, encouraged Charlevoix to judge Indian behaviour in a relatively evenhanded fashion. Although he remained ethnocentric in his evaluation of the ways of life of non-Europeans, he interpreted historical events in such a fashion that natives were portrayed neither as saints nor as demons, but as human beings motivated by universally comprehensible concepts of self-interest. For all of its obvious shortcomings, no more balanced view of the behaviour of native peoples was to be achieved in a historical study of Canada until well into the twentieth century.

Later writers who had little, if any, contact with native people used Charlevoix as a source of information about them but altered his interpretations to suit their own purposes. In his widely read critique of the ancien régime, *Histoire philosophique et politique des établissemens et du commerce des Européens dans les deux Indes*, Guillaume-Thomas Raynal (1713–96) portrayed the North American Indians as noble savages. Like Rousseau and Voltaire, he sought to see in them proof of the essential goodness of human nature when uncorrupted by the evils of civilization. Raynal highlighted Charlevoix's positive characterization of Indians and Indian life. He portrayed them as hardy, stoical, brave, and magnanimous individuals who prized their freedom and independence above all else. Indian men were intrepid hunters and bold warriors, but also mild and sagacious in their everyday life. They loved their families, passionately mourned their dead children, and were unswerving in their loyalty to their friends. Friendships were not spoiled by greed nor were their lives ruined by the pursuit of riches or titles. Sexual obsessions were curbed by their need to work hard to stay alive. Even the torturing of prisoners was explained as an understandable extension of their martial valour. Their main shortcoming was their childlike understanding, which allowed them to be tormented by superstitious fears and made them vengeful (Raynal 1795). The more religiously orthodox François-René de Chateaubriand (1768–1848), who also used Charlevoix as a source, similarly praised Indian life and morals, though condemning their paganism (D. Smith 1974:11). During a visit to the United States in 1791 he had travelled with fur traders and had briefly encountered Indian groups.

Although generally dismissed as a badly organized and derivative work, *Beautés de l'histoire du Canada*, which was published under the pseudonym D. Dainville (1821), provides the first indication of the impact of the romantic style on the writing of Canadian history. The book has been attributed to the French businessman Adolphe Bossange, who had commercial interests in Montreal and who might have written it with a French-Canadian audience at least partly in mind, although his picture of contemporary French-Canadian society at the end of the book was far from flattering. Although based largely on Charlevoix and generally adhering to the view that Indians were independent, generous, and committed to individual liberty, Dainville emphasized to an unprecedented degree their fiery passions, lack of self-control, and love of warfare and vengeance. His insistence that they were an equal blend of the most generous and the most atrocious of human characteristics was a retreat from the eighteenth-century ideal of the noble savage.

In his introduction, Dainville stressed that the main theme of his book was the conflict between savagery and civilization. No land, he melodramatically informed his readers, had been more bloodied by the encounter between transplanted European civilization and native barbarism than Canada had (1821:ii). He denounced Europeans for stealing Indian land, spreading diseases, encouraging the consumption of alcohol, corrupting Indian life, and teaching native people to scorn their ancient traditions. The wars waged by Indians were shown to be largely attempts to defend themselves against European oppression. Yet Dainville sought to engage his readers' interest with gory and detailed descriptions of tortures and massacres committed by both sides, but mainly by the Indians. He implied that cruelty and violence were basic aspects of human nature, which if not curbed by the authority of the state would overwhelm even the most civilized societies. Such views reflected the growing pessimism about human nature that had undermined the faith of the middle class in reason throughout western Europe after the French Revolution. Dainville also may have calculated that an emphasis on Indian warfare and bloodshed would appeal to his French-Canadian readers. He stressed that missionaries had been forced to suffer greatly to convert even the Hurons, whom he described as a capricious, ignorant, and fierce people. Dainville included a section on contemporary native Americans, stressing that their character remained the same, despite the changing circumstances in which they lived. This too reflected the tendency of the romantic movement to regard human behaviour as innate rather than as the product of historical circumstances.

The earliest histories of Canada written in English were largely digests of Charlevoix's work and their portrayals of native people were strongly influenced by him. They were also conservative works in the sense that they were little influenced, as Dainville had been, by current European literary fashions. The first of these was published by the deputy postmaster general of British America, George Heriot (1766–1844), in 1804. He saw the early history of Canada as being closely linked to that of the Iroquois, and Indians featured as prominently in his narrative as in Charlevoix's. He described them as having an unshakeable attachment to their tribe, a strong respect for the memory of dead friends, and an implacable hatred of their enemies. He regarded the Iroquois, whom he described as allies of the British, as the most warlike as well as the most politically astute of all natives on the continent and contrasted their promptness and energy with the indolence and folly of the Hurons. While not minimizing the cruelty or deceitfulness of the Iroquois, Heriot argued that these qualities were equally evident in the manner in which the French had treated them.

The loyalist William Smith's (1769–1847) *History of Canada* was printed in 1815, but because of his debts to the publisher, it was not released for sale until 1826. A long section on Indian customs noted their lack of hygiene, moral depravity, and religious ignorance. He concluded that they did not have even the most rudimentary notion about God. They loved freedom and desired military glory. Their attachment to their tribal territories indicated that they had well-developed concepts of property. Smith also argued that most natives did not retreat westward when the Europeans arrived but fought to remain in their ancient territories until they were destroyed by European diseases, vices, and warfare (1815:48–9). Although he paid little attention to the motives of individual Indians or Europeans, he believed that native people were guided by the same passions and desires as Whites. They had greeted the first Europeans warmly and had fed, housed, cured, and guided them. When their friendship was requited by "deceit, treachery, and cruelty," the Indians sought in vain to expel the newcomers. Smith also suggested that the French had inspired most of the acts of "barbarism" that the Indians had committed against the English, a view that made it easy to explain why tribes that formerly had fought the British were now their allies.

The final work in this tradition of early English-Canadian historical writing was *The History of Canada from Its First Discovery to the Present Time* written by Brockville publisher John Mercier McMullen (1820–1907) and published in 1855. McMullen based his treatment of early Canadian history on the writings of Heriot and Smith. Like them, he praised the Indians for being bold in war, skilful at hunting, stoical in adversity, eloquent in council, and capable of forceful and dignified action. He was even prepared to endorse, at second or third hand, the opinions of the seventeenth-century Jesuits that the Iroquoians were more intelligent than the peasants of Europe and that their love of country rivalled that of the classical nations of antiquity. Yet he also described native people as rude, improvident, destitute of all arts and industry, and unable to improve the part of the world in which they lived. He urged readers not to regret that the rule of the "fierce Indian" had passed away forever and that possession of the soil of Canada had been transferred into the hands of Anglo-Saxons (1855:xiv). He was grateful that Providence in his wisdom had swept away the aboriginal races of southern Ontario and Quebec and left these rich regions to be inherited by a more fortunate people who, unlike their American neighbours, did not have to atone for any crimes or injustices against native peoples. When Heriot and Smith wrote their histories, Indian tribes were important allies in the struggle between Britain and the United States for control of major sections of North America; by the 1850s these tribes had lost their political importance and for the most part were confined, subject to White tutelage, on Indian reserves. As contacts between Indians and the White population of Ontario became less frequent and increasingly unequal, stereotypes of native people were more strongly shaped by the newspapers and books that flooded into the province from the United States.

The first history to be written in the French language in Canada was Joseph-François Perrault's (1753–1844) *Abrégé de l'histoire du Canada*, a five-volume elementary school manual published in the early 1830s. The period prior to 1752 was covered in only forty-three pages, which depended heavily on Charlevoix and Smith. Although Perrault had been a fur trader and had been tortured by the Indians, he had little to say about them. The first detailed account of the French regime written by a French Canadian was published by Michel Bibaud (1782–1837) in 1837. Bibaud presented a generally favourable view of native peoples, which ignored local folklore but was in accord with Charlevoix and Raynal on whom he relied heavily as sources. The pro-British sympathies of both Bibaud and Perrault adversely affected the reception of their work as nationalism became the dominant ideology of middle-class French Canadians (Ouellet 1982:47–8).

## NATIONALIST HISTORIES

The nationalist school of French-Canadian historiography began with François-Xavier Garneau's (1809–66) three-volume *Histoire du Canada* (1845–8); a work which won instant acclaim, appeared in successive revised editions, and was published as a textbook from 1856 to 1881 (Lefebvre 1945; Lanctôt 1946). The main theme of this book, which was written from a rationalist perspective, was the British Conquest of Canada and the struggle of French Canadians to maintain their cultural identity thereafter (Ouellet 1982:48–9). In spite of this, he provided extensive coverage of the French regime and of relations with native peoples at that time which was based on first-hand knowledge of early printed sources and of the most important manuscripts available in Quebec. He thus became the first historian to examine Charlevoix's sources and ponder the quality of his work. Unlike Charlevoix, he had little, if any, direct knowledge of native people.

Garneau reproduced many of Charlevoix's positive stereotypes about Indians. He praised their respect for the dead and their eloquence and denied that they were naturally inferior to Whites or could not be civilized; they were simply dwelling in mental darkness. He also adopted Charlevoix's stereotypes of individual tribes, lauding the Iroquois as intellectually superior to other native peoples and the Micmacs for their gentleness and bravery. The Hurons were seen as equal to the Iroquois in courage but inferior in discipline, and the Fox were condemned for their cruelty.

Garneau's portrayal of Indian life, however, was generally darker than former ones had been. Like Dainville, he saw Canada as an arena of bloody conflict between civilization and barbarism (1882–3, 1:vi). He stated that war was a habitual source of uncontrollable joy for young native men, who waged it without reason. Hence, when the French engaged "cruel hordes of barbarians" to fight their wars, they were merely employing the Indians' natural tendencies for their own purposes (ibid.). Yet he accused the English of sharpening the Iroquois' natural instinct for war. He also stressed the habitual vindictiveness of Indians, scalps being torn from prostrate bodies, slow tortures, and bloody sacrifices. He went further than previous Canadian historians in implying that Indians were sexually promiscuous, enslaved their women, took inadequate care of their children, and before the arrival of Europeans had lived solely by hunting and fishing. He suggested that the Hurons had taken up agriculture only after they had fled to Quebec in 1650. Garneau also believed that their languages were inferior to European ones, since they appeared to lack abstract terms, and claimed that this reflected the intellectual limitations of the Indians themselves, who were not given to abstract thought. Even the idea of a supreme deity, which had long been attributed to them, was interpreted as a product of missionary influence. In his descriptions of French defeats by the Iroquois, he resorted to language that is reminiscent of Dainville. The Jesuit missionaries were slain with tortures that only devils could inflict, while at Lachine the Iroquois revealed themselves to be pitiless butchers and fiendish murderers.

Garneau also praised the moral and physical superiority of Europeans. French missionaries and fur traders could control large numbers of Indians not only because of European technological superiority but also because their hardiness and bravery elicited the latter's natural respect. The Indians believed the first Europeans they encountered to be gods and thereafter the Europeans lived charmed lives. Yet Garneau was prepared to admit that the Europeans had repeatedly wronged and despoiled native peoples (Gagnon 1982:29–32).

Garneau's ambivalence about native peoples is already evident in his early poetry. In "Le dernier Huron" he mourned the passing of the noble savage; in "Le vieux chêne" he recalled folk images of savage tortures (Huston 1893:172–5, 206–9). In his historical writings, he continued to reflect Charlevoix's vision of Indians as rational human beings; but he also went further than Dainville in portraying them as primitive savages. No doubt he sought to glorify the founders of New France by emphasizing the degree to which their existence had been threatened and the many trials they had had to overcome (D. Smith 1974:28–9). Yet that does not appear to be the whole explanation. Lacking personal knowledge of native people, Garneau turned for information not only to Charlevoix but also to prestigious American ethnologists and historians. From their works he absorbed, sometimes reluctantly, the evolutionary and racist perspectives that were colouring scientific as well as popular views of native people in the United States. This reinforced his belief that the Indians were a primitive race doomed to extinction. Despite his extensive coverage of native people, he treated them more schematically and anonymously than Charlevoix had done. Moreover, he often explained specific Indian actions in terms of innate tendencies, or not at all, instead of trying to understand them rationally. Thus, in Garneau's treatment of native people, as in that of McMullen, one finds a heterogeneous mixture of influences from the French Enlightenment and the contemporary United States. Indians had diminished in importance to the point where they could now be regarded as merely part of the background against which the early history of New France had been enacted. This peripheral role did not encourage a resolution of the resulting contradictions.

The growing influence of the Roman Catholic church in Quebec reinforced the clerical and conservative aspects of historical writing after 1850 (Gagnon 1982:2–8, 39; Ouellet 1982:49). This is reflected in the work of historians such as Jean-Baptiste-Antoine Ferland (1805–65), Etienne-Michel Faillon (1799?–1870), and Henri-Raymond Casgrain (1831–1904), who stressed the role of the church in guiding the development of New France. Ferland, a priest who later taught Canadian history at Laval University, had in the course of his religious duties visited Indian bands in Quebec and Labrador, but although he devoted almost fifty pages to discussing native cultures, these experiences did not noticeably lessen his ethnocentric prejudices. He believed that Indians had long been sunk in depravity and were victims of their own brutal passions and degrading vices. They were unwilling to work with regularity, and their much-praised generosity and hospitality were offset by dishonesty, pride, and an excessive desire for vengeance. In his historical writing he viewed the Indian missions as a heroic struggle between Christian civilization and barbaric superstition and argued that only the church offered the Indians the means to escape from their degraded condition, a conclusion that was consonant with the renewed missionary zeal of the period when he was writing. Although they had been reluctant to abandon their undisciplined ways, under Jesuit and Sulpician guidance even the ferocious Iroquois had become models of gentleness and Christian good conduct (Ferland 1882).

Despite his negative views of Indians, Ferland (1882:36) acknowledged that it had been wrong of Cartier to kidnap Donnacona and carry the old chief from a land that must have been dear to him. He also condemned Champlain's seemingly unprovoked attacks upon the Iroquois (ibid., 148) and the dishonest practices of French fur traders, who, he believed, cheated the Indians more than English ones did. Ferland displayed a residual respect for the resourcefulness and national pride of the Iroquois and, as a sensitive nationalist, attributed the failure of Indians to make substantial moral and material progress after their conversion to Christianity to the loss of their native languages and the sense of dignity associated with them (Gagnon 1982:58–64).

Faillon, a French priest who lived in Canada for some time, produced a narrative history of Montreal to 1675. He emphasized the religious and moral ignorance of native people, their enslavement to witchcraft and superstition, and their strong resistance to the work of Christian missionaries; documenting how their everyday life was corrupted by paganism. No people, he asserted, could have been harder to convert than the Hurons. They not only lacked writing, a sense of history, and any idea of God as the ruler of the world, but also permitted divorce and failed to execute murderers or even to discipline their own children. Faillon believed that French merchants, especially Huguenot merchants, had corrupted the Indians and that the fur trade had resulted in the expansion of intertribal wars. He also denounced the folly of French officials who on a number of occasions had goaded the Iroquois to attack New France. By contrast, priests had always sought to promote peace, not only between the French and the Indians but also among the various Indian tribes, so that they could more easily spread the gospel. While Indian actions were often branded as perfidious, cowardly, or traitorous, Faillon attempted to a much greater degree than Garneau did to understand in rational terms why Indians behaved as they did (Faillon 1865–6).

The influence of the pejorative views that the Canadian public had of Indians, as well as the impact of American scholarship in communicating a "scientific" version of such prejudices to Canadian historians, was already evident in historical writing by the middle of the nineteenth century. These developments played a major role in making French- and English-speaking historians and the general public in English Canada receptive to Parkman's colourful but biased portrayals of native Americans. It was all the easier for historians to succumb to his influence, since in the final decades of the nineteenth century many of them were not professionals but rather clergymen, lawyers, and journalists who wrote historical works as a hobby.

In French Canada, the Abbé Casgrain drew attention to Parkman's work. Like many other French-Canadian historians, he admired Parkman but doubted that as a Protestant and an American he could truly understand the significance of what he was studying (Wade 1942:420). French-Canadian historians appear, however, to have been receptive to Parkman's portrayals of native people and to have drawn inspiration from them. They began to rival one another not only in glorifying the habitant as the true foundation of French Canada but also in stressing the vices of Indian life and in portraying the Indians as enemies of the faith and of civilization. Donald Smith (1974:36–43) documents how, while Casgrain delighted in detailed and often fanciful descriptions of the Iroquois torturing priests, Benjamin Sulte (in a denunciation of Jesuit fanaticism in their missionary endeavours), J.-E. Roy, and Ernest Gagnon systematically extended these descriptions to cover the martyrdoms of ordinary settlers: men, women, and children. In his massive *Histoire des Canadiens-français*, Sulte (1882–4, 3:144) assured his readers that their ancestors had been carried off, tortured, and burned by the Iroquois. Most historians did not try to understand why the Iroquois had treated these "pioneers of faith and civilization" so brutally. Even a priest who had worked for many years among the Algonkians chronicled the gluttony, fiendishness, perfidy, and cruelty of their ancestors (Maurault 1866). Indians were habitually portrayed as simple hunter-gatherers, and historians contrasted the radiance of converts with the wretchedness and corruption of paganism. Sulte saw the natives as "hardly more civilized than animals" (Gagnon 1982:96). Smith (1974:40) concludes, "From Casgrain on, all positive references to native people disappear," a statement that catches the spirit of these works, even if it is not literally true. The history of New France increasingly came to be seen as a victorious struggle by priests, soldiers, and ordinary farmers against Indians who threatened the very existence of the colony, just as industrialization and Anglo-Saxon supremacy were seen as threatening French Canada in the late nineteenth century (Walker 1971:36–7).

Towards the end of the nineteenth century, racist theories began to influence the evaluation of native peoples in French-Canadian historical accounts. Even so, Quebec was the last region of North America to be invaded by the intellectual racism that had prevailed in Europe and the United States during most of the nineteenth century. In the 1880s Sulte described French Canadians as a homogeneous race and proclaimed their biological superiority over the Métis and Indians (Gagnon 1982:71, 90–1). Soon after, politicians, such as Henri Bourassa, began to refer to the instincts of race in their speeches, and articles were published alleging the biological inferiority of blacks and native people (D. Smith 1974:55–6). This thinking differed from earlier ethnic stereotypes by interpreting behavioural variations among human groups as being the result of unalterable biological differences.

During his graduate studies at Fribourg and in Paris, the French-Canadian historian Lionel-Adolphe Groulx (1878–1967) was influenced by the followers of the French racial theorist Joseph-Arthur, comte de Gobineau. For Groulx, race became the most powerful historical force and the main one that determines the life of a nation. He pictured French Canadians as a pure race that had survived French misrule and British tyranny (Wade 1956:868–9). It is therefore not surprising that in 1919 he lashed out even more vociferously than Sulte had done in the 1880s against suggestions that French Canadians were a product of extensive interbreeding with native peoples. While this outburst was occasioned by what he correctly viewed as deliberate slurs by Frenchmen and English Canadians against French Canadians, his response was in accord with racist thinking elsewhere. Rather than denying the racial inferiority of native people or the bad effects of interbreeding, he chose only to refute the fact that such interbreeding had happened (Dickason 1982). He clearly regarded the Indians as being biologically inferior to the French. For him their alleged status as a "less evolved race" sufficed to explain why for thousands of years they had been condemned to follow the same degrading way of life (Groulx 1919). While Groulx was criticized by some of his contemporaries for his attacks on racial mixing, leading French- and English-Canadian historians continued to maintain, as late as the 1960s, that Canada was fortunate to have been spared the complications that were alleged to have arisen in Latin America and elsewhere as the result of racial mixture between native peoples and European immigrants (Lanctôt 1963:330; Morton 1963:60–1).

The traditional nationalist school persisted in Quebec until after World War II when a new generation of professionally trained historians brought different interests as well as new methods to the discipline (Ouellet 1982:51–5). Most of them sought to study the effects of the Conquest and the subsequent social and economic development of Quebec. Only Gustave Lanctôt and Marcel Trudel continued to work mainly on the Heroic Period, and they were primarily concerned with the internal affairs of the French community. While increasingly aware of new trends in native American studies and shunning the flagrantly anti-Indian rhetoric of the past, Quebec historians on the whole avoided the serious consideration of native people.

In the latter part of the nineteenth century and thereafter, amateur English-Canadian historians expounded their own patriotic versions of Canadian history. Their style and their treatment of French Canadians and Indians were strongly influenced by Parkman. They portrayed Indians as living an animal-like existence amidst filth and vermin, indulging in immoral behaviour, and brutalizing their womenfolk. Their technology and scientific knowledge were emphasized to be of the most primitive form. Stephen Leacock (1941:19), in one of his historical works, stated, "The Indians were too few to count. Their use of the resources of the continent was scarcely more than that by crows and wolves, their development of it nothing." In other works they were said to possess only the most elementary religious beliefs, depicted as living in sleepless suspicion of their neighbours, and portrayed as being dark and sinister in their retaliations. Even their love of freedom, which had formerly been greatly admired, was now qualified as being only of a "wild primeval form" (Hopkins 1901:44). Leaders who had played an important role fighting alongside the British were generally treated as exceptional individuals who were more intelligent and humane than other Indians and morally superior to them. As James Walker (1971:26–7) has pointed out, ordinary native people implicitly suffered by such comparisons. Even attractive features of Indian life, such as their generosity and personal dignity, were construed to be aspects of a primitive way of life that could not withstand the onslaught of civilization (ibid., 23). In the evolutionary perspective of the time, the Indian was at best a noble animal, at worst a primitive scourge or a butcher. It should be noted, however, that more dogmatic evolutionists, such as Sir John

Lubbock (1865, 1882), in their efforts to demonstrate the extent of human progress, were unwilling to attribute any good qualities to the simpler cultures.

While accepting and propagating this negative image of native peoples, Canadian historians, such as J.C. Hopkins (1901:43), also felt compelled to point out that their American counterparts exaggerated the cruelty and treachery of the "white man's enemy" and did scant justice to the Indians' noble qualities. Memories of "midnight scalping raids" had caused them to forget that there was much to admire about Indian life. Hopkins asserted that the Indian was a being of contrasts and then inadvertently noted the good qualities that Parkman had ascribed to them as evidence of this (ibid., 43–4). He also proudly claimed that in Canada Indians had not suffered from racial antagonism, treaty-breaking, removal from their reserves, wrong treatment by vicious White men, or failure to receive legal justice; and that there was no prouder page in the country's history than its treatment of its "Indian wards" (ibid., 65). He maintained that because Indians were "natural monarchists" and "believers in aristocracy," they preferred the British system to the American (ibid.). This curious assertion appears to have been based on the statement by the missionary John Maclean (1896:371–2) that while Indians rejected an aristocracy of wealth, they embraced one of personal ability, valour, and character.

Canadian historians were prepared to admit that Indians were not naturally inclined to be hostile to Whites and that early European settlers had mistreated them. Hopkins even saw fit to repeat Charlevoix's observation that it had never been the policy of the Iroquois to destroy the French (1901:61–2). Early missionaries were portrayed as being able to alter "savage nature" to an extraordinary degree by restraining lawless passions and "reviving" natural human tenderness (ibid., 72). There was also a tendency to describe the dispirited Indians living on reserves as an emasculated product of modern civilization, who were very different in nature from the original native people. This suggests a continuing vacillation between an eighteenth-century view, which saw the character of native peoples as a product of education and environment, and the racist views of the nineteenth century, which considered it to be biologically innate and hence immutable. Yet historians and the public generally agreed that the Indians were an inferior race doomed to extinction as a result of its inability to respond to the demands of civilized life. No serious attempt was made to explain the condition of the Indian in the nineteenth century as a product of 300 years of colonial history.

*Wacousta.* This illustration, from an edition of John Richardson's novel published in Montreal in 1867, reflects the stereotype of the Indian as a satanic figure. Courtesy Department of Rare Books and Special Collections, McGill University Libraries, Lawrence M. Lande collection.

The same ambivalence about native people is evident in Canadian novels and poems written in the nineteenth century. In these works, the symbolic status of the Indian is even more clearly marked than in historical writing. As Margaret Atwood (1972:87–106) has observed, Indians, whether portrayed as good or bad, were inevitably viewed as more primitive than White men and therefore closer to nature. It was also agreed that Indians, like nature itself, were destined to make way for civilization. Some authors treated them in a sentimental fashion. Charles Mair glorified Tecumseh as a national folk hero in his celebrated verse drama, and others often depicted Indians as a whole as warrior heroes or as living an arcadian life before the coming of Europeans. They were also portrayed as friends and guides for the Whites or as people waiting to be rescued by Christianity from the terrors of their own primitive cultures. The latter included romantic fantasies about human sacrifice or suicide involving Indian girls who were being forced to marry men they did not love. Yet many stories represented them simply as the savage and irredeemable enemies of the White man (Monkman 1981).

The development of professional historiography in English Canada after 1900 saw a growing emphasis on constitutional history, as a result of which less attention was paid both to the French regime and to native people. Carl Berger (1976:183) suggests that English-Canadian academic history was born in a rebellion against the late nineteenth-century glorification of New France. Yet the pejorative stereotypes and confusions about native peoples persisted and possibly were intensified in the writings of the leading historians of this period. Indians continued to be caricatured as savage, cruel, treacherous, bloodthirsty, dirty, cowardly, lazy, fiendish, superstitious, gluttonous, and untrustworthy (Walker 1971:22). Even the development of economic history in the 1920s did not alter the situation. Harold Innis has been described as placing Indian culture at the centre of the fur trade and being the first Canadian scholar to explain its disintegration under the impact of European capitalism (Berger 1976:100). He clearly appreciated the important role that Indians had played in this trade. Yet he paid little attention to the Indian end of it. He ignored cultural differences and social organization as factors shaping the role played by native groups. Instead, he considered that Indians had been linked to the fur trade by rational calculations of economic self-interest (Innis 1930). Others who were attracted to economic history, such as Donald Creighton, paid even less attention to the Indians than Innis had. Growing interest in political biography and the tendency of Canadian history to assert its autonomy of the other social sciences in the 1950s (Berger 1976:160) resulted in an ever-diminishing interest in native peoples.

## VICTORIAN ANTHROPOLOGY IN CANADA

Anthropology developed slowly in Canada in comparison with England and the United States. There were no professionals until 1887 when David Boyle (1842–1911), a former teacher and bookstore owner, received a salary from the Ontario government for curating an archaeological collection that became part of the Provincial Museum (and later the Royal Ontario Museum) (Killan 1983). For a long time there were no journals, apart from newspapers, in which scientific material of any kind could be published. In the 1850s, however, natural history societies became active in Ontario, Quebec, and the Maritime provinces and sponsored journals in which professional men with scientific interests could publish reports on various kinds of research, including archaeological and ethnographic subjects. The most important of these was the Canadian Institute in Toronto, which published the *Canadian Journal* (Killan 1980). There were as yet no large public museums, such as had been founded in major cities in the United States, in which native American artifacts could be studied and displayed. Even private collections were few in number. Much of the ethnographic material that became available for sale at this time found its way into collections in the United States (Cole 1982). Although Boyle encouraged archaeological research in Ontario, it was not until the Canadian government established a separate anthropology department within the Geological Survey of Canada, in 1910, that a team of professional anthropologists was employed anywhere in Canada. No anthropologist taught the subject full time in a Canadian university until T.F. McIlwraith (1899–1964) came to the University of Toronto in the 1920s (Trigger 1981*a*). Nevertheless a number of professional anthropologists lived and worked in Canada in the second half of the nineteenth century. At least three of these had international reputations.

Daniel Wilson (1816–92) had come from Edinburgh to Toronto to teach history and English at University College in 1853 and was president of the University of Toronto from 1887 until his death in 1892. When he arrived in Toronto, he was already a celebrated archaeologist, whose *The Archaeology and Prehistoric Annals of Scotland* (1851) had won him an honorary doctorate from the Uni-

versity of St Andrews. In this book, Wilson broke with the traditions of British antiquarianism, which had been dominated by a
concern with classical antiquities and a sterile desire to identify
all other archaeological remains as the relics of historically known
peoples. Instead, he saw the work of Danish archaeologists, who
interpreted prehistoric times as an evolutionary sequence of Stone,
Bronze, and Iron Ages, as constituting the foundations of archaeology as a science. He was inclined to adopt this view as a result
of his familiarity with the works of the great Edinburgh philosophers and historians of the eighteenth century, who had espoused
the ideals of the French Enlightenment, including the concept of
cultural evolution and the capacity of human beings for cultural
development through the exercise of reason. He was also committed to the monogenist position that all human beings are members of a single species, a view championed in England in the
nineteenth century by James Prichard (1843).

Wilson was quick to appreciate that the Canadian wilderness
was a laboratory of great interest to a prehistorian. For him, the
pioneers who were pushing back the forest had much in common
with the early medieval inhabitants of northern Europe, while the
Indians were a living example of what European society must have
been like in prehistoric times. Because of this, his interests quickly
expanded to embrace all branches of anthropology. In 1862 he published *Prehistoric Man: Researches into the Origin of Civilization
in the Old and the New World*, which appeared in a second edition
in 1865 and was revised and enlarged in 1876. This book, which
was widely read in the United States (Starr 1892), used archaeological and ethnographic data to compare the parallel development
of civilization in the Old and New Worlds. It was a worthy suc-
cessor to Scotland's first major contribution to the study of the
native cultures of the New World, William Robertson's *The History
of America*, published a century earlier (Hoebel 1960).

Wilson rejected the polygenist and racist views prevailing in
American physical anthropology when he arrived in Canada. He
believed that primitive peoples had the same inherent intellectual
abilities as civilized ones and that the latter appeared more intelligent only because they had more opportunity to cultivate their
talents. He also pointed out that much of the same behaviour that
was denounced as cruel and barbarous among Indians was praised
as evidence of vitality and manliness when encountered in the
historical records of early European peoples. While he agreed that
Prescott made the indigenous civilizations of Mexico and Peru
seem unduly like European ones, he interpreted them as analogous

to the early civilizations of Egypt and the Near East and as evidence that the peoples of the New World had been able to evolve their own high cultures. He argued that the triumph of Europeans over other races was due less to constitution than to acquired civilization and rejected the view that Indians and Negroes were inferior to Whites.

In Wilson's opinion, the vigorous Métis population of the Canadian West was living proof that racial interbreeding was not harmful. Races were not necessarily entities of great antiquity but groupings that had been created and perished even in historical times. Contacts between different peoples played a major role in disseminating knowledge and promoting cultural development. Wilson opposed all forms of segregation, such as the separate schools for black children in Canada and New England that were maintained on the grounds that their learning patterns differed from those of Whites. He believed that prolonged government tutelage might prove harmful for Indians and looked forward to the day when they and the White race would mingle to form a single and distinctive Canadian people. While these views have resulted in Wilson's being branded an apologist for White expansion in the West (McCardle 1980:129), their contemporary significance can be judged only by comparing them with the widely held beliefs that native peoples were inherently inferior to Whites, incapable of adapting to civilized life, and biologically doomed to extinction as civilization spread westward.

John William Dawson (1820–99), principal of McGill University from 1855 to 1893, was an eminent geologist, whose conservative views on religion led him to oppose the concept of evolution in both the natural and the cultural realms. His attention was drawn to anthropology by his study of Iroquoian pottery in the collection of the Natural History Society of Montreal and by his rescue and publication of material from an Iroquoian archaeological site near the McGill campus in 1860. His most important anthropological work, *Fossil Men and Their Modern Representatives* (1880), subscribed to the same general premise as Wilson's *Prehistoric Man* had done eighteen years earlier: that the culture of contemporary Indian peoples could shed light on the nature of life in Europe in prehistoric times. Unlike Wilson, however, he argued that there was no proof that cultures at all different levels of complexity had not coexisted throughout history. Sites containing crude stone tools might be workshops or hunting camps belonging to more advanced settlements nearby and stratigraphic evidence suggesting cultural development might have only local significance. He maintained that degeneration was as characteristic of human history as was progress and believed that all the languages of the world showed traces of their common origin, as did humanity's widespread conception of a supreme being and their belief in immortality. In these respects, Dawson revealed himself to be the intellectual heir of Lafitau. He also argued that human physical variations were produced more by cultural differences than by long separation and natural selection. Hence he viewed cranial differences, which were crucial to the racial classifications of his time, as "more an indication of lowness of culture and civilization than of difference of race" (1880:179). He rejected any notion of biological evolution, although he accepted that peoples could become physically as well as morally degraded. While he regarded Hinduism, polygamy, and other non-Western patterns of behaviour as degenerate, his conservative rejection of the evolutionary and racist views popular in his time led him to view anthropological studies as a way to widen sympathies with men of all periods of human history and to demonstrate a unity in the hopes and aspirations of all mankind.

The third outstanding amateur anthropologist, Horatio Hale (1817–96), was born in New Hampshire. After graduating from Harvard University, he did important linguistic and ethnographic research in Oregon and Polynesia as a member of the Wilke Exploring Expedition, a scientific mission sponsored by the United States government. In 1856 he moved to Clinton, Ontario, where his energies were absorbed by his law practice for over two decades. In 1870 he visited the Six Nations Reserve near Brantford, and began to collect information about Iroquoian languages and traditions. His publication of The Iroquois Book of Rites in 1883 was the major scholarly achievement of his career. In the oral literature of the Iroquois, he saw evidence of noble feeling, political wisdom, and literary skill that long pre-dated any European influence. He argued that anthropology had to reject the claims that superior culture implied superior capacity and that our own race and language were the best of all. J.W. Gruber (1967:18) has noted that Hale's anthropology of the 1880s was a relic of the ethnology of the early nineteenth century. In that respect, Hale was not unlike Wilson and Dawson. Each in his way was committed to a view of an undivided humanity that antedated the development of a close link between evolutionary anthropology and scientific racism. The old-fashionedness of their views about human nature led all three to reject what modern anthropologists regard as some of the most abhorrent views of nineteenth-century anthropologists. Through his supervision of the research that the young German ethnologist

Franz Boas carried out for the British Association for the Advancement of Science among the Indians of British Columbia in 1888 and 1889, Hale appears to have played a significant role in purging American anthropology of its racist and evolutionary predilections (ibid., 31–4).

While these scholars had international reputations, a more effective popularizer of anthropology within Canada was the missionary John Maclean (1851–1928). His two books, *The Indians* (1889) and *Canadian Savage Folk* (1896), are rambling works embellished with tales of the torturing of European captives, cannibalism, scalping, and other gruesome Indian customs. Yet, after living among the Blood Indians for nine years, he realized that native peoples were badly misunderstood. Like Hale, to whom his first book was dedicated, he believed that Indians possessed noble characteristics that White men would do well to emulate. Their myths appeared foolish only to those who did not understand them. He also found admirable beliefs in native religions and saw great hope for the betterment of Indians in their strong commitment to religion. He pointed out that in some respects Whites had changed Indian life for the worse and that their ways must be understood if more harm was not to be done to them. Nevertheless, he did not hesitate to brand native peoples and their cultures as primitive and inferior to Europeans. He looked forward to the complete emancipation of their bodies, minds, and souls from their barbaric past, and believed this could be done only by having them adopt White customs and religion. Indians would also have to be taught how to earn their bread by hard work. White Canadians had still to discover how they could best educate them and accept that it would take a long time to complete the process. He approved of the forcible suppression of native practices, such as the potlatch, which, he claimed, retarded progress.

Maclean feared that not all natives would be able to survive the transition to civilized life. Despite these Darwinian reservations, he, like Wilson, looked forward to a time when a single Canadian nationality would emerge which shared a common language and religion. Maclean's work was an unstable mixture of popular stereotypes, mostly unfavourable to native peoples, and more positive views derived from Hale and Wilson. His banal assertion that "under the blanket and coat of skin there beats a human heart" (1896:iii) was a reaffirmation of the eighteenth-century belief in the intellectual and spiritual unity of man, while his statement that native people judge Whites from their own point of view, just as Whites judge them from theirs, was as much an echo of Hale's old-fashioned beliefs as it was of the new cultural relativism being preached by Boas (Stocking 1974). Maclean tried to steer a middle course in his estimate of the degree to which immutable biological factors accounted for Indian behaviour. As a result of increasingly detailed knowledge of native cultures, it was now understood that Indians acted on the basis of premises that were very different from those of Whites. That this middle course was shared by most Canadian historians in the late nineteenth century indicates that the more prestigious Canadian anthropologists had scored at least a limited success with their efforts to resist the racially based evolutionary theories that had coloured Parkman's portrayal of native peoples.

In French Canada, no scholar of the stature of Wilson, Dawson, or Hale showed a sustained interest in the study of native peoples. Nevertheless Maximilien Bibaud (1824–87), son of the historian Michel Bibaud, published two important works on the Indians, a romantic book titled *Biographie des Sagamos illustres de l'Amérique septentrionale* in 1848 and a long, scholarly article, "Discours préliminarie sur les origines américaines," in 1855. Like the English-Canadian anthropologists, Bibaud rejected the fashionable racist notions that Indians constituted a separate species from Whites or that head size was a measure of intelligence. He noted that native people cultivated the arts of peace no less than those of war and had made considerable progress towards civilization prior to the arrival of the Europeans, a fact which by itself refuted the claim that they could not be civilized. Thirty years later, a Quebec civil servant, Napoléon Legendre (1841–1907), took up the same themes in a paper titled "Les races indigènes de l'Amérique devant l'histoire" (1884), which was published in the *Transactions* of the newly founded Royal Society of Canada. He attacked the prevailing view that native peoples had rewarded the disinterested efforts of Europeans to civilize them with acts of murder, pillage, and arson by showing that Europeans had repaid the warm welcome the Indians had given them by occupying their lands without permission, cheating them in the fur trade, and telling them they had to become Christians. In resisting the invaders, the Indians had sought in a justified fashion to defend their country and their families. The atrocities committed in Europe in the sixteenth and seventeenth centuries outweighed any reproaches about the cruelty of native peoples. In 1894 the writer Charles Gagnon published a collection of articles dealing with various aspects of New World archaeology. These works were insufficient, however, to counter the growing tendency of Quebec historians to regard Indians as savages.

## RECENT TRENDS

*The Conflict of European and Eastern Algonkian Cultures, 1504–1700* (1937) by A.G. Bailey (b. 1905) marked a turning point in the historical study of native peoples. It was the first major work in North America that had as its central theme the changing reactions of native people to European encroachment. Bailey's work will be discussed in chapter 4. In 1947 the lawyer and novelist Léo-Paul Desrosiers (1896–1967) published volume 1 of his *Iroquoisie*, which investigated for the first time the history of the native peoples of New France in its own right. Unfortunately, this book was almost totally ignored and Desrosiers had to publish his second volume as a series of papers. Shortly before *Iroquoisie* appeared, Ringuet (Philippe Panneton, 1895–1960), the author of the novel *Trente arpents*, published *Un monde était leur empire* (1943). In it, he drew attention to the Maya and Inca civilizations and urged French Canadians to relate their own history more closely to the land in which they lived and its original inhabitants. In 1945 the biologist Jacques Rousseau (1905–70) vigorously attacked notions of racial superiority and inferiority in his book *L'hérédité et l'homme*. Rousseau spent much of the last twenty years of his life demonstrating that native people were worthy of respect (D. Smith 1974:84–8). His work introduced French Canadians to the values of contemporary North American anthropology, which since the time of Boas had been spearheading the scholarly opposition to racist interpretations of human behaviour and which had also rejected the belief that the worth of a people and their culture can be determined by their alleged evolutionary status.

In recent years, insofar as Quebec historians have written about native peoples at all, they have done so with increasing politeness and in some cases with genuine respect. Marcel Trudel (1968) has drawn his readers' attention to anthropological studies of native people and has tried to treat them in an objective fashion. André Vachon's (1960) study of the effects of brandy on seventeenth-century native peoples was a major contribution to understanding this problem in terms of native values and beliefs. More recently, John Dickinson (1982) has demonstrated that Iroquois warfare did not have the negative effect on the development of New France that nationalist historians have claimed. More far-reaching studies are now in progress that attempt to consider from a unified theoretical perspective the roles played by European colonists and native peoples in Quebec and North American history (Delâge 1981).

On the other hand, the more religiously orientated writings of Lucien Campeau (1967, 1979) continue to manifest a considerable amount of ethnocentric bias.

Historical works published in English have shown a similar tendency to excise negative stereotypes, and some of them have portrayed native people as playing a significant role in Canadian history. Stanley Ryerson (1960) treated the Indian from a Marxist perspective as the chief victim of the struggle between French and English for control of the fur trade. Unlike G.F.G. Stanley (1960), who saw the Métis as a semi-primitive society doomed to national extinction in its struggle with civilization, W.L. Morton (1957) demonstrated that the Métis and the Sioux had played a major role in shaping the development of western Canada. In his treatment of relations between the Indians and the French, W.J. Eccles (1973) returned to the imagery of the noble savage. He observes that the Indians found the French way of life inferior to their own, had a religion adequate to their needs, and were better nourished than the European settlers were. Monographs by historians dealing with native peoples have been appearing with increasing frequency, including Robin Fisher's (1977) study of relations between the Indians of coastal British Columbia and successive waves of European traders and settlers; P.S. Schmalz (1977) on the Saugeen Indians; L.F.S. Upton (1979) on the Micmacs; and F.W. Rowe (1977) on the Beothuks. These works carry forward Bailey's effort to document and understand the nature of early interaction between Indians and Whites.

Yet most historians continue to regard native people as peripheral to the mainstream of Canadian history. The situation has not changed markedly from a decade ago when James Walker (1971:21) suggested that few of his colleagues regarded Indians or their societies as worth serious historical analysis. Studies of relations between native people and Whites generally are viewed, even by historians who study native people, as an extension of historical research into a new field rather than as an integral part of research on Canadian society. Moreover, there is a tendency to favour spectacular but partial interpretations of native behaviour, such as G.T. Hunt's (1940) view of it as economic man writ small or Calvin Martin's (1978) belief that it was controlled by systems of thought wholly alien to our own. Only a detailed anthropological understanding of native cultures allows a reasonable balance to be struck between the distinctive qualities of native cultures and the equally important characteristics shared by all human beings. There is also little awareness that more about native history can or need be studied than only their relationship with Europeans. Because of the restricted interest in native peoples, there is ample scope for confusing, contradictory, and incomplete views about them to persist, as they have done in various guises for centuries, without attracting scholarly notice. In Quebec the continuing preoccupation with "national" history (Vincent 1978a, 1978b; Vaugeois 1978), and in English Canada a continuing insistence on disciplinary autonomy that makes cooperation between history and the other social sciences difficult, have further encouraged the divorce of native peoples from the mainstream of Canadian history.

Since the nineteenth century, school textbooks have been even more important than popular literature in influencing views about native people. While these publications have been stripped of their more pejorative stereotypes in recent years and efforts have been made to convey a more anthropological view of native peoples, the shortcomings of historical research continue to be reflected in them (Vincent and Arcand 1979). The development of native cultures in prehistoric times is treated in an extremely cursory fashion, if at all, and inadequate attention is paid to the dynamism and diverse accomplishments of native people prior to the coming of the first Europeans. Canada's history is considered to have started only with the arrival of the Europeans; and Indians continue to be treated only as part of the setting in which the story of these newcomers unfolds (Walker 1971:27). The Indians teach Europeans how to survive in North America, share their herbal lore with them, aid their explorations, fight alongside them in their wars, and provide furs for trade. Sometimes they are credited with influencing the decisions of White administrators. Yet the Iroquois are still portrayed as murdering Jesuit missionaries and harassing European settlers in such a manner that their ferocity emphasizes the Europeans' heroism (ibid., 36). Very little attention is paid to how or why native people had either friendly or hostile relations with Whites or to the problems that the coming of the Europeans posed for them. Even when Indians are lauded as natural ecologists (the most recent version of the noble savage concept [Martin 1978:157–88]), their way of life is still depicted as equivalent to that of Europeans in prehistoric times. While featured in accounts of early European settlement, they disappear almost completely in works on more recent times. Even though the Plains Indians are generally treated sympathetically in discussions of the Northwest Rebellion of 1885, they are greatly overshadowed by the Métis (Walker 1971:30). Hence the impression is still wrongly given that these first inhabitants of Canada have faded into insignificance as White settlement has progressed.

CONCLUSION

In 1888 William Kingsford (1887–98, 2:166) wrote that the study of Indians was "totally independent of the History of Canada, except so far as it bears upon the relations of the European and Indian races." Despite a growing interest in Indian history, we must conclude that conditions have not changed greatly since that time. In the nineteenth century historians and anthropologists concurred that native people had played at best a marginal and passive role in North American history. Anthropology itself began as a study of peoples who were thought to lack history and hence were doomed to disappear as a result of the spread of European civilization. Anthropology, no less than history, was deeply coloured by White prejudices and unconsciously helped to rationalize the European colonization of North America by reaffirming White stereotypes of Indians as primitive people who were incapable of progress.

Since that time, native people have not vanished. White archaeologists, ethnologists, and historians have slowly overcome the racist biases in their disciplines and have begun to understand native people as resilient actors on the stage of history. Canadian scholars, such as Alfred Bailey and Léo-Paul Desrosiers, played a significant role in combating traditional views. Archaeologists are currently revealing that the prehistory of Canada was a complex mosaic of cultural adaptation and change, while ethnologists, historians, and geographers are learning to cooperate in studying changes in native societies since European contact. In the course of doing so, they are not only documenting the dynamism of native societies but also revealing injustices in the treatment of Indians by White colonists that were not evident to previous generations of researchers.

Despite these advances, historians still tend to study native peoples only in terms of their relations with Europeans during the early periods of European settlement; while studies of more recent times are left to sociologists and anthropologists. Moreover, historians who seek to do justice to native peoples frequently end up merely replacing unfavourable stereotypes with what White society regards as flattering ones; and ethnohistorians see themselves studying aspects of history that lie outside the main focus of historical concern. Historical research thus mirrors the social alienation of native peoples from the society that occupies the land that was once exclusively their own.

The view that native people have played more than an insignificant role in shaping the national history of Canada must be entertained if scholars are to overcome their own heritage of racism and ethnic bias. A more objective understanding cannot be achieved simply by inverting old prejudices but must be based on detailed insights into the social, political, and economic relations, as well as the differing cultural values, that governed the reciprocal interactions between specific groups of native people and European settlers. Such studies almost certainly will provide the basis for a more complete and objective understanding of Canada's historical development. It is also highly likely that as native people increasingly assert their place as part of the Canadian mosaic, such an approach will come more easily.

## CHAPTER TWO

# Before History

Scholars divide the human past into a historical era, which is studied by professional historians using written records, and a prehistoric one prior to adequate written documentation. The beginning of the historical era varies from as early as the third millennium BC in Egypt and the Near East to the time of European discovery in North America and the South Pacific. In Europe archaeology has been viewed as an important source of information about the things human beings have made and used from earliest times to the present. Classical, medieval, and industrial archaeology are valued because they provide information that can supplement the written record of European history. Prehistoric archaeology is acknowledged to be the principal source of information about human origins and for chronicling the development of societies everywhere in the world before the dawn of written history.

In the nineteenth century archaeologists traced human progress primarily in terms of the successive appearance of more sophisticated stone, bronze, and iron artifacts. Because technological progress was accompanied by more complex subsistence economies, denser populations, more hierarchical societies, and more elaborate art and architecture, the archaeological record was valued as evidence that progress in the broadest sense had characterized European society in prehistoric times no less than in the historical period. Archaeologists also sought to trace the origins of particular European nationalities and to demonstrate their greatness in prehistoric times. Hence historians and archaeologists working in Europe shared common objectives, despite their different data and methods. They sought to document the accomplishments of European peoples at successive stages of their development. Although archaeology was closely linked to anthropology and evolutionary theory in the nineteenth century, there was no dichotomy between history and archaeology when it came to studying the European past.

In North America the situation was very different. From early times Indians had been stereotyped as primitive peoples. As the theory of degeneration was abandoned, their way of life was universally interpreted as representing the infancy of the human race. By the nineteenth century one of the principal reasons given for studying native North American cultures was that this would help anthropologists to understand how Europeans had lived during the Stone Age. As proof of this, the archaeological record was expected to show that Indian cultures had not altered significantly in the past. This interpretation was maintained despite the discovery of powerful evidence to the contrary.

As European settlement spread westward in the late eighteenth century, huge mounds and earthworks containing graves filled with sophisticated pottery, copper, silver, and mica ornaments, and worked marine shell were found throughout the Ohio and Mississippi Valleys. This discovery produced widespread speculation that in the remote past Norse, Toltecs, Hindus, or lost tribes of Israelites had established a flourishing and peaceful civilization in North America that later had been destroyed by savage hordes of Indians. Such speculations not only denied creativity to the Indians but also reinforced the widespread belief that they were murderous and destructive. In addition they romantically justified White aggression against native people as a crusade to avenge the Mound-builders. During the nineteenth century, amateur archaeologists played a significant role in elaborating such ideas. Even when the professional archaeologist Cyrus Thomas (1894) demonstrated that the Moundbuilders were not a single people, that mound building had continued into historical times, and that ancestors of the North American Indians were responsible for these works, he made his case seem plausible by denying any special accomplishments to the Moundbuilders and arguing that their way of life was essentially similar to that of the disrupted tribal groups that had lived in the eastern United States in the eighteenth century (Silverberg 1968).

### STUDIES OF PREHISTORY

Historians find prehistoric archaeology a disconcerting discipline. They are used to discovering written documents that have escaped notice and reinterpreting old ones. Because their findings generally do not bulk large in relation to what is already known, the work of a single historian rarely completely alters the understanding of a period. By contrast, archaeological data have been recovered at an accelerating rate in recent decades, and new methods of interpretation are constantly providing fresh insights into their significance. An archaeological understanding of the past is never more than a provisional one that is doomed to be superseded, in whole or part, as new data and new interpretative techniques become available. All too often, however, in stating their conclusions archaeologists fail to specify adequately the limitations of their current knowledge and to this degree they may mislead historians as well as themselves. For example, it was long believed that the addition of beans to the Ontario Iroquoian horticultural complex around AD 1300 had resulted in a rapid increase in population and in the complexity of Iroquoian culture (Noble 1969). Today it is known that beans were introduced into southern Ontario at least two centuries earlier and hence do not explain the massive changes that occurred around AD 1300. If archaeologists are not to obscure the understanding of the past, they must learn to leave many questions unanswered and to offer alternative hypotheses to explain their data.

There are other significant differences between archaeology and history. Written documents reveal the thoughts and actions of individuals and groups who lived in the past. Archaeologists can study only what human beings made or used, not what they thought or did. They are further limited to material remains that have survived the recycling of worn-out objects. They may have no information about the context in which the objects were used because they were disposed of as garbage, and they lack a complete record, since some categories of goods have been destroyed naturally in the soil. This introduces many systematic biases into our understanding of the past. For example, archaeological evidence indicates that trading between different societies has gone on for many millennia in North America. Yet archaeologists generally recover only nonperishable materials, such as copper, shell, and mica, which were mostly used to make luxury goods. They are left to guess, with the help of ethnographic examples, how many more mundane but perishable commodities, such as food, tobacco, nets, basketry, and fancy furs, accompanied these exchanges. Despite these handicaps, the goal of archaeology is to transform its data into a record of human behaviour that can be used as a basis for understanding the past. To do this, archaeologists must constantly strive to learn more about how human behaviour is reflected in the archaeological

record (Schiffer 1976; Binford 1983a). To most historians and ethnologists this endeavour seems highly unpromising. Yet archaeology remains the principal, and in many cases the only, source of
information about human behaviour from earliest times to the
beginnings of written records.

There are, however, important auxiliary sources of information
about human activities in prehistoric times. Linguists have developed reliable techniques for tracing historical relationships among
languages and reconstructing significant aspects of the unrecorded
ancestral languages from which related modern ones are derived.
By comparing the degree of similarity among related languages,
they can estimate approximately how long ago these languages
diverged, although methods that claim to yield specific dates, such
as glottochronology, remain controversial (Hymes 1960). By
examining the vocabulary of an ancestral language, it is possible
to learn something about the environmental setting in which it
was spoken, as well as the way of life that was associated with it
at a particular stage in its development. It is also thought possible
to estimate where an ancestral language was spoken by examining
the distribution of its modern branches and mathematically cal-
culating the fewest and shortest moves that would account for this
distribution (Dyen 1956; Diebold 1960). Using these techniques,
historical linguists can sometimes associate particular languages
with archaeological cultures, although the continuing disputes about
the original homeland of the Indo-European languages illustrate
the problems involved in making such equations (Gimbutas 1963;
Thieme 1964).

The history of languages and cultures does not inevitably follow
a parallel course. In the American Southwest and on the Great
Plains, common cultural patterns were shared by native groups
who spoke totally unrelated languages. Just as modern Finns,
Magyars, and Basques follow the same industrial way of life as
their Indo-European-speaking neighbours, these native groups came
to share a common way of life, which in the case of the Plains
Indians developed after they had acquired Spanish horses early in
the eighteenth century. Nor does the spread of a language signify
the total replacement of one people by another. In France, native
Celtic-speakers, and later German invaders, learned to speak the
language of the Roman Empire. Finally, while linguists have assumed that the ancestral form of any language family must have
been spoken by a single people and therefore over only a relatively
small tribal territory, it has recently been suggested that these
proto-languages may have been spoken in varied forms by more

than one group, thereby allowing for greater geographical continuity in the areas occupied by language families (Snow 1980:27–8). This idea has not yet been endorsed by historical linguists. The only reliable way to establish continuity of language and ethnicity in the archaeological record is to trace individual communities backward in time from the early historical period. In the Eastern Woodlands of North America, the zone of deciduous forest that stretches from the Mississippi Valley to the Atlantic Ocean and from the Gulf of Mexico as far north as southern Ontario, such continuities so far have not been carried back much before AD 1000 (Fitting 1978:15).

Physical anthropology provides another important source of information about the past, primarily through the study of skeletal material recovered by archaeologists. Physical anthropologists now reject the view that racial variations remain fixed over long periods of time or that they can be defined by taking a few measurements on skulls. Many physical characteristics are clearly influenced by cultural behaviour: height can be affected by nutrition, while the robustness of the jaw tends to be reduced and the shape of the face altered once soft vegetable foods have replaced meat as the major component in a person's diet (Schindler et al. 1981). It used to be believed that in Ontario and New York State the transition from the Middle to the Late Woodland period, which occurred about AD 500, was accompanied by the replacement of a round-headed (Walcolid) population by an oval-headed (Lenapid) one (Neumann 1952). More detailed skeletal analyses by James Anderson (1963:108–9) suggested that on the contrary the Middle Woodland population of southern Ontario developed slowly into the Iroquoian type as a response to genetic and dietary modifications. Today, studies of large numbers of skeletal traits that are sufficiently detailed to reveal physical differences between one prehistoric community and another are beginning to address the problems of continuity and discontinuity among populations at a local as well as a regional level (Molto 1979, 1983). Where whole cemeteries have been excavated, it is also possible, by comparing male and female skeletons, to identify that exogamous marriage customs required that partners of one sex be recruited regularly from outside the band or community (Kennedy 1981).

The data recovered from cemeteries also provide important information about mortality rates and the composition of populations according to age and sex. Medical examinations of skeletons can reveal certain causes of death, evidence of injury, and some information about standards of nutrition. The latter have been found to vary even within relatively egalitarian populations according to age, sex, and social status. Chemicals in skeletons may provide information about aspects of diet, such as the relative consumption of meat and various types of plants (van der Merwe and Vogel 1978; Chapman et al. 1981:123–44). Thus physical anthropological data tell us much not only about demography but also about social organization, access to resources, warfare, and violence. Such information, while still scarce for prehistoric Iroquoians, can supplement what can be learned from archaeological analysis in many important ways.

Comparative ethnology studies historically recorded distributions of cultural traits in an attempt to trace the origin and spread of customs or perishable items that are not documented in the archaeological record. The comparative study of mythology reveals motifs and patterns common to many groups (Lévi-Strauss 1981). Studies of prisoner sacrifice throughout the Western Hemisphere have yielded important information about the history and nature of this practice (Knowles 1940; Rands and Riley 1958). In the case of domesticated plants and animals, it is possible, by pinpointing where wild varieties occur naturally, to locate probable points of origin even without archaeological data. For most human inventions, this is not possible. One also cannot assume, as many anthropologists used to, that items that have wide distributions are necessarily older than those with narrower ones; that would make Coca-Cola bottles and steam engines older than Palaeolithic hand-axes. Nor can one assume that products that look much alike necessarily share a common origin (Binford 1972:81–4). Archaeological evidence now indicates that cone-shaped pottery marked with simple cord or fabric decorations, which was once thought to have a single origin (Edmonson 1961), was invented repeatedly in many different parts of the world. For theories about the origin and spread of customs or about items of material culture not generally preserved in the archaeological record to be credible, archaeological evidence must show that there was contact between the regions involved at an appropriate time (Binford 1972:91–6).

A final source of information that can supplement archaeological data is oral traditions. While such information, gathered directly from native people, can be extremely valuable for studying the recent past, orally transmitted accounts frequently are altered over time. Hence claims about the more remote past cannot be accepted without independent confirmation. The use of oral traditions will be discussed in more detail in chapter 4.

While historical linguistics, physical anthropology, comparative ethnology, and oral traditions provide important information about prehistoric times, archaeological research constitutes the main source of data and provides the framework within which all other types of information can be integrated to produce a holistic view of the past.

## EARLY NORTH AMERICAN ARCHAEOLOGY

The first historical question that Europeans asked about the native peoples of the New World was where they had come from. Between the sixteenth and nineteenth centuries, scholars speculated that the Indians might be descended from Carthaginians, Israelites, Canaanites, or Tartars. They were also supposed to be survivors from the lost continent of Atlantis. For several decades in the nineteenth century, polygenists maintained that they were a separate species of human beings that had been created in the Western Hemisphere (Stanton 1960). At the same time, however, there was growing support for the theory, first expounded in 1589 by the Jesuit priest Joseph de Acosta in his *Historia natural y moral de las Indias*, that the Indians had crossed the Bering Strait as primitive hunters and, after spreading throughout the New World, had developed the varied cultures found there by the Europeans (Fagan 1977:21–2). All these arguments were based on comparative ethnology and physical similarities, not on archaeological data. Certain resemblances were later noted between Amerindian languages and those of Siberia. Edward Sapir hypothesized a link between Na-Dené (Athabaskan, Haida, and Tlingit) and Sino-Tibetan (Swadesh 1960:895). Today, apart from Inuktitut, which is spoken by the Inuit on both sides of the Bering Strait, there are no generally accepted historical connections between the languages spoken in the Old and New Worlds.

It was generally assumed that the Indians had not arrived in the New World long prior to its discovery by Europeans. The Biblical chronology allowed at most only a few thousand years for human beings to have lived in the Western Hemisphere. Scholars also believed that their recent arrival explained why the population density of the New World was significantly lower than that of the Old. Later, although some archaeologists searched for an American equivalent to the Palaeolithic period and some interpreted fraudulent platform pipes depicting elephants as evidence that the Moundbuilders had coexisted with extinct Pleistocene animals, the ease with which these arguments were refuted suggests that there was little support among professional archaeologists for the arrival of Indians more than 10,000 years ago (Willey and Sabloff 1980:47–50; Meltzer 1983).

The natural history orientation of early anthropology also mitigated against studies of change. It was assumed that soon after their arrival in the New World, native people lived in the same fashion as they did in historical times. As late as 1909 the ethnologist A.L. Kroeber stated, concerning the archaeology of North America in general, that "the civilization revealed by it is in essentials the same as that found in the same region by the more recent explorer and settler. The material dealt with by archaeology and ethnology is therefore the same" (1909:3–4). He also argued that the native cultures of California were so primitive in the historical period that it was impossible to believe that archaeologists could detect any signs of development in the prehistoric record (ibid., 16). The principal variations in culture that archaeologists believed they could study were, not changes over time, as in Europe, but differences among ethnic groups and cultural areas. Because there appeared to have been so little change, archaeologists also thought they could use ethnographic data in a straightforward fashion to interpret archaeological findings. This connection seemed especially close in the southwestern United States, where anthropologists moved easily between studying living Pueblo Indians and investigating their prehistoric remains (Willey and Sabloff 1980:50–1). During a long formative period, which lasted from about 1800 until 1910, the interpretation of archaeological data was modelled on ethnographic research. We call this the period of ethnographic archaeology.

## ETHNOGRAPHIC ARCHAEOLOGY

The nineteenth century saw the gradual development of archaeology as a scientific discipline in the United States. Already, towards the end of the previous century, the American Philosophical Society, which had been founded in 1743 by Benjamin Franklin and which had maintained a continuous interest in Indian languages and ethnology, had begun publishing papers on the Moundbuilder controversy (Wissler 1943). The establishment of scientific academies in many American cities during the nineteenth century encouraged the systematic collection of artifacts and the publication of accounts of investigations by amateur archaeologists. In 1812 Isaiah Thomas founded the American Antiquarian Society, the first association devoted primarily to the study of American archaeology. The first volume of the society's *Transactions*, published in 1820, contained Caleb Atwater's detailed account of ancient earthworks in the Ohio Valley. The Smithsonian Institution, founded in 1846, played an especially important role in the development of American archaeology. Its secretary, the physicist Joseph Henry, encouraged scientific rigour in the institution's publications by requiring archaeologists to delete what he regarded as unwarranted speculation. The effect of this supervision was particularly evident in E.G. Squier and E.H. Davis's *Ancient Monuments of the Mississippi Valley*, which was published in 1848 as the first volume of the Smithsonian Contributions to Knowledge series. Henry also commissioned more general studies, such as Samuel Haven's *Archaeology of the United States* (1856), a critical review of the development and state of American archaeology that was intended to improve the standard of work in this field (Hinsley 1981:34–40).

In the second half of the nineteenth century, major museums were founded throughout the eastern United States that provided employment for archaeologists and expanded opportunities for the collection and study of archaeological data. These included the Peabody Museum of Harvard University (1865), the American Museum of Natural History in New York (1869), the National Museum in Washington (1879), and the Field Museum of Natural History in Chicago (1893). It is indicative of the views held about American Indians at this time that their artifacts were assigned, along with geological specimens, fossils, and stuffed animals, to museums of natural history rather than to museums of fine arts, which exhibited the cultural achievements of the civilizations of Europe and Asia. Nevertheless, museums played a major role in the professionalization of prehistoric archaeology. Despite its name, the Bureau of Ethnology (later renamed the Bureau of American Ethnology), founded in 1879 under the direction of the renowned geologist John Wesley Powell, promoted archaeological research on a large scale. The establishment of professorships of American archaeology in leading universities was the final step in the emergence of prehistoric archaeology as a scholarly discipline. Hitherto, scholars had come to archaeology after having been trained in other disciplines; now it was possible for students to receive formal training in the subject.

During the nineteenth century, professional archaeologists were interested mainly in studying artifacts. Many of these made their way into museum collections after being found by farmers, construction workers, or amateur archaeologists. Even the excavations sponsored by museums were intended primarily to recover artifacts rather than to record the circumstances in which they were found. Hence the provenience data for these artifacts were generally very poor. Archaeologists wanted to determine how artifacts had been made and what they had been used for, and they relied heavily on ethnographic data and duplicative experiments for this purpose. This orientation is exemplified by Daniel Wilson's "The Huron-Iroquois of Canada, A Typical Race of American Aborigines" (1884), in which archaeological evidence was used merely to illustrate what was already known about the Hurons from ethnographic and historical sources.

Later archaeologists became interested in studying regional variations in their data. W.H. Holmes (1903) defined a series of pottery regions for the eastern United States, while J.D. McGuire (1899) established zones for native pipes and W.K. Moorehead (1910) did the same for stone tools. Cyrus Thomas (1898) and Holmes (1914) both attempted to use archaeological data to delineate a set of general cultural areas covering the whole of North America. These efforts imitated similar ones by ethnologists such as Otis T. Mason (1896) and Clark Wissler (1914). Archaeologists tended to stress the primitive nature of native American technology by claiming that it was easy for White scholars to duplicate and improve on the techniques that had been used to manufacture native goods and that especially elaborate artifacts had been manufactured only after European contact (Hinsley 1981:88–91).

Archaeologists also sought to learn from artifacts about how people had lived in the past. Harlan Smith (1872–1940) used the material he had excavated from the Fox Farm site in Mason County, Kentucky, to illustrate life in a native community in late prehistoric times. The archaeological evidence was presented in terms of standard ethnographic categories, including plant and animal materials, securing and preparing food, habitations, tools used by men and women, processes used to manufacture tools, games, religious objects, pipes, warfare, dress, arts, injuries and diseases, and burial practices. Although ethnographic analogies were used to determine the functions of many artifacts, guesswork played an important role in assigning them to these classes. Smith appropriately called his final report "The Prehistoric Ethnology of a Kentucky Site" (1910).

Throughout this period, American archaeologists showed little interest in changes that had occurred over time. It has been argued that this lack of interest reflected the absence in American prehistory of major technological transformations, such as the transition from the use of stone to that of bronze and iron, that characterized the archaeological record in Europe and the Near East. It has also been suggested that American archaeologists had not yet realized the basic principle of seriation: that regularities in minor stylistic changes can be used to construct cultural sequences (Willey and Sabloff 1980:76–81). Yet American archaeologists were by no means unaware of what was happening in European archaeology (Morlot 1861). Some who had excavated coastal shell mounds had observed significant cultural changes between levels, while others had tried to use stylistic trends to date neighbouring shell mounds containing different cultural material. Cultural chronology of this sort failed to be applied more extensively, not because archaeologists did not know how to arrange their material in temporal sequences, but because they saw no point in doing so (Trigger 1980:664). Where changes were obvious in the archaeological record, they were generally assumed to have resulted from one tribe occupying another's territory rather than from internal changes in the way of life of an individual people. Writers from Parkman (1927:3) to G.T. Hunt (1940:13) described these migrations as aimless tribal movements on a large and thinly populated continent. Thus they denied that the changes they brought about were the purposive subject matter of true history and continued to subscribe to the view that native people had been unable or unwilling to change.

In New York State and Ontario, archaeological research followed the same pattern as in other parts of North America, although its development tended to lag somewhat behind major innovations elsewhere. In the late 1880s and 1890s, Boyle visited many parts of Ontario, surveying for sites, trenching mounds, and persuading farmers and amateur collectors to donate their finds to the Provincial Museum. In 1887 he founded *The Annual Archaeological Report for Ontario*, the first Canadian journal devoted primarily to archaeology. In it, artifacts received by the museum were recorded and archaeological work done throughout the province was described. By the time he died, in 1911, he had established a collection of more than 32,000 artifacts from across Ontario. He had classified these artifacts in terms of provenience, material, and probable use but had showed little interest in establishing their relative age (Killan 1983).

Boyle also encouraged a group of serious amateur archaeologists to carry out site surveys and examinations in southern Ontario. Andrew F. Hunter (1863–1940) systematically recorded 637 sites in northern Simcoe County, the historical homeland of the Hurons. He noted the location of each site, classified it according to function, estimated its size, and sought to determine, as a clue to its age, whether it yielded many, few, or no European artifacts (Kidd 1952:71–2). This was the most comprehensive survey of a historical tribal area so far carried out in North America. At the same time, in a study of sites in Blenheim Township, Oxford County, another member of Boyle's group, William J. Wintemberg (1876–1941), distinguished between "Neutral villages" and "pre-Neutral campsites" (Trigger 1978b:7–8).

Into the early twentieth century, archaeology in Ontario and New York State remained largely museum-oriented, although, in New York State, Arthur C. Parker (1881–1955) was recording middens (trash heaps), post moulds, and the find spots of individual artifacts in his field notes and was publishing monographs describing his research at specific sites (Parker 1907). William Beauchamp (1830–1925) wrote a series of monographs on the prehistoric pottery, chipped and polished stone, horn, bone, shell, and wooden artifacts of the Indians of New York State, as well as others describing European trade goods. These monographs dealt mainly with the Five Nations Iroquois. About the same time, Wintemberg published papers on fish weirs, bone tools, and the use of shells, chert, and cords by the Indians. After he was employed by the National Museum of Canada, he carried out large-scale excavations at six major prehistoric Iroquoian sites across Ontario. The artifacts from each site were studied using the format that Harlan Smith had established in his report on the Fox Farm site. Wintemberg's publications abound in observations of a functional nature. He discussed what foods were eaten, how handles were attached to clay pots, what stages could be recognized in the manufacture of stone tools by observing unfinished specimens, how beaver incisors were used as chisels, and how pipes were made. Yet, although he succeeded in delineating the palisades that surrounded Iroquoian villages, he failed to reconstruct the ground plans of houses by observing patterns of post moulds. Nor did he systematically record the distribution of artifacts within sites, as at least one nineteenth-century Canadian archaeologist had done (Matthew 1884). Thus he failed to advance archaeology in any significant way beyond the traditional museum-oriented approach to the study of artifacts (Trigger 1978b).

During the nineteenth century, archaeologists showed little interest in learning how the Iroquoian cultures of the St Lawrence lowlands had developed. Yet anthropologists wished to know where the Iroquoian people had originated. Many of them believed, as the Jesuit missionary to the Hurons Father Jérome Lalemant had done 200 years earlier (Thwaites 1896–1901, 21:193–5), that in the not distant past all Iroquoian-speakers had been a single people, who later became separated from one another geographically as well as in loyalties, material culture, and dialects. Because they lacked adequate archaeological data, these scholars had to rely on historical records and oral traditions to resolve the question of Iroquoian origins.

Some noted that in the early sixteenth century French explorers had visited a number of Iroquoian-speaking communities in the St Lawrence Valley between Tadoussac and Montreal; yet by 1603 these people had vanished and the Five Nations Iroquois and northern Algonkians were locked in a struggle to control their abandoned homeland. On these few historical facts was constructed the theory that the St Lawrence Valley was the original home of all Iroquoian-speaking peoples.The supposed retreat of the St Lawrence Iroquoians westward from the valley was viewed as only the last of a pattern of tribal movements. Lewis Henry Morgan and Horatio Hale found support for this theory in a seventeenth-century tradition, recorded by Nicolas Perrot, to the effect that the Iroquois had lived in the vicinity of Montreal before being forced to retreat into New York State by the Algonkians (Trigger 1972:48–50). Hale (1883b) also suggested that because their words were the least contracted, Huron and Mohawk were the two least-altered Iroquoian languages, and therefore these peoples must have remained longest in their place of origin, probably in the vicinity of Montreal.

In 1899 W.D. Lighthall (1857–1946) noted that the Jesuits reported that some Hurons claimed to have lived on the shores of Georgian Bay for 200 years prior to 1640. Knowing no other claim of similar antiquity, he suggested that the Iroquoian peoples had originated in the Huron country before migrating south to form the other Iroquoian tribes. Both the Laurentian and Huronia hypotheses were abandoned around the beginning of the twentieth century, when there was a growing consensus that scanty historical records and inadequately recorded native traditions, often of unknown origin, were an inadequate basis for reconstructing Iroquoian prehistory.

Gradually archaeologists in New York State recognized prehistoric sites that were significantly different from those of the historical Iroquois. The pottery from these sites more closely resembled that assumed to have been produced by Algonkian-speaking groups living to the north and east. Hence it was believed that these sites had belonged to an Algonkian people that had been expelled from the region by invading Iroquoians. In 1920 Parker identified a still earlier culture without pottery that he thought exhibited affinities with the modern Inuit. Wintemberg (1931) soon recognized a similar prehistoric succession in Ontario.

New directions were given to speculations about Iroquoian origins as a result of an increasing awareness of the ties between the northern Iroquoian languages and Cherokee, which was spoken in the southeastern United States. In due course, Cherokee was classified as an Iroquoian language (Powell 1891). In 1901 H.M. Lloyd argued that the Iroquoian peoples had originated in the southeastern United States. His work inspired Parker's influential paper "The Origin of the Iroquois as Suggested by Their Archaeology" (1916). Parker argued that many Iroquoian myths, especially those that spoke about a tree with long swordlike leaves, suggested a southern origin. He also noted that many features of northern Iroquoian culture, including their crops, the torture of prisoners, and the distinction between peace and war chiefs, seemed to have originated in the south. Parker interpreted these, as well as a possible relationship between the Iroquoian and Caddoan languages, which also had a southern distribution, as evidence that the Iroquoians had come from the south. While he carefully reviewed the archaeological evidence from New York State, his aim was to prove that Iroquoian culture had been in the north only for a short time before the arrival of the Europeans.

Yet, already in 1907, Parker had noted some stylistic differences between earlier and later Iroquoian sites in western New York State, and in 1921 Alanson Skinner was to distinguish an earlier "Archaic Iroquois culture" from that found on later sites in Cayuga territory. In 1916 Parker allowed that the Iroquoians might have manufactured different styles of pottery when they first arrived in the north than they did later; hence he appears to have been willing to recognize at least minor internal changes in Iroquoian cultures. In southwestern Ontario, Wintemberg (1939:60) correctly interpreted the Uren, Middleport, and Lawson sites as representing a developmental sequence, which he divided into three stages of increasing cultural complexity. He was unwilling, however, to question Parker's theory of the southern origin of Iroquoian culture. He interpreted the "Algonkian" attributes of early Iroquoian culture, not as evidence that it had evolved locally from "Algonkian-like" beginnings, but rather as modifications brought about when an invading Iroquoian group had come into contact with and temporarily absorbed elements from an indigenous Algonkian culture.

All these theories of Iroquoian prehistory assumed that those features common to all the Iroquoian tribes were the oldest, while traits shared by fewer tribes represented more recent differentiations. They therefore also assumed that the main characteristics of Iroquoian culture pre-dated the various tribal divisions and that tribal, linguistic, and cultural differentiation had all followed a parallel course. Such a view ignored the possibility that many of the traits shared by all the northern Iroquoian peoples might have been passed from tribe to tribe in relatively recent times. These included ones that were said to indicate that Iroquoian culture had originated in the south. The role of diffusion, which meant the spreading of ideas from one group to another, was still limited to explaining the sporadic dispersal of Iroquoian-style pottery and agriculture among neighbouring Algonkian peoples. Even early Iroquoian sites that appeared to exhibit evidence of extensive Algonkian influence were interpreted as products of ethnic mixture between native Algonkians and Iroquoian invaders rather than purely in terms of diffusion. The minimizing of cultural change resulting from either internal development or diffusion continued to subordinate archaeological to ethnological research, since it suggested that nothing about native cultures could be learned from studying the former that could not more easily be ascertained from the latter.

## CHRONOLOGICAL ARCHAEOLOGY

After 1910 the systematic application of techniques of stratigraphy and seriation to sites in the American Southwest produced a growing awareness of the importance of cultural change in prehistoric times. Alfred Kidder's *An Introduction to the Study of Southwestern Archaeology*, published in 1924, provided the first culture-historical synthesis of archaeological data for a major region of North America. Kidder discussed the archaeological material for nine adjacent river drainages in the Southwest in terms of four shared phases of cultural development: Basketmaker, Post-Basketmaker, Pre-Pueblo, and Pueblo. He argued that the Southwest owed little more than the "germs" of its culture to the outside and that its development had been a local and almost wholly independent one that was cut short by the "devastating blight of the white man's arrival" (1962:344). While most archaeologists did not share Kidder's faith in internal development, his book played an important role in stimulating a concern for the systematic investigation of cultural change elsewhere in North America. It was the first major work of synthesis reflecting the interest in chronology that dominated American archaeology from 1910 into the 1950s (Willey and Sabloff 1980:83–129).

During this period archaeologists undertook as their primary goal to delineate cultural sequences for each region of North America. Their acceptance that changes had occurred in prehistoric times reflected a growing awareness of temporal, as well as ethnic and geographical, variation, which had become more self-evident as the archaeological record came to be known in greater detail. It also reflected, however, the less hostile view of native peoples that developed following the establishment of effective White control over the whole territory of the United States by the end of the nineteenth century and the confinement of the last free native peoples on government reservations (Rawls 1984). Equally important, this view was encouraged within anthropology by the overt stand against racism that Boas was taking (Harris 1968:290–300).

Nearby archaeological sites that contained similar inventories of artifacts were grouped to form archaeological cultures, which were usually called phases or foci. These were assumed to be entities equivalent to tribes in ethnology. The geographical and temporal extent of archaeological cultures had to be defined individually, since they varied considerably. Cultures in the same region were dated relative to each other by means of stratigraphy and seriation. More distant ones were considered to be contemporary if they shared a few highly distinctive types of artifacts that were presumed to constitute evidence of trade or other forms of cultural contact. Cultures sharing a considerable number of traits were grouped to form hierarchies that were assumed to reflect various kinds of historical relations. The only one of these larger groupings to survive is the culture area, which embraces cultures that shared a similar adaptation to the same environmental zone (Willey and Sabloff 1980:104–8).

There was now a general tendency to explain cultural change not only in terms of migration, as had been done previously, but also in terms of diffusion. This presupposed the more tolerant view of Indians as being flexible enough to make use of new ideas, even if they were still generally believed to be uninventive. Major innovations, such as pottery, agriculture, and burial mounds, were rarely attributed to the North American Indians. Instead, each was traced to a presumed point of origin in Central America or Siberia, whence it was believed to have been brought into North America by a fresh incursion of migrants.

A major problem that confronted archaeologists before radiocarbon dates became available in the 1950s was the calendrical dating of archaeological sequences. In the arid regions of the American Southwest, where logs were preserved as elements of buildings, tree-ring studies allowed precise dates to be assigned to sites as far back as the beginning of the Christian era. In eastern North America this method could not be applied. Instead, a guesswork chronology was accepted in which Late Archaic cultures, now dated between 4000 and 1500 BC, were dated no earlier than AD 300 (Ritchie 1944). The rapid succession of major changes that appeared to be documented in the archaeological record seemed reasonable so long as these changes were thought to have been brought about by population movements and cultural diffusion, since the intervals between them were too brief to allow much time for internal developments. The dating system thus continued to reflect limited faith in the cultural creativity of native people. Radiocarbon dating not only relieved archaeologists from having to depend almost entirely upon stylistic criteria to work out relative chronologies, but also revealed that they had grossly underestimated the age of most prehistoric cultures in eastern North America. The new chronology slowed the rate of cultural change to the point where it seemed as likely to result from internal processes as from diffusion and migration.

The growing preoccupation with the study of cultural chronologies led many archaeologists to abandon their earlier interests in determining how artifacts had been made and what they had been used for. Instead, they sought to define archaeological cultures in terms of formal trait lists and to align them on chronological charts in which horizontal columns represented chronological periods and vertical ones geographical divisions (Taylor 1948:73–80). For most archaeologists, the reconstruction of culture history became "little more than an ordering of the archaeological remains of a given area in a spatial-temporal framework" (Willey and Sabloff 1980:110). To define cultures it was necessary to recover a representative sample of artifacts from each archaeological site. Yet it was generally assumed that any part of a site was representative of the whole; therefore excavations were carried out in those areas that would yield the most artifacts for the least effort. This most often meant digging middens. In the 1930s and 1940s, only small portions of archaeological sites were generally excavated in Ontario and New York State, and almost no attention was paid to settlement patterns, except by Wilfrid Jury, who had learned about archaeology by working for Wintemberg (Trigger 1981b:10–13).

The chronological approach encouraged the study of the "pre-Iroquoian" archaeology of New York State. In 1944 William A. Ritchie divided the prehistory of that area into three periods: Late Prehistoric (now called Late Woodland), Intermediate (Middle Woodland), and Archaic. He defined the archaeological cultures from various parts of the state that belonged to these periods by providing a comprehensive list of the types of artifacts associated with each culture. He also described a selection of archaeological sites and summarized the human skeletal evidence for each. Ritchie used shared features to try to establish a more detailed chronological arrangement of these cultural units. He generally assumed that each culture or set of closely related cultures represented a separate people. Hence he interpreted the Owasco culture, which is now known to have been an early stage in the development of the Five Nations Iroquois and some neighbouring groups, as being at least partly coeval with early Iroquoian sites and probably belonging to an Algonkian-speaking people. While Ritchie accepted internal changes and diffusion as possible explanations for some aspects of the archaeological record, he invoked population movements to account for the appearance of many cultural configurations. He agreed that the Archaic pattern was of Asiatic origin. He also showed almost no interest in environmental changes or their effects on prehistoric cultures. This is not surprising, however, since the oldest Archaic cultures were not believed to date earlier than AD 300.

Although most archaeologists, including Ritchie, continued to believe that Iroquoian culture, with its horticulture, incised pottery, and small triangular arrowheads, had been brought into the lower Great Lakes region by a migration from the south, the growing emphasis on diffusion provided the basis for a new understanding of its origins. In the late 1930s some archaeologists took note of Wintemberg's evidence that the culture of the historical Neutral Indians of southwestern Ontario had slowly evolved there from antecedents that in significant respects resembled still earlier cultures ascribed to the supposedly Algonkian inhabitants of that region (Pearce 1984:35–6). They also noted that no ancestral version of Iroquoian culture had been located anywhere in the southeastern United States, nor had any evidence of their migration northward been found in the Ohio Valley. They began to speculate that Iroquoian culture might have developed among a population already living in the north, with diffusion accounting for its southern characteristics. In 1944 James B. Griffin suggested that the historical Iroquoian cultures probably had evolved from a regional variant of Hopewellian culture that had already moved north from the Ohio Valley in the Middle Woodland period.

Eight years later Richard S. MacNeish (1952) established what has come to be called the in situ theory of Iroquoian origins with his publication of *Iroquois Pottery Types*. He sought to demonstrate that the pottery styles associated with the historical Iroquoian peoples had evolved from local Middle Woodland antecedents that archaeologists had hitherto wrongly associated with Algon-

kian-speakers. He concluded that after AD 1000 the Middle Woodland Point Peninsula culture had given rise to four regional variants,
which represented the first differentiation of the Iroquoians into
tribal groupings. The most easterly variant in New York State was
probably ancestral to the Mohawks and the central one produced
the Oneidas and Onondagas. In western New York State, a third
sequence led to the Cayugas and Senecas, while in Ontario a variant
of Owasco produced the Neutral and Huron cultures.

Basic to MacNeish's theory was the rejection of the migration
model that had dominated Iroquoian studies until that time. In
place of it, Iroquoian culture was seen as developing amongst people already living around the lower Great Lakes. The various cultural features shared by the northern Iroquoian peoples were perhaps
to a small degree a residue from the Point Peninsula culture, but
the most distinctive ones had been acquired by them at a later
time. Using pottery types, MacNeish felt able to trace the development of local groups, each of which had evolved a distinctive
culture within a broader field of shared cultural development. Probably because of his concentration on pottery types and on tracing
the origin of tribal groups, he chose to stress local lines of development rather than the important interconnections among different Iroquoian peoples. The result was a model that rejected migration
and emphasized local development, leaving unresolved the further
question of the relative importance of the roles played by on-the-
spot innovation and diffusion. This encouraged archaeologists to
ignore interactions between prehistoric Iroquoian cultures and
neighbouring non-Iroquoian ones, especially those to the south.

In 1966 James V. Wright drew upon the archaeological research
of Thomas Lee, J. Norman Emerson, and Frank Ridley to modify
and refine MacNeish's view of Iroquoian development in southern
Ontario. He proposed that two Iroquoian cultures had evolved from
Middle Woodland antecedents in Ontario about the same time as
the earliest Iroquoian cultures had developed in New York State:
the Glen Meyer culture in southwestern Ontario and the Pickering
culture north of Lake Ontario. Later the distinction between these
two cultures disappeared, as a result, Wright argued, of the conquest
of the Glen Meyer people by the Pickering. For about 100 years
southern Ontario remained culturally unified as it developed through
what Wright called the Uren and Middleport substages. Then its
cultural unity again broke down as the historical Neutral tribes
evolved out of the Middleport culture in southwestern Ontario and
the Huron and Petun tribes did the same north of Lake Ontario.

Since 1966 the Princess Point culture has been defined in southwestern Ontario (Stothers 1977). It is ancestral to Glen Meyer and
appears to mark the transition from a hunting and gathering economy to one relying significantly on food crops. Research has also
progressed on the in situ evolution of the St Lawrence Iroquoians,
whom MacNeish wrongly believed represented a temporary expansion of the Onondagas and Oneidas to the northeast (Pendergast
1975). Finally, William Noble (1969) took the first steps towards
understanding the social changes involved in the development of
Iroquoian culture in Ontario with his study of the evolution of
settlement patterns, subsistence strategies, burial practices, and
pipes, which he assumed had special social significance.

SPATIAL ARCHAEOLOGY

In the 1950s American archaeology began to change radically.
Archaeologists switched from trying to account for cultural change
in terms of external stimuli – diffusion and migration – to understanding it as a process of internal transformation. Environmental
changes and processes within individual societies were seen as
playing a major role in promoting the changes observed in the
archaeological record. Archaeologists also were coming to believe
that pottery, burial mounds, copper working, and agriculture had
evolved independently in many cultures when conditions were
favourable. Even when traits were known to have diffused from
one culture to another, it was thought more important to understand why and how they had been internalized into the recipient
culture than to determine where they had come from. All this
encouraged an interest in the variability in the archaeological record as expressed in spatial distributions of artifacts in relationship
to houses and sites and of sites in relationship to one another and
to their environmental setting (Caldwell 1959).

One of the first manifestations of this new orientation was the
growing attention paid to cultural ecology. Archaeologists began
to interpret their data as evidence of how prehistoric societies had
adapted to their natural environments. In *Trend and Tradition in
the Prehistory of the Eastern United States*, Joseph Caldwell (1958)
argued that ecological adjustments to the disappearance of big game
at the end of the last Ice Age had resulted in more complex patterns
of food collection, which in most regions of North America supported a larger human population and promoted increasing seden-
tariness. These developments encouraged the acquisition of heavier

and more diverse types of equipment than had been used previously, including ceramic cooking vessels. Caldwell stressed not only the internal capacity for change among the cultures of the Eastern Woodlands, but also the need to understand the roles that artifacts had played as part of adaptive systems.

The development of settlement archaeology also moved prehistoric archaeology away from a preoccupation with artifacts and towards the study of household composition, community patterns, and general social organization. This line of thinking received substantial expression in the unilinear scheme of types of community patterning devised in 1955 at the Seminar on Functional and Evolutionary Implications of Community Patterning (Beardsley et al. 1956). As a result of this seminar, concepts such as free wandering, restricted wandering, central-based wandering, and semi-permanent sedentary were used to describe the prehistoric settlement and subsistence systems of the Eastern Woodlands.

William Ritchie began an extensive investigation of Iroquoian settlement patterns in New York State in the 1950s (Ritchie and Funk 1973). Sites dating from Owasco times to the early historical period were studied in the area between Buffalo and Albany. Yet, in general, only small portions of any one site were excavated. While a few longhouses were totally cleared, others were only partially dug. Their remaining outlines were traced with slit trenches, which were also used to follow village palisades and establish total village sizes. As a result, many interpretations of village plans remained tentative. As an extension of this research, James Tuck (1971) sought, by determining the sequence of Iroquoian sites in the Syracuse area, to trace the development of the historical Onondaga tribe.

Increasing emphasis on cultures as adaptive systems and on changing social organization helped to eliminate the widespread disbelief in the creativity of native peoples. These trends were consolidated by the New Archaeology, a movement that began in the United States in the 1960s. Lewis Binford (1972), in particular, impressed upon archaeologists the need to view prehistoric cultures, not as collections of isolated traits, but in terms of integrated behavioural patterns relating peoples to their environment. He drew attention to the internal complexity of cultures and the need to study archaeological data as a record of the many kinds of activities in which groups of people had been engaged. Binford also stressed the need to treat archaeological data as a record of total cultural systems and not simply of technology or subsistence activities.

Archaeologists henceforth spent more time trying to reconstruct palaeoenvironments and to determine how prehistoric societies had adapted to them. They sought to learn as much as possible about prehistoric diets; seasonal variations in the production and use of food; the division of labour according to age, sex, and other criteria; tool kits as indications of economic activities; and settlement patterns as evidence of strategies for the use of resources. The extensive use of flotation to recover small organic remains from pits and middens greatly expanded knowledge of food sources. All of this helped archaeologists to discover at what time of year and for what purpose each archaeological site had been used. More systematic attention was also paid to studying the movement of goods from one site to another in order to define regional trading patterns. Trace-element analyses were employed to pinpoint the origin of raw materials, such as obsidian, native copper, and pottery clay. The distributions of luxury items were also examined within sites to document differential access to such goods.

Demography and social organization became important areas of investigation. Household composition was studied by examining the internal arrangements of dwellings and plotting the distribution of artifacts in relationship to them. By doing this, it was sometimes possible to determine how many people had lived in a house, how these people had been related to each other, and what activities had been carried out in and around houses (Hayden 1979; Clermont and Chapdelaine 1983). This research also provided data for studies of spatial and temporal variations in the size and plans of houses (Dodd 1984). Village plans and regional settlement patterns were interpreted as evidence of social and political organization. Much of this research was focused on determining relative social status and social hierarchies by establishing variations in access to goods and services. Burial customs were studied as another source of information about social status (Chapman et al. 1981). These developments have revolutionized the archaeological techniques employed throughout North America. Archaeologists no longer treat a sample of material from a single site as if it were representative of a whole community or a whole culture. They are also increasingly aware of the vast range of potential variability within and among sites.

In 1971 James Wright (1974) took a major step forward in Iroquoian studies with his total excavation of the Nodwell site, a fourteenth-century Iroquoian settlement near Southampton, Ontario, which was being threatened by a housing development. This work documented an unanticipated amount of diversity within the settlement. Internal arrangements displayed striking variations in the population densities of houses. Differing amounts of miniature, often crudely made, pottery suggested significant fluctuations in the number of children living in different longhouses. Refuse from ceramic manufacture was found in all but three of the twelve long-houses, but the amount varied considerably in relationship to the size of the houses and the number of finished vessels discovered in each. Wright also used the stylistic variations in ceramics to divide the houses into three groupings that may have been clans or lineages. For the first time, it was possible to study correlations between artifact distributions and features over an entire Iroquoian habitation site. This permitted archaeologists to ask questions concerning Iroquoian social behaviour that they had not previously considered.

The almost total excavation of the prehistoric Huron Draper site, near Pickering, Ontario, carried forward the work begun at Nodwell. Work at that site permitted the recovery of nearly the entire plan of an exceptionally large and complex village; data concerning its repeated expansions; the locations, spacing, orientation, and internal features of longhouses and other structures; and the locations and extent of middens, both within and around the edges of the site. Special attention was paid to subsistence practices, especially the use of floral resources. Unlike many other Iroquoian sites, a large portion of this one had never been ploughed. Undisturbed floor deposits were screened for four complete and thirteen partial houses, while more were examined in the ploughed area. As a result of this research, an unparalleled amount of information is now available for a single site about variations in house plans, as well as in the amounts of different types of artifacts found in middens, house floors, and open spaces (Finlayson and Pihl 1980). Efforts to match fragments of broken pipes found throughout the site have provided valuable information about how these objects were reused and disposed of after breakage (von Gernet 1982). The work at Draper has stimulated the total, or nearly total, excavation of many Iroquoian village sites elsewhere in Ontario. This research has been synthesized in Gary Warrick's (1984) study of changes in village planning from Early Iroquoian to protohistoric times in Ontario.

Iroquoian archaeologists have also become aware of the importance of regional surveys for defining settlement patterns for different periods and studying changes in them over time. This requires that special purpose sites, those used seasonally for hunting, fishing, gathering nuts, tending crops, and mining flint, be distinguished from communities that were inhabited throughout the year (Williamson 1983a). Such information is necessary to prevent overestimating populations, to avoid erroneous conclusions about the locations of major settlements, and to define the subsistence patterns of various Iroquoian groups; in brief, it is a prerequisite for any general study of Iroquoian population size or ecology (Pearce 1984). It seems clear, as a result of these studies, that the evolution of Iroquoian subsistence patterns was a more complex process than had been previously believed. Comprehensive regional surveys are also required to define political groupings and to study trade and warfare in prehistoric times.

The interpretation of such findings requires greater chronological precision. Demonstrating that sites coexisted as part of a settlement pattern demands more exact dating than does the building of general cultural chronologies. It has also become desirable to distinguish what happened to an Iroquoian site during the several decades that it was inhabited: Did the economy change as the surrounding environment was degraded by intensive use? Did the population of such a community increase or decrease? How did the occupation patterns of individual houses change? Answering such questions requires that archaeological data (including the proveniences of radiocarbon samples) be recorded ever more minutely and studied in greater detail (Timmins 1984). This makes archaeological research increasingly labour intensive and expensive. Yet the result is an understanding of the past that is conceived, not, as formerly, in terms of cultures defined as collections of artifacts, but rather in terms of the social systems that were the means by which groups of human beings wrested a living from their environment and satisfied their own socially defined needs (Pearce 1984).

## SYMBOLIC ARCHAEOLOGY

In recent decades American archaeologists have concentrated on establishing universal generalizations that would permit them to infer human behaviour from archaeological data. Because of this, they have mainly investigated ecological adaptation and social organization, the two spheres of human activity that appear to be most susceptible to generalizations of this sort. Even the study of burials has been directed almost exclusively towards the study of social organization. Relatively little attention has been paid to prehistoric cosmology, religious beliefs, or iconography. Most work on these topics has been done by archaeologists not closely associated with the American New Archaeology (Dewdney and Kidd 1967; Vastokas and Vastokas 1973). Mainstream American archaeology has also tended to regard these aspects of culture as epiphenomena that are of little importance for explaining change.

Yet, long ago, V.G. Childe (1956) argued that the incorporation of these spheres of human activity into a general explanation of human behaviour was essential even for the development of a successful materialist research strategy. In recent years the advocates of so-called structural or symbolic archaeology have claimed that archaeologists must pay systematic attention to the cognitive aspects of human behaviour if they are to explain cultural change adequately (Hodder 1982a, 1982b; Renfrew 1982).

Evolutionists can generalize about the characteristics of knowledge and beliefs that are associated with societies at the same level of development, but these are such high-level generalizations that they explain only a small portion of the regularities that can be observed in the archaeological record. The specific content of knowledge and beliefs is highly variable, even among societies at the same stage of development; yet within individual societies this content is by no means random or unstructured (Gellner 1982). Hence as archaeologists begin once more to take account of the complexity of human phenomena, they are realizing that universal principles do not explain all of the regularities that characterize human behaviour. It is possible, for example, to formulate significant generalizations about the canons of beauty in ancient Greek or Egyptian art (Schäfer 1974). Generalizations about aesthetic standards and to a lesser degree about iconography can be derived from formal studies of material remains alone. Yet, when contemporary written records are not available, an understanding of the significance of archaeological evidence concerning religious beliefs can generally be recovered only by means of the direct historical approach.

The importance of the latter sort of studies for the prehistoric archaeology of eastern North America has recently been illustrated by R.L. Hall and George Hamell. Hall (1979) has drawn upon ethnographic and ethnohistorical evidence concerning native religious beliefs and symbolism in eastern North America to explain the internal structure of Adena burial mounds as well as why certain classes of artifacts were included in Middle Woodland burials. Hamell, in a series of provisional studies, has addressed the problem of why certain exotic materials, such as native copper, quartz crystals, and marine shell, were utilized in burial rites that persisted, with fluctuating intensity, from Late Archaic times to the historical period. On the basis of comparative analyses of historical Iroquoian, Siouan, and Algonkian mythology and religious beliefs, he has concluded that these and certain other natural substances found beneath the ground or in the water were thought to possess supernatural powers that promoted spiritual and physical vigour among the dead no less than among the living. For this reason, it was desirable to place these substances in graves (Hamell 1980, 1982). Despite the well-known problems involved in equating symbols and beliefs over long periods of time, Hamell's evidence is particularly convincing because the archaeological record shows the continuous use of these materials in funerary contexts from their first occurrence into historical times. Both anthropologists offer explanations of significant regularities, which could not be accounted for by cross-cultural generalizations.

The symbolic approach is of special importance because it encourages a more holistic view of prehistoric cultures than conventional American archaeology does. Even more importantly it directs attention to the unique features of these cultures as well as to the properties that they share with human societies in general or with societies throughout the world at the same stage of development. Together with a reviving concern to determine the ethnic identity of prehistoric cultures and their historical relationship to modern native peoples, such studies enhance the historical significance of prehistoric archaeology at the same time that they expand the range of a scientific approach to studying prehistory.

The remaining sections of this chapter will survey current interpretations of Iroquoian prehistory in order to understand that society at the time of European contact. Because of the rapid pace of archaeological discoveries, no synthesis of this sort can long remain unchallenged. I have therefore emphasized innovative trends in research and problems that remain unanswered. Despite the provisional nature of most archaeological interpretations, the broad outlines of Iroquoian prehistory have been emerging with greater clarity, especially in southern Ontario, where more work has been done than elsewhere in recent decades.

## PREHISTORIC HUNTER-GATHERERS

For various reasons, archaeologists know considerably less about early prehistoric periods than about later ones. The earliest evidence of human beings in upper New York State and southern Ontario dates sometime after the retreat of the last glaciation. During the Palaeo-Indian period, which probably lasted in this area from about 9000 to 8000 BC, the southern front of a continental glacier ran across central Ontario, and the Champlain Sea filled the St Lawrence Valley. The whole of southern Ontario probably supported only one or two hunting bands that subsisted mainly by exploiting local herds of caribou (Roosa and Deller 1982; Storck 1984). As the climate grew warmer, tundra and open spruce parkland were transformed into boreal forest, and hardwood trees spread north into central Ontario. Along with these changes, nonmigratory deer replaced caribou as the principal game animal. Environmental conditions roughly approximating those of modern times were reached by about 4000 BC.

Native people appear to have gradually exploited a wider range of natural resources. Net fishing and weir fishing and the extensive use of nuts and other vegetable foods supplemented big game hunting at least by the Late Archaic period (4000–1500 BC), and they were relied on to a still greater degree during the Early (1500–500 BC) and Middle (500 BC–AD 500) Woodland periods (Cleland 1982). Accompanying these developments, there appears to have been a progressive increase in population, as a result of which individual band territories became restricted to single river valleys and to portions of the larger ones. There is also evidence of increasing contact among neighbouring bands. Beginning in the Late Archaic period, exotic materials, such as native copper, which is found in the Lake Superior region, and marine shells from the Atlantic and Gulf coasts of the eastern United States were exchanged from one group to another over most of eastern North America. These exchanges, along with intermarriage, probably helped to maintain friendly relations among neighbouring bands. There is relatively little archaeological evidence of blood feuds or warfare among hunter-gatherers in the St Lawrence lowlands, such as might have resulted from competition for scarce resources (Ritchie 1965:123).

There is evidence of a general continuity in the development of economies and social life in the St Lawrence lowlands from Palaeo-Indian times to the historical era. Yet, until after AD 800, when the continuity of various Iroquoian-speaking groups is well attested archaeologically, we still do not have enough evidence to demonstrate a corresponding continuity in population. The supporters of in situ development have assumed that there was a continuity of population from Middle Woodland into later times throughout the entire region. Almost everywhere, however, the evidence for local continuities remains inconclusive.

Although some pottery first appeared in New York State during Early Woodland times (it had been used in the southeastern United

States more than a thousand years earlier), it first became common throughout the lower Great Lakes region at the beginning of the Middle Woodland period. Small cooking pots with pointed bottoms were manufactured by the coiling method and decorated with stamped and cord-marked patterns. The increasing use of pottery appears to reflect a less migratory pattern of life than had prevailed hitherto. The overall population is believed to have increased, as well as the number of bands, each occupying a smaller territory. As in earlier periods, bands of between 100 and 300 people gathered at fishing stations along lakes and rivers during the spring and summer. It was at this time of year that burial rituals were performed in special cemeteries adjacent to fishing camps and probably the time that members of different bands visited each other to exchange goods, join in celebrations, and arrange marriages. The friendly ties thus established among neighbouring groups helped to ensure that their subsistence activities were not disrupted by warfare and made it possible for individuals to shift from bands with increasing populations to less prolific ones.

The natural resources of the region were utilized more efficiently in the Middle Woodland period than they had been in the past. Autumn-spawning fish were exploited and more nuts, molluscs, and wild rice were consumed (Ritche 1965:203–12). It has also been suggested, on the basis of tooth-wear patterns, that horticulture may have begun to play an incipient role in some late Middle Woodland economies in Ontario and New York State, as it had already been doing for some time to the south and west (Molto 1979:40–1; Patterson 1984:325). Recently, carbonized maize kernels have been recovered from what appears to be a very late Middle Woodland feature at the Dawson Creek site at Rice Lake, Ontario. This feature has been radiocarbon dated to AD 545 ± 60; when calibrated to take account of fluctuations in carbon 14, the date becomes AD 615 ± 25 (Jackson 1983; Timmins 1984:85). At present, these are the oldest known cultivated plants from Ontario. The more intensive utilization of natural resources in certain especially rich areas may have allowed the members of some bands to remain together, or at least to stay in intermediate-sized groups, for a longer period than they had done previously (Finlayson 1977:563–78; Spence et al. 1979:117).

Ethnologists have argued that while hunter-gatherer groups, such as the Bushmen, enjoy coming together periodically in large groups, tensions soon develop which lead to their dispersal (Turnbull 1968). The problem is the lack of any authority to resolve conflicts. In historical times, however, the Algonkians of central Ontario had chiefs whose position tended to be hereditary in particular families. Although they had no coercive power, these chiefs appear to have been able to resolve conflicts so that bands of several hundred people could remain together from spring until late autumn (Cleland 1982:775). Similar chiefs may have existed in southern Ontario in Middle Woodland times and may have been the antecedents of Iroquoian peace chiefs. Yet no naturally occurring food was sufficiently abundant or dependable from one year to the next to permit the development of sedentary life (Keene 1981). However much food was collected, sooner or later in the autumn the bands had to divide into smaller extended family groups which moved into the forest to hunt game. The winter hunting season was the time of greatest hardship, danger, and mortality for the whole society.

Archaeologists generally have assumed that in Middle Woodland times men remained in the same band for life, while adult women normally left their band to marry men from other groups. If the greatest challenge was to survive the winter, it was essential that hunters, upon whose skill and cooperation the survival of their families depended, were able to work together effectively. This was best achieved by having a man and his adult sons, or several brothers and cousins, live and cooperate as members of the same group (Murdock 1949:213–14). This interpretation has been challenged by the work of the ethnologists R.B. Lee and I. DeVore (1968) and Lee Guemple (1972), who suggest that hunter-gatherers typically have more flexible and variable patterns of marriage and residence. Other anthropologists have argued that matrilocal residence patterns (whereby a man goes to live with his wife's family), such as are found among some of the coastal hunter-gatherer peoples of British Columbia, may have developed in some parts of the St Lawrence lowlands in the Middle Woodland period as a result of heavy reliance on fishing (Clermont and Chapdelaine 1982:120). Yet an analysis of human skeletons from the Rice Lake area of southern Ontario suggests a closer biological affinity among the male than among the female members of local groups (Spence et al. 1979). The regular movement of women from one band to another upon marriage would also explain why pottery styles are distributed much more homogeneously throughout the Great Lakes region than are stone tools and copper artifacts, which tend to vary locally within the same culture. It is assumed that women made pottery in Middle Woodland times as they did in this part of North America in the historical period. David Brose (1970:67–8) has argued that it was the rapid spread of new pottery styles as a result of such marriage practices that formerly gave archaeologists the impression that a new ethnic group had swept into the area at the beginning of the Middle Woodland period.

At least three broadly contemporary Middle Woodland cultures have been defined in the St Lawrence lowlands on the basis of stylistic differences in pottery and some other artifacts: Saugeen, in southwestern Ontario; Ontario Point Peninsula, in the central and eastern parts of southern Ontario; and other variants of Point Peninsula culture in southern Quebec and upper New York State. The Laurel culture flourished in northern Ontario and adjacent parts of Manitoba, Michigan, and Minnesota at this time (Wright 1967:95–125). Each culture would have embraced a number of adjacent bands. It is not yet clear to what degree these cultures were sharply bounded or intergraded with each other. The fact that skeletons associated with the Saugeen and Ontario Point Peninsula cultures can be clearly distinguished from one another indicates some degree of genetic heterogeneity, and hence ethnic distinctiveness, among the inhabitants of different parts of southern Ontario in Middle Woodland times (Molto 1979:49–50; 1983).

Both the Ontario and the New York Point Peninsula cultures were influenced by the Hopewell interaction sphere. This movement, which was centred in the Ohio Valley, was a vast elaboration of the intertribal exchange and burial ceremonialism that had begun in eastern North America in Late Archaic times. It was characterized by marked status differences, the construction of large burial mounds and geometrical earthworks, the manufacturing of luxury goods which reached an artistic level not afterward equalled in the region, and the exchange of raw materials drawn into the area from all over eastern North America. Many different groups were involved to varying degrees. Between 100 BC and AD 300, this included Ontario Point Peninsula bands that spent the summers along the shores of Rice Lake and nearby waterways. It appears that once or twice in a generation, when the chief of a band died, a mound would be erected in which goods of Hopewellian type, including copper beads and conch pendants, cut mica, perforated shark's teeth, and metal panpipes, would be buried with the dead. The fact that the lavish grave goods found alongside the principal interments are associated primarily with men and children has been interpreted as additional evidence for the patrilineal organization of these groups (Spence et al. 1979). A similar bias in historical Seneca burials must, however, call this interpretation into question, since the Senecas were both matrilocal and matrilinear. It appears that hereditary chiefs controlled the exchange of these luxury items and that Rice Lake was the point where nuggets of

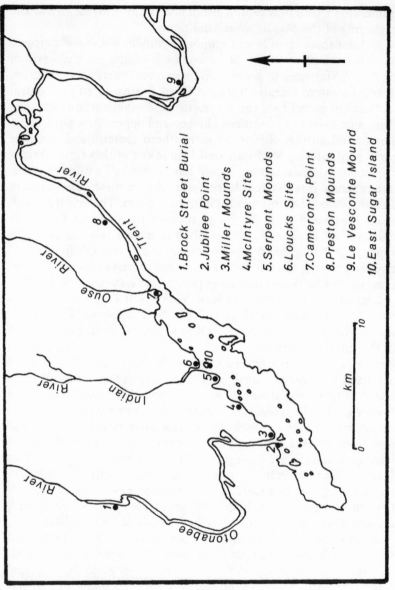

1. Brock Street Burial
2. Jubilee Point
3. Miller Mounds
4. McIntyre Site
5. Serpent Mounds
6. Loucks Site
7. Cameron's Point
8. Preston Mounds
9. Le Vesconte Mound
10. East Sugar Island

Middle Woodland burial mounds in the Rice Lake area of southeastern Ontario.

native silver coming from the Cobalt area, in northern Ontario, entered the Hopewell interaction sphere (Spence 1982). The Rice Lake sites seem to display Hopewellian influences that reached southeastern Ontario by way of New York State, although what has been found in New York has been described as constituting only "attenuated examples of Hopewellian practice" (Johnston 1968a:29). These ideas had only a short-lived and tenuous influence on the cultures of southern Ontario.

Since 1952 archaeologists have tended to assume that Iroquoian-speaking peoples had lived around the lower Great Lakes for a long time. James Tuck (1977), while admitting gaps in the archaeological record, would trace the Iroquoians back through the Point Peninsula culture to the Laurentian Archaic of Ontario and New York State. James Wright (1972, 1984) agrees but extends the area of their occupation westward to include the Middle Woodland Saugeen and earlier Inverhuron Archaic cultures of southwestern Ontario. Douglas Byers (1961) and, more recently, William Haviland and Marjory Power (1981:74, 273) equate the arrival of the Iroquoians with the earliest manifestations of the Lamoka culture in New York State during the Late Archaic period. This hunter-gatherer culture has long been believed to have many features in common with contemporary ones in the southeastern United States. Dean Snow (1977) has linked the arrival of the Iroquoians to the later Frost Island culture, which he interprets as ancestral to Meadowood and Point Peninsula.

David Stothers (1977), by contrast, rejected the claim that there was ethnic continuity between Middle Woodland and later cultures in the lower Great Lakes region. He derived the historical Iroquoian peoples from Hopewell groups that originally lived in Michigan, Illinois, and Wisconsin and equated their arrival in Ontario with the early Princess Point or still earlier Weaver culture. In New York State they were equated with the Clemson's Island culture, which, as noted by Ritchie and Funk (1973:187), had some "still obscure" relationship with Early Owasco. Stothers saw the intrusive Iroquoians as possessing only a rudimentary form of horticulture and a way of life that was little different from that of the Middle Woodland peoples they supposedly superseded. Yet they might have brought with them a very different, possibly matrilocal, social organization. Stothers has since withdrawn this proposal about Iroquoian origins as a result of a better understanding of the prehistory of the region south and west of Lake Erie and he now maintains that they developed from local Middle Woodland antecedents (Stothers and Graves 1982).

Linguists date the separation between Cherokee and the other Iroquoian languages between 3,500 and 4,000 years ago, and the separation between Nottoway and Tuscarora, Iroquoian languages formerly spoken in Virginia and North Carolina, and the other northern Iroquoian languages about the beginning of the Christian era (Lounsbury 1978:334–6). The principle of least moves indicates that the Iroquoian languages originated in the north. This conclusion accords with the results of lexical studies of Iroquoian by Buell (1979) and Mithun (1984), which suggest that the Proto-Iroquoian languages were spoken in an environmental setting resembling the northeastern North American Woodlands. Floyd Lounsbury (1978:336) suggests a long occupation in central New York State, north-central Pennsylvania, and perhaps northeastern Ohio, with expansion or migration first to the south and then to the immediate north and west. Unfortunately, no linguist has yet dated the separation between Huron and the Five Nations Iroquois languages.

Frank Siebert (1967) has argued, on the basis of a careful study of plant and animal terms, that Proto-Algonkian was spoken between Georgian Bay and Lake Ontario between 2,000 and 3,000 years ago. This would equate the origin of the Algonkian language family with an Ontario manifestation of the Laurentian Archaic culture. These two lines of linguistic evidence suggest that Iroquoian-speaking peoples might have entered Ontario sometime after the Late Archaic period and perhaps not before the end of the Middle Woodland stage. Yet such conclusions are regarded by linguists as highly speculative. J.E. Molto (1983:234) argues persuasively that the physical anthropological data indicating a continuation of the population of southern Ontario between Middle Woodland and historical times constitute prime evidence supporting the continuity hypothesis. The use of the Serpent Mounds site, on Rice Lake, as a place of burial in Early Iroquoian times also suggests cultural continuity going back to the Middle Woodland period (Johnston 1968b:48–50).

Yet archaeologists do not have to chose between a total replacement of population and complete continuity. It is possible that small migrating groups helped to disseminate new ideas and practices without ejecting indigenous populations. Such newcomers might even have been sufficiently influential that their languages were able to supplant those of the earlier inhabitants. In any case, the suggestion that Iroquoian-speaking peoples may have expanded into new areas of the St Lawrence lowlands during the late Middle Woodland period does not represent a return to the migrationary theories of former times. H.M. Lloyd and A.C. Parker saw the invading Iroquoians as possessing a well-developed horticultural way of life that was totally different from that of Algonkian hunter-gatherers they replaced. Today it is clear that any newcomers would have possessed a culture that was only a little different from that of the indigenous population and that most of the distinctive characteristics of the Iroquoian way of life evolved after they were settled in the general vicinity of their historical homelands.

## TRANSITION TO FOOD PRODUCTION

Sometime after AD 500, reliance on horticulture in the St Lawrence lowlands initiated a series of cultural changes that eventually produced the way of life associated with the historical Iroquoians. Archaeologists refer to this as the Late Woodland period. This period in turn is divided into the Early, Middle, and Late Iroquoian time spans. The use of the term Iroquoian does not any longer imply that Iroquoian-speaking peoples did not inhabit the St Lawrence lowlands prior to the Late Woodland period.

The Early Iroquoian period marks the transition from a predominantly hunter-gatherer economy to a largely horticultural one. In southwestern Ontario this period is represented by the successive Princess Point and Glen Meyer cultures; in south-central Ontario by the Pickering culture; and in New York State by the Owasco culture, which in turn is subdivided into three phases. The corresponding stage of Iroquoian development in the St Lawrence Valley remains poorly understood. It has been suggested that it was initiated when the Pickering culture spread among the indigenous inhabitants of this region or was carried there by migrants from south-central Ontario. Yet an Owasco-like culture also seems to have been ancestral to some St Lawrence Iroquoian groups (Pendergast 1975; Chapdelaine 1980). Physical anthropological evidence supports a Pickering ancestry for at least some St Lawrence Iroquoian populations (Molto 1983:256). It also suggests that the Pickering and Glen Meyer populations are continuations of earlier Ontario Point Peninsula and Saugeen ones (ibid., 253).

For a long time the Early Iroquoian period was believed to have started about AD 1000. In recent years there has been a tendency to date it earlier. It is now suggested that the Glen Meyer culture began as early as AD 500 and Princess Point perhaps 200 years before that (Molto 1983:53–4). A recent study of radiocarbon dates by Peter Timmins (1984) shows that after calibration all but one of the Princess Point dates fall between AD 800 and 1000, the exception being an AD 505 ± 55 date for the Mohawk Chapel site. The Porteous site, which most researchers would agree is transitional between Princess Point and Glen Meyer, has produced a series of highly variable dates that Timmins averages to AD 830 ± 75. The other Glen Meyer dates range from AD 1000 to 1300. A rather poor array of radiocarbon dates for the Pickering culture falls between AD 850 and 1335, with most of them coming after AD 1000. These dates do not support a proposed extension of the Pickering culture as far back as AD 700 (ibid., 92). In New York State, the terminal Middle Woodland Hunter's Home culture calibrates to AD 900 to 1100, while the following Carpenter Brook (Early Owasco) culture appears to date from AD 1100 to 1150. Stothers (1977:140–2) observes that the elongate to globular ceramic vessels, as well as the pipes and stone tools of these two cultures, are strikingly similar to those of Princess Point, although horticulture is definitely associated only with Princess Point and Early Owasco. The following Canandaigua and Castle Creek phases of Owasco (Middle and Late Owasco) span the periods from AD 1150 to 1230 and AD 1230 to 1330 respectively. No radiocarbon dates are available that shed light on the earliest horticulture in the St Lawrence Valley.

Although Timmins stresses the limitations of the radiocarbon dates that are currently available, especially those relating to the early periods, they strongly suggest that the initial manifestations of Early Iroquoian culture appeared in southwestern Ontario, even if the beginnings of the Princess Point culture do not now seem as early as some researchers have maintained. This area, which is part of the Carolinian biotic province, has a longer growing season and hence was ecologically more favourable for horticulture than either upper New York State or the area north of Lake Ontario. Whether horticulture spread to New York State from there or from the Ohio Valley or Pennsylvania remains to be determined. Archaeological data would suggest that the Hunter's Home and Early Owasco cultures were influenced by Princess Point rather than the reverse.

Variants of the Princess Point culture were formerly believed to extend over all of the warmer, southern part of southwestern Ontario. The archaeologist William Fox (1982) now argues that it was confined to areas lying within and to the east of the Grand River Valley and along the northwestern shore of Lake Ontario. The extreme southwestern part of Ontario appears to have been occupied by Western Basin tradition sites, which also occur in eastern Michigan and which may have been associated with Algonkian-speakers.

The early Princess Point summer campsites were located on river flats, sheltered inlets, or streams close to rivers. Many of these sites, as well as later Early Owasco ones such as Roundtop (Ritchie and Funk 1973:179–94), would have been extremely exposed and uncomfortable in winter and flooded in the spring. Stothers (1977:122–6) suggests that the Iroquoians grew corn and fished at these sites during the summer and autumn but dispersed into the interior of southwestern Ontario to hunt sometime during the winter. Thus, despite the introduction of corn, the general cycle of life remained much as it had been in the past. The need to guard corn crops against birds and wild animals throughout the growing season may have required at least some women to remain at these summer camps more consistently and for longer periods than in the past, but even that is not certain. The surplus corn probably allowed bands to remain together longer into the autumn.

Corn appears to have spread north from the Ohio and Illinois areas, where a small-cobbed flint corn, or popcorn, usually with twelve or fourteen rows of kernels, was grown in small quantities prior to 100 BC, and eight-rowed Northern Flint maize, which appears to have been adapted to the shorter growing season, is attested after AD 700. While it is not clear which sort was the first to appear in Ontario, eight-rowed maize has been found at the Princess Point site and it predominates in a significant sample from the Glen Meyer De Waele site (Yarnell 1964:101–25; Sykes 1981).

Yet the mere presence of a suitable cultigen does not explain why it was adopted as part of the Iroquoian subsistence pattern at this time. It may be speculated that corn initially played a role similar to that already played by wild rice, acorns and other nuts, and dried fish. It could be stored to be eaten at base camps into the early winter or carried in small quantities to winter hunting camps. Thus it lessened the danger of starvation during the winter. Even a poorly adapted strain of corn would have been more reliable than wild rice, which because of its vulnerability to flooding, wind, drought, and hail produces an abundant harvest only about one year in three (Hickerson 1970:106). Corn could also have been planted near many productive fishing stations where rice did not grow and stands of nut trees were not close at hand. Its greater dependability and versatility would have made it a welcome addition to a subsistence pattern already oriented to the collection and storage of wild plant foods.

Small multifamily houses, often with several hearths arranged down the centre, have been found associated with the Princess Point and Early Owasco cultures. It is assumed that a single family lived on either side of these hearths, as Iroquoian families did in historical times. Patterns of overlapping post moulds suggest that houses were rebuilt, often many times, in the same place. Especially on sites that were flooded in the spring, rebuilding may have occurred annually when a band returned for the late spring and summer. It is also possible that fields located on mudflats were exhausted less quickly than those located on sandy loam soils and hence sites were occupied for longer periods than was the case later when the Iroquoians no longer built on mudflats. The small multi-family dwelling was not an innovation of this period. Households composed of two or three families are evidenced in the Great Lakes region by Middle Woodland times, and some of these extended families were living in small longhouses that closely resemble Early Iroquoian ones. The best studied example comes from the Summer Island site, an Algonkian fishing camp in Lake Michigan that dates from the second or third century AD (Brose 1970).

Princess Point and later Early Iroquoian villages are estimated to have had between 100 and 400 inhabitants. If the Iroquoians were not intrusive, it seems likely that these communities were continuations of the hunting bands of the Middle Woodland period. Their small size suggests that separate bands had not yet joined together to form larger communities. If these bands remained exogamous, the resulting marriage patterns would have promoted the rapid diffusion of horticultural practices and pottery styles from one community to another.

With the evolution of the Princess Point culture into Glen Meyer, further changes are evident. Transitional sites, such as Porteous, are located on higher ground, palisaded, and appear to have been inhabited at least to some degree year-round. At present the earliest evidence that beans and squash were grown in Ontario comes from the Glen Meyer culture; in upper New York State these cultigens are first attested in the roughly contemporary Early Owasco culture (Ritchie and Funk 1973:186). Sunflowers and tobacco were also part of the horticultural complex by this time. Corn, while rich in carbohydrates and varying in the total amount of protein, is deficient in certain amino acids that are abundant in beans. Any diet in which corn and beans are both present is adequate for all but the most protein-sensitive members of a population, namely, nursing mothers and newly weaned babies. The combination of corn and beans as staples in the Iroquoian diet therefore reduced their dependence on fish and meat (Kaplan 1967:202–3). It would appear that enough surplus food was produced by early Glen Meyer times to permit at least some members of each community to continue living in their summer camping locations throughout the year. The need for the band to divide into small family hunting parties in order to survive the winter had been eliminated.

Glen Meyer villages are found as far west as the London, Ontario, area. It is currently believed that an expanding Iroquoian population pushed in that direction, displacing the people of the Western Basin tradition, who still appear to have been coming together in the spring and dispersing during the winter (Fox 1982). The Iroquoians established their year-round villages in areas of easily worked sandy loam soils, such as are found on the Norfolk and Caradoc sand plains. These communities appear to have evolved into the Iroquoian populations that lived in southwestern Ontario in late prehistoric times.

The Glen Meyer culture has traditionally been interpreted as one of established village life, such as characterized the Iroquoian peoples in the historical period (Wright 1966:22–40, 52–3). Their main settlements covered an average of only 0.6 hectares. Each community appears to have been separated from neighbouring ones by more than 10 kilometres and to have inhabited a separate drainage system or minor physiographic region. The community that occupied the Caradoc sand plain near London located its main village in the midst of large maple-beech stands on the western side of the plain, rather than in the oak forests to the east, so that land for cornfields could more easily be cleared (Williamson 1983b). Longhouses remained small and were arranged in no particular order within the villages. A high incidence of overlapping structures and low pit densities inside houses suggest that these structures continued to be flimsy and had to be rebuilt frequently (Warrick 1984:54–65). Unlike the larger Iroquoian settlements of the historical period, which had to move to new locations every few decades, these communities may have remained at the same site for some time, since they would have depleted adjacent soils, game, and sources of firewood less rapidly. Even in this period, as in historical times, however, many other factors, including hygienic considerations, were probably involved in determining relocations (Starna et al. 1984).

Large numbers of fishing camps along the north shore of Lake Erie and numerous hunting and nut-processing camps farther inland suggest that the population was neither as sedentary nor as dependent upon horticulture as it was later. Food-processing stations often had fences around them, perhaps to keep out wild animals while work was in progress (Williamson 1983*b*). Acorns, chestnuts, and wild rice, where it was available, may have been as important sources of food as horticultural crops were.

Some of the population, especially the elderly, probably lived year-round in the main villages and the women likely grew their crops in adjacent fields. Yet teams composed of men, women, and children appear to have left these settlements for considerable periods during the warmer months to hunt, fish, and gather nuts in camps some distance away. Many hunting and food-collecting camps on the Caradoc sand plain were located in the oak forests, and there is some evidence that these people visited fishing camps on the shores of Lake Huron. The Glen Meyer people would have transported the surplus food processed in these camps back to their main villages (Williamson 1983*b*). Large groups of men may also have left for long winter hunts, as was done among the semi-horticultural Ottawa bands in historical times (Fitting and Cleland 1969:295–6). Similar settlement patterns are associated with the Owasco and Pickering cultures. On average, Pickering villages may have been smaller and more widely dispersed and the population less dependent on horticulture than was the case with Glen Meyer and Owasco (Wright 1966:22). On the other hand, provisional studies of isotopic evidence from skeletal remains from the Snell site suggest a "surprisingly high" dependence on maize by the Middle Owasco period, which may indicate that horticulture was adopted "with remarkable rapidity and efficiency" in New York State (Vogel and van der Merwe 1977). A high incidence of dental caries suggests considerable dependence on horticulture in the Pickering culture, although other dental features indicate that gathered food products remained significant (Patterson 1984:312–14, 324–5).

While all Iroquoian pottery was now made by the superior paddle-and-anvil method rather than by coiling, the various Iroquoian cultures were distinguished by the different styles decorating their vessels. Stone and bone artifacts also varied and pipes tended to be more elaborate in New York State than in Ontario at this stage. Despite these differences, which in some cases reflected earlier ethnic divisions, all these cultures were evolving a basic pattern of life that can only be interpreted as being the result of major shared experiences.

Robert Whallon (1968) postulated that associations of particular design elements would be strong on pottery produced in a community in which the knowledge of pottery making was transmitted within matrilocal family groups. Under these conditions it seems likely that each household would perpetuate its own favourite combinations of designs. His study of pottery from New York State suggested that matrilocal residence was practised in the Early Owasco period and became increasingly important in later phases of Iroquoian development. Much more research is needed, however, to determine what residence patterns were associated with each phase of Iroquoian development and in particular when matrilocal residence developed. If women were remaining in the main villages for longer periods, helping each other to tend the crops and care for the children, while men were increasingly absent from these communities hunting and fishing, it would have made sense for women rather than men to live together and form the core of extended households. Moreover, when small family hunting groups were no longer required to survive the winter, the main justification for male blood relatives living together permanently would have vanished. It has been observed that sisters, or closely related women, generally find it easier to live together than unrelated women do (Ember 1973). Hence a shift from patrilocal to matrilocal residence would have eliminated a key factor, discord, that had restricted the size of extended families in the Middle Woodland period. This may account in part for the modest expansion of longhouses in the Early Iroquoian period. Matrilocal residence would have been reinforced in later times by the changing division of labour: women and children left the neighbourhood of their villages ever less frequently, while parties of men more often went far away to hunt, fish, trade, and wage war. The village and its adjacent clearing increasingly became the domain of, and their welfare the concern of, the Iroquoian women. Men's interests were largely oriented towards what went on beyond the bounds of the clearing, including relations with other groups. As a result, by historical times Iroquoian women had a dominant voice in all matters concerning the welfare of their community, although public business and dealings with other groups were conducted by male spokesmen (Trigger 1978c).

Throughout the Early Iroquoian period, most communities continued to number only a few hundred people, as had the macrobands of the Middle Woodland period. They probably consisted of single bands, which appear to have survived into the historical period in the form of localized matrilineal clans. Each band had its own chiefs, remained exogamous, and was identified with one of a number of totemic animals. Under these circumstances, village government would not have been different from that of earlier times. Intermarriage, whether based on the movement of men or women, would have continued to cement friendly relations between neighbouring communities. While villages were surrounded by palisades, these were lightly constructed and do not suggest protracted or intensive warfare. Curiously, there is very little evidence for the exchange of exotic luxury goods at this time, which in earlier periods appears to have helped to promote friendly contact among neighbouring groups. This may be the result of factors affecting longdistance trade outside the Iroquoian area or it may reflect the decline of the mortuary ceremonialism with which most of these goods were associated.

The presence of two small cemeteries at the Sackett site in New York State has been interpreted as evidence that more than one clan or band was inhabiting some Owasco communities (Ritchie 1965:295; Ritchie and Funk 1973:220). Yet, while multiple cemeteries were common among the Five Nations Iroquois, burial in clan cemeteries is not demonstrated for historical times (Stern 1933:139). The emergence of a homogeneous biological population across most of southern Ontario before AD 1350 suggests considerable movement of population from one community to another and between the Glen Meyer and Pickering cultures. At least one of these traits indicates gene flow from west to east across southern Ontario (Molto 1983:232). This appears to rule out a prevalence of endogamous villages. While no statistical study has yet been carried out, it would appear that at least in southwestern Ontario there was considerable diversity in pottery styles among communities, even though new techniques and designs diffused from one community to another. This may suggest a pattern of residence that was primarily matrilinear (as Whallon [1968] suggested for New York State), with men moving from one community to another.

Among the Iroquois of New York State, individual burial in cemeteries was, and remained until historical times, the normal form of interment. While the dead were buried near, or even inside, villages north of Lake Ontario, a series of Pickering multiple interments at the Point Peninsula Serpent Mounds site indicates not only that the traditions of Middle Woodland ceremonialism remained but also that the attachment of Iroquoians in this area to their villages was not as strong as it was in later times (Johnston 1968b:48–50). In and around Pickering villages, a number of graves, or ossuaries, were found, some containing as many as thirteen skeletons (W. Kenyon 1958:21–3). A few of these skeletons are the remains of intact bodies but most of the bodies were badly decayed or mere bundles of bones prior to burial. It would appear that villagers who had died in the course of the year were buried in a common grave, possibly in the spring. Although these practices may prefigure some aspects of the ossuary burial practised by Ontario Iroquoians in historical times, the paucity of grave goods in early Iroquoian burials reflects the diminution of burial ritualism that had played such an important role from Late Archaic times into the late Middle Woodland period. Year-round village life may have reduced the need for these rituals to express band solidarity.

As yet very little is known about rates of cultural change during the Early Iroquoian period. Ritchie (1965:271) assumed that the Owasco phases marked a gradual transition from the hunter-gatherer cultures of Middle Woodland times to Iroquoian village life, which was already in existence by the end of this period. More recent evidence from southwestern Ontario suggests a marked cultural change between Princess Point and Glen Meyer times, which appears to be correlated with an increased dependence on horticulture. It is not yet clear whether this change resulted from the introduction of a new strain of maize that was better adapted to a shorter growing season, an increasing population, or other causes. Evidence from the Caradoc sand plain suggests that there was little cultural change during the 150 or more years of its occupation in the Glen Meyer period. In particular, pottery styles changed very little during this time. Yet a study of five villages on the plain that appear to have been inhabited in succession by a single community suggests that later sites were chosen with greater care than earlier ones to ensure proximity to good agricultural soils (Williamson, personal communication).

### CONSOLIDATION OF VILLAGE LIFE

There is growing evidence that the fourteenth century witnessed a dramatic revolution in Iroquoian life throughout most of the St Lawrence lowlands. This transformation, known to archaeologists as the Middle Iroquoian period, is associated with the sequential Uren and Middleport cultures, found across southern Ontario west of Kingston, and the Oak Hill horizon or culture in New York State. In recent writings there is a tendency to abandon the term Uren and to use Middleport to designate the whole of the Middle Iroquoian period in Ontario (Pearce 1984). This period has recently been studied in detail in the vicinity of London, Ontario. There two or three small Glen Meyer communities, including the one on the Caradoc sand plain, appear to have joined together to form a single large community along Oxbow Creek, which flows into the Thames River. This new community was located farther from productive oak forests than its predecessors had been. It was also surrounded by heavier soils that were harder to cultivate but less susceptible to drought than were the sandy soils that had been cultivated in Glen Meyer times. Hence it is reasonable to assume that its inhabitants depended more heavily upon horticulture (Pearce 1984). Indeed, it is unlikely that a community of this size could have supported itself without doing so.

Although few other areas have been studied in similar detail, other Iroquoian peoples now appear to have been living in larger communities than previously. The largest settlements covered more than two hectares. Houses became longer and were inhabited by many more families. The length of the houses varied greatly. They were located closer together and began to be aligned parallel to one another in groups that may have been occupied by related matrilineages or individual clans. Villages were surrounded by more elaborate fortifications, and at least some of the village planning may have been intended to reduce the amount of palisades that had to be constructed and manned in order to defend a settlement (Noble 1969:19). Higher frequencies of house extensions and of interior house post densities suggest that individual houses were being occupied for longer periods than previously. This would also have encouraged sturdier construction.

Horticulture appears to have been providing most of the food eaten by the Iroquoians by this time, as in the historical period. Yet numerous hunting and fishing camps attest to the continuing pursuit of these activities. Even in the historical period, hunting, fishing, and to a lesser extent food gathering remained important and not all tribes relied on horticulture to an equal degree. The Mohawks and Neutrals appear to have depended more on hunting than the Hurons and the Senecas did, while the St Lawrence Iroquoians who lived in the Quebec City area in the sixteenth century relied as much on hunting and fishing as the Ottawa or Algonkin bands did a century later. Fishing expeditions composed of men, women, and children travelled as far east as the Gaspé Peninsula each summer, while male hunting parties were absent for long periods during the winter (Trigger 1963). The way of life of these Stadaconan Iroquoians must have had much in common with that of all Iroquoians during the Early Iroquoian period. Because of a lack of archaeological evidence, we do not yet know if the Stadaconans had preserved an archaic Iroquoian way of life in an area only marginally suitable for growing crops or if a more horticultural group had reverted to such a pattern after moving into that region.

A marked increase in the number of villages and campsites known for the Middleport period has traditionally been interpreted as evidence for a substantial increase in population at that time (Wright 1966:59). Survey data from Elgin County, Ontario, indicate significantly more Middleport than Glen Meyer village sites in that area (Poulton 1980:10). Until more detailed studies of settlement patterns have been carried out, it is impossible to confirm that this increase occurred. Pearce's (1984) work around London and Tuck's (1971) study of the area occupied by the historical Onondagas do not indicate a major increase in population. They suggest instead that larger villages resulted from the amalgamation of neighbouring communities.

The increasing number of local clans living in the same community would have necessitated the development of more formal village councils, with spokesmen from each clan. In historical times, these offices were hereditary in each local clan and there were separate chiefs for peace and war, a pattern also found among many tribes in the southeastern United States. The peace chiefs, in consultation with the adult members of the households belonging to their respective clans, settled disputes within the village, directed community work projects, organized rituals and celebrations, and conducted negotiations with other groups. War chiefs had the more limited authority to organize and lead raiding parties, to dispose of prisoners, and to kill suspected witches. These offices were hereditary in particular family lines within each clan, but were a source of prestige rather than power. A chief could act only as a spokesman for his clan; he could not order its members or anyone else to do anything. His immediate family had to work especially hard to provide the extra food that allowed him to validate his status by providing hospitality and entertainment to villagers and strangers alike. Since there was no rule of primogeniture, brothers and cousins competed with one another for these offices by trying to show themselves to be brave warriors, good hunters, clever traders, generous hosts, and good speakers (Trigger 1969:69–72).

The reasons for the variability in the size of the houses and the larger extended family households remain obscure, but Gary Warrick (1984:66) has suggested that at this transitional phase there may have been considerable rivalry among lineage groups as they struggled to control the affairs of the expanding villages. This may have encouraged greater lineage solidarity, which expressed itself by families belonging to the same lineage forming larger households. In later times this solidarity and the size of houses declined, although hereditary chiefs continued to live in large houses which served as public meeting-places. There is no archaeological evidence that at this time or in the future large households monopolized more wealth than smaller ones (ibid., 41). There is also ethnographic evidence that in historical times households and clans continued to resist efforts by other groups to interfere in their internal affairs.

Beginning in Middle Iroquoian times, the Feast of the Dead became, among many Iroquoian groups living north of Lake Ontario, a community ritual that was celebrated each time a sizeable village shifted to a new location. The communal reburial of the bones of those who had died while the village had been inhabited symbolized the solidarity of a community inhabited by clans and lineages that continued to maintain a considerable degree of autonomy. The other Iroquoian groups, who continued to bury their dead in smaller groups or individually, probably emphasized other less archaeologically tangible rituals as expressions of community solidarity. No Iroquoian group buried significant offerings with the dead at this time.

The fundamental changes that occurred in Iroquoian social organization during the Middle Iroquoian period were accompanied by equally far-reaching changes in material culture. Iroquoian pottery became progressively more globular and collars and castellated rims more pronounced. This completed a process whereby the small elongated pot with roughened exterior surface that had predominated in Middle Woodland times, and which appears to have been suitable for the slow-boiling of meats (Linton 1944), was gradually transformed into a larger vessel mainly used for boiling corn soup. The more elaborate patterning on the bodies of pots also disappeared, and incised rather than other forms of decoration came to predominate around the rim (Ritchie 1965:302-3; Wright 1966:57-62).

The movements and realignments of population occurring at this time may have encouraged the dissemination of innovations throughout the whole northern Iroquoian culture area. Physical anthropological evidence indicates that there was more homogeneity in human physical type across southern Ontario by the Middle Iroquoian period than there had been in Middle Woodland times (Molto 1983:241-3). This suggests movement of people between southwestern and south-central Ontario, perhaps beginning in the Early Iroquoian period. The development of multiclan villages in Middle Iroquoian times would have lessened the need for spouses to move from one village to another. On the other hand, the relocation and combining of whole communities sometimes involved major migrations of population. The nearest areas from which the settlers at the Nodwell site could have come were located 100 kilometres to the east or south. It has been suggested that they moved to the foot of the Bruce Peninsula in order to trade for native copper with the Algonkians of northern Michigan (Wright 1974:304–5). Resettlement may have been a major factor promoting the increasing cultural homogeneity of the Middle Iroquoian period.

While it is hazardous to equate social and stylistic phenomena in any simplistic fashion (Hodder 1982c), it is possible that the transformation of Iroquoian society occurring at this period encouraged a general willingness to abandon traditional ways. While the adoption of new decorative motifs may correspond with a new sense of community identity, this does not necessarily indicate that the individual communities that were joining together were losing their sense of identity. It may have been their self-confidence rather than the reverse that made such innovations acceptable.

There is also evidence of an increasingly elaborate pipe complex throughout the Iroquoian area. While it used to be believed that the pipe types that appear in the Middleport period diffused to Ontario from the Oak Hill culture of New York State (Wright 1966:62–3), there is now evidence that the Ontario Iroquoians participated in the development of these more elaborate pipe styles (Kapches 1981:211–13). The production of more elaborate pipes may reflect the evolution of more formal political behaviour. While smoking was an aspect of everyday life in historical times, it was also of great ceremonial importance in political deliberations. Here too there may be a link between social and cultural change.

The Middle Iroquoian period has generally been dated between AD 1300 and 1400 (Wright 1966:64) and hence has been recognized as a time of rapid cultural change. In recent years some archaeologists have proposed to extend this period from AD 1250 to 1450, which would considerably slow the rate of change (Kapches 1981:310, 316; Dodd 1984:192). Yet Timmins's (1984:162–4) calibration of radiocarbon dates suggests that the Middle Iroquoian period may have lasted only fifty years. It also indicates that this phase began and ended earlier in the west than it did farther east. Middleport sites near London, in the western part of southwestern Ontario, date between AD 1300 and 1340. Farther east in southwestern Ontario and north of Lake Ontario they fall between 1325 and 1380, while the Oak Hill culture in New York State dates from 1330 to 1375 (ibid., 163). Although based on a small number of radiocarbon determinations, this conclusion is supported by the fact that these dates are tightly bracketed by late Early Iroquoian and early Late Iroquoian ones. Hence the Middle Iroquoian period may have been a brief phase of major transition that began in southwestern Ontario and quickly spread in a wavelike fashion to the Iroquoian groups to the east. While much remains to be learned about the cultural sequence in the St Lawrence Valley, it appears that the cultural and ethnic affinities that had linked this region with the Pickering culture were severed by this time. The St Lawrence Iroquoians henceforth developed separately from their western neighbours.

Various explanations have been advanced to account for the Middle Iroquoian transition. According to Wright (1966:53–65), around AD 1300 the Pickering culture conquered and absorbed Glen Meyer to produce a homogeneous culture that stretched across southern Ontario west of Kingston. Wright's conquest theory has not generally been accepted, in part because no direct evidence of large-scale military operations or of major disruptions is evident in the archaeological record of southwestern Ontario (White 1971). It also runs counter to the chronological evidence that the Middle Iroquoian phase began earlier in southwestern Ontario than in the area of the Pickering culture. Moreover, there is growing evidence that the Pickering and Glen Meyer cultures were not as distinctive as archaeologists had formerly believed (Pearce 1984). Finally, despite the massive spread of new forms of social organization and material culture, archaeologists in Ontario are now able to trace the local development of some Iroquoian communities with distinctive cultural traits from Early into Late Iroquoian times (Sutherland 1980). The situation is similar in New York State. There, although Owasco is followed by the widespread Oak Hill culture, local lines of development can be discerned within both periods that eventually emerge as the five Iroquois tribes.

Evidence suggests that increasing warfare may have played a key role in the changes that were occurring at this time. Although the elaborate palisades that surround villages indicate a growing concern for defence, many villages continued to be built on dry ground along streams or rivers rather than in defensive positions remote from navigable waters, as became general practice later. Nevertheless, a significant new dimension to warfare was added in the form of cannibalism. In Ontario the earliest witness to this practice found so far is a small quantity of fragmented human bone recovered from the middens at the Uren site. More fragments occur in refuse from later Middleport sites and thereafter they become increasingly

Torture of a war captive. Detail from the map *Novae Franciae Accurata Delineatio* attributed to F.J. Bressani and engraved by G.F. Pesca, 1657. Courtesy Public Archives of Canada.

common in Iroquoian sites throughout southern Ontario (Wright 1966:56–7, 60, 64). Some of these bones exhibit signs of having been cut, cooked, and split open to extract the marrow.

In historical times cannibalism was an integral part of a cult in which male prisoners of war were tortured to death. War was waged, at least in theory, to avenge the killing of a member of one's own group by an outsider. Someone belonging to the group responsible for the killing was seized so that he or she could be adopted as a replacement for the victim or, failing this, the enemy was slain and his head or scalp brought home as a trophy (Friederici 1907). Women and children who were captured were usually permitted to live; men were more frequently slain in an elaborate ceremony as a sacrifice to the sun, who was also identified as the tutelary spirit of war and the fertility of nature. Certain key elements, including the use of prisoners, the removal of the heart, the killing of the victim on an elevated platform and in view of the sun, and finally the cooking and eating of all or parts of his body, connect this northern Iroquoian ritual with ones practised in the southeastern United States and in Mexico by the Aztecs, although many specific differences remain. It would appear that the fundamental ideas of this ceremony diffused northward from Mesoamerica, as did corn, beans, and squash (though not perhaps at the same time), and were used by various groups which developed their own version of it (Knowles 1940; Trigger 1969:42–53).

Why did warfare become increasingly important among the Iroquoian peoples as they came to depend more heavily on growing corn? It has been suggested that a possible shift to a cooler and drier climate around AD 1300 may have produced more summer droughts and soil depletion. As a result the Iroquoian populations living on the sand plains of southwestern Ontario may have moved inland in search of heavier, moister soils and the Iroquois in New York State may have abandoned the elevated and cold Allegheny Plateau (Warrick 1984:65). The harvesting of smaller corncobs around AD 1400 has been proposed as evidence of environmental stress, although Sykes (1981:29) believes that it more likely signifies greater dependence on horticulture. These relocations could have led to increased competition over strategic, localized resources (Warrick 1984:65–6). As yet, however, there is no solid evidence for environmental changes on a scale that could have brought about the effects described.

In the absence of major ecological changes, increasing pressure on existing resources does not provide a satisfactory explanation for warfare. Even if we assume the rapid depletion of the fertility of fields by Iroquoian slash and burn cultivation (cf. Sykes 1980), conflict over resources is unlikely, since the overall population density seems to have remained low and only a small fraction of suitable land was ever used by them. Even in the areas of highest population density, such as the historical Huron country, there is no evidence that soil was being exhausted at a rate beyond natural recovery (Heidenreich 1971:189–200). Quarrels about deer hunting territories might have produced conflict as a growing population required more skins to make clothing (Gramly 1977). Yet the number of deer probably increased as exhausted cornfields provided more clearings for them to graze. The fact that in historical times many neighbouring tribes not only were at peace with each other but also shared their hunting grounds suggests that such pressure was not a cause of warfare. Traditions record that among the Iroquois the visiting tribe was expected to leave the skin for the residents, although the visitors kept the meat.

Sociocultural factors may account for warfare during this period. We are handicapped by a lack of detailed knowledge of the extent and motivation of warfare in Early Iroquoian times. The putative intermarriage between neighbouring communities should have dampened conflict. Yet it is possible that, in spite of this, warfare increased as it became the principal means by which a young man could win individual prestige. In Middle Woodland times, the ability of a hunter to bring his wife and children through the rigours of winter must have constituted the supreme test of his skill, courage and personal initiative. While hunting, fishing, and forest clearance were important activities among the later Iroquoians, they had become collective tasks, carried out by larger groups. Hence they did not provide a dramatic setting for displaying resourcefulness and winning individual prestige. While, in historical times, there were many ways by which a man could win acclaim, the Iroquoians universally agreed that the most important was valour in warfare. John Witthoft (1959) has argued that as hunting became a less satisfactory way to gain male prestige, warfare became more important. Disputes proliferated as the young men of every community sought excuses to wage war and eventually it became impossible for any group not to have some enemies.

Could such warfare have reached the point where it stimulated at least a few neighbouring communities to unite in self-defence? The development of this sort of militarily more powerful community might have begun on the western frontier of Iroquoian settlement, where warfare with the Central Algonkians was commonplace. This development in turn could have had a snowballing effect that produced radical changes in Iroquoian society across their whole region.

The formation of larger communities probably intensified rather than dampened the spiralling incidence of warfare. The need for either men or women to marry into neighbouring villages would have been reduced. As a result important ties between communities that had hitherto helped to reduce conflict would have been weakened. The increasing reliance on horticulture necessitated by larger communities also may have encouraged men to turn to warfare to recover prestige. The men may have felt threatened by the growing importance of horticulture, since it was a female concern. Under these conditions, prisoner sacrifice would have been welcomed as an additional reason for waging war. The belief that the sacrifice of prisoners encouraged the growing of crops also enhanced collective male prestige in a society that increasingly valued horticulture.

Much remains to be found out about the Middle Iroquoian period and future discoveries can be expected to alter greatly what has been said here; and even this is very different from what I would have written a year ago. Because of the interdependent nature of cultural systems, satisfactory solutions to most problems will depend upon a more rounded understanding of environmental change, subsistence patterns, social organization, warfare, and religious beliefs. In particular, much more will have to be learned about what

Longhouse or field cabin with women pounding corn and carrying firewood and water (?). Detail from *Novae Franciae Accurata Delineatio.*

happened in local sequences before the seemingly dramatic changes that occurred at this time can be explained. At an even more fundamental level, extensive research is required on problems of chronology.

### PREHISTORIC FLORESCENCE

The revolutionary changes of the Middle Iroquoian period created a pattern that had considerable potential for further development in the following Late Iroquoian period. Over the next 200 years Iroquoian culture appears to have slowly increased in social complexity and to have experienced gradual change. After AD 1400 a major cleavage became apparent, in terms of pottery styles, house types, burial practices, and other aspects of material culture, between the Ontario Iroquoians living north of Lake Ontario and those north of Lake Erie (Wright 1966:66–8). This division, which led to the historical Petun-Huron and Neutral cultures respectively, appears to have reopened the earlier division between Pickering and Glen Meyer. In New York State cultural groupings ancestral to the historical tribes of that region – including the Five Nations Iroquois – also become more clearly defined. Archaeologists are only beginning to define the cultural differences among the various Iroquoian groups that occupied the upper St Lawrence Valley at this time.

In all these areas many communities continued to increase in size, probably mainly as a result of the union of two or more existing ones. Many settlements had 1,500 inhabitants. While houses became shorter, they still differed considerably in size. Village planning became more elaborate, with open spaces being provided as work areas and for the disposal of garbage (Warrick 1984:67–8). Because larger communities consumed nearby land and sources of firewood more rapidly than smaller ones, they probably had to be relocated more often. As a result the amount of work men had to do clearing fields and building houses and palisades would have increased. In settlements of more than 2,000 inhabitants (or more than six clan groups), it seems that factionalism stretched the regulatory mechanisms of Iroquoian society to their limits and quarrelling broke out. Hence few settlements remained larger than this for long (Heidenreich 1971:129–34; Johnson 1981). The largest known Iroquoian settlement in Ontario is the Draper site, which appears from calibrated radiocarbon dates to have been inhabited for a few decades sometime in the fifteenth century (Timmins 1984:110–12). It covers eight hectares and is estimated at its maximum development to have had 2,000 to 3,000 inhabitants.

There is also widespread evidence at this time of neighbouring and hitherto autonomous settlements clustering close to one another to form "tribes." The best documented example is Tuck's (1971:214–16) demonstration that two villages, one small and the other much larger, settled within a few kilometres of each other between AD 1450 and 1475 to found the Onondaga nation. The larger village was itself the result of an earlier fusion of two small ones. This drawing together of communities to form larger settlements and tribes led to the abandonment of many formerly settled areas and produced more widely separated clusters of human habitation. It also created new political groupings, each of which embraced more people than any previous ones in this part of North America had. In New York State clusters of settlements can be observed that are ancestral to the five Iroquois tribes. A larger number of similar clusters stretching from the London area into the Niagara Peninsula appear to be in whole or part ancestral to the historical Neutrals. Clusters that are related to the prehistoric Hurons and Petuns are found dispersed in Simcoe County, along the rivers flowing into the north shore of Lake Ontario, in Prince Edward County, and in the Trent Valley area (Ramsden 1977). So far, however, archaeologists have not established a direct link between specific prehistoric clusters and any of the tribes that made up the historical Huron and Neutral confederacies. There was more population movement and tribal regroupings in Ontario than in New York State during the sixteenth century, perhaps because these populations lived on the frontiers of semi-sedentary life rather than in the midst of horticultural communities, as the Iroquois

Huron (?) council. Detail from *Novae Franciae Accurata Delineatio.*

did. Hence much research will be required to link prehistoric tribal groups in these areas to those that are known in the historical period.

Tribal councils must have been formed, as an extension of community ones, to regulate the affairs of emerging tribal groupings. At the same time, clans named after the same totemic animal may have recognized a special kin-like affinity that cut across village, and later tribal, boundaries (Fenton 1978). It is possible that already in Middle Woodland times members of different bands that were named after the same animal did not intermarry (Tooker 1971). In the historical period Iroquoian clans that bore specific names were grouped to form associations, or phratries, that regulated many aspects of ceremonialism, including the burial of the dead. For example, among the Hurons it appears that the bear and deer clans formed the bear phratry; the turtle and beaver clans the turtle phratry; and the wolf, hawk, loon (or sturgeon), and fox clans the wolf phratry. It is also possible that, for certain ceremonial purposes, where only two groupings were required, the bear and turtle phratries constituted a single unit, while the wolf phratry constituted another (Steckley 1982). The resulting interdigitation of loyalties to village and tribe and to clan and phratry helped to consolidate these expanding societies.

Membership in medicine societies, which engaged in curing the sick, probably also cut across clan and village divisions in prehistoric as well as historical times. These links must have helped to consolidate tribal societies, as did games of chance and lacrosse,

which brought the inhabitants of neighbouring settlements together in friendly rivalry (Tuck 1971:213). Lacrosse also channelled
some of the aggressiveness and prestige-seeking of young men along
peaceful lines. Mortuary rituals, although centred on the dead of
single communities, drew neighbouring groups together, at least
among the prehistoric Hurons and Petuns. So far, only mortuary
rituals have received anything approaching systematic archaeological study.

It has been suggested that large communities, such as Draper,
and presumably tribal clusters as well, developed so that their
inhabitants could dominate and control local resources and trade
routes (Hayden 1978; 1979:7–9). Yet support for this argument has
not been forthcoming. In historical times the Huron communities
most deeply involved in the fur trade varied greatly in size. For
example, Ihonitiria was a small village, while Ossossané was a large
town; yet both were heavily involved in trading with the French.
We have also observed that the creation of larger settlements posed
serious economic and social problems. It seems more likely that
warfare was the major factor encouraging the extension of political
alliances, and that when individual communities had reached their
maximum practical size, these alliances were expanded in the form
of tribes and confederacies. Among the historical Hurons, only the
communities that were directly exposed to Iroquois attacks along
the southern and eastern borders of their zone of settlement were
large ones. In late prehistoric times major settlements were located
on hilltops or high ground and often surrounded on all but one side
by forked streambeds. There are also indications of increasing cannibalism, which, Wright (1966:91) estimates, reached a peak in
Ontario during the sixteenth century. Fortifications became more
complex, with multiple rows of palisades sometimes strengthened
with earthworks. Among the Iroquois, these palisades were constructed of large tree trunks for the first time (Ritchie 1965:318).
By encouraging the growth of larger communities and settlement
clusters, which depleted natural food resources more rapidly, warfare probably continued to make the Iroquoians more dependent
on horticulture.

The development of tribal groupings made up of two or more
communities can be traced in the archaeological record. It is less
certain when the earliest confederations, which aimed to suppress
blood feuds and hence warfare among member tribes, were formed.
Various discordant traditions of the Five Nations Iroquois date the
founding of their confederacy between AD 1400 and 1600 (Tooker
1978b:418–22). Apart from Tuck's evidence that the Onondaga

tribe likely did not exist as a political entity before AD 1450, archaeology has not shed additional light on this problem (Engelbrecht 1974). Since confederated tribes normally did not move closer to each other, settlement data are of little help.

Many anthropologists dogmatically assume that Indian confederacies developed as a response to conditions arising from European contact (Hunt 1940; Tooker 1964:4; Brasser 1971). Those who adhere to this position date the formation of the Iroquois confederacy to the sixteenth century. On the other hand, while the Hurons claimed, in the 1640s, that two of the four tribes that made up their confederacy had joined it about the beginning of the seventeenth century, they asserted that the other two had established it 200 years earlier (Thwaites 1896–1901, 16:227–9), which may simply have been a Huron way of saying "long ago." A confederacy such as that formed by the Attignawantan and Attigneenongnahac tribes would have been basically an extension of the Huron tribal structures that were developing in the fifteenth century. Such an association was intended to achieve a very limited number of common goals. There is no reason to believe that, where there was a need, confederacies could not have evolved in prehistoric times as easily as in the early historical period.

It is generally asserted that there was little intertribal trade among the prehistoric Iroquoian peoples. Ritchie (1965:293) has described the Owasco culture as "very provincial, self-sufficient and locally orientated." Yet in Ontario and New York State a small number of beads made from native copper and marine shell, as well as a few other exotic goods, are found in Early Iroquoian sites. This suggests that at least to a limited degree intertribal trade was supplying the same ritually valued materials that it had been since Late Archaic times, although these items were not being used for burial rituals at this time. Archaeologists appear to encounter more marine shell as well as a considerable number of native copper ornaments in Late Iroquoian villages, although quantification of the copper ornaments is complicated by the fact that trace-element analyses are sometimes needed to distinguish ornaments made from native copper from ones manufactured from European sheet metal. We know from the accounts of Jacques Cartier's voyages that, early in the sixteenth century, native copper was being traded from Lake Superior east to Lac Saint-Jean and from there down the Saguenay River to the St Lawrence Valley (Biggar 1924:106, 171). More than 770 pieces of native copper found in the most recent levels (AD 1200 to 1400) of the Juntunen site, on Bois Blanc Island in the Straits of Mackinac, indicate that marginally horticultural

Algonkian groups were already playing a major role in the copper trade of the upper Great Lakes several centuries earlier (McPherron 1967:106). Pickering-style ceramic vessels and an ossuary containing thirty-four human bodies at this site have been interpreted as evidence of either direct or indirect contact with the Iroquoian peoples of southern Ontario. The predominance of Ontario Iroquoian-style pottery at the stratified Frank Bay site, on Lake Nipissing, also indicates close contact between the Algonkian-speaking people who lived there and the inhabitants of southern Ontario from Pickering times onward (Ridley 1954). A considerable amount of native copper may have travelled south and been distributed throughout southern Ontario as part of diplomatic relations among tribes that were not at war with one another.

In historical times Iroquoian tribes exchanged goods, as an integral expression of goodwill, with all neighbouring groups with whom they were not at war. Although marine shell beads are not common on prehistoric St Lawrence Iroquoian sites, Cartier's account of his visit to Canada in 1535–6 mentions large quantities of them. After he had kidnapped Donnacona, he was presented with twenty-five strings of beads to influence him to treat the old chief well (Biggar 1924:228–33). These beads, although not manufactured in the same style as later wampum beads, which were shaped with iron tools, probably came from the same localities along the Atlantic coast and were traded north along the Hudson Valley. A more detailed study of the archaeological record is required before an accurate picture can be drawn of Iroquoian trade in late prehistoric times.

It has generally been believed in recent decades that warfare, like political organization, was limited in prehistoric times, while the genocidal conflicts among native groups in the historical period have been interpreted as being a consequence of the fur trade (Sauer 1971:304; Salisbury 1982). This claim is motivated by a creditable opposition to viewing Indians as bloodthirsty savages. Yet it errs too far in the direction of a naive "noble savage" interpretation of their behaviour. It also continues to imply that Indian history, in the sense of substantial change, was a consequence of the arrival of the Europeans.

The most important clues to major warfare patterns in prehistoric times are provided by the exotic styles of pottery found in many Iroquoian sites. To be recognized as such, these styles have to come from far enough away so that they can be distinguished from local styles of pottery. Hence pottery does not tell us much about conflicts between nearby groups that manufactured essentially similar vessels. Some recognizably foreign pottery also may have been carried from one community to another by traders or visitors. It is now becoming possible to distinguish this pottery from locally made versions of foreign styles by analysing the chemical composition of pottery clays (Trigger et al. 1980). Most locally produced exotic pottery was probably made by foreign women living at a site or by their female descendants. These women could have arrived as peacefully acquired brides, as refugees, or as prisoners of war. Intermarriage was probably not common among widely separated Iroquoian tribes, and when it occurred, more likely the men rather than the women moved. When refugees are involved, their pottery will be found abundantly in the sites they fled to, while their hosts' pottery is less likely to be found in any considerable amount in the villages the refugees abandoned. In the case of blood feuds, when prisoners were taken over a long period, archaeologists can expect to find small to medium amounts of foreign-style pottery in sites on either side.

In recent years it has become fashionable for archaeologists to argue that the Iroquoian peoples inhabiting the St Lawrence Valley between Quebec City and Lake Ontario were wiped out during the sixteenth century by Hurons, who were angered by the efforts of those Iroquoians to profit from or block the passage of European goods into the interior of North America (Ramsden 1977:293; Wright 1979:71–5). This historical interpretation was encouraged by the misdating of certain key archaeological sites as the result of the faulty identification of native copper objects as European trade goods (Bradley 1980:113). Yet it was clear from the beginning that large amounts of St Lawrence Iroquoian-style pottery were being found in Huron-Petun sites in Prince Edward County, the Trent Valley, and farther west that dated prior to any evidence of European goods. To claim that the inhabitants of these sites were engaged in prolonged warfare to gain European goods but failed to obtain any is to tax the imagination unduly. Recent chemical analyses of alleged fragments of European copper or brass indicate that at present no European objects are securely associated with any St Lawrence Iroquoian site west of Montreal, including nearly sixty sites in Jefferson County, just south of the head of the St Lawrence River (Pendergast 1982a). These include the burials at the Roebuck site, where such goods are likely to have been left as offerings if it dated from the early period of European contact. A number of problematical calibrated radiocarbon dates suggest that the latest of the St Lawrence Iroquoian sites west of Montreal may date from the early sixteenth century (Jamieson 1982; Timmins 1984:

141–55). Yet the presence of considerable amounts of Ontario-style pottery in some St Lawrence sites, corresponding to the St Lawrence-style pottery in prehistoric sites west of Kingston, suggests prolonged warfare between at least some Huron groups and the St Lawrence Iroquoians. This warfare probably ended prior to the penetration of European goods into the St Lawrence low-lands, with the defeat of the St Lawrence Iroquoians west of Mon-treal and their incorporation into Huron and Petun communities, including the Draper site. That left the easternmost St Lawrence Iroquoian tribes, who lived in the vicinity of Montreal and Quebec City, as the only members of this grouping to survive into the historical period.

It has also been assumed that the Neutrals abandoned their set-tlements west of the Grand River and moved farther east to be closer to the fur-trading routes. Yet no European goods have been found in any Iroquoian sites in the area abandoned, which suggests that they had relocated prior to the arrival of such goods in this part of Ontario. There is now also much archaeological evidence of warfare after AD 1400 between Iroquoian groups in the London area and the Fort Meigs culture, found in extreme southwestern Ontario and around the western end of Lake Erie. According to D.M. Stothers and J.R. Graves (1982; Bowen 1980), the Fort Meigs culture is a manifestation of the Sandusky tradition that spread through the western Lake Erie region replacing the Western Basin tradition. As a result of these hostilities, after AD 1500, the Fort Meigs people retreated towards the Lake St Clair lowlands, while the Ontario Iroquoians withdrew east of the Grand River. The Fort Meigs people appear to have been ancestral to at least some of the Central Algonkians who were known collectively as the Assista-ronons. Hence the warfare between the Neutrals and the Central Algonkians which continued into the 1640s might have been the final stages of a conflict that had begun in the prehistoric period.

The individual causes of the instances of large-scale warfare in-ferred for late prehistoric times remain obscure. The conflict be-tween the Neutrals and the Central Algonkians may have been initiated by the intrusion of a new group into southwestern On-tario, although it does not appear to have occupied any Iroquoian territory. More generally, these wars may relate to the need for young men seeking prestige to find new enemies, as the growth of tribes and confederacies curtailed traditional warfare closer to home. Yet, by forcing some groups to abandon large areas of settlement and dispersing others, this warfare was significantly altering the distribution and composition of tribal groups in the St Lawrence lowlands. It thus had an impact that went far beyond that of the minor blood feuds, which until recently were thought to have been the normal form of warfare prior to the fur trade. As political alliances expanded and warfare was directed against more remote and often alien peoples, the possibility of conflict escalating into genocidal warfare may have increased. It should be noted that there is little evidence of warfare between Hurons and Five Nations Iroquois or Hurons and Neutrals in prehistoric times.

Archaeological evidence increasingly demonstrates that Iroquoian cultures were changing rapidly in late prehistoric times. Larger settlements were appearing, tribes and possibly confederacies were evolving, and in some cases warfare was being waged on an expanded scale and with more intensity and destructiveness that ever before. Until recently most anthropologists viewed the growth of large tribes and confederacies as well as destructive warfare as responses to indirect European pressure upon the native societies of eastern North America. It now appears that, as a result of believing this and concentrating too heavily upon changes in subsistence patterns, archaeologists may have oversimplified the late prehistory of the Iroquoian peoples and underestimated the dynamism of their cultural pattern and its capacity to generate new forms of creative and destructive behaviour. The Iroquoians now seem to have evolved the essential features of their way of life before the first Europeans appeared along the east coast of Canada.

## THE PATTERN OF PREHISTORY

Archaeological coverage of the prehistory of eastern North America remains extremely uneven. Much less is known about earlier periods than about more recent ones. There is still too great a tendency to conceptualize the past in terms of abstract and often arbitrarily defined cultural units. Much more must be learned about the local sequences that either disappeared or gave rise to specific native communities of the historical period.

Archaeologists are also only beginning to investigate why the changes observed in the archaeological record took place. They need to be much better informed about changes in demography and subsistence patterns before they can understand the relationship between these factors. It has generally been assumed in recent years that population pressure led to the adoption of a horticultural economy, which in turn played an important role in shaping Iroquoian social organization (Ritchie 1965:296; Whallon 1968; P. Smith 1972:418). It is argued that as populations became more sedentary the birthrate increased, since the physical stresses of mobile existence, which produced a high incidence of natural miscarriages and allowed a woman to tend only one child in arms at a time, no longer applied (Binford and Chasko 1976). Yet, in the seventeenth century, Europeans noted with surprise the small size of Iroquoian families and observed that women abstained from sexual intercourse for two or three years while they breast-fed each child (Thwaites 1896–1901, 8:127). The horticultural Iroquoians appear to have been practising the same birth-spacing methods as were the Algonkian hunter-gatherer populations to the north.

Community size increased during the course of Iroquoian prehistory, but since we know that some settlements grew as a result of two or more smaller ones amalgamating, it is not clear to what degree the population as a whole increased. Moreover, at the same time that tribal clusters grew larger, many areas that formerly had been inhabited were abandoned. Until detailed regional surveys have been carried out to reveal the number, size, and function of sites for each period and enough is known about the internal density of village sites to permit the number of inhabitants to be inferred in greater detail than at present, actual population trends will remain unknown (Clermont 1980). Without such data, the possibility must be left open that population increases were not the driving force behind the development of more intensive subsistence patterns, including horticulture. The main reason for adopting a horticultural economy may have been to reduce and finally to eliminate the need to disperse in small hunting groups during the winter. If archaeologists are to understand Iroquoian prehistory, they must study more than Iroquoian subsistence and settlement patterns. They must seek to know more about their social organization, including their residence patterns, political organization, and warfare patterns, as well as about their rituals at different periods. Only as these individual facets of Iroquoian culture are known in more detail will it become possible to understand the development of Iroquoian culture from a broader perspective.

Yet despite its current limitations, archaeology has radically altered our understanding of the history of the St Lawrence lowlands prior to the coming of the Europeans. It has shown it to be a long history, not a short one as was once generally believed. It has also been demonstrated that internal change and development characterized all the native societies of this area and that some of these societies changed rapidly. Crops of Mesoamerican origin played an important role in the development of Iroquoian culture and some religious concepts that were derived from that region apparently did so as well. Yet these borrowings were effective because local people used them to transform their own societies. Archaeology does not offer a picture of prehistoric native people that conforms with the ideal of the noble savage or with any other stereotypes that White men have entertained about them. Instead it shows specific groups of human beings facing and solving problems in a distinctive and effective manner. By doing this, archaeology demonstrates that it is able to produce a history of peoples rather than merely a chronicle of objects.

Because prehistoric archaeology can aspire to explain why changes have occurred in the past, it can claim an integral role in the study of Canadian history. It provides the only substantial source of understanding of what Canadians were doing for 10,000 years or more. Yet, despite the existence of parallels and direct links between the prehistoric cultures studied by archaeologists and the historical ones studied by ethnologists, archaeology does more than explain local sequences of development. Some archaeological cultures are radically different from those known in historical times, and the variety of cultures from the historical period is much less than that found in the archaeological record. Hence archaeology also enhances our appreciation of the richness and diversity of native cultures.

## CHAPTER THREE

# The Approach of the Europeans, 1497–1600

Until recently ethnologists and ethnohistorians generally believed that the detailed accounts of native life that Europeans had recorded in eastern North America during the seventeenth century referred to cultures that were basically unaltered by European contact. It was acknowledged that many groups probably had been enriched or transformed in limited ways by the acquisition of European goods, but these changes were not thought to have influenced prehistoric styles of life to any significant degree (Tooker 1964:4; Trigger 1969, 1976; cf. Hunt 1940:4–5). Ethnologists generally assumed that their reconstructions were valid for the sixteenth as well as the seventeenth century, while archaeologists, with notable exceptions (Wedel 1936; Strong 1940), limited their studies of cultural change to prehistoric times.

Anthropologists were unchallenged in these views because of the restricted nature of historical studies of European activities in North America during the sixteenth century. In the nineteenth century historians were discouraged by the lack of detailed narrative material, which for eastern Canada was limited to the fragmentary accounts of the voyages of Jacques Cartier. Maps, contracts, and government documents allowed the activities of European explorers, fishermen, and fur traders to be studied but, after the pioneering works of H.P. Biggar (1901) and W.F. Ganong (papers reprinted as a book 1964), little original research was carried out on such topics until recent work by D.B. Quinn (1977), Selma Barkham (1980, 1982), and J.A. Tuck (1982). Thus the sixteenth century, which saw the first extensive contacts between Europeans and native people in eastern North America, remained the stepchild of both history and anthropology.

## BOASIAN ANTHROPOLOGY

The belief that native North American cultures had not changed significantly in the sixteenth century also conformed with the orientation of American anthropology in the first half of the twentieth century. American anthropology was dominated from the 1890s into the 1950s by the work of Franz Boas (1858–1942). The first prominent anthropologist to hold a teaching post in an American university, Boas trained most of the anthropologists who worked in the United States during the first half of the twentieth century and, in so doing, he decisively altered the character of anthropology in that country (Stocking 1974:1). Born in Germany, he studied physics and geography but soon became interested exclusively in human behaviour. In 1883–4 he investigated the Inuit of Baffin Island, after which, under the supervision of Horatio Hale, he worked among the Indians of British Columbia for the British Association for the Advancement of Science. In 1896 he began to teach at Columbia University in New York City, where he remained employed for the rest of his life. In addition to his studies of the ethnology, folklore, and art of the North American Indians, especially those of the West Coast, he made significant contributions to the understanding of Indian languages and physical anthropology and encouraged archaeological research (Kroeber et al. 1943; Herskovits 1953; Goldschmidt 1959; Rohner 1966; Harris 1968: 250–421; Stocking 1974, 1982:133–60, 195–233, 270–307).

Boas was strongly influenced by the German romanticism of the late nineteenth century. Among other things, this caused him to deny that any simple regularities accounted for the development of culture. It also led him to oppose the evolutionary anthropology that was being championed by the Bureau of American Ethnology and its director, John Wesley Powell. He rejected the distinction that evolutionary anthropologists had drawn between civilized and primitive cultures as being unacceptably ethnocentric. Contrary to evolutionists, who viewed cultural variations as representing the degree of development of different societies, he sought to document the immense variability of cultures and the numerous and unpredictable ways in which different economic, social, and religious practices might combine. He saw in the diversity of these combinations a direct refutation of the deterministic views of evolutionary anthropologists. Like German geographers, notably Friedrich Ratzel, Boas assumed that each culture was a unique accretion of elements that had come together as the result of a largely random process of diffusion. As belief in evolution waned, cultural change was attributed less to the independent development of similar features among unrelated cultures than to the diffusion of ideas from one culture to another. The conviction that diffusion was largely an unpredictable process, rather than one that could be explained in terms of general principles, encouraged the view that the development of cultures was also random. This position has been labelled historical particularism.

Boas rejected the tendency of American anthropologists to investigate the development of individual items of culture, such as pottery or the bow and arrow, in isolation from the specific cultures of which they were a part. He stressed that if cultures were products of diffusion, they were also patterns or configurations of elements that satisfied basic human needs, including a need for psychological consistency. The nature of such consistency was explored in Ruth Benedict's celebrated *Patterns of Culture* (1934). Underlying such concerns was an interest in understanding how individual elements were joined together to form total cultures. Boas encouraged his students to try to record entire cultural patterns rather than simply specific aspects of cultures that happened to interest them. The ideal of Boasian ethnography was to write a monograph that portrayed the traditional way of life of a specific tribe or people.

Boas also opposed the scientific trend of the period to explain differences in human behaviour in terms of innate biological factors. He sought to demonstrate that all races of human beings shared an equal capacity for change and development and that differences in human behaviour were the result of historical rather than biological factors. This view struck a responsive chord among immigrants from central and eastern Europe who were entering the United States in large numbers in the late nineteenth century and encountering ethnic and racial prejudice among Americans of Anglo-Saxon origin. Later, he was to play a major role in combating the racist doctrines of the National Socialist movement in the United States.

He also championed the concept of cultural relativism, which rejected the idea an absolute scale of values existed that was applicable to all societies or by which they could be judged in relationship to one another. He argued that each culture evolves to satisfy the needs and wishes of its own people and as a result of this process develops its own system of values. The morality or propriety of any aspect of human behaviour can therefore be evaluated only in terms of the ethical principles of the society in which it occurs, not in terms of any universal standard, however scientific such a standard may appear to be. This view was tempered in practice by the belief that some aspects of behaviour were universal responses to basic human needs. In particular, the concept of cultural relativism denied that people of European origin could objectively evaluate the morality or religious beliefs of peoples living elsewhere in the world by comparing them with their own. It was also directed against the view that technologically less developed societies were socially and morally inferior to Western ones.

Boasian anthropology had its share of shortcomings. Yet by opposing racism, stressing a holistic view of cultures, and denying that one culture can be used as a standard for evaluating the rest, it emphasized, as only a few anthropologists had done before, the dignity of native peoples and of the ways of life they had evolved before the coming of the White man.

### THE ETHNOGRAPHIC PRESENT

Like most evolutionary anthropologists, Boas believed that native American cultures were disintegrating and native groups dying out. He was no more interested than his predecessors had been in systematically studying, or even recording, the consequences of White hegemony over native people. Instead, he stressed the need to note as much as possible about traditional ways of life before they became extinct: the material culture, subsistence patterns, social organization, myths, and rituals of tribal groups. Although he had not been a student of Boas, the Canadian anthropologist T.F. McIlwraith (1948) produced one of the most successful monographs of this sort with his study of the Bella Coola Indians of coastal British Columbia.

Yet by the late nineteenth century most native cultures had been significantly altered and disrupted by European contact. On the Great Plains, along the west coast, and in the southwestern United States, anthropologists relied on native informants to recall how people had lived in their youth, when it was believed that native cultures had been disrupted only slightly. In eastern North America it was generally acknowledged that historical data were required to help determine traditional ways of life. Lewis Henry Morgan (1851) pioneered the combined use of historical and ethnographic information in his efforts to reconstruct the traditional culture of the Five Nations Iroquois. Regardless of the materials he used, the aim of the ethnographer was to eliminate distortions resulting from European contact and to compensate for the decay of native cultures in order to come as close as possible to describing them as they had existed prior to the arrival of the first Europeans in North America. Boas's students pursued such research with great energy.

Because of extensive reliance on native informants and historical documents, native cultures were not viewed as groups of people interacting with each other and with their environments. Rather, each culture was conceptualized as a distinctive pattern of norms which governed the behaviour of its members, as these were recollected by individuals. This encouraged an idealist rather than a behavioural view of culture. Although Boasian anthropologists were interested in the role that diffusion had played in shaping individual cultures (Sapir 1916), they had rejected an evolutionary view of cultures and had little motivation to study what had happened to them from a historical perspective. Native cultures were assumed to have been stable prior to European intervention, not because native people were uncreative, but because each cultural pattern represented a successful and hence stable adaptation of a people to its natural environment. Each culture, regardless of when it had existed, was a witness to human diversity and therefore a basis for attempting to understand such diversity. For that reason it was thought appropriate to describe all traditional cultures in the present tense, even though the description was often based on what was assumed to have existed in the past rather than what could be observed at present. This convention became known as the ethnographic present.

Ethnologists regarded cultures described in this way as a reliable basis for comparative studies of human behaviour. In 1949 G.P. Murdock statistically analysed a sample of 250 societies from around the world in order to draw some general conclusions about the nature of kinship terminology. Since then many ethnologists have used the information about cultures classified in the Human Relations Area Files to study worldwide regularities in many aspects of human behaviour (Moore 1961; Ford 1967). H.E. Driver and W.C. Massey (1957) employed ethnographic data on trait distributions among North American Indian tribes to determine the degree to which diffusion or functional constraints within cultures account for these patterns. Archaeologists have also made use of cross-cultural studies of ethnographic data; for example, L.R. Binford (1980) utilized them in his examination of the spatial organization of hunter-gatherers in tropical and high-latitude environments. Ethnohistorians have also tended to assume that ethnographic descriptions of "traditional" cultures constitute a baseline for measuring changes brought about by contact with Europeans. I did this in my early work on the Hurons (Trigger 1960) and continued to do so to a significant degree when I wrote *The Children of Aataentsic* (Trigger 1976). The same has been done for Indian tribes across the continent (Spicer 1961; Leacock and Lurie 1971).

Anthropologists have always been prepared to believe that certain kinds of changes had occurred in native life as a result of European contact. Confederacies and genocidal warfare were often viewed as post-contact developments. There was also a prolonged debate about the origin of family hunting territories among the Montagnais and other northern tribes, which developed significant political connotations. Marxist anthropologists, who did not believe that private property could be associated with classless societies, generally championed a post-contact origin, while more conservative scholars, including most Boasians, sought to demonstrate the opposite.

Later F.R. Eggan (1966:15–44) showed that complex variations in kinship terminology among the Indians of the southeastern United States did not reflect an aboriginal diversity of cultures, but were the result of varying degrees of acculturation to European ways. Ethnologists studying the Algonkians of southern New England also became increasingly uncertain that the political structures documented in the seventeenth century could be projected into the period prior to the great epidemics of 1616–19 (Salwen 1978:168). No less important has been W.N. Fenton's (1953:199–201) demonstration that many traits that used to be cited as evidence for the southeastern origin of the Iroquois, including the Eagle Dance, were transferred northward as a result of contact between the Cherokees and the Iroquois in the eighteenth century.

Still more recently archaeological research has revealed that significant changes took place in settlement patterns and other aspects of native life between the first appearance of European goods and the earliest substantial historical records. In many areas this interval, which is now generally called the protohistoric period, lasted a century or longer (Wilcox and Masse 1981). At the same time ethnologists are recognizing the need to view their descriptions of cultures in a historical context. They are also realizing that because most native cultures were described in detail only after they had been altered as a result of European contact, these descriptions can no longer be used as a baseline for studying changes brought about by such contact. Where changes are known to have been occurring rapidly in late prehistoric as well as protohistoric times, still more care is required in using the ethnographic record to interpret archaeological evidence.

Some ethnologists and ethnohistorians now claim that almost every facet of native culture was transformed as a result of responses to early and largely unrecorded European activities. T.J.C. Brasser (1971) has argued that social organization in eastern North America remained on a village level prior to the sixteenth century and that tribal structures, confederacies, widespread religious cults, and major trading institutions developed as responses to direct or indirect European contact. He also assumed that the emphasis on curing rites among the historical Iroquoian and Algonkian peoples was a reaction to the unprecedented spread of European diseases, while other religious movements embodied native resistance to the expanding European frontier. Harold Hickerson (1970) has similarly argued that the Ojibwa Midewiwin, or Medicine Lodge society, was a response to the fur trade, although many Ojibwas reject this interpretation and there is now some archaeological evidence to support their objections (Kidd 1981). Cara Richards (1967) and Brian Hayden (1979:182) have cast doubt on the traditional interpretation of Huron society as being matrilinear and matrilocal, while Wallis Smith (1970) has argued that it was matrilocal but this pattern disintegrated rapidly as a result of the development of the fur trade. Harold Blau (1966) has proposed that the Iroquois False Face society originated among the Hurons during the epidemics of the 1630s and was introduced to the Iroquois by Huron refugees in the 1650s. It has also been observed that the calendrical thanksgiving rituals that have been central to the religious practices of the historical Iroquois were not described for either the Hurons or the Iroquois prior to 1650 and therefore may not have been introduced into northeastern North America until the second half of the seventeenth century (Tooker 1960). Family ownership of trade routes has been interpreted as developing as a result of the fur trade (Brasser 1971).

Although changes obviously occurred, it is dangerous to view all but the most basic native institutions as being responses to European influences. This point has already been noted in discussions of genocidal warfare and confederacies in chapter 2. If, in the past, many ethnologists overestimated the amount of cultural continuity from the prehistoric into the historical periods, today some appear to be going to the opposite extreme by claiming without reasonable evidence that almost every aspect of native cultures was radically altered during the protohistoric period. Such gratuitous revisionism is no less misleading than the discredited assumption of cultural immutability that it seeks to replace.

Some questions may be resolved by means of a better understanding of oral traditions or of the historical significance of ethnographic data. Yet it is clear that most of what we can hope to
know for certain about changes that occurred in native cultures as
a response to a European presence in North America but prior to
historical records must be learned from archaeological data. Archaeologists are coming to regard the protohistoric period as an
important focus of study. Much can be learned archaeologically
about changes in settlement patterns, material culture, access to
wealth, and ritual practices, especially burial customs. Other issues, such as the ownership of trade routes, which are of interest
to ethnologists may never be resolved archaeologically. Yet, despite
these limitations, archaeology offers the only hope for defining a
substantial baseline for studying the initial changes brought about
by European contact. In eastern North America, archaeological data
from the sixteenth century are vital for understanding the nature
of native cultures prior to the arrival of the Europeans and of the
changes that followed. Whatever reservations ethnologists and ethnohistorians may have about the adequacy of archaeological data
or about their compatibility with historical or ethnographic data,
they must recognize archaeology as being the major source of information concerning cultural change that is required to set early
ethnographic information into an adequate historical context. Reliable archaeological data are clearly preferable to unverified ethnographic speculations.

## EARLY EUROPEAN CONTACT

In 1535 Gonzalo Hernandez de Oviedo y Valdéz speculated that
the New World had been discovered long before the Christian era
by Carthaginian merchants or still earlier by Iberian explorers.
Later claims were made that Israelites, Hindus, Romans, and many
other nationalities had visited it centuries before Columbus (Fagan
1977:16–18). The most recent of these unsubstantiated speculations is Barry Fell's (1982) proposal that Indian petroglyphs near
Peterborough, Ontario, are a record of Scandinavian expeditions to
obtain copper ore from the Lake Superior region in the second
millennium BC. There is also continuing interest in the possibility
of Irish settlement in eastern North America in the wake of its
alleged discovery by St Brendan in the fifth or sixth centuries AD
(Ashe 1971:22–50). Yet there is no solid evidence that Europeans
reached North America prior to the Viking landfalls. Timber and
occasionally native boats were accidently carried in the Gulf Stream

from North America to the northwestern coasts of Europe (Quinn 1977:66). Hence, much more indirect evidence of the existence of North America must have reached Europe than that which travelled in the opposite direction.

Although the sagas recounting the Scandinavian discovery of North America differ substantially in detail, there is no doubt that Norse seafarers reached the New World about AD 1000 and attempted to establish there a westward extension of Eric the Red's Greenland colony over at least a ten-year period (Quinn 1977: 20–40). Archaeological confirmation of such settlement has been found at L'Anse aux Meadows in northern Newfoundland (Ingstad 1971). The Norse sagas indicate sporadic contact with native people, who could have been either Inuit or Beothuks. After observing the Norse for some time, these natives brought bales of sables and other furs which they sought to exchange for metal weapons and red cloth. When the Norse would not sell them weapons, they accepted cloth and milk instead (Quinn 1979, 1:39, 51). Later, for reasons that are not explained, relations between the two groups deteriorated and native hostility became an important factor leading to the abandonment of the Norse settlements in North America. While the Norse may have continued to trade with the Inuit in the high Arctic for several centuries (McGhee 1982a, 1984), apart from that found at L'Anse aux Meadows and perhaps an eleventh-century Norwegian coin discovered in an Amerindian archaeological site in coastal Maine (McKusick and Wahlgren 1980:9), there is no convincing evidence of a Norse presence in North America. Nor is there any evidence of Norse influences on native cultures. In terms of later Canadian history, the most interesting aspect of the sagas is the importance they accord to furs as an item of exchange between native people and Whites and their mention of the bales of furs that the native people had ready or were soon able to collect for trade.

European contact with North America in the late fifteenth century was preceded by over 100 years of exploration and commercial expansion during which the Portuguese, backed by Genoese capital, took the lead in seeking to discover and exploit overseas sources of gold, slaves, fish, and agricultural land. Later they began to search for a route that would lead them to the spices and other riches of the Orient (Wallerstein 1974:15–63). These explorations carried the Portuguese south along the west coast of Africa and westward into the Atlantic Ocean where they searched for islands suitable for agriculture, fishing, and sealing. The Canary Islands, near the coast of Africa, were discovered before 1400, while the Madeira group was reached before 1420 and settled about five years later. The Azores were discovered in 1427 and settlement began there about 1440. As early as 1452 sailings, such as the one by Diogo de Tieve, were being made westward from the Azores in search of other islands. Elaborate but unsubstantiated claims have been advanced that a Portuguese landfall was made in North America during the 1470s.

Portuguese interest in Atlantic exploration subsided after Bartolomeu Dias rounded the Cape of Good Hope in 1488 (Quinn 1977:50–60). Yet it appears that knowledge of Portuguese explorations led English fishermen from the port of Bristol, who were being harassed by Hanseatic vessels off the coast of Iceland, to search for islands farther west in the Atlantic for use as fishing stations. This may have led to the discovery of the Grand Banks off Newfoundland during the 1480s or early 1490s (cf. ibid., 60–4 and Morison 1971:208), or even earlier (Davies 1984). In 1474 the cosmographer Paolo Toscanelli urged a search for islands farther west in the Atlantic that could be used as staging posts for commercial voyages from Europe to the Far East, which he estimated were only about 10,000 kilometres apart. His theories inspired the voyages of exploration of his fellow Italians, Christopher Columbus and John Cabot (Giovanni Caboto), and hence the European discoveries of the Caribbean and the northeastern extremity of North America. By the end of the fifteenth century, Europeans were visiting the New World in search of trade routes to the riches of the Orient, fishing grounds, and mineral wealth.

In the sixteenth century Europe was very different from what it had been like in the Viking period. Although many groups in North America had themselves made considerable material progress in the intervening 500 years, the technological gap between the two continents had vastly widened. By the sixteenth century European swords, spears, armour, cavalry equipment, and projectiles of earlier times had all undergone considerable technical improvement, while cannons and hand guns had been added to the military arsenal. The latter weapons had a shock effect that was to be highly advantageous in encounters with native people. Ships had also changed, becoming longer, narrower, and more manoeuvrable. The number of masts increased and new types of sails made it possible to utilize side winds. Multiple decks provided better accommodation and allowed larger cargoes to be carried. New navigational instruments and improved techniques of mapmaking permitted longer, safer, and more profitable voyages. During the sixteenth century the Portuguese were considered to be the best pilots and

Italians the best mapmakers (Parry 1966:13–25; 1981:3–23; Quinn 1977:71–107).

The sixteenth century also witnessed a marked increase in productivity in western Europe and the development of companies that could amass large amounts of capital for investment in ships, cargo, and equipment for foreign voyages. As D.B. Quinn (1977:102) observes, profitable trading and the exploitation of natural resources were the main incentives that made European activity in North America continuous and systematic. In addition the sixteenth century was a time of growing centralization and increasing royal power in western Europe. Kings encouraged enterprises that yielded profits to support their expanding armies and government bureaucracies. Because European society was strongly hierarchical, it was taken for granted that men of superior social status would take command in wars and foreign settlements. The exploitation of the New World thus provided opportunities for impoverished members of the nobility to recover their fortunes and to enhance their status (ibid., 100).

European religions, though ecumenical in spirit, were exclusive and intolerant, as well as hierarchically organized and controlled. While sectarian differences complicated and exacerbated national rivalries within Europe, Christianity gave Europeans a strong and rarely questioned sense of superiority over peoples who did not share their religious faith. Increasing scientific knowledge, which allowed them to construct mechanical instruments and predict eclipses, added to this sense of superiority. It also provided them with further means to impress and intimidate peoples who did not possess such knowledge. A growing awareness of history gave Europeans a heightened sense of the importance of what they were doing and of their fitness to dominate and exploit other peoples (Quinn 1977:106–7). While all non-Christian societies were viewed as morally and technologically inferior to European ones, tribal societies were also viewed as politically inferior. With such societies there was no thought of equal dealing (Dickason 1979). On the other hand, Europeans often knew less than they thought they did about the newly discovered regions of the world to which their enterprise was taking them.

Very little is recorded about the earliest contacts between Europeans and native peoples along the eastern shores of North America. This in turn has allowed the proliferation of a large body of speculative literature. For reasons that are not entirely clear, access to the east coast of North America between latitudes 26° and 35° North was seldom gained by a direct voyage from Europe prior to

the seventeenth century. Ships sailed either westward to Newfoundland or by way of the Canary Islands and the Caribbean to
Florida. For that reason, both the northern and southern extremities
of eastern North America were more frequented by Europeans than
the central coast of the United States was (Quinn 1977:90).

Perhaps beginning as early as the 1480s, English ships were exploring the northeastern tip of the continent. In 1497 John Cabot
traversed the east coast of Newfoundland, possibly starting at Cape
Breton, in an unsuccessful search for a sea route to the Orient.
Bristol sent out more expeditions from 1501 onward. The return
of a vessel bearing what appear to have been specimens of the now
extinct Carolina parakeet (*Conuropis carolinensis*) suggests that
by 1505 at least one ship had penetrated as far south as New England (Quinn 1977:129). In 1508–9, following a search for a northwest passage, Sebastian Cabot appears to have ranged considerably
farther south along the east coast of North America. Perhaps while
exploring indentations in the coast for possible routes to the Orient,
he had some friendly encounters with native people (Quinn 1979,
1:124–6).

In 1499 the Azorean João Fernandes, who had trading connections with Bristol, obtained from the Portuguese king a grant making him governor of any islands that he might discover in the
Atlantic. The following year a similar grant was made to another
prominent Azorean, Gaspar Corte-Real. In 1500 Corte-Real reached
Greenland and the next year he explored the coasts of Labrador,
Newfoundland, and part of the mainland to the south. The Cort-
Reals' voyages ceased after Gaspar's flagship was lost in 1501 and
his brother Miguel's the following year. By 1520 João Fagundes, a
native of Viana, Portugal, had explored the coast from Maine to
Sable Island (Sauer 1971:49–51).

While the English and Portuguese were investigating the northeastern coasts of North America, the Spanish were active in the
far south. Juan Ponce de Leon explored the southern coasts of Florida in 1513 searching for slaves and lands where he might make
his fortune. Between 1517 and 1519 it was discovered that Florida
was not an island but part of a mainland extending southwestward
to Mexico. Lucas Vázquez de Ayllón explored the east coast of the
United States as far north as South Carolina between 1521 and
1525 (Sauer 1971:26–72).

After the Magellan-Elcano expedition had circumnavigated the
world in 1522, it was evident that no sea passage joined the Atlantic
and Pacific Oceans between Florida and the storm-ridden southern
tip of South America. A spate of activity aimed at locating such a

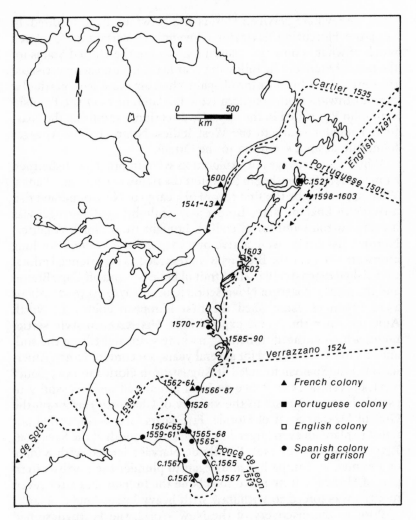

European exploration and settlement of the east coast of North America during the sixteenth century.

strait somewhere between Florida and Newfoundland resulted. In 1524 the Florentine navigator Giovanni da Verrazzano explored much of what is now the eastern seaboard of the United States for the king of France. The following year Estevão Gomes investigated the same coasts for the king of Spain, charting them with particular care northward from southern New England. In 1527 the Englishman John Rut sailed in the opposite direction, examining the coast from Labrador south to the West Indies. None of these voyages found the desired sea route to the Orient.

While these voyages of exploration were in progress, fishermen from western Europe began to exploit the riches of the Grand Banks. What appears to be the first record of a cargo of Newfoundland fish arriving in England dates from 1502, while by 1506 Portugal was levying customs duties on codfish brought from North America. Norman fishermen were active by 1504, and the Bretons not long afterward. By 1511 the Bretons were regarded as experienced pilots; they fished extensively in the Strait of Belle Isle and off Cape Breton and the nearby coasts of Nova Scotia (Quinn 1979, 1:156–7). About 1521 Fagundes established the first European colony in North America since the Norse explorations. His Azorean-style settlement, which engaged in fishing, making soap, and tilling the soil, appears to have survived for several years, a record for North America until the Spanish founded St Augustine in Florida in 1565 (Sauer 1971:49–51). In 1521 Ponce de Leon attempted unsuccessfully to establish 200 colonists in the vicinity of Charlotte Harbor on the Gulf of Mexico coast of Florida. Five years later Ayllón tried but failed to plant an even larger colony near the mouth of the Savannah River in Georgia. In 1528 Pánfilo de Narváez landed with a force of 400 men at Tampa Bay and began to plunder the northwestern part of Florida, but he failed to subdue the Indians and after seven months was forced to withdraw with heavy losses (ibid., 36–46).

Prior to the discovery of the New World, the Portuguese had encountered many different types of non-Western societies along the west coast of Africa. Usually they gave the native people presents to establish goodwill and sought to trade with them for gold, slaves, and other commodities. Not all of the early encounters in the New World were so peaceful. On his voyage of 1501 Corte-Real kidnapped a large number of Indians, who were offered for sale as slaves in Portugal (Quinn 1979, 1:148–51). Not long after, Spanish entrepreneurs in the West Indies, who were experiencing a shortage of labour because the local natives were dying in such large numbers, began to raid the Bahamas as a source of slaves. In 1521 about seventy Indians were lured aboard two ships along the coast of South Carolina and carried off to Santo Domingo (ibid., 248). Gomes also abducted many native people, probably along the Penobscot River. Fifty-eight of them were still alive when he returned to Spain (ibid., 275-6). The high mortality rate among Indian captives, probably even more than the Spanish government's opposition to the illegal enslavement of native people, kept the number of mass kidnappings low.

A more common practice was to abduct one or more Indians as trophies of a voyage or in the hope that they might learn a European language and later be useful as interpreters. In 1502 three Indians in native costumes were presented at the court of Henry vii, where at least two of them were still living two years later (Quinn 1979, 1:110). In 1509 Thomas Aubert of Rouen is reported to have brought seven Indians to Normandy, although elsewhere it was claimed that these Indians had been rescued from a canoe drifting in the Atlantic Ocean (ibid., 157). Along the eastern seaboard of the United States, Verrazzano kidnapped a young boy and tried unsuccessfully to carry off a young woman (ibid., 283). There is no evidence that any of these native people were returned home. As late as 1605 Indians were being abducted; in that year Captain George Waymouth seized five men as potential informants and interpreters along the coast of New England (ibid., 3:374).

One of the Indians that the Spanish had carried off from South Carolina in 1521 was baptized Francisco de Chicora. He lived comfortably among his captors for five years, enjoyed favourable attention at the Spanish court, and won the trust of his master Ayllón. Yet when he returned to South Carolina with Ayllón's settlers in 1526, he and other Indian interpreters managed to elude the colonists and rejoin their people (Quinn 1979, 1:261). Another Indian, Don Luis de Velasco, who had been captured on Chesapeake Bay in 1561, was carefully educated by the Spaniards and became the confidant of Pedro Menéndez de Avilés, the Spanish commander in Florida. Nevertheless, in 1571, he played a leading role in murdering the Jesuit priests whom he had accompanied back to his homeland (ibid., 2:556–66). Familiarity with Europeans and the apparent adoption of European beliefs and habits did not signify that the loyalty of these captives had been won.

We have almost no contemporary information about how native North Americans perceived the Europeans whom they encountered in the early sixteenth century. Yet oral traditions that were recorded at a later date may provide some insights into their initial reactions. Native people had no idea that other lands lay beyond the ocean, an area that they tended to associate primarily with the supernatural. Nor was it easy for them to understand the technological significance of much of what they were experiencing for the first time. The Montagnais and Micmacs believed that the first European ships they saw were floating islands (Rand 1894:225; Thwaites 1896–1901, 5:119–21). In 1634 New England Indians added that they had thought the sails of such a ship to be white clouds and the discharge of its guns to be thunder and lightning (Wood 1634:77). In 1761 elderly Delawares informed the missionary John Heckewelder (1841:71–2) that their ancestors had admired the white skins and fancy clothes of the first Europeans they met, especially the shiny red garments worn by a man who gave them presents. They concluded that the ship was a house or canoe belonging to their supreme being and prepared sacrifices, food, and entertainment for him. According to George Hamell (1982:45), the Micmacs probably believed that their culture hero, the White Rabbit Manbeing, was aboard the first ship they saw, although by the nineteenth century their folklore had transformed him into a missionary wearing white robes.

If Hamell is correct, what probably shaped the impressions of native people the most was the abundant supply of metal and of glass beads that the newcomers possessed, some of which were given to them as presents. The Delawares claimed that, not knowing the function of some of the items, their ancestors had worn the axes and hoes as ornaments and had used stockings as tobacco pouches (Heckewelder 1841:74). Hamell believes that the Indians thought European metal was equivalent to their own native copper and glass beads to natural crystals. These substances, which came out of the earth, were thought to possess supernatural powers. The European visitors were therefore equated with the spirits who were the keepers of shell, copper, and quartz and who had the power to cure the sick and confer health, longevity, and good fortune on human beings (Hamell 1980, 1982). Yet these same spirits could use their powers to harm humanity. When native people experienced outbreaks of diseases following European visits, they probably interpreted them as manifestations of such supernatural powers. In 1587 English colonists in Virginia reported that because Indians had died in each town they had passed through and they themselves had not become sick, they were regarded as spirits of the dead returning to the world (Quinn 1979, 3:152–3). As reports of kidnappings circulated early in the sixteenth century, these too must have inspired fear of Europeans, who were thought in this way to be carrying people into the realms of the dead.

Despite these fears, native people along the east coast, especially chiefs, appear to have been eager to obtain European glass beads and metalware probably because they regarded these goods as sources of supernatural power that could reinforce their personal authority. As early as 1508 native people along the northeastern coast of North America were observed to possess copper ornaments (Quinn 1979, 1:125). Later in the century it was reported that Indians of high status in Virginia wore copper bands and earrings (ibid., 3:278). It is not clear in either case how much of this copper came from Europe and how much from North American sources. Already in 1501 the Indians that Corte-Real enslaved were found to possess a piece of a broken gilt sword and two silver rings of Venetian origin (ibid., 1:151). Later descriptions specify that the Indians had objects made from both red and paler metals and that they preferred the darker, presumably because they more closely resembled native copper. The paler metals were almost certainly tin, brass, and other European alloys; however, the red metal was not necessarily native copper, since Europeans began to sell copper to the Indians after they had learned about their preference (ibid., 1:285; 3:293, 298, 351).

It is also clear that native attitudes towards Europeans quickly changed as a result of repeated or prolonged contact. In Florida native people were soon fighting Spanish invaders and defeating them by means of ambushes and a scorched-earth policy. Spaniards who were often shipwrecked along the southeast coast of the United States were enslaved by native headmen, who, it was reported, used them as human sacrifices. In 1566 the Calusa chief in the Charlotte Bay region of Florida was reputed to have captured more than 200 Spaniards over the previous twenty years, most of whom he had killed (Quinn 1979, 2:339, 480, 515). In 1527 John Rut's Italian pilot was slain when he went ashore somewhere in the northeast (ibid., 1:192); a very different treatment from the friendly reception that was accorded to a member of Verrazzano's crew who had fallen alone into the hands of native people along the Hatteras shore only three years before (ibid., 283).

In eastern Canada the most frequent and intimate contacts were established between coastal peoples and Europeans who landed to dry codfish or render whale oil. Indians in the vicinity of work sites were pacified with presents and occasionally some of them were employed there. The main link, however, almost from the beginning, appears to have been a casual trade in animal pelts. Early in the sixteenth century this trade was conducted on a small scale and involved fancy furs as well as moose and walrus hides. Contact of this sort is attested in the Strait of Belle Isle where a large wooden enclosure constructed in the Baie des Chasteaux indicates that whaling was already under way in 1529 (Quinn 1977:354), and we know that codfishing had begun there still earlier. In the summer of 1534 Jacques Cartier encountered Montagnais Indians who had come from farther up the St Lawrence to meet and trade with Europeans in that region (Bigger 1924:22–3, 76–7). Some of these Indians may already have been carrying European goods as far inland as the St Lawrence Iroquoian settlements near Quebec City. There is also some evidence that the St Lawrence Iroquoians were engaged, either directly or indirectly, in trading furs around this time. In 1535 Cartier encountered Indians amassing muskrat pelts between Quebec City and Montreal (ibid., 147). When Donnacona, a chief from the Quebec City area, was carried off to France the following year, his followers gave him three bundles of beaver and seal skins, presumably to trade with the French (ibid., 233). Yet the fact that no fur trading between the French and the St Lawrence Iroquoians was recorded over the winter of 1535–6 suggests that it was still limited (although the fragmentary nature of the historical record must also be considered).

Fur trading of this sort almost certainly went on at an equally early date in Newfoundland, in the Cape Breton area, where the Portuguese settlement had been located in the 1520s, and as far north as Chaleur Bay, where the Micmac Indians had furs and knew how to conduct trade with Europeans prior to Cartier's arrival in 1534 (Biggar 1924:49–57). Around 1540 a Portuguese agent claimed that many thousands of animal skins were being brought to France from the New World (Quinn 1979, 1:329).

As native people came to know Europeans better, they became more familiar with the range of goods that they could hope to obtain in exchange for their furs. While they continued to seek copper and tin ornaments and glass beads, they also began to value iron cutting-tools, which they recognized as being superior to their own stone and bone implements. We do not know if the ornaments that were treasured by the Indians Verrazzano encountered in Narragansett Bay in 1524 were made of copper from Europe, and hence evidence of still earlier European trade, or if they were made of native copper (Quinn 1979, 1:285). While largely unsubstantiated claims have been made that they were one or the other (cf. Morison 1971:306; Sauer 1971:61; and Bradley 1979:367), until more archaeological work has been done on the protohistoric period in Rhode Island, this question cannot be satisfactorily answered. Yet it seems significant that while these Indians avidly sought to obtain bells and other small metal objects and blue glass beads, they were not interested in tools made of steel or iron. They also rejected mirrors, perhaps for supernatural reasons, and did not value gold because of its light colour. By contrast, the native people that Verrazzano encountered farther north along the coast of Maine were much more wary and rude in their dealings with him, perhaps reflecting previous bad experiences with Europeans. They accepted only knives, fish-hooks, and sharp-edged metal in return for their goods, although they were observed to be wearing small "paternostri" beads of copper in their ears (Quinn 1979, 1:287). These contrasting attitudes seem to reflect the differing frequencies with which the Indians of southern New England and coastal Maine were encountering Europeans in the 1520s as a consequence of their varying proximity to areas where European fishermen were active. They probably also represent successive stages in the development of native views of Europeans and European goods. A reference to quantities of ironware being taken to the Strait of Belle Isle to trade for marten (*Mustela* sp. ) and other furs suggests that in that region the stage of more discriminating contact had been reached by 1537 (Biggar 1930:453).

### JACQUES CARTIER

By the 1530s it had become evident that no sea route to the Pacific Ocean was located between the Straits of Magellan and Cape Breton, and because of ice and cold any northwest passage was probably unnavigable. The Gulf of St Lawrence appeared to offer the last hope of finding a navigable sea route. In 1534 Jacques Cartier, an experienced navigator from Saint-Malo, was commissioned to explore that region to see if he could find a sea passage to the Orient or, failing that, mineral wealth that French colonists might exploit. Cartier was said to have already visited Brazil and Newfoundland (Trudel 1966c:165). In Brazil he had probably encountered the Tupinambas, a fierce and warlike people with whom the French had traded for dye-wood (Dickason 1984b). On his voyage to the Gulf of St Lawrence Cartier took with him a supply of trinkets as presents for native people he might encounter along the way. These probably were the same kinds of goods that were traded for furs, but with an emphasis on the cheaper items.

The direct course that Cartier followed suggests that not only the Strait of Belle Isle but also most of the Gulf of St Lawrence was already known to men aboard his ships. Besides searching for a passage westward, he was to chart the region. In Chaleur Bay he met and traded with a large gathering of Micmacs (Biggar 1924:49–57). These Indians insisted on trading with Cartier's crew, although they did not have a large number of furs with them. Encounters with European ships were probably still intermittent in this area, but it is possible that these Indians were already trading periodically with European fishermen farther south, probably in the vicinity of Cape Breton Island. Although they were friendlier than the Indians Verrazzano had encountered along the coast of Maine a decade earlier, their interest in obtaining iron knives and hatchets was similar.

Farther north, in Gaspé Harbour, Cartier met a group of St Lawrence Iroquoian families from the village of Stadacona, at Quebec, who had come to fish for mackerel along the Gaspé Peninsula. These Indians were led by Donnacona, who was the head chief of their village. Unlike the Micmacs, they had nothing with them to trade, which led Cartier to describe them as the "sorriest folk there can be in the world" (Biggar 1924:60). As we have already seen, however, it would be wrong to assume that these Indians had no knowledge of Europeans and had not already been receiving at least small quantities of European goods. Indeed, the manner in which they greeted the French suggests that they had. Though initially cautious, they eagerly accepted the trinkets, glass beads, and knives the French gave them. Before leaving, Cartier, like many explorers before him, seized two teen-age Indians, who were the sons or nephews of Donnacona, so that they might serve as guides and interpreters on future voyages. Unable to rescue the boys and no doubt troubled that Cartier, in Iroquoian fashion, had not left French youths with him in exchange, Donnacona accepted the presents (ibid., 64–7). He must have hoped that Cartier would return his sons the following year and he could then conclude an alliance with the French that would make European goods more accessible to his people. Sailing past the eastern tip of Anticosti Island, Cartier discovered a passage leading westward. When he returned to France and it was possible to converse with his captives, he learned that a ship could sail far to the west in this passage. Not realizing that he had discovered the St Lawrence River, he hoped that a route to the Orient had at last been found.

Cartier returned to Canada in the summer of 1535 with three ocean ships and enough provisions to spend the winter there. As he travelled up the St Lawrence, he was disappointed to discover that it was a river rather than an arm of the ocean. Yet he hoped, as other Europeans were to continue to do for over a century, that it might take him near enough to the Pacific Ocean that it could be used as a trade route to the Orient. Upon arriving in the Quebec City area, Cartier docked his ships and established a winter camp without obtaining permission from the nearby villages of Stadacona and Sitadin (Dickason 1977b). In addition he offended Indian customs by announcing that he intended to visit the town of Hochelaga, on Montreal Island, without first concluding an alliance with Donnacona or obtaining that chief's permission to travel upriver through Stadaconan territory. Cartier was angered by the increasingly obvious hostility of Donnacona's two sons. Like Francisco de Chicora and Don Luis de Velasco, they had evidently not enjoyed their captivity among Europeans. Although neither had been baptized and Cartier probably believed that he had treated them indulgently, European discipline must have been oppressive to youths who had grown up in a society in which physical punishments and public humiliation were not used to control even the youngest children.

In the early autumn Cartier and some of his men travelled upriver without any native guide or interpreter to visit Hochelaga. This fortified Iroquoian town had a much larger population and was more dependent on horticulture than were the settlements in the vicinity of Quebec City. Cartier was ecstatically received at Hochelaga and distributed numerous presents to its inhabitants. He was asked to lay hands on the sick, no doubt because the metal objects and glass beads he brought with him were interpreted as evidence that he possessed great supernatural power. In spite of this, he did not trust the Hochelagans, whose community probably reminded him of those of the Tupinambas. He therefore rejected their hospitality, and after a view from the summit of Mount Royal had convinced him that he could not get his longboats above the Lachine Rapids, he left Montreal Island. The visit had lasted less than a day (Biggar 1924:152–72).

During the winter Cartier and his men were harassed by cold, sickness, and their fear of the Indians. Cartier became convinced that Donnacona and his sons were plotting to massacre the French. After an epidemic had broken out in Stadacona in December, he ordered the Iroquoians to stay away from his encampment (Biggar 1924:204). Later, he interpreted a large number of men leaving on a winter hunting expedition as a force gathering to attack him (ibid., 216–19). When the French were stricken by a severe outbreak of scurvy, Cartier tried to conceal it because he feared that knowledge of their weakened condition would invite an attack. Yet, upon learning of their illness, the Indians showed them how to cure

Canadian Indians using snowshoes. From André Thevet's *La cosmographie universelle* of 1575. While the costumes and the background appear to be mainly a product of the artist's imagination and the snowshoes are based on an inadequate verbal description, the scene is considerably more realistic than the nude hunters on snowshoes that appear in a French engraving of 1708 (Gagnon 1984: 71). Courtesy John Carter Brown Library, Brown University, Providence, RI.

scurvy with a drink rich in vitamin C made from the fronds of white cedar (*Thuja occidentalis*) (ibid., 210–15). Despite bad relations, at various times the St Lawrence Iroquoians exchanged fish, eels, and fresh meat for knives, awls, and beads (ibid., 187–8).

During his stay at Quebec, Cartier was given to understand that Donnacona had visited a Kingdom of Saguenay that lay to the west. It was said to be rich in gold, silver, and other precious items and inhabited by White men who wore woollen clothing. Because of these stories, some historians have suggested that the Stadaconans knew about the Spanish who were in Mexico and that some of them might even have visited the Spanish settlements there (Trudel 1963:109). Almost certainly, however, the core of facts that was embroidered in these tales refers to the sources of native copper around Lake Superior and possibly also to the Hurons of northern

Simcoe County who lived not far from the copper trade route leading from Lake Superior to the Saguenay River.

These tales led Cartier to change his objectives. He now knew that there was no sea passage, or even an easy river route, across Canada from the Atlantic to the Pacific Oceans, but he saw that a French colony on the St Lawrence could be used as a base for exploring the interior. The hope of discovering and conquering a kingdom in the heart of North America that was as rich as Mexico or Peru would provide a major stimulus for financing such an enterprise. To further his plans Cartier decided to kidnap Donnacona and his sons and carry them back to France so that they could tell their stories to the French king and other interested officials. Disagreement among the Stadaconans about how to deal with the French also led him to hope that, with Donnacona gone, a chief who was friendlier to him might gain control of the village. Altogether he carried off ten Iroquoians when he returned to France in May 1536 (Biggar 1924:225–40). Cartier's behaviour towards native people clearly became more cynical and opportunistic as his objectives shifted from peaceful exploration to the conquest and control of North America.

Francis I was impressed by Donnacona's stories and his promises to guide the French to the Kingdom of the Saguenay. These promises were no doubt made in the hope that they would get him and his sons back to Canada, although the French seemingly had already decided never to permit this (Trudel 1963:113, 142). Eventually the French king decided to challenge Spanish claims to North America by establishing a settlement on the St Lawrence. The proposed colony was placed under the control of a nobleman, Jean-François de La Rocque, sieur de Roberval, who was granted vice-regal powers.

In 1541 Cartier was dispatched with several hundred colonists of both sexes. He established a settlement at Cap Rouge, a short distance west of Quebec, again without permission from the Stadaconans. By this time only one of the Iroquoians he had taken to France in 1536 remained alive and to hide this fact it was thought best not to return her to her people. Cartier undertook another reconnaissance of Montreal Island that autumn without incident, but once again he failed to get his boats above the Lachine Rapids, which suggested there would be problems pushing into the interior the following year. During the winter his settlement was besieged by Indians. The opposition to the French came not only from the Stadaconans but also from hitherto friendly groups, such as the inhabitants of Achelacy, near Portneuf (Biggar 1924:259). The next summer Spanish Basque fishermen were informed by Indians who had come to the Strait of Belle Isle to trade "deer" and "wolf" skins for axes, knives, and similar items that more than thirty-five of Cartier's settlers had been killed by the St Lawrence Iroquoians. The shipowner Clemente de Odeliça specified that this information came from a group that lived upriver and included a chief from Canada (Stadacona) (Biggar 1930:462–3). Research by Selma Barkham (1980:53) has emphasized the reliability of these Spanish depositions. With a growing number of European fishermen and whalers frequenting the Strait of Belle Isle, the Stadaconans had a dependable if distant source of European trade goods. This must have made them all the more willing to attack and try to expel the French intruders who had kidnapped their chiefs and young people and settled without permission in their midst.

Cartier and his surviving party decamped in the spring of 1542, but in July of that year Roberval rebuilt the abandoned settlement and established approximately 150 colonists there. Because they, unlike Cartier, did not know how to control scurvy, more than a third of them died over the winter. The colonists also suffered from food shortages, and in June 1543 seventy of them sent fifty-five kilograms of cornmeal downriver to their settlement from Montreal. Though the surviving fragmentary sources suggest that Roberval was on better terms with nearby native groups than Cartier had been, the cornmeal may have been plundered rather than purchased from the Hochelagans (Biggar 1924:270), just as René de Goulaine de Laudonnière later stole corn for his hard-pressed colony in Florida and Champlain was planning to steal it from the Iroquois during the winter of 1628–9 (Biggar 1922–36, 5:304–5). If so, by this time conflict between French and Iroquoians had spread throughout the St Lawrence Valley and the Hochelagans may have suffered significant losses (Beaugrand-Champagne 1948). Whatever happened, Roberval's hopes of being able to penetrate farther into the interior faded and Donnacona's tales about the Kingdom of the Saguenay must have been revealed as an invention.

In 1543 Roberval and his surviving settlers returned to France, and European efforts at colonization in this region were abandoned until the following century. Cartier and Roberval had failed to discover a rich kingdom in the interior of Canada and the gold and diamonds alleged to exist near Quebec turned out to be only iron pyrites and quartz. Canada was no longer of interest to kings or noblemen who hoped to become rich by emulating the Spanish explorers and conquistadores. For the rest of the century less ambitious entrepreneurs were to draw profits from New France in the form of fish and furs. The abortive efforts at settlement near Quebec left a heritage of bad relations between the French and the St Lawrence Iroquoians. According to·later sources, the Indians living around Quebec did not permit Europeans to travel west of Tadoussac until the 1580s (Hakluyt 1589:723; Gaffarel 1878:423). No doubt, they were well supplied with equipment that the French had abandoned and could obtain fresh supplies from downriver.

## EUROPEAN ACTIVITIES, 1540–1600

Very little is known about European activities in Maritime Canada during the sixteenth century. Quinn (1977:348) suggests that small-scale trading for skins and furs was one inducement for European fishermen to congregate in the Cape Breton area beginning early in the sixteenth century. European explorers also traded with the Indians. For example, Gomes's pilot and possibly other members of his crew brought sables and other valuable furs back to Spain in 1525 (Quinn 1979, 1:274). After 1550 growing competition with the English for the fishing grounds off Newfoundland caused many French fishermen to frequent the shores of Nova Scotia and the Gulf of St Lawrence. Later the decline in Spanish fishing during that country's wars with England opened a new export market for the French, but one that preferred dry rather than wet processed cod. This land-based operation encouraged additional movement into the gulf, where conditions were more favourable for drying fish, and this produced still more contact with native people (Innis 1940:46). A French ship was specifically recorded as trading for furs in the vicinity of Cape Breton in 1569 (Biggar 1901:31). French Basques became involved in whaling and killing walrus for their hides on the Magdalen Islands towards the end of the century, and an unsuccessful English settlement was attempted there in 1597 (Quinn 1977:471). The Portuguese released cattle on Sable Island in 1568 to prepare the island for future settlement.

There is no documentation of the number of furs that were traded in the Maritimes during the sixteenth century, but the volume probably increased steadily. While many different kinds of furs and skins were purchased prior to 1580, there was growing emphasis on beaver during at least the last two decades of the century. This development was connected with an increasing demand for felted beaver hats among the nobility and middle classes of western Europe. More research is needed to determine whether the felting industry expanded more because of the new fashions, which increased the demand for beaver pelts, or because of the growing availability of the pelts (Crean 1962). The pelts best suited for this process were ones that had been trapped during the winter and worn by the Indians with the fur next to the body for fifteen to eighteen months. This removed the long guard hairs, leaving only the short barbed underhair (Innis 1956:12–14). The demand for beaver pelts was to the advantage of native hunters, since beavers were more economical to hunt than other fur-bearing animals. On average beaver meat yields seven times the number of calories that must be expended to capture it. While this is far less than the 24- to 40-fold yield from moose, it is much greater than the negative 0.7 to 0.1 yield from other animals with fancy furs (Feit 1973).

During the sixteenth century, European, and in particular French, fishing activities extended along the western coasts of Nova Scotia and Maine and there too fur trading began with the Indians. French pirates returning from Florida and the Caribbean joined in this trade. As early as 1524 the Indians of coastal Maine knew how to trade with Europeans, and in 1545 the French navigator Jean Alfonse noted that large quantities of furs were available there (Biggar 1901:31). In 1580 an English vessel under the command of Simon Fernandes visited the coast of New England and brought back sample hides, probably of moose. The same year, the crew of another vessel, commanded by John Walker, raided an Abenaki village along the Penobscot River and carried off 300 hides (Quinn 1977:387). Three years later the French explorer Etienne Bellenger attempted to found a fur-trading post and mission station on the Bay of Fundy or along the Maine coast. Although an Indian attack frustrated his plans, he returned to France with a profitable cargo of hides, marten, otter, and lynx pelts, and enough beaver to make 600 hats. He also brought back a supply of beaver civit, or castoreum, a reddish-brown oil extracted from beaver glands that was used to make medicine and perfume (Quinn 1979, 4:307). From the seventeenth century until the present, castoreum has been a significant sideline to the North American fur trade (Longley and Moyle 1963:15). Its exploitation at this early date suggests a systematic development of the beaver trade already by 1583.

In 1602 Bartholomew Gosnold and in 1603 Martin Pring, both English explorers, built trading enclosures in southern New England, but nowhere along the coast of New England could enough furs be obtained in one place to justify the expense of establishing permanent posts. It was more profitable for ships to reconnoitre the coast each summer, collecting furs where they were available.

There is evidence, however, from 1603, that Maliseet or Abenaki groups from Maine were travelling north each year to trade at least some of their furs at Tadoussac (Biggar 1922–36, 1:103; Quinn 1979, 3:422). This suggests that trading encounters between native people and Whites were not yet as dependable along the coast of Maine as they were along the St Lawrence River or in the Gulf of St Lawrence.

Sustained contact between native people and Whites in Maritime Canada must have greatly altered native life during the sixteenth century. Unfortunately, few archaeological data are yet available for this period and substantial written documentation begins only in the early seventeenth century with the publications of Champlain, Marc Lescarbot, and Pierre Biard (Bailey 1937). As the fur trade became more important, Indian groups in the Maritimes seem to have begun to fight with adjacent bands in order to secure larger hunting territories. The Micmacs, who were better armed with iron weapons than their neighbours, were able to extend their territories westward. By the 1620s some of the Maliseets had been forced to seek refuge among the Montagnais who hunted in the St Lawrence Valley (Sagard 1866:149–50; Biggar 1922–36, 1:295–6). It is also possible that the Micmacs took advantage of having prior access to iron weapons to drive the St Lawrence Iroquoians from their fishing grounds in the Gaspé Peninsula. Cartier learned that the Stadaconans were at war with the Toudamans, a people who lived south of the St Lawrence River, and that while they were travelling to the Gaspé Peninsula in the summer of 1533, many Stadaconans had been massacred by those people (Biggar 1924:177–8). It has been suggested that the Maliseets were responsible for the massacre (Lighthall 1899), but it was more likely an episode of what later Micmac traditions were to recount as their wars with the Kwedech (Rand 1894:200–22). We do not know if this war was part of an attempt by the Micmacs to enlarge their hunting territories or to pay off old scores, which was facilitated by their new weapons. The evidence of genocidal warfare in prehistoric times warrants suspending judgment until more evidence becomes available. By the beginning of the seventeenth century the Micmacs had occupied and were exploiting the Gaspé Peninsula.

As contacts between native people and Europeans became more frequent, so did the number of occasional disagreements and injuries. Native people also became more critical and demanding in their commercial dealings. In the 1580s at least some Micmacs had a reputation for being "subtle" and "cruel" (Quinn 1979, 4:307), a view adumbrated by Verrazzano's description of the Indians of Maine as *mala gente*.

Increasing emphasis on trapping also altered the subsistence patterns of the Micmacs and their neighbours. In this part of North America the sea was richer than the land; native people traditionally camped along the coasts during the warm months and retired into the interior to hunt moose and beaver only during the winter (Bailey 1937:55–7). As the fur trade became more important, a longer period of each year had to be spent hunting. Also, during the summer, because of trade, less time was available to gather and preserve meat and wild plants for the coming winter (Burley 1981). The resulting reduction in the local food supply was compensated for by purchasing dried peas, biscuits, meal, and other vegetable products from Europeans or by trading European goods for cornmeal as well as furs with the Indians of southern New England (Biggar 1922–36, 1:395–6). In 1602 Gosnold encountered a masted European shallop along the coast of Maine that was filled with Micmacs travelling south either to plunder or to trade with the Indians of New England. The leader of this party wore European clothes (Quinn 1979, 3:348). While D.B. Quinn (1977:392) has suggested that this boat had been stolen from Basques in Newfoundland, it is possible that these Indians were working for them. Between 1607 and 1615 the Micmacs and the Abenakis fought over which group should be intermediaries in the trading of European goods from Nova Scotia with the Indian tribes of New England (Snow 1976b). Extensive contacts with Europeans as well as increasing disruptions of traditional food-procurement systems probably resulted in epidemics and a considerable population decline during the sixteenth century (Miller 1976, 1982).

Many problems beset our understanding of the development of contacts between native people and Europeans in the St Lawrence Valley, especially before 1580. Breton fishermen were already visiting the Strait of Belle Isle early in the sixteenth century. In the late 1530s Spanish Basques were fishing and hunting whales in that area, and from the 1540s until the mid-1580s they had a near monopoly of the whaling activities there. Over 1,000 men lived and worked for at least six months of the year in the Baie des Chasteaux, Red Bay, and neighbouring coves and occasionally some of them remained involuntarily over the winter (Barkham 1980:56). Except for one possible skirmish in 1574 (ibid., 54), relations between Basques and Montagnais appear to have been cordial, to the extent that shallops could be left in Labrador over the winter without fear they would be stolen or broken up to secure iron nails. Although little archaeological evidence has yet been found of Indian-White contact in this area, written sources suggest that at least a few Indians assisted in activities associated with the whaling industry in return for food and metal goods. It was probably at this time that they adopted the Basque words that were still part of the lingua franca used for trading in that area in the seventeenth century (Lescarbot 1907–14, 2:24). Trading for furs is already attested in the 1530s, while moose hides are apparently mentioned in the will of a sailor from Orio, in Spain, in 1557 (Barkham 1980:54). Around 1580 English merchants also sought to trade and hunt whales there (ibid., 57–8). A considerable amount of European goods probably made its way from the Strait of Belle Isle north and west into the interior of North America throughout the sixteenth century, but especially between 1540 and 1585.

Quinn (1977:466) suggests that as early as the 1560s French Basques may have been hunting beluga and walrus west of the Strait of Belle Isle, while Bretons were moving deeper into the Gulf of St Lawrence from their fishing grounds on Cape Breton Island. He does not see evidence that the Bretons were ranging up the St Lawrence River as far as Tadoussac until the 1580s or that the French Basques were trading there before the 1590s. He admits, however, that combined whaling and fur trading may have gone on in the Tadoussac area prior to that time (ibid., 523). The name Tadoussac (Thadoyzeau) first appears in André Thevet's unpublished "Le grand insulaire," which was being worked on as late as 1588 (Trudel 1963:240). Yet in 1610 elderly seamen referred to the arrival of ships at Tadoussac as being the earliest in sixty years (Biggar 1922–36, 2:117), which suggests that Europeans had been visiting the area since 1550. Until detailed archaeological work has been carried out at Tadoussac and at "Basque" whale-processing stations known to exist at Les Escoumins and on various islands in the St Lawrence River, the likelihood that European whaling, fishing, and casual fur trading were already under way at or around Tadoussac by the middle of the sixteenth century should not be ruled out (Gaumond 1979; Turgeon 1982). This region might have been supplying some of the 6,000 hides that in 1565 Pedro Menéndez de Avilés claimed were arriving annually at La Rochelle (Quinn 1979, 2:400).

It was almost certainly the profits already being derived from the fur trade at Tadoussac that induced a Breton syndicate to send a small ship to the St Lawrence Valley in 1581 specifically to trade for furs. The following year a larger ship was sent and a fourteenfold profit was made from selling the furs to a Paris skinner. In 1583 three ships were dispatched, one of which seems to have carried Jacques Noël, a nephew of Jacques Cartier and the heir to his patents from Francis I. There is also evidence that, beginning in the early 1580s, French traders were operating farther upriver, especially around Lac Saint-Pierre and Montreal Island (Hakluyt 1589:723; de Poli 1894:48–53; Le Blant and Baudry 1967:246–7). Either in 1583 or in 1585 (Trudel 1963:221–3), Noël travelled up the St Lawrence River to Montreal Island, although it seems certain that he did not make his way above the Lachine Rapids at this time (Quinn 1979, 4:305–6). In 1583 Richard Hakluyt saw in a Paris depot furs from Canada, which were estimated to be worth 15,000 livres. In 1584 merchants from Saint-Malo sent five ships to the St Lawrence, and the following year they planned to send twice as many. The Normans and French Basques also remained active in the fur trade. As early as 1584 Indians were being brought to Saint-Malo, apparently so that they could learn French and might help to forge closer relations between their own people and the traders of that city. Like many Indians taken to France in the seventeenth century, the two brought in 1584 were probably the sons of chiefs who were already on good terms with French traders and who were confident that they would be returned the following year (Trudel 1963:215; Quinn 1977:468).

The merchants of Saint-Malo claimed that considerable numbers of French traders continued to visit the Montreal area into the early seventeenth century (de Poli 1894). Yet the fact that large numbers of Algonkins were coming from the Ottawa Valley to Tadoussac to trade at this time suggests that the trade at Montreal may not have been either as regular or on as large a scale as the Malouins had implied. Nor would the warfare going on in the upper St Lawrence Valley between the Iroquois and the Algonkians have been conducive to routine trading there. There is also some very tenuous evidence that on a later voyage Noël may have explored the St Lawrence River above the Lachine Rapids (Quinn 1979, 3:169), and D.B. Quinn and A.M. Quinn (1983:177) have speculated that he or his sons Michel and Jean may have visited the west end of Lake Ontario in 1587 or later. The existence of Lake Ontario was well known to Jacques Noël from native accounts, and it was hoped that it might provide easy access to the Pacific Ocean and the riches of the Orient. While the Noëls thus may have had a strong incentive to explore the St Lawrence Valley, the evidence for any European penetration west of Montreal Island in the sixteenth century remains unconvincing.

By the end of the sixteenth century, Tadoussac was clearly the most important fur-trading centre in North America. It stood at the head of a large number of native trade routes leading into the interior of the continent. In return for European goods, the Montagnais Indians who lived there were receiving furs that had been traded from tribe to tribe from as far north as James Bay and as far west as Ontario. There was also a vast potential for increasing the number of furs arriving from these directions. Some Indians themselves were coming each summer to trade from as far west as the Ottawa Valley and from Maine (Biggar 1922–36, 1:123–4). Neither the Strait of Belle Isle, nor any other point in Atlantic Canada or the northeastern United States, could supply furs in quantities that rivalled that at Tadoussac. By 1580, if not before, Tadoussac must have replaced the Strait of Belle Isle as the major source from which European goods were reaching the regions to the north and west of the St Lawrence Valley. It is also a reasonable assumption that the amount of European goods reaching the interior increased significantly after professional traders had begun to operate there in the early 1580s.

Contact between native people and Europeans also intensified along the east coast of the United States during the sixteenth century. In coastal Florida and Georgia, Indians recovered much metal and other European goods from wrecked Spanish galleons. Early in the century the Spanish explorer Antón de Alaminos discovered the Gulf Stream and made it the regular route by which ships returned from the Caribbean to Spain (Sauer 1971:29). Hernando de Soto and his men plundered their way through the interior of the southeastern United States between 1539 and 1543, searching vainly, as Cartier and Roberval had done, for native kingdoms to conquer that were as rich in gold and precious stones as Mexico and Peru had been. They destroyed many villages, spread diseases, and probably murdered several thousand people. Yet they left behind large quantities of European equipment, as well as pigs, which ran wild throughout the southeastern United States and which provided a new source of food (ibid., 157–85). At the town of Cofitachequi near Augusta, Georgia, the Spaniards found beads, rosaries, and iron axes that had apparently come from Ayllón's abortive colony. They were also presented at various places with marten and deer skins, which the Indians recognized as something that Europeans valued (Quinn 1979, 2:457).

In the 1520s French pirates began to prey on Spanish shipping, first on the high seas but later with increasing frequency in the

Caribbean and along the coast of Florida (Quinn 1977:241). Such vessels took on supplies of water and firewood along the east coast of the United States and, while doing so, traded with the Indians. One French ship is reported to have bartered knives, fish-hooks, and shirts for 1,000 marten skins in Chesapeake Bay in 1546 and to have obtained an equal number of furs farther south (Quinn 1979, 1:218). In 1560 official Spanish documents claimed that French privateers were visiting the southeastern coast almost every year to trade for gold, pearls, and marten skins (ibid., 217).

Settlements brought Europeans and native peoples into ever-closer contact. The two fortified but short-lived colonies that the French successively established in South Carolina and Florida in 1562 and 1564 provided a new source of European goods for the Indians, as these items were used as payment for food. The material left in these settlements when the former was abandoned and the latter was destroyed by the Spanish would also soon have been appropriated by local natives. The Spanish community of St Augustine, founded in 1565, became the first enduring European settlement in North America and thereafter Spanish forts and missions were established along the coasts of the southeastern United States. In 1568 Dominique de Gourgues, a French privateer seeking to avenge his countrymen's losses in Florida, supplied daggers, knives, and other presents to the Indians and encouraged them to attack the Spaniards (Quinn 1979, 2:568–9). Despite Spanish efforts to exclude them, French privateers continued to trade in the region throughout the 1590s (Quinn 1977:429).

In 1570 fear that the French might try to settle on Chesapeake Bay and from there discover a short overland route to both Lake Ontario and the Pacific Ocean led to the establishment of a short-lived Spanish Jesuit mission, probably located on the York River. It too was a source of European goods for the Indians in return for food and provided them with booty when they wiped it out in 1571 (Quinn 1979, 2:556–66). The English Roanoke settlement, which was founded in Virginia in 1585 after a reconnaissance the previous year, traded European goods for corn, fish, and deerskins, which the English visitor Thomas Harriot observed could be purchased cheaply from the Indians (ibid., 3:142). Both the Roanoke settlers and the later ones at Jamestown noted that the Indians were especially anxious to obtain copper.

How much European goods was available along the Atlantic seaboard of the United States during the sixteenth century? When the Spanish official Hernando Manrique de Rojas found some European goods in Indian villages north of Florida in 1564, he correctly attributed them to recent visits by French colonizers (Quinn 1979, 2:311–13). Copper and brass ornaments seem to have been more common along the east coast of North America in the late sixteenth century than they had been earlier. Yet in the early 1580s the Indians of coastal Virginia were reported to possess only a few iron tools that they had obtained from a wreck twenty years earlier (ibid., 3:150, 278), and as late as 1607 a single iron axe was still regarded as a rich present. By 1610, however, the illegal trading of copper had so glutted the market that it and other English goods were losing their value in coastal Virginia (ibid., 5:300, 314). In 1608 the Virginian ruler Powhatan received valuable presents from the English as part of his formal installation as a ruler tributary to James I (ibid., 325). He was also accused of stealing hatchets and swords to arm his soldiers (ibid., 331) and amassing iron and copper to give to his neighbours as encouragement to fight the English (ibid., 297).

At the same time, however, Captain John Smith observed that the Susquehannocks, an Iroquoian tribe living north of Chesapeake Bay, were supplying Algonkian groups who lived between them and the Powhatan realm with hatchets, knives, and pieces of iron and brass (Quinn 1979,5:322). This southward movement of European goods suggests the continuing importance of the pattern of trade centred on the lower St Lawrence Valley and the Maritime provinces which antedated the appearance of the more abundant supplies of European material along the central coast of the United States.

Still farther north, in 1609 Henry Hudson's crew believed that they were the first Europeans to ascend the Hudson River, although Lynn Ceci (1977:145–51) proposes that Gomes had already done so in 1525. At present there is little archaeological evidence pertaining to the Hudson River during the sixteenth century (Bradley 1979:374). The hostility of the Indians living at the mouth of the river, as opposed to the friendliness of those who lived upriver, does not necessarily imply that the former were protecting a monopoly of the fur trade. Like the Stadaconans, they may have been simply seeking to prevent the formation of a political alliance between Hudson and tribes living farther inland, while the furs possessed by the interior tribes may have been collected for trading to the north, or east, rather than to the south. The earliest European goods in coastal New York have been dated between 1570 and 1595 (Ceci 1982:97).

According to J.W. Bradley (1982), only a small amount of European material turns up in archaeological sites in Massachusetts prior to about 1575. It consists mainly of pieces of sheet brass or copper, brass beads, and only rarely glass beads. After 1575 tubular brass or copper beads, plates or gorgets of sheet brass or copper, and iron celts become more common, although glass beads remain infrequent. Other European implements and utensils also occur occasionally. This suggests that, prior to about 1580, European goods were not routinely available along the coast of New England. Although in the future more detailed archaeological data may alter an interpretation based largely on historical sources, it currently appears that the Indians of Atlantic Canada and Florida were able to obtain more abundant and more regular supplies of European materials than those who lived along the coast between New England and the Carolinas.

### THE DISAPPEARANCE OF THE
### ST LAWRENCE IROQUOIANS

The most important historical event in eastern Canada following Cartier's visits was the final disappearance of the St Lawrence Iroquoians. Unfortunately, nothing was recorded about this event during the sixteenth century. Early anthropologists believed that the St Lawrence Iroquoians were ancestral to the Mohawks, Onondagas, Oneidas, or some other tribe that was known in the seventeenth century and that they had moved to their historical homeland sometime after 1543. Even R.S. MacNeish (1952:84–9), although he was a champion of in situ development, believed them to be Onondagas or Oneidas who in prehistoric times had spread into the St Lawrence Valley before retreating to their ancestral territories in New York State. In the 1960s, however, first linguists and then archaeologists came to view the St Lawrence Iroquoians as separate Iroquoian groups that had evolved in the St Lawrence Valley while other Iroquoian groups had developed in southern Ontario and New York State (Trigger 1968; Lounsbury 1978).

Until recently most archaeologists attributed the disappearance of the St Lawrence Iroquoians to attacks by the Hurons (Ramsden 1977; Wright 1979:71–5), while ethnohistorians attributed it to Iroquois aggression (Trigger 1972). It now seems possible that the evidence cited by these two groups refers to different periods. As was explained in chapter 2, most of the St Lawrence Iroquoian groups appear to have vanished prior to the protohistoric period, possibly as a result of wars with their Huron neighbours, leaving

Warfare along the St Lawrence. From André Thevet's *La cosmographie universelle* of 1575. Smoke is being used to overpower the enemy. Although the houses resemble Iroquoian ones, they are almost certainly based on conventional French representations of South American native dwellings. Courtesy John Carter Brown Library, Brown University, Providence, RI.

only the easternmost groups at Montreal (Hochelaga) and in the vicinity of Quebec City (Stadacona). The dearth of any verified protohistoric sites west of Montreal seems to rule out the idea that the upper St Lawrence was a major artery along which European goods were reaching the lower Great Lakes area in the early and middle parts of the sixteenth century. It also vitiates the suggestion that Hurons living in the Trent Valley or along the north shore of Lake Ontario had reason to attack the St Lawrence Iroquoians because they were blocking trade or seeking to profit unduly from it.

The earliest historical reference attributes the disappearance of the St Lawrence Iroquoians to an attack by the Iroquois, which Pierre Erondelle's seventeenth-century English translation of Lescarbot dated around AD 1600 (Lescarbot 1907–14, 3:267–8; Hoffman 1961:203). Denis Jamet, a Recollet priest writing from Quebec in

1615, placed the event nearer the time of Cartier's visit. He also claimed to know or know of an aged Huron who remembered seeing the St Lawrence Iroquoian villages prior to their destruction by the Iroquois (Jouve 1914:437–8; Le Blant and Baudry 1967:350). A tradition that was recorded later claimed that an Algonkin tribe, the Petite Nation, or a branch of it had been driven from Montreal Island by the Hurons (Thwaites 1896–1901, 22:215–17). This tale could be relevant to the disappearance of the St Lawrence Iroquoians if some of the survivors had found refuge among the Algonkins, just as, according to the same account, others did among the Iroquois and Abenakis. Caution is required, however, since what appears to be another version of this tale claims that the Petite Nation were driven into the Ottawa Valley by another Algonkian-speaking group (Trigger 1972:79–80). Still later anachronistic traditions about tribal conflicts in the St Lawrence Valley prior to French settlement show how easy it was to invent such stories (ibid., 80–3).

If the Dawson site in downtown Montreal actually dates from the sixteenth century, the presence of small amounts of Huron pottery might suggest that warfare continued between the St Lawrence Iroquoians and the Hurons and that the Hurons destroyed Hochelaga as they did the prehistoric St Lawrence Iroquoian settlements farther west. Yet it is no longer certain that the European metal goods recovered from the site in 1860 are from the same period as the Iroquoian material, while a recent archaeological study, in agreement with MacNeish's (1972:302) earlier conclusions, would date the latter prior to the sixteenth century (Jamieson 1982). Therefore archaeologists cannot depend even on this evidence.

Champlain's account of the St Lawrence Valley in 1603 indicates that there were no St Lawrence Iroquoians living there at that time. Instead, the region had been turned into a no man's land as the result of warfare between the Algonkins and Montagnais who lived north of the river and the Mohawks and perhaps other Iroquois groups who lived to the south. At least as far downstream as Quebec, the Iroquois were terrorizing their enemies, although the Iroquois had made no effort to settle there. On the other hand, there is no record that Hurons were visiting the St Lawrence Valley prior to 1609 (Biggar 1922–36, 1:125–57). Champlain suggests that this war had begun around 1570, although such dates must be treated as rough estimates (ibid., 5:78). It is reasonable to assume that the St Lawrence Iroquoians were among the early casualties of the war. While Jacques Noël encountered Indians on Montreal Island in the 1580s, he mentions no large settlements and the Hochelagans seem to have been dispersed by then. A.G. Bailey (1933:103) has suggested that the destruction of the Stadaconans rather than any change in their attitude was responsible for the resumption of European travel and trade west of Tadoussac in the 1580s.

Contrary to earlier suggestions (Innis 1956:12–15), it seems more likely that the Stadaconans and the Hochelagans were attacked and dispersed by the Iroquois than by the Montagnais and the Algonkins. The corn that these Iroquoians produced, even if limited in the case of the Stadaconans, is likely to have made them friendly trading partners rather than enemies of the northern hunting peoples, just as the Hurons of northern Simcoe County were friendly with the Nipissings and the Algonkians of southern New England traded with the Micmacs. The suggestion that the Agojuda, or "Evil Folk," whom Cartier apparently found at war with the Hochelagans, were Algonkins is not necessarily a sound one (Biggar 1925:171). The Agojuda may have been Hurons or Iroquois and the relevant passage may mean that they were warring among themselves rather than with the Hochelagans. Another factor to be considered is that the Hochelagans may have attacked the Stadaconans in an effort to gain unimpeded access to European traders on the lower St Lawrence. It is also possible that the Stadaconan economy was adversely affected by lower temperatures, which made horticulture more difficult after 1550, as well as by their expulsion from their fishing grounds along the Gaspé Peninsula by the Micmacs. About 200 Stadaconans were killed by the Micmacs in 1534 (Biggar 1924:178). Many more may have died fighting the Micmacs or as a result of epidemics of European diseases that may have swept the St Lawrence Valley at various times in the sixteenth century. While none of these factors is directly attested by historical or archaeological evidence, some or all of them may have weakened the St Lawrence Iroquoians prior to the Iroquois invasion of the St Lawrence Valley.

Champlain recorded in 1609 that the Mohawks were still obtaining iron axes by capturing them in war (Biggar 1922–36, 2:96). These implements would have been especially valued as weapons because they made it easier to cut through defensive palisades and to pierce traditional wooden body armour. By the late 1570s the Mohawks may have felt threatened by a lack of such implements, especially if their Algonkian and St Lawrence Iroquoian neighbours were more reluctant to trade iron implements than they were to sell them fragments of copper kettles. The Mohawks may have decided to try to obtain more of these items by attacking and dispersing the St Lawrence Iroquoians and trading directly with the Europeans. This would not have been the first war of annihilation among native peoples in eastern Canada, as it was once thought to be. While the Mohawks succeeded in dispersing the remaining St Lawrence Iroquoians and their raiding parties penetrated down the St Lawrence River past Quebec, they did not drive the Montagnais from Tadoussac or gain the right to trade there. They may, however, have been able to trade with French boats that travelled farther upriver after 1580. By 1603 the Algonkins and Montagnais, who had united to oppose the Iroquois, were seeking to gain control of the St Lawrence (ibid., 1:107–9).

The Hurons were not affected by these developments. European goods were traded from tribe to tribe inland from Tadoussac to Lac Saint-Jean and then along the old copper trade route that snaked across the interior waterways of southern Quebec to the Ottawa Valley. From there some of them were exchanged with Iroquoian groups in southern Ontario for cornmeal, fishing nets, tobacco, and beaver skins. Some European materials were traded by the Kichesipirini Algonkins, who lived in the upper part of the Ottawa Valley, to the Nipissings, who in turn carried them to the Huron settlements in northern Simcoe County. Before the end of the sixteenth century, however, the Hurons and the Kichesipirinis were probably visiting and trading directly with one another. Other goods seem to have passed from the Kichesipirinis to the Petite Nation Algonkins, who lived in the southern part of the Ottawa Valley and who carried them along the St Lawrence or South Nation Rivers to Lake Ontario and from there to the various Iroquoian tribes that bordered that lake: the Hurons of the Trent Valley, the Neutrals, and probably the Onondagas and Senecas. Some of these trading expeditions may even have reached the shores of Lake Erie (Biggar 1922–36, 1:153–61). Detailed information about the geography of the upper St Lawrence Valley and Lake Ontario collected by Jacques Noël from native informants suggests that this trade might have begun by the early 1580s (Quinn 1979, 4:305–6). If St Lawrence Iroquoian refugees, especially recent ones from Hochelaga, had found shelter among both the Hurons living in the Trent Valley and the Petite Nation, they may have encouraged especially close relations between these two groups. In the seventeenth century, after these Hurons had resettled in northern Simcoe County, the Petite Nation, by way of Lake Nipissing, continued to visit and trade with the Arendahronons, who had come from the Trent Valley. The trade route along which the Algonkins reached Lake Ontario seems to have been closed by Oneida and Mohawk attacks towards the end of the sixteenth century.

## SIXTEENTH-CENTURY ONTARIO

During the 1970s opinions about when and how European goods penetrated the interior of North America altered radically. Until recently archaeologists did not believe that European goods were arriving in southern Ontario in traceable amounts prior to about 1580 (Noble 1971). Comparing the large number of Huron sites in northern Simcoe County containing large amounts of European material and which seem to date between 1615 and 1650 with the fewer found throughout Simcoe and Victoria Counties that contain smaller amounts, and hence are presumably earlier, there appeared to be only enough sites to extend back to about that time (Trigger 1976:237–42).

Yet by tracing what they believed were sites successively occupied by the same community back from historically dated ones and estimating that each site was occupied for fifteen to twenty-five years, C.F. Wray and H.L. Schoff (1953) calculated that European goods had first appeared among the Senecas as early as AD 1550. A few iron axes and knives, some brass ornaments, and an occasional round or oval glass bead were found in the earliest Seneca sites. It also appeared that the volume of European goods increased rapidly and that by 1590 polished stone axes and flint knives had largely given way to their iron equivalents. Gunflints were thought to be present as early as 1615–30 (ibid., 57), although Wray (1973:9) later dated them after 1640. Peter Pratt (1976:117, 139) and Donald Lenig (1977:73) both accepted 1550 as a probable date for the earliest appearance of European goods in Oneida and Mohawk sites. More recently, however, Wray and Don Cameron found additional early Seneca sites containing European material, which they believe date as early as 1525 (Bradley 1979:358). J.W. Bradley accepts this date for the first appearance of European goods on Onondaga sites and among the Five Nations Iroquois generally (ibid., 358–9). Unlike Wray and Schoff, he notes that most of the early evidence consists of ornaments made from brass and smelted copper and that iron was scarce before 1550. Complete iron axes and other iron goods did not become "abundant" until after 1600 (Bradley 1980:109–10).

In the late 1970s many Ontario archaeologists began to assume that European materials had started to appear in Iroquoian sites in southern Ontario early in the sixteenth century and reinterpreted the history of the sixteenth century accordingly. When bark that lined the Huron Sopher ossuary, which contained an iron celt, was

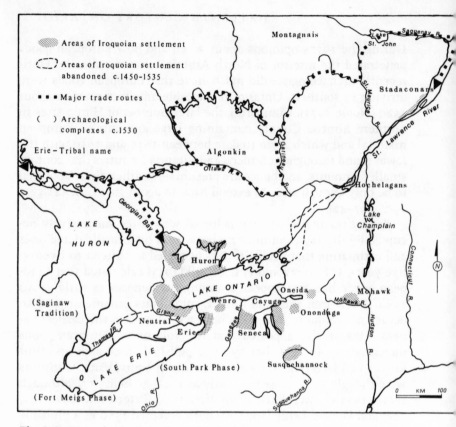

The St Lawrence lowlands in the sixteenth century.

assigned an uncalibrated radiocarbon date of AD 1505 ± 85 and the Cleveland Neutral site, which yielded a similar celt, was dated 1540 ± 90, W.C. Noble (1982:180) suggested a date close to 1500 as marking the beginning of the protohistoric period. At the same time, European material, often in the form of copper or brass, was noted on many sites located north of Lake Ontario that previously had been presumed to be prehistoric (Ramsden 1977). Increasing numbers of beaver bones and scrapers in some protohistoric sites were also cited as direct evidence of the growing importance of the fur trade (ibid., 274). Large settlements, such as Draper and Benson, were interpreted as a defensive response to the war that was assumed to be in progress because of Huron efforts to break a St Lawrence Iroquoian monopoly and win control of the St Lawrence River as an artery of the fur trade (ibid., 293). Alternatively, they were seen as "gateway communities" seeking to control and profit from trade routes that had assumed new importance as a result of the fur trade (Ramsden 1978; see also Hayden 1978). Communities were also interpreted as coming together, splitting apart, and shifting northward as beaver stocks became exhausted north of Lake Ontario (Ramsden 1977:292).

Today the necessity for greater caution in interpreting this evidence has become clear. The copper artifacts found on the Draper site, which were the only evidence of European material, now appear to be made of native copper (Fagan and Carlson 1982:7–8), while a series of calibrated radiocarbon dates assign that site to the fifteenth century (Hayden 1979:27; Timmins 1984:110–12). Likewise, spectrographic analysis of two metal artifacts from the Barnes site, which had been believed to be the oldest Onondaga site to contain material of European origin, has shown them to be made of native copper (Bradley 1980:113). Other sites in Ontario and New York State that have been assigned to the protohistoric period only because of artifacts made of copper assumed to be of European origin may likewise turn out to be prehistoric. It now appears probable, as noted previously, that the wars between the Hurons and the St Lawrence Iroquoians began and were largely, if not wholly, fought during the late prehistoric period.

Small quantities of European goods may have reached southern Ontario intermittently early in the sixteenth century (Trigger 1976:449 n40). Yet much archaeological work will have to be done before the amount and sources of these goods can be ascertained. Research currently in progress on chronologies of European materials indicates that prior to about 1580 only small amounts of such goods were reaching Iroquoian sites in Ontario. Often only an iron celt or a few rolled brass beads are found (Fitzgerald 1982*a*, 1982*b*, 1983). It is curious that no glass beads are reported for this period, since historical records indicate that they were among the presents that Cartier distributed to the St Lawrence Iroquoians. This may reflect the lack of involvement of the St Lawrence Iroquoians in the trading networks reaching southern Ontario at this time. More likely, however, it indicates that coastal peoples were generally screening out more valuable items and passing along only the more worn or common items to the tribes that lived in the interior. Beads were not reaching New England as well at this time.

After 1580 larger amounts of European material appear in Ontario burial sites, such as the Neutral Carton and Snider cemeteries or the Kleinburg ossuary, which may be Huron, and in villages, such as Fonger, which is dated between 1580 and 1610. Intact axes, iron knives, and a diverse assortment of glass beads are found associated with burials (Kenyon and Kenyon 1982). On the other hand, in contemporary habitation sites, axes tend to be fragmentary and ornaments, such as rolled beads and tinkling cones, made from scraps of copper and brass predominate. While these scraps appear to have been cut from kettles, there are no iron rim bands to indicate that whole kettles were yet reaching southern Ontario. Scraps of iron, though much rarer, were also being refashioned as tools. This reuse demonstrates that metal of all sorts was highly valued (Fitzgerald 1982*a*:233, 245, 246, 296). Beads made of shell from the east coast of the United States were present in larger quantities than they had been before, although far fewer glass and shell beads were reaching southern Ontario at this time than they would be early in the seventeenth century (Fitzgerald 1982*a*, 1983).

Comparisons of glass bead types between Ontario and New York State, which generally seem to be the same until between 1615 and 1625, suggest that archaeologists in New York State have tended to date late sixteenth and early seventeenth century sites containing European goods about thirty-five years too early and because of this have overestimated the rapidity with which these goods became part of the culture of the Five Nations Iroquois. Ian Kenyon and Thomas Kenyon (1982) have suggested a date around 1620 for sites in New York State such as Dutch Hollow (Seneca), Pompey Center (Onondaga), and Cameron (Oneida), which are usually treated as late sixteenth century. This does not, of course, rule out the possibility that limited amounts of European goods were reaching some Iroquois sites in New York State early in the sixteenth century, as they appear to have been in Ontario.

Much has to be learned archaeologically about the routes along which European goods entered southern Ontario and upper New York State. Bradley (1979:359–80), noting the lack of European goods along the upper St Lawrence for the sixteenth century, has expressed doubts about H.P. Biggar's view that at that time such goods were reaching the Five Nations Iroquois from the Gulf of St Lawrence. Bradley suggests that the Hudson, Delaware, and Susquehanna Rivers should be considered as alternative routes along which European material moved to the lower Great Lakes region. While he admits that there is little archaeological or historical evidence that such goods were moving inland along either the Hudson or the Delaware Rivers, he believes that the situation is different for the Susquehanna. Ear spools and tubular beads made from what appears to be European brass or copper have been found in Shenks Ferry sites along the lower course of the river. These are believed to date from the first half of the sixteenth century. Seemingly contemporary sites along the north branch of the Susquehanna, which are associated with the Iroquoian-speaking Susquehannocks, contain glass beads, as well as copper beads and ear spools. Apparently about the middle of the sixteenth century, the majority of the Susquehannocks moved south displacing the Shenks Ferry people. It has long been suggested that they relocated to gain easier access to the European goods thought to be available on Chesapeake Bay (Hunter 1959). In their new location, it has been stated, the Susquehannocks were receiving European goods in quantities similar to those being obtained by the Iroquois. Approximately 70 per cent of the graves at the Shultz site, which was formerly dated between 1579 and 1595 and is now believed to have been occupied from 1550 to 1600, contain European goods (Bradley 1979:379). These dates depend, however, on the accuracy of those assigned by Wray and Schoff to the Seneca sequence and hence may be too early.

European materials, as we have already noted, were reaching the entire east coast of North America throughout the sixteenth century, though in varying quantities and with differing degrees of regularity, as presents, from shipwrecks, or in payment for food, furs, and other goods. Sporadic European trade is reported on Chesapeake Bay in the 1540s and it became more frequent and regular, especially after 1585. It is also possible that European goods were making their way north from Florida, where Europeans were active throughout most of the sixteenth century. These materials could have been distributed widely throughout the interior of eastern

North America along established intertribal trading networks. Like other rare and exotic items, they would have featured prominently in intertribal trade and diplomatic exchanges between chiefs. Hence it is possible that some European goods entered New York State and Ontario from the south.

Yet European materials do not appear to have been abundant in coastal Virginia in the early 1580s, while the fact that the Susquehannocks were providing their southern neighbours with such goods early in the seventeenth century suggests that they were obtaining their own supplies from the north. It is possible that in the sixteenth century European goods were being traded from the Maritime provinces or the St Lawrence Valley to the headwaters of the Hudson River, which had been part of a major north-south trade route in the 1530s. Participation in such trading networks might explain why Mahican groups in the upper part of the Hudson Valley had marten and beaver skins available for trade when Hudson visited them in 1609, while the Indians at the mouth of the river had only tobacco and maize (Quinn 1979, 3:484–8). Some European goods (though perhaps not iron axes) may have passed from this trading network west to the Iroquois. Others may have been carried overland to the Delaware Valley where the Susquehannocks came to trade in the seventeenth century. It is also possible that some European goods were being carried from Ontario south to the Susquehannocks in the sixteenth century, although the bead types in the two areas are considerably different and large quantities of marine shell did not begin to move in the opposite direction prior to the early seventeenth century (Fitzgerald 1982a).

John Smith reported that the Susquehannocks and neighbouring tribes were being attacked by the Massawomekes, who lived across the mountains and by an inland sea, had bark canoes (unlike the Algonkians of Virginia), and got European goods from the St Lawrence Valley. It was also said that the Massawomekes were raiding the Susquehanna Valley and the headwaters of some of the other rivers flowing into Chesapeake Bay (Arber 1910:117, 367). If they are indeed the Iroquois, as seems most likely (Barbour 1964:452), it would appear that they were attacking the Susquehannocks for the same reason they were raiding the St Lawrence Valley: to obtain European goods. This suggests that the Susquehannocks may have moved south in the sixteenth century, not to be able to trade more easily on Chesapeake Bay, but to escape Iroquois attacks. All of this conforms to what is known about relations between the Susquehannocks and the Iroquois after 1615.

While European goods probably circulated at first from tribe to tribe in small quantities as did native-made "luxury goods," in the latter part of the sixteenth century the growing emphasis on the fur trade in the Maritimes and along the St Lawrence would have made larger quantities of European goods available. At the same time, furs rather than native luxury goods would have become the primary commodity that tribes living near the coast began to solicit from their inland neighbours. In general the volume of exchange along routes leading to the coast probably increased, while trade along traditional north-south routes remained static or declined in importance. There was also probably a small but significant increase in the volume of European goods reaching the Iroquoian tribes of the lower Great Lakes region after trading had become regular at Tadoussac around the middle of the sixteenth century and again after Europeans had begun to trade specifically for furs after 1580. Yet it was likely only during the last two decades of the sixteenth century that furs were a significant item being exported from the lower Great Lakes region in return for European goods. Hence, until a more detailed and accurate chronology is constructed, alternative explanations should be considered for reports of increasing amounts of beaver bones on Iroquoian sites that are dated prior to that time (McGhee 1982b:21), as well as for shifts of settlement in the early and middle parts of the sixteenth century that have been assumed to be related to the trapping of more beaver. The amount of European material found even on late sixteenth-century sites seems small by comparison with what occurs on later ones. Nevertheless, it would be wrong to treat the volume as being an accurate measure of the importance to native people of the European goods being exchanged at this time.

Most European goods that the Iroquoians possessed during the sixteenth century are found in graves rather than habitation sites. Because of this, archaeologists tend to recover the earliest traces of such goods from cemetery sites or ossuaries (Bradley 1979:359). If George Hamell (1982) is correct, scraps of European copper and brass and, when they became available, glass beads were associated with concepts of health, vigour, and survival after death. Since these goods were equated with natural substances from the earth, it would have been appropriate to return them to the ground to ensure the well-being of the dead. Such goods would have had additional prestige if it was understood that they had been obtained from strangers whom coastal peoples originally believed to be deities or returning spirits of the dead. The spread of European goods also stimulated a growing exchange of marine shell, which had similar religious connotations (Beauchamp 1901; Fenton 1971; Ceci 1982).

In the late sixteenth century the more widespread exchange of exotic goods of both European and North American origin appears to have been associated with an elaboration of funerary ritualism that was in some ways analogous to that found in eastern North America during the Middle Woodland period. Research by Hamell and R.L. Hall (1979) suggests that many of the basic concepts underlying Hopewellian ritual survived into historical times as part of the religious beliefs of the Algonkian, Iroquoian, and Siouan peoples. These beliefs may have provided the basis for the resurgence of burial rituals at this time. James Axtell (1981:110–28) has noted that, in the protohistoric period, from New England to as far west as the Senecas the dead tended to be buried with their heads pointed to the west, although in prehistoric times there was no uniform orientation of bodies among the tribes of this area. Among the Senecas the westward orientation appears to have quickly become predominant sometime early in the seventeenth century. At this time also grave offerings, which had hitherto included iron axes and knives as well as items made from sheet brass, became much more common. By the middle of the seventeenth century almost all bodies were buried with their heads pointing to the west (Wray and Schoff 1953:56–8; Wray 1973:27). The evidence suggests that a burial cult may have diffused westward across the northeastern United States. While the full cult did not reach southern Ontario, an analogous elaboration of burial rituals occurred there too, involving the interment of European goods in individual graves and ossuaries. The Huron belief that the villages inhabited by the dead were located in the west, which in historical times was (still?) not universal (Thwaites 1896–1901, 8:117–19), may reflect the influence of the more widespread cult.

While chiefs and their families may have wished to monopolize European goods and their spiritual powers, as they appear to have done to some extent in the more hierarchical societies of coastal Virginia, the presence of European material in many Iroquoian graves suggests that the economic egalitarianism and insistence upon redistribution that characterized Iroquoian society prevented this from happening. Of interest is Wray and Schoff's (1953:55) observation that in the earliest Seneca cemeteries to contain European goods, offerings were largely restricted to men and children, while "seldom was anything buried with an adult female." During the seventeenth century, among the Senecas, men continued to be better provided with grave goods than women were (ibid., 58). This may partly reflect the tendency for Iroquoian traders to acquire more European goods for male than for female use, as well as the Iroquoian fondness towards children. It may also reflect a general Iroquoian tendency to relate foreign things to men and to associate village matters with women.

The protohistoric period was also a time of major social and political change, especially in southern Ontario. Sometime in the sixteenth century, the southern Hurons abandoned the fertile lowlands north of Lake Ontario and shifted north across the Oak Ridges moraine to join the Attignawantans and possibly the Attigneenongnahacs who in whole or in part had long resided in Simcoe County. According to Huron traditions, the Arendahronons moved from the Trent Valley to west of Lake Simcoe about 1590. Finally, about 1610, the Tahontaenrats, who may have been living in Innisfil Township, resettled in northern Simcoe County. These relocations created the dense settlement cluster that was to characterize the Huron confederacy until 1649. This pattern, which involved more than 20,000 people inhabiting less than 2,100 square kilometres, was able to survive, in part, because in their new location the Hurons could produce large amounts of surplus corn and exchange it for meat and fish with the Algonkian peoples living to the north. Bringing so many people together in a small area was a unique achievement among the northern Iroquoian peoples (Trigger 1963).

The traditional explanation for the formation of the Huron confederacy, as it was known in the seventeenth century, is that the Hurons were driven northward to escape attacks by the more powerful and aggressive Five Nation Iroquois (Heidenreich 1967:16). Historians have imagined the Hurons as cowering on the shores of Georgian Bay when they were first contacted by the French. Champlain himself claimed that the Arendahronons had abandoned the Trent Valley because of Iroquois aggression (Biggar 1922–36, 3:59). Yet, while the Hurons were at war with the four western Iroquois tribes (the Senecas, Cayugas, Onondagas, and Oneidas), there is no evidence that early in the seventeenth century they were militarily inferior to the Iroquois.

It seems more likely that various Huron groups moved into Simcoe County to be close to the major trade route along which European goods were entering southern Ontario (Trigger 1962). The Arendahronons may have abandoned the Trent Valley after the Oneidas and Mohawks severed the St Lawrence River as an artery of trade; thus forcing the Petite Nation to visit them by way of

Lake Nipissing and Georgian Bay, as previously noted. The Arendahronons may therefore have moved west because of warfare, as Champlain claimed, but not because they had been defeated by the Iroquois. The Hurons who lived near Lake Ontario may have moved north still earlier to be located closer to the northern trade route. This confirms that more European goods were reaching southern Ontario in the middle of the sixteenth century by way of Lake Nipissing than from the south. To obtain these benefits, Hurons who were moving into Simcoe County from the south had to be prepared to live in an area that had more snow and a shorter growing season than the one they were leaving. Historical Huronia was the northernmost region in Ontario where corn could be grown securely, but it had the best location for along-shore canoe travel to reach and trade with the people who inhabited the rocky and lake-covered terrain to the north. The principal canoe trail they used, which hugged the eastern shore of Georgian Bay, also joined the main trade route along which goods travelled between Tadoussac and the upper Great Lakes.

As yet we know very little about the social and political events that accompanied these relocations. Because the Hurons who moved into northern Simcoe County settled on land that had been occupied by other Huron groups for many hundreds of years, the latter probably shifted westward to make room for the newcomers. They must also have familiarized the newly arrived Hurons with the northern trade routes and given them permission to use them. All of the land that had been abandoned as far south as Lake Ontario and as far east as the St Lawrence River remained Huron hunting territory. In return for permitting the newcomers to settle on their land, the inhabitants were allowed to use that hunting territory. We do not know if the expansion of the Huron confederacy and the consolidation of Huron settlement occurred peacefully or if threats and even warfare were required. Presumably the Hurons living in northern Simcoe County would not have been happy to share lucrative trade routes with neighbouring groups. Considerable pressure may have been required to win their consent for this.

There is no evidence that the four or five Huron tribes that were known in the historical period existed prior to the seventeenth century. These tribes may have been formed as associations of geographically contiguous villages and of former tribal groupings as these became re-established in their new areas of settlement (Ramsden 1977:295–6). Considerable reorganization must have been necessary to create councils to manage the affairs of these new tribes. The Huron confederacy was also expanded, if it did not come into existence, at this time, which required establishing a new level of coordination and decision-making capable of handling the affairs of over 20,000 people, who were now living close to one another and sharing a common trade. It also involved setting up a more complex hierarchy of chiefs and more elaborate rituals of consultation. Much discussion was probably needed to decide in which clans the offices of village, tribal, and confederacy chiefs would be hereditary. The creation of this new political order may have generated considerable tension, which, if it became acute, would have enhanced the power of war chiefs at the expense of that of peace or council chiefs, as later happened among the Iroquois in times of crisis (see also Thwaites 1896–1901, 15:53). The Huron social and political organization of the seventeenth century was fashioned by the Hurons themselves, largely by elaborating an older and simpler structure to serve new ends. Yet, what Champlain described in 1615 was not a social and political organization that had been in existence for hundreds of years. Instead, it was the product of a recent period of instability and major changes (Trigger 1984). This may help to explain why the Hurons in the 1630s remembered the council chiefs as having relatively low status (Thwaites 1896–1901, 10:231–3).

The Petuns are also viewed as a creation of the late sixteenth century in the sense that no Iroquoians appear to have lived in their historical homeland in prehistoric times and they themselves seem to have been an amalgamation of various groups that had moved into the area from the south and east (Garrad 1980). The main reason for their settlement south of Nottawasaga Bay may have been to exploit the rich beaver hunting grounds in the nearby swamps at the headwaters of the Grand River (Ramsden 1977:274; Prevec and Noble 1983). These swamps are located above the Niagara Escarpment in an area that has too short a growing season for corn. Historical sources report that there were fierce wars between the Petuns and Hurons in late protohistoric times (Thwaites 1896–1901, 20:43). No reason is given for this warfare but it may have resulted from Petun efforts to share in the trade with the north.

The Petuns were never admitted to the Huron confederacy, nor did the Hurons allow them to travel north through their country or along their coasts to trade with the Nipissings and the French. They obtained European materials from the Hurons and also from the Ottawas who wintered to the west of them, in return for furs, nets, and tobacco. They also exchanged European material with the Neutrals, as the Hurons did, for furs and a variety of native goods. The Neutrals traded with the Eries and the Susquehannocks, and probably also with the Senecas, since Iroquois as well as Hurons visited the Neutrals freely (Thwaites 1896–1901, 21:221–3). Thus the Neutrals may have played an important role in transferring exotic goods between hostile Iroquoian groups. The acceptance by both the Petuns and the Neutrals of a primary role for the Hurons in trading between southern Ontario and the north ensured peace among the Iroquoian tribes of southern Ontario. Yet the peace was not strong enough to prevent a threat of warfare between the Hurons and Neutrals in 1623 (Wrong 1939:156–8). Because the acquisition of individual prestige among the Iroquoians required more or less continuous warfare, the intensification of intertribal trade in southern Ontario externalized conflict rather than ended it. The Hurons and the Five Nations Iroquois, in particular the Senecas and the Cayugas, began to raid each other with increasing regularity, while the Petuns and Neutrals carried on warfare with the Central Algonkians of eastern Michigan. Thus, by the beginning of the seventeenth century, most of the basic patterns of trade and warfare that were to persist throughout the first half of the seventeenth century in the lower Great Lakes region had been established.

Prior to the sixteenth century the Hurons who lived in northern Simcoe County had probably exchanged cornmeal, nets, tobacco, marine shell, and various luxury items from the south for meat, dried fish, and copper with the Algonkian tribes who lived on the Precambrian Shield to the north. Relations appear to have been especially close with the Nipissings, whose sites contain Ontario Iroquoian-style pottery from Pickering times onward (Ridley 1954). This long-standing relationship, which cut across a major ecological boundary and which involved trading in staple subsistence items as well as luxury goods, was almost certainly a crucial beginning for the later development of the Huron fur trade. In the early sixteenth century small amounts of European goods probably were added to the material that the Nipissings had available for exchange. As trade intensified in the late sixteenth century, the Hurons no doubt began to trade beaver skins to the Nipissings and the Algonkins. The greater prominence of beaver bones and scrapers on some Huron and Petun sites of this period is probably sound evidence for the increasing exploitation of beavers in southern Ontario (Savage 1971a:167; 1971b:176). In the early seventeenth century Petite Nation bands were spending the winters on the outskirts of Arendahronon villages and trading European goods for cornmeal, which made it easier for them to survive a season when even hunting was often unproductive. Nipissings likewise wintered among the Attignawantans, an arrangement that made it unnecessary to transport large amounts of corn over long distances.

The Five Nations Iroquois, who were surrounded by other horticultural tribes and hence did not have a reciprocal trading relationship in staple products with any of their neighbours, may have had a more difficult time getting the European goods they wanted. Neighbouring groups may have been prepared to trade ornamental prestige goods but less willing to supply them with iron cutting-tools that could be used as weapons. First the Mohawks and then possibly the other Iroquoian tribes sought to obtain these weapons from their neighbours in battle, a method of procurement that was still being employed as late as 1609. According to Bradley (1979), early protohistoric Onondaga sites contain only a few scraps of iron, which were used as cutting or scraping tools. Later sites contain iron celts that were apparently reworked from broken iron axes, while scraps of iron continued to be extensively recycled throughout the sixteenth century (Bradley 1980). Common interests in obtaining such goods, or at least in minimizing local quarrels so that tribes to the north and east might be raided more easily, led to the formation or strengthening of the Iroquois confederacy. Reconciling tribal, village, and lineage jealousies to construct a workable confederacy council must have involved numerous difficulties, even though the Iroquois faced fewer problems than the Hurons did, since each of their tribes remained in its own territory instead of relocating as the Huron ones had done. These obstacles are remembered in the traditions of the tortuous negotiations that led to the founding of the confederacy (Wallace 1946; Fenton 1949). The redistribution of European goods may have played an important role in the early strengthening of the confederacy, especially if the member tribes had unequal access to them. Iroquoian confederacies were not intended as offensive leagues but as mechanisms to prevent blood feuds that freed member tribes from the threat of war with each other.

## CRISIS AND TRANSITION

Archaeology has revealed the sixteenth century as a time of significant cultural change in eastern North America. In so doing, it has altered many older views of this period. Among the Hurons and Petuns major changes have been observed in protohistoric settlement patterns that suggest significant alterations in social and political organization. European goods appeared, at least in small quantities, at a much earlier date than was formerly believed and were used in hitherto unsuspected ways. Much more must be learned about when European goods appeared in each area, what kind they were, along what routes they travelled, and how and in what social contexts they were used. All this requires more refined typologies of European goods, better chronologies, and more information about where they were manufactured and how they reached North America. Archaeologists are responding to this challenge. In the near future we can expect many surprising discoveries about the protohistoric period.

Even now it is clear that the first European goods to appear in the sites of the northern Iroquoians and their neighbours were mostly scraps of copper, brass, and iron and very rarely glass beads. The impact of these goods was out of all proportion to their economic or technological significance. A disproportionate amount of them was interred in burials and they may have been associated with new burial rituals in some areas. Traditional native values were transferred to European commodities and with this came the revival of an interest in mortuary ceremonialism that had generally remained dormant since the Middle Woodland period. This supports I.W. Brown's (1979) general observation that at first European artifacts were incorporated into aboriginal cultures in non-European roles; only later did they come to be used in the same fashion as in the donor society.

Archaeology also reveals that the changes at this time were not as far-reaching as the more radical revisionists have imagined them. Large communities and destructive warfare were both present before the protohistoric period and Huron burial rituals had already become more elaborate prior to that time. The productive subsistence economy and large towns that had developed in prehistoric times provided a receptive setting for the increase in ritualism stimulated by the arrival of European goods. There also appears to have been a significant revival of intertribal trade in the late prehistoric period and it was along the networks that supplied traditional prestige goods that European materials first seem to have reached the interior of eastern North America.

Yet European goods became an agent of economic change. As they grew more plentiful, they must have been traded to an increasing degree for furs, especially beaver pelts, which were supplying a growing European demand. By the end of the sixteenth century, the greater importance of the fur trade not only was increasing the volume of goods in intertribal exchanges but also was altering the importance and directions of that trade. Hamell (1982:63) has suggested that native people initially may have equated the Europeans with deities who controlled copper and other life-giving substances that came from below the earth; their demands for the skins of water-dwelling creatures over which they were also the keepers in return for these goods seemed totally reasonable. Only in the latter decades of the sixteenth century is there evidence that the military and technological importance of European goods was beginning to be appreciated in the interior as it probably had been considerably earlier in coastal areas where native peoples had long been in direct contact with Europeans. European goods ceased to be a factor mainly promoting ritual alliances and became instead an object of increasing competition and conflict. While these goods and the impact of White activities raced ahead of European exploration and settlement, they did not totally transform native life, as Hunt (1940:5) and some other historians have suggested. Throughout the century, native cultural values continued to play a major role in determining responses to change.

It is also evident that in this region traditional ethnographies do not describe cultures uninfluenced by European contact. The earliest written accounts are of Iroquoian cultures that had already responded to an indirect but significant European presence. The baseline for studying changes resulting from contact must be a reconstruction of Huron and Iroquois society derived from archaeological data. It is no longer acceptable to treat ethnographic descriptions of societies that are divorced from their historical background as representing general stages of development or examples of adaptations to broad natural areas. On the contrary, seeing each culture in its specific historical context is a prerequisite for understanding its adaptive or comparative significance. The resulting dynamic and enriched perspective more than compensates anthropologists for the loss of comfortable illusions.

## CHAPTER FOUR

# Traders and Colonizers, 1600–1632

At the beginning of the seventeenth century, eastern Canada emerges into the full light of history, as this term is traditionally understood. Champlain, Lescarbot, Sagard, the authors of the *Jesuit Relations*, and numerous lesser sources provide a contemporary chronicle of European (mainly French) exploration and settlement. They also offer the most detailed descriptions of Indian cultures and of relations between Indians and Europeans that are available for all of eastern North America between 1600 and 1650. These writings have provided the basis for understanding the early European colonization of Canada. Yet Canadian historians have generally treated native people as part of the setting for European activities, instead of studying them for their own sakes, while ethnologists used the ethnographic information contained in these works only to try to determine what native cultures had been like prior to European contact. The systematic use of these data to study native American history had to await the development of ethnohistory.

## ETHNOHISTORY

Ethnohistory uses written sources of information and oral traditions to study the history of nonliterate peoples. It began in North America with A.G. Bailey's *The Conflict of European and Eastern Algonkian Cultures, 1504–1700: A Study in Canadian Civilization* (1937). This book was the first to have as its central theme the changing responses of native peoples to early European encroachment. Although Bailey wrote it as a history student at the University of Toronto, he was influenced there by the economist Harold Innis and the ethnologist T.F. McIlwraith (Bailey 1977). His work remains remarkable for its clear view of the many cultural as well as economic factors involved in early Indian-White relations. Unfortunately, this highly innovative study was published in an obscure Canadian series just before World War II and did not receive the attention that it deserved until it was reprinted by the University of Toronto Press in 1969.

Since the time of L.H. Morgan, American ethnologists have used historical documents, in conjunction with varying amounts of archaeological, linguistic, and ethnographic evidence, to reconstruct traditional native cultures and to trace the origins and interconnections of their various features. In the twentieth century researchers working in this fashion, such as John R. Swanton, Frank Speck, and William N. Fenton, immeasurably enriched the understanding of the traditional cultures of eastern North America. Their work, however, used written records for purposes of historical ethnography rather than for the systematic study of what had happened to native cultures after European contact.

An awareness of the importance of understanding changes in native American cultures following European contact gradually occurred as a result of studies of acculturation in the United States. In the 1930s well-intentioned anthropologists sought to learn more about how native peoples had responded to different forms of European domination in order to help government agencies formulate more effective and humane policies for dealing with them. Robert Redfield, Ralph Linton, and M. J. Herskovits's "Outline for the Study of Acculturation" (1936), Linton's *Acculturation in Seven American Indian Tribes* (1940), and E.H. Spicer's *Perspectives in American Indian Culture Change* (1961) as well as his monumental *Cycles of Conquest* (1962) were milestones in the development of studies of acculturation into what by the 1950s had come to be called ethnohistory. The most important theoretical innovation of this period was the distinction that Linton (1940:501) drew between directed and nondirected contact situations, a distinction based on the amount of power that European settlers had to influence and change native behaviour.

With the development of ethnohistory came a growing realization that the study of native history was not only a source of generalizations useful for formulating Indian policy but also the only means of discovering how specific peoples had changed since protohistoric times. Ethnohistorical research intensified and a stronger emphasis was placed on the use of archival materials when anthropologists in the United States became involved in the 1950s in gathering evidence for land claims litigation. Many of them learned to work for and alongside native peoples.

For a long time the theoretical foundations and aims of ethnohistory remained part of the broader discipline of anthropology (McBryde 1979). In recent years, however, more ethnohistorical research has been done by professional historians, as well as by economists and geographers. These researchers are bringing new skills and fresh theoretical perspectives to the study of native American history. The development of ethnohistory has also been encouraged by a growing popular interest in native Americans that is a response to the increasingly dynamic role they are playing in North American society.

Ethnohistorians seek to understand the changes that have occurred in native societies from earliest recorded European contact until the present. As the study of native American history, ethnohistory takes up where prehistoric archaeology leaves off. Ethnohistory thus covers essentially the same time span as historical studies of White activities in the New World. It adds a new historical dimension to American anthropology that rectifies the omission of such an approach in the nineteenth century.

Ethnohistory has been variously described as a separate discipline, a branch of anthropology or of history, a technique for analysing particular kinds of data, and a convenient source of information for other disciplines (McBryde 1979:147). It has been debated whether it is closer to anthropology or to history and whether it is a bridge or a no man's land between these two disciplines. There is also disagreement about whether historical ethnography, or the reconstruction of early historical cultures, and the study of changes in native societies are separate branches of ethnohistory, as many ethnohistorians maintain (Lurie 1961), or whether only the latter activity constitutes ethnohistory in the strict sense (Hickerson 1970). It is worth noting, however, that historical ethnography was not designated as ethnohistory prior to the development of an interest in studying cultural change. In recent years it has been suggested that labelling a field of historical investigation "ethnohistory" perpetuates an ethnocentric and unjustifiable distinction between the study of literate and nonliterate societies. In this view, to which I subscribe, the term ethnohistory should be confined to labelling a set of techniques that are necessary for studying native history (Trigger 1976:12; 1982c).

It is generally agreed that ethnohistory uses documentary evidence and oral traditions to study changes in nonliterate societies.

It is further agreed that while ethnohistorians must master the skills of professional historians, they must also be able to cope with the special problems that are involved in interpreting historical data about non-Western peoples that have been collected by representatives of an alien culture.

The use of oral traditions to understand historical events requires a detailed understanding of their derivation and a critical comparison of alternative versions of the same story (Vansina 1965). While oral traditions may provide a valuable record of former beliefs and values, caution is needed in interpreting that sort of information historically. Anthropological research in North America and elsewhere indicates that tribal societies generally have little interest in conserving an accurate knowledge of the past over long periods of time for its own sake. What pass as historical traditions are often mythical charters explaining and validating current social relations and these change as social relations change. Early in the twentieth century A.C. Parker (1916) found to his surprise that the Iroquois did not remember the palisaded villages and longhouses that their ancestors had lived in 200 years before. Similarly, in the traditional history of his people that he published in 1870, the Wyandot Peter Clarke showed no awareness that they had ever been more numerous or that their way of life had ever been different from that in the eighteenth and early nineteenth centuries. On the other hand, George Copway's (1850) folk history of the Ojibwas recorded important historical data preserved as oral traditions from the late seventeenth century that have since been corroborated by seventeenth-century historical documents (Eid 1979; see also Day 1972).

The small populations of tribal societies, and their general lack of concern with the inheritance of private property, tend not to produce the systematic variations in oral traditions that are useful for evaluating their historical authenticity. The recording of oral traditions as well may be suspect. The few committed to writing in eastern Canada prior to the late nineteenth century were done in an extremely cursory fashion and from poorly identified sources (Trigger 1972:71–83). At least some of these oral traditions appear to have been heavily influenced by White historical narratives, missionary propaganda, and even anthropological publications (Hamell 1982:45). They also frequently reflect knowledge of periods later than those to which they are alleged to refer. In general, some kind of independent verification is required before such traditions can be accepted as accurate historical accounts.

Another highly specific set of problems is involved in interpreting the records that Europeans have left of their early dealings with native peoples. These visitors had a variable but almost inevitably a deficient understanding of the behaviour they were observing. Hence while many of them recorded what they saw accurately, the motives that they ascribed to native peoples and their interpretations of what these people were doing are often erroneous and ethnocentric. Because of this, it is very difficult to ascertain with any certainty why particular native people acted as they did or what specific policies they were pursuing. Even factual descriptions of native behaviour are sometimes too brief and too contaminated by European literary conventions to be either trustworthy or useful as anthropological documents.

Historical records can be interpreted only when the cultural values of both the observer and the observed are understood by the historian. In the study of modern Western history, the experience of everyday life may suffice to supply such knowledge. Yet this implicit approach does not provide an adequate basis for understanding the behaviour of people in earlier times or in cultures radically different from our own. It is normally possible for a historian who studies literate people to learn enough from their writings about their philosophy, religious beliefs, and values to be able to interpret their behaviour with some degree of accuracy. It is nevertheless clear that the written records of societies are generally much more informative about the thinking of the upper classes than of the illiterate peasants and labourers who constituted the bulk of the population. Because of this, ethnohistory shares many problems with the history of the lower classes in ancient, medieval, or even early modern times.

Ethnohistorians can cope with this difficulty to some degree by utilizing a detailed ethnographic knowledge of the descendants of the groups described in the historical records or of tribes that shared closely related ways of life. Such information provides a balanced view of whole cultures that is useful for evaluating old sources, which invariably describe only fragments of them. Yet anthropologists are becoming increasingly aware of the pervasiveness of change in native cultures and hence know that it may be misleading to employ detailed studies of the recent past as a basis for understanding much earlier stages of the same culture. It is necessary to work systematically back through the historical records and to note changes over time, before knowledge about modern native cultures can be used to infer the beliefs and values that influenced behaviour in the more remote past.

To interpret the former actions of native peoples, each group must be situated in a specific cultural context. Yet, like historians, ethnohistorians cannot assume that behaviour is automatically dictated by shared cultural patterns. These patterns constitute a framework in terms of which decisions are made by individuals and groups. Nevertheless, in concrete situations members of the same culture may decide to pursue goals diametrically opposed to one another, either because the individuals occupy different positions in the society and therefore have different personal interests or because for idiosyncratic reasons they perceive the situation that they are confronting differently. Only rarely is enough historical information available about nonliterate peoples to permit historians to understand behaviour at the level of the individual (Spicer 1962). Even our knowledge of well-documented native leaders, such as Pontiac or Tecumseh, is inadequate for the detailed biographical treatment accorded to prominent Whites of the same period.

On the other hand, it is possible to do more at the level of the interest group, as this concept has been defined implicitly or explicitly by sociologists and historians (Homans 1962:182–91; Sartre 1963; Lanctôt 1967). While many ethnohistorians have used this concept implicitly, I first drew attention to it as an analytical device in The Children of Aataentsic (Trigger 1976:23–5). There I stated that interest groups are not abstract categories established by social scientists for comparative research, but specific groupings that emerge within societies as a result of common interests shared by people in concrete historical situations. Some of these groups had a recognized corporate existence; others are constructs of the historian. Yet for such a group to be valid, its members must at least implicitly have shared common goals and supported one another in collective actions.

Within individual Indian tribes, various groupings based on clan membership, sex, age, trade, waging war, communities, and political factions had opposing interests in dealing with one another, with other tribes, and with Europeans. Europeans also competed with one another and with native people not only as national groups but also, within colonies, as interest groups. Fur traders, government officials, farmers, and religious orders often pursued incompatible and even conflicting goals. Common interests cut across ethnic divisions and united various Indians and Europeans in opposition to their own people. By carefully analysing historical documents, in favourable situations the ethnohistorian can define the more significant interest groups, native and White, and offer reasonable explanations for why they behaved as they did. These explanations seek to account for reciprocal interactions in which competing interest groups sought to achieve their own goals or to thwart those of opponents. It must not be forgotten, however, that, as a result of idiosyncracies or for personal reasons, an individual may not adhere to the interest group to which he or she is expected to belong.

In practice an unlimited number of interest groups can be defined and these vary greatly in scale and nature. Some may form within individual families, guilds, or communities; others may ramify, either as a single entity or as a network of small groups, across a whole society. Some are evanescent; others endure over generations. Some have very limited and explicit goals; others, like modern political parties, simultaneously pursue a broad range of objectives. These include not only profit, status, and power but religious causes and other culturally specific goals for which some individuals may be willing to suffer great personal hardship. The historian will naturally pay most attention to interest groups that are of historical, rather than static social or cultural, significance. Men and women, as well as various age groups, are assigned different and often unequal roles vis-à-vis one another in individual societies. These roles promote group solidarity and chronic intergroup rivalry. Yet they become significant for explaining historical change only if their relationship to the society as a whole begins to change. The kinds of groups that the historian will choose to study are strongly influenced by the scale of the social networks he is investigating. Since historians most often study whole societies, rather than communities or families, they tend to be concerned with groups whose interactions affect the entire society.

Seventeenth-century European societies were divided into a hierarchy of social classes that were an official expression of rank and status. While individuals sought to enhance their status, social classes were concerned to protect their corporate political and economic privileges. This does not mean, however, that classes and interest groups are congruent. Struggles between rival groups within privileged classes are often no less important than struggles between classes. French merchants were members of a small middle class; yet different associations of merchants competed with one another to control the Canadian fur trade. In so doing, they often sought the favour and patronage of influential members of the nobility. It is therefore the investors in these rival companies, not the middle class itself, that constitute interest groups. On the other hand, the Jesuits, who were recruited from both the middle class and the lesser nobility, made common cause against officials, traders, and members of rival religious orders recruited from their own classes. While it is probably true that in complex societies interest groups that cut across widely divergent classes tend to be weaker and more ephemeral than ones made up of members of a single class, class homogeneity does not guarantee that an interest group will not be wracked by internal dissension.

In classless native societies, the most important cleavages were between different lineages, clans, and tribes. Chiefs and their supporters competed for prestige with other groups. Because prestige was derived in various ways from the conduct of foreign relations, chiefs within a tribe or confederacy often formed two or more factions that pursued alternative foreign policies, each faction hoping to benefit from its choice. In Iroquoian society there was also frequent opposition between war chiefs and peace chiefs (although one of each belonged to each localized clan), since their prestige was derived from the successful conduct of foreign policy by warlike and peaceful means respectively. These were probably the two kinds of native interest groups most easily visible to Europeans.

While the concept of the interest group is certainly worthy of more detailed epistemological analysis (Gadacz 1982:158–60), its main utilitarian value for ethnohistorical research is to provide a generally useful minimal level at which the behaviour of native people can be studied. While insufficient data are available to analyse the behaviour of individual native people as such, what is recorded concerning the conduct of various individuals may be sufficient to define an interest group. This kind of approach is particularly rewarding if rival European interest groups left accounts of their dealings with the same native people. Yet, all too often, not enough information is available for more than a vague and uncertain picture to emerge.

Ethnohistory began as an activity within ethnology and, if it is now widely recognized as a separate branch of anthropology or even a separate discipline, the ties between these two subdisciplines remain especially close. In North America ethnohistorians continue to be recruited mainly from ethnology rather than from other branches of anthropology. Ethnohistory's original relationship to archaeology involved the use of historical ethnography to interpret late prehistoric archaeological sites, a technique that was developed particularly effectively by archaeologists working on the Great Plains in the 1930s (Strong 1940). Archaeologists thus saw themselves as consumers of ethnohistorical data. Now many ethnohistorians acknowledge the need to learn what native societies were like in the late prehistoric and protohistoric periods, since changes had oc-

curred, and realize that this can be done only by means of archaeological data. They also note that archaeology provides vital
information about the material culture of the early historical period, which is often poorly described in contemporary written accounts. For these reasons, archaeological findings are now being
recognized as essential for ethnohistorical studies.

Ethnohistorical analysis is a complex procedure that cannot be
reduced to a simple formula or set of rules. Like all forms of historical investigation, it must be taught and learned by example.
The rest of chapter 4 and chapter 5 attempt to promote an understanding of the practice of ethnohistory by surveying the current
state of research on the Iroquoian peoples who inhabited the St
Lawrence lowlands in the seventeenth century.

## TRADE AND WARFARE, 1600–1615

Late in the sixteenth century French officials developed an increasing interest in Canada. Henri IV sought to promote colonization
by granting wealthy merchants an exclusive right to trade with the
Indians in return for establishing French settlements there. In 1599
Pierre de Chauvin de Tonnetuit, a merchant of Honfleur, obtained
a monopoly of the fur trade, and in 1603 Pierre Du Gua de Monts,
a trader who had already visited Canada several times, received a
new ten-year grant. In an effort to secure as many furs as possible,
both men sought to cultivate good relations with the Montagnais
who lived around Tadoussac and controlled the trading there. In
1600 Chauvin obtained permission from them to build a trading
post at Tadoussac, where he left sixteen men to spend the winter.
Because of sickness, quarrelling, and lack of provisions, only five
survived, those who did being fed and cared for by the Montagnais
(Biggar 1901:42–4). From 1603 to 1607 efforts at colonization were
directed towards Acadia. During this period trading on the St Lawrence was confined to summer meetings as it had been in the past.

Over the winter of 1601–2 Chauvin's trading company received
royal approval for its plans to broaden its relations with the native
peoples along the St Lawrence River (Biggar 1922–36, 1:99–101).
That these plans had been discussed with the king indicates how
important obtaining the goodwill of the Montagnais was regarded
at that time. Because of the major role that Champlain was later
to play in executing these plans, it should be noted that they were
devised before his involvement with Canada and embodied the
experience that French merchants had acquired from trading along
the St Lawrence over the previous twenty years.

The leader in encouraging the expansion of Indian trade appears to have been Chauvin's partner François Gravé Du Pont, who had already been active in Canada for some time. In 1602 and 1603 he brought three young relatives of Montagnais chiefs to spend the winter in France and by his generous treatment of them won their elders' approval. While in France, they visited the royal court and were presented to the king. As a sign that they recognized him as their ally, in 1603 the Montagnais gave Gravé Du Pont an Iroquois woman whom they had captured to take back to France with him (Biggar 1922–36, 1:99–100, 188).

The French traders already knew that the furs arriving from north of the St Lawrence were superior in quality to those coming from elsewhere. Because of the complex network of rivers flowing into the St Lawrence from the north, furs coming from that direction could also be collected in larger quantities than those from the south. While the French would have liked to trade with all tribes, the commercial advantages of trading with the Montagnais and Algonkins were so great that they ensured that if a choice had to be made, the French would deal with these groups rather than with the Mohawks, who lived in New York State. The French traders also noted that Mohawk raids in the St Lawrence Valley made it difficult for native people living west of Tadoussac to trade there. To develop the St Lawrence River as a major artery for trade and to promote good relations between themselves and the Montagnais, the French thought it desirable to help these Indians fight the Iroquois. Chauvin had promised them that the French would settle among them and either compel the Iroquois to make peace or help to destroy them (Biggar 1922–36, 1:100). After 1601 the traders assisted the Montagnais by supplying them with iron knives, hatchets, and other weapons that would allow them and their Algonkin allies to defeat Mohawk war parties. By 1603 the Montagnais and Algonkins were winning victories as far south as Lake Champlain (ibid., 107–9, 141).

Chauvin's company also wished to contact and make alliances with tribes that lived farther west. The Montagnais at Tadoussac were receiving furs from as far north as James Bay and as far west as southern Ontario (Biggar 1922–36, 1:121–4; 2:18–19). Yet the volume of furs that these Indians required, even as middlemen, to supply their own needs for European wares must have been limited and did not provide them with a strong incentive to expand their trade with the interior. On the contrary, their semi-nomadic style of life must have imposed severe restrictions on the amount of goods that they could handle or would want. Nevertheless, as late as 1635, they killed a group of Montagnais from the interior who attempted to trade directly with the French (Thwaites 1896–1901, 8:41). To the extent that they prevented other tribes from visiting Tadoussac in order to protect their own position as intermediaries, the Montagnais were probably curtailing the growth of the fur trade. This is a point that was not appreciated in former analyses of the fur trade, which have generally assumed that the Montagnais were seeking to maximize their profits.

Yet the Montagnais needed help to fight the Iroquois. Their principal allies at the beginning of the seventeenth century were other Montagnais and Algonkin groups who lived north of the St Lawrence River from Tadoussac as far west as the Ottawa Valley. To avoid the Iroquois, many of these groups probably travelled to and from Tadoussac along the old copper route rather than along the St Lawrence River. In 1603, in order to reaffirm his friendship with the Kichesipirini Algonkins, who lived in the upper part of the Ottawa Valley, and to gain their support for a raid against the Mohawks, Anadabijou, the principal chief at Tadoussac, presented them with French axes, swords, kettles, ornaments, and dried food (Biggar 1922–36, 1:109). These allies also appear to have enjoyed the privilege of trading directly with the French at Tadoussac, which probably cost the Montagnais very little if they were already obtaining sufficient furs from central and northern Quebec to purchase what they needed from the French. In return, Anadabijou was recognized by his Indian allies as an intermediary between themselves and the French, a role from which he and his descendants derived considerable prestige (ibid., 5:64). The French traders encouraged this alliance, which they perceived as a device not only for repelling Iroquois raiders but also for expanding trade with the interior without offending the Montagnais.

In 1607 the advocates of free trade had de Monts's privileges revoked as of the following year. In an effort to retain control of the fur trade west of Tadoussac while he tried to obtain a new monopoly, he decided to found a new trading post on the St Lawrence in the summer of 1608. Champlain, who had worked as an explorer and cartographer for de Monts in the Maritimes since 1604, established this post on the north side of the Narrows of Quebec, a location from which it was possible to prevent illicit traders from travelling upriver. Before doing this, however, he and Gravé Du Pont no doubt secured permission from the Montagnais at Tadoussac, who would have welcomed such a settlement as additional protection against Iroquois attacks. The presence of armed Frenchmen also made it possible for the Montagnais to fish and take eels in the vicinity of Quebec despite their dread of Iroquois raiders. Although they had won some victories earlier in the decade, the Montagnais and their allies continued to fear the Mohawks, who outnumbered them and were more formidable and experienced warriors. If their winter hunting was unproductive, native bands could also come to Quebec and request food from their French allies (Biggar 1922–36, 2:50–6).

De Monts's company was now determined to put an end to the Iroquois menace along the St Lawrence River, so that native people living in the Batiscan, St Maurice, and Ottawa Valleys could use it freely to trade at Quebec. Henceforth armed Frenchmen were to accompany allied war parties in an effort to defeat the Iroquois. It was also hoped that more active involvement in warfare would enhance the prestige of de Monts's men and therefore assist them to compete with independent traders. In addition his men would have an excuse to explore the interior and contact more tribes (Biggar 1922–36, 2:63–9).

In 1608 Champlain agreed to accompany a party of Montagnais and Petite Nation Algonkin warriors on a raid up the Richelieu River the following summer. Iroquet, the Petite Nation chief who was to be part of this expedition, spent the winter among the Arendahronons and while there invited his Huron trading partner, Ochasteguin, to participate in the raid. Ochasteguin accepted this invitation and in 1609 he and his men became the first Hurons to contact the French in the St Lawrence Valley (Trigger 1976:246–7). Huron custom prescribed that because Ochasteguin had pioneered a new trade route, he and his family would become its owners and have the right to determine which Hurons could use it, a privilege normally accorded only in return for a share of the profits (Thwaites 1896–1901, 10:223–5). Ochasteguin or the chief of his clan was therefore theoretically in a position to acquire great wealth by Huron standards and perhaps to become a leading Huron chief.

The Hurons and Algonkins spent five or six days feasting and trading at Quebec and inspecting the European buildings. Early in July Champlain and two other Frenchmen armed with muskets accompanied sixty Montagnais, Algonkin, and Huron warriors southward. As a sign that they were the oldest and therefore the closest allies of the French, the Montagnais insisted that on military expeditions the French should continue to travel in their canoes, not those of other tribes (Biggar 1922–36, 2:97). Near Point Ticonderoga, at the south end of Lake Champlain, the expedition intercepted and defeated a raiding party of 200 Mohawk warriors. In this first recorded encounter of the Iroquois with European fire-

Battle of Lake Champlain, 30 July 1609. The hammocks, palm trees, and nudity of the Indians were borrowed by Champlain's engraver probably from Theodor de Bry's illustrations of South America. Courtesy Public Archives of Canada.

arms, about fifty Iroquois, including two chiefs, were slain and ten or twelve more taken prisoner (ibid., 98–101). Ochasteguin promised that the following summer more Hurons would visit the St Lawrence and that, after a raid against the Iroquois, they would lead Champlain into the interior and show him their country.

In 1610 Champlain traded with the Indians on Ile Saint-Ignace, near the mouth of the Richelieu River. He had designated this island as a trading place the year before, hoping that it would lie within a new monopoly zone or at least be far enough upriver that rival traders would not find it. On both scores he was to be disappointed. Of greater long-term importance, this new location allowed the Algonkins to trade directly with the French rather than at the discretion of the Montagnais and was a first step towards founding a permanent French settlement in Algonkin territory. Yet, although the Algonkins greatly desired it, a year-round trading post was not established on their territory until one at Trois-Rivières was started in 1634. A few days before the main party of Hurons and their Algonkin allies arrived to trade at Ile Saint-Ignace, Champlain and the Indians who had already assembled attacked a fortified Mohawk war camp located a short distance up the Richelieu River. Of the hundred warriors in this camp, fifteen were taken prisoner and the rest killed (Biggar 1922–36, 2:125–34). This was the last time that the Mohawks were a serious threat along the St

Lawrence River until the 1630s. Having suffered major losses in two successive encounters, they were henceforth anxious to avoid armed Frenchmen.

Another event is equally important for explaining the withdrawal of the Mohawks from the St Lawrence Valley. In 1609 Henry Hudson had sailed the *Half Moon* up the Hudson River and had noted the wealth that could be derived from trading for furs in the Albany area. The next year Dutch trading vessels began to visit the upper part of the Hudson Valley. Hereafter the Mohawks found it preferable to steal or purchase European goods from their Mahican neighbours, who lived in the Hudson Valley, or to acquire them directly by selling furs to the Dutch. Iroquois raiders, probably mainly Oneidas, continued to plunder European goods along the Ottawa River as long as the French did not go there regularly (Wrong 1939:261).

After the battle of the Richelieu River, Champlain persuaded Iroquet to allow a young employee of the trading company, unnamed but almost certainly Etienne Brûlé, to spend the winter with his people. This arrangement was intended to strengthen the ties between the French and the Petite Nation Algonkins. It would also give Brûlé a chance to learn a native language and gather valuable information about the geography and peoples of the interior. In exchange, Champlain agreed to take Savignon, the younger brother of a Huron chief, to France (Biggar 1922–36, 2:138–42). Iroquet almost certainly spent the winter in the Huron country and it seems likely that Brûlé himself lived with Savignon's family rather than among the Petite Nation. Thus it appears that the ties that Iroquet had to his Arendahronon hosts were very close. By introducing the Hurons to the French and allowing Brûlé to live with them, he was promoting a close relationship as well between these two groups.

Champlain does not state why he did not act on Ochasteguin's invitation to visit the Huron country in 1610. It may have been because of a minor wound that he had suffered in the battle with the Iroquois or because of his desire to return to France quickly to do what he could to persuade de Monts's partners not to abandon the trading post at Quebec. Almost certainly, however, the Algonkin groups who were profiting as intermediaries in the trade between the Hurons and the French, and in particular the Kichesipirinis, were opposed to any action that would seal a closer alliance between these two groups. As a result, Ochasteguin and his Algonkin trading partners may not have had enough strength or influence to ensure Champlain a safe passage through the upper part of the

Ottawa Valley. The Montagnais had prevented Champlain from travelling up the Saguenay River in 1608 (Biggar 1922–36, 2:19), and the Indians in the Trois-Rivières area thwarted his plans to explore the St Maurice River in 1610 and again in 1611 (ibid., 119, 173–4). When native groups stood to gain from being middlemen in the fur trade and no alliance was urgently needed against the Iroquois, they did not permit leading Frenchmen to visit trading partners who lived farther inland so that no trading alliances could be concluded with such groups. Champlain arranged to trade with the Algonkins and Hurons the following year at the Lachine Rapids. He hoped that by moving the trading place still farther up the St Lawrence River he might outdistance rival traders (ibid., 175).

In June 1611 about 200 Indians arrived at the Lachine Rapids. Many of them were Huron traders who had not come downriver previously. The Huron chiefs met secretly with Champlain and Gravé Du Pont and presented them with four strings of shell beads and fifty beaver skins. Presumably one string of beads was from each of the Huron tribes and one beaver pelt from each of the council chiefs. The Hurons explained that these gifts came from the principal Huron chiefs, who like themselves wished for an alliance with the French that would eliminate the Algonkins as intermediaries in the fur trade. The Hurons seem to have implied, however, that to conclude such an alliance Champlain would have to visit their country and confer with the fifty council chiefs, who could not all leave home at the same time (Biggar 1922–36, 2:194–6).

We can surmise that between 1609 and 1611 the recently expanded Huron confederacy was grappling with the political and economic challenges posed by the opportunity for trading directly with the French. This trade was clearly too important to be monopolized by Ochasteguin and his family; hence it must have been agreed that it should be shared with his tribe, the Arendahronons. This meant that the chiefs of all the local clans that made up the tribe would control it. Relations with the French henceforth became the special responsibility of Atironta, the chief who was the principal spokesman of the Arendahronons. It was equally clear, however, that if the Arendahronons tried to monopolize this trade for themselves, the resulting grievances and hostility would tear apart the newly constituted confederacy. The Arendahronons must have consented to share the regulation of this trade with all Huron chiefs, provided that Atironta was recognized as the principal Huron ally of the French and as the spokesman for all the Hurons in high-level negotiations with them. All Huron council chiefs were thus in a position to acquire large amounts of European goods that they could redistribute as a means of enhancing their prestige. In this way, they could bolster their status, which probably had been undermined during the period of turmoil that had led to the expansion of the confederacy. While there appeared to be no way that Champlain could visit the Huron country in 1611, he promised to ask the French king to send forty or fifty men with him the following year who would help the Hurons fight their enemies.

Champlain did not visit Canada in 1612, but stayed in France where he lobbied successfully for the re-establishment of a monopoly for the fur trade. Because many native traders had been harassed by rival groups of French merchants in 1612, only a few of them came to trade at Montreal Island in 1613. Since the new monopoly came into effect that year and Champlain was once again responsible for relations with the Indians, on his return he decided to travel up the Ottawa River to renew his friendship with the Algonkin bands and encourage them to trade with licensed French merchants. He also wanted to discover if it was possible to travel north from the Ottawa Valley to James Bay. He was halted, however, when Tessouat, the wily chief of the Kichesipirinis, persuaded him that Nicolas de Vignau, a young man who had wintered among his people to learn their language, was lying when he claimed to have travelled to the shores of a northern ocean with the Nipissings, a tribe that lived between the Ottawa Valley and Georgian Bay and traded as far north as James Bay each summer. As a result of the ensuing imbroglio, which was carefully orchestrated by Tessouat, Champlain was prevented from contacting the Nipissings (Biggar 1922–36, 2:282–307).

In 1612 a large number of warriors had embarked on a campaign against the Iroquois (Biggar 1922–36, 2:253–4). Most of these were Algonkins and their aim was no doubt to avenge Oneida attacks on the Ottawa Valley; however, Arendahronon traders who had suffered from these attacks probably joined this expedition. The aim of the Oneidas was still to seize European goods and their attacks were probably aimed mainly against native traders travelling upriver. Champlain did not visit Canada in 1614. Nevertheless, when he reached Montreal Island in 1615, he was informed that the Hurons were organizing yet another major military campaign against the Oneidas. The Indians invited him to keep his promise to help them against their enemies. Most likely the Hurons once again wanted to avenge losses they had suffered at the hands of the Oneidas, either while travelling in the Ottawa Valley or fighting alongside their Algonkin trading partners. The Algonkins

The Iroquois town attacked by Champlain and his allies in 1615. The symmetrical design of the settlement is the invention of the French artist. Courtesy Public Archives of Canada.

could not object to Champlain's visiting the Huron country on this occasion since they themselves had agreed to join this expedition. The Hurons thus manoeuvred the Algonkins into letting him travel inland and meet their council chiefs.

Champlain reached the Huron country on 1 August and toured their settlements where he was entertained with great ceremony. Because he did not understand Indian protocol, he does not appear to have realized that in the course of these receptions he had concluded an alliance with each of the Huron chiefs. On 1 September about 500 warriors set out from the Arendahronon town of Cahiagué and travelled south of Lake Ontario where they laid siege for two weeks to the only Oneida settlement. Champlain thought that the campaign was a dismal failure because he and his men did not capture and destroy the town, but his Huron and Algonkin allies seemed pleased by the large number of Iroquois that had been slain in skirmishes. For them the raid had gone as they had wanted. The Hurons refused, however, to return Champlain to Quebec that autumn by travelling down the St Lawrence River. Winter was near at hand and for a small party the danger of encountering Oneida or Mohawk warriors was too great. Champlain spent the winter at Cahiagué. He was allowed to visit the Petuns but they did not permit him to contact the Neutrals, and the following spring the Nipissings reneged on a promise to show him the northern ocean. The Hurons and their neighbours clearly did not wish him to contact any of their trading partners living farther to the north and west. In the spring Atironta accompanied Champlain to Quebec where he visited the French settlement. This visit reciprocated Champlain's and sealed the alliance between the Hurons and the French (Thwaites 1896–1901, 20:35; 23:167; Biggar 1922–36, 3:168–72). It also demonstrated to the Hurons that among them Atironta, rather than Ochasteguin, was now recognized by the French as their principal ally and trading partner.

Many Algonkins, especially the Kichesipirinis, did not approve of this alliance, but because of the Hurons' numerical superiority and their own increasing reliance on them for corn and military support, they could not stop them from trading with the French. They did, however, have the right to charge Huron traders tolls for passing through their band territories along the Ottawa River. The Kichesipirinis, who were described as the richest and proudest of all the Algonkin bands, were particularly assiduous in collecting these dues. The Algonkins also did all they could to sow mistrust between the Hurons and the French, in the hope that the Hurons would trade through them rather than risk their lives in direct annual encounters with the French (Wrong 1939:262–4).

Between 1608 and 1615 the French had in this way extended their direct trading relations to include the Algonkins and the Hurons. They had undercut the role of the Montagnais as middlemen by establishing summer trading stations farther up the St Lawrence Valley within Algonkin territory. Direct trade with the Hurons required concluding a formal alliance that gave the Hurons the confidence needed to dispense with Algonkin intermediaries. During this period the Iroquois showed little overt hostility towards the French. Neither the Mohawks nor the Oneidas sought blood revenge for their heavy losses, although they may have renewed their attacks on Huron and Algonkin traders using the St Lawrence River for a brief time early in the 1620s (Sagard 1866:760). The Mohawks and Oneidas were no doubt frightened of the French. Yet when Brûlé was captured by the Senecas in 1616, the council chiefs and old men rescued him from being tortured in the hope he might arrange for them to trade with the French (Biggar 1922–36, 3:224).

The French would have liked to trade with the Iroquois as well as the northern tribes. In the 1620s this further trade could have added 7,500 pelts to the 12,000 to 22,000 being exported through Tadoussac each year (Thwaites 1896–1901, 4:207; Trelease 1960:43). The Mohawks would also have been pleased to trade with the French as well as the Dutch, since the competition would have increased the amount of European goods they received for their furs. The French feared, however, that if peace prevailed, their native trading partners would be drawn to the Dutch. The Mohawks also feared that if the Dutch began to trade with northern tribes, who could provide more and better quality furs than the Mohawks could, the Dutch would be led to conclude political alliances with these tribes. The Mohawks therefore might once again find themselves cut off from a secure source of furs.

To prevent this from happening, in 1624 the Mohawks made peace with the Montagnais, Algonkins, and French. Then, assured of at least a temporary supply of European goods, they attacked the Mahicans and in a long and hard-fought war expelled those groups that lived around the Dutch trading post which was now at Fort Orange on the west bank of the Hudson. As a result of their victory, in 1628 the Mohawks extended their control over the land surrounding Fort Orange and henceforth forbade the northern tribes to cross their territory to trade with the Dutch (Trigger 1971a). The Dutch then informed the Mohawks that during the war the Algonkins and Montagnais had accepted Dutch presents urging them to support the Mahicans. This revelation led to a renewal of warfare between the Mohawks and the northern tribes, once the Mohawks had assured themselves of a continuous supply of European goods from the Dutch.

After 1610 when the Dutch had begun to trade along the Hudson River, a two-tier network developed in which the Hurons, Algonkins, and Montagnais traded with the French, while the Iroquois traded with the Dutch and later the English. It is frequently asserted that the Dutch and French became locked into two previously existing chains of mutually hostile alliances (Rotstein 1972). There is evidence of warfare between the Mohawks and Oneidas on the one side and the Montagnais and Algonkins on the other already in the late sixteenth century and the Hurons seem to have been fighting the three western Iroquois tribes by then as well. Yet conflict between the Hurons and the Mohawks and Oneidas probably arose still later as a result of the historically documented fur trade, while the main patterns of warfare in earlier times involved the St Lawrence Iroquoians.

Although many neighbouring tribes probably traded with one another, there is no evidence that ones living as far apart as the Montagnais at Tadoussac and the Kichesipirinis or the Algonkins and the Hurons were doing so directly prior to the development of the fur trade. It is also obvious that the fur trade would not have produced the patterns of exchanges and alliances found in the St Lawrence lowlands after 1609 if rival groups of European traders had not established themselves along the Hudson and St Lawrence Rivers. While pre-existing patterns of trade and warfare, as well as regional geography and ecology, played a role in the development of the two-tier trading system, its main features were determined by the fact that neither the French traders nor the Mohawks could afford to permit the Hurons, Algonkins, and Montagnais to trade with the Dutch. Such trade would have put the prosperity of the French and the security of the Mohawks at serious risk. These factors, which had not influenced tribal relations previously, made it impossible for the French and the Iroquois to conclude a lasting peace with each other during the seventeenth century. Yet, while the French had to protect their native allies, neither the French traders nor the Iroquois had any pressing reason that would cause one to seek to destroy the other. On the contrary, the vested interests of both parties dictated the other's continued existence.

## THE NATURE OF INDIAN TRADE

The interpretations of historical events offered in the previous section depend largely on current anthropological views about how native people acted as middlemen and about their economic behaviour generally. C.H. McIlwain (1915), H.A. Innis (1930), and G.T. Hunt (1940) in turn used the concept of middleman as a basis for understanding the development of trade and intertribal politics in eastern North America in early historical times. They assumed that native groups who were suitably located profited as intermediaries in exchanging European goods for furs between the coast and the interior and that these groups were prepared to fight to maintain that role. They also assumed that middlemen would exploit their position to derive maximum gain for themselves. For the most part, this interpretation was elaborated in terms of purely economic arguments and without significant reference to anthropological data or native values. In the works of Innis and Hunt, native peoples remained economic stereotypes only minimally disguised in feathers. Hunt (1940:4–5), in particular, justified this approach by arguing that the imperatives of the fur trade quickly rendered former relations among native peoples obsolete. On the other hand, scholars interested in native cultural history, such as Bailey (1937) and Fenton (1940), did not pay much attention to exchange networks. In *The Children of Aataentsic*, I noted that traditional values greatly influenced intertribal relations but did not systematically review the concept of native middlemen.

During the last twenty-five years a lively debate has developed about the nature of the fur trade in Canada, based mainly on the abundant records concerning the operation of the Hudson's Bay Company during the eighteenth century. This debate is part of a broader controversy, among economists and economic anthropologists, about how the evolution of economic behaviour is to be understood. On the one side, the formalists claim that the economic activities of native North Americans can be understood in terms of theories of market behaviour that apply equally to peoples at all levels of development. Alternatively, the substantivists, basing themselves largely on the work of Karl Polanyi, interpret all precapitalist economic activity as being embedded in and controlled by political and economic structures rather than being shaped by market forces (Dalton 1968). They treat the fur trade as an example of treaty or embassy trade, which they claim characterized all precapitalist intergroup exchanges. So far very little attention has been paid by this debate to the trade that is documented, however imperfectly, for the St Lawrence Valley during the seventeenth century. Important information is provided concerning native economic behaviour by these data.

E.E. Rich (1960), following Innis, recognized that groups such as the Crees and the Assiniboines functioned as professional traders to the extent that they did little trapping but obtained most of the furs they traded with Europeans from interior tribes in exchange for European goods. They were not professional traders in the sense that they depended wholly on that activity for their livelihood; they and their families continued to produce their own food and other basic necessities. Yet they obtained the European goods they needed by charging the tribes who lived farther inland more than they themselves had paid for such goods. Rich also observed that if rival European suppliers were present, the Indians would increase the prices that they charged for their furs. They exploited markets, however, not to maximize gain but to supply their limited wants more easily. They also insisted on trading goods with any one group at a fixed rate and would object if Europeans tried to haggle or to raise the prices that they charged for their wares. In return, they did not seek more favourable exchange rates if furs became scarce. Rich maintained that, in general, native people succeeded in imposing their pre-existing trading customs on European fur buyers.

Abraham Rotstein (1970, 1972) carried Rich's interpretations further along substantivist lines. He argues that all tribes technically were at war unless a formal alliance had been established between them. Trade and exchange of gifts were important elements in initiating and maintaining such alliances. Identical rituals were used for intertribal trade and for reinforcing alliances and the same meetings often served both purposes. According to Rotstein, tribes that were trading partners were required to support one another against their enemies. He also suggests that exchange rates were fixed as part of the political alliance and because of that did not vary over long periods. The major features of market exchanges in modern Western societies were all conspicuously lacking: prices were not determined by the operation of supply and demand in a situation where internally competing groups of buyers and sellers were interacting with one another. Instead, factors such as the relative status of trading groups and the need for military support played an important role in fixing the price of goods.

A.J. Ray and Donald Freeman (1978) have used their statistical analyses of Hudson's Bay Company trading records to call into question many of Rich's and Rotstein's conclusions. They point out that Indian traders sought European goods to supply their own needs and those of their kinsmen as well as to engage in intertribal trade. They also cast doubt on the importance of alliances as Rotstein has described them. The Hudson's Bay Company did not provide military assistance to their Indian trading partners, and the latter were prepared to trade with rival groups of Europeans if it were economically advantageous to do so. Traders generally were not paramount chiefs and in any case the loose political organization of Cree bands would have made it impossible for them to fulfil the terms of any military alliance with the English. Trading rituals were often quite informal and the Indians' speeches normally contained only requests to be given good value for their furs. Finally, Ray and Freeman assert, Indians and Whites paid only lip service to the concept of fixed exchange rates: the Europeans tried to give short measure or to provide goods of inferior quality, while the Indians sought more than the standard measure for their furs. Native people also calculated marginal costs. For example, they were willing to pay more for European goods if they did not have to carry them so far. Ray and Freeman do not contest Rotstein's portrayal of traditional Indian trade but suggest that the trade described in the Hudson's Bay Company records was of a transitional, not a traditional, type and that its nonmarket features were a survival from the past that continued to colour it rather than ones that any longer determined its basic nature.

It is clear that in historical times all neighbouring tribes either were at war or traded with one another. Archaeological evidence reveals that for millennia trading, perhaps in many instances only of luxury goods, had been an important mechanism for maintaining peace and friendly contacts among tribes. It is also evident that intertribal trading did not take place in the absence of political alliances.

Each summer when the main party of Huron traders visited the French, an elaborate ceremony was performed to reaffirm the alliance between their two nations. Before meeting the French, the Hurons would paint their faces and put on their best clothes. During an initial round of speeches, feasts, and ceremonies, the Huron chiefs presented rich gifts of furs to the French administrators and asked them to see that the Huron traders obtained high-quality goods at reasonable prices. Then individual Hurons exchanged their furs with the French traders. More feasts and ceremonies followed and the French officials gave the Huron chiefs presents equal in value to those they had received and invited them to return to trade the following year (Thwaites 1896–1901, 32:185–9). Unless major chiefs had performed this ceremony, the ordinary Hurons who accompanied them or who came later in the season to trade felt uncomfortable in their dealings with the French.

In 1623, when the captain of one of the company trading vessels offered the Montagnais chief Erouachy too small a present after he had arrived at Tadoussac, Erouachy threw the present in the river and ordered his men to board ship and carry off whatever they needed, leaving in return only what they wished. Rather than risk a disruption of trade, the French allowed the Montagnais to plunder their vessel. They were more than pleased when the Montagnais returned that evening and friendly relations could be restored (Wrong 1939:45–6). This incident illustrates both that native people attached great importance to these rituals and that they could enforce their observance at this time.

The Indians who inhabited the St Lawrence lowlands valued formal and long-standing alliances, especially ones that involved exchanges of military assistance as well as of goods. Yet even these alliances were not exclusive. The Montagnais and Algonkins traded with the Dutch as well as the French until the Mohawks prevented them from doing so in the 1620s. In this they were acting no differently from the Crees of northern Ontario, who in later times traded with the French to the south and with the English along the coast of Hudson Bay and James Bay. The Neutrals traded with both the Iroquois and the Hurons, despite the almost perpetual warfare between these two groups. The Montagnais consistently dealt with independent and clandestine European traders as well as with the official company, notwithstanding their alliance with Gravé Du Pont and Champlain. Nevertheless they were careful not to offend Champlain, since he, unlike the other traders, was prepared to help them fight the Iroquois (Biggar 1922–36, 2:201–3).

It is not true that trading partners were invariably committed to helping one another militarily. The Neutrals were so named because they scrupulously avoided siding with either the Hurons or the Iroquois. After 1615 some armed Frenchmen continued to live in the Huron country, and in 1624 a number of these volunteered to fight alongside the Hurons in a projected war against the Neutrals (Wrong 1939:157). Yet there is no record of Frenchmen actually joining Huron raiding parties after 1615. Champlain believed that various Indian tribes had agreed to trade with the French in return for his promise to continue helping them in their wars (Biggar 1922–36, 3:225–7). Nevertheless, even when he later refused repeated requests to join native expeditions against the Iroquois, after he had been forced against his will to spend the winter of 1615–16 among the Hurons, the Hurons and Algonkins continued to trade with the French. Many Montagnais and Algonkin groups traded with the French, even though for many years no Frenchmen lived with them or assisted them militarily. The solidity of the alliances between the French and their Huron and Algonkin trading partners is suggested by the fact that Champlain, although recognized as the chief spokesman for the French, does not appear to have attended the annual trading sessions which were held on the upper St Lawrence after 1615. He does not even appear to have been present when peace was concluded with the Iroquois in 1624.

Where contact was limited, as between the Hurons and the French along the St Lawrence River, the annual ritual at which the bulk of goods was exchanged was a highly formal one, which also served to renew their alliance. As a result of this renewal, smaller groups of Huron traders could do business with the French while observing less elaborate rituals. Among groups that lived closer to one another, such as the Hurons and the neighbouring Petuns, Neutrals, and Algonkins, chiefs appear to have visited one another periodically to exchange gifts and renew alliances. Intertribal alliances were also strengthened at periodic celebrations such as the Huron Feast of the Dead. This made it possible for ordinary members of these tribes to trade with one another at any time on an individual basis. Normally such traders had formal partners in other tribes with whom they lived when they went to trade. These partners sometimes exchanged children for varying periods of time, thereby strengthening the ritual kinship on which their relationships were founded (Trigger 1976:911). There are numerous references to individual Huron traders visiting the Petuns and Neutrals as well as neighbouring Algonkian-speaking groups. The Nipissings and Algonkins also traded with the Hurons while they spent the winters living on the outskirts of their villages.

The Hurons clearly despised haggling over the price of each skin and were angered when French traders tried to do so (Wrong 1939:140). The stable price paid for furs during the period of the Huron missions, despite marked fluctuations in prices in France (Le Blant 1972), may also reflect the need to conform to a standard accepted by Indian trading partners. In spite of this, the substantivists err in claiming that no profit motive was involved in native trade. As Rich (1960:40) pointed out, Indian middlemen did not hesitate to charge trading partners more for goods than they had paid for them. Exact figures are not available for trade in the St Lawrence Valley during the seventeenth century, but what is known makes it clear that the situation was not significantly different from that farther north in later times, when Indian middlemen exchanged an iron hatchet that they had obtained from the English for only one beaver skin with tribes living farther inland for up to ten skins (ibid.). In the interior, where monopolies were easy to maintain, many tribes used European tools before passing them along in worn-out condition to their trading partners for as much as or more than they had paid for them. This practice, as we have already seen, appears to have become general in the sixteenth century. In these ways tribes that could act as middlemen in the fur trade were able to profit from exchanging furs they did not have to trap for European goods they did not have to manufacture.

European traders clearly made huge profits from the fur trade. They charged native people high prices for goods that were often of poor quality. As native peoples became dependent on these goods, they depleted their environment and were drawn into destructive intertribal wars in an effort to obtain adequate supplies of them (Delâge 1981). It is often cited as evidence of Indian naivety that they were prepared to trade valuable furs for European goods of little value. Anthropologists object, however, and claim that to Indians furs were commonplace, while European goods were scarce and valued for their utility, beauty, and perhaps for their supernatural significance. Yet there is evidence that from an early date native people sought to learn the value that goods had for Europeans and to alter the exchange rate they received for their furs accordingly. In 1535 the two boys that Cartier had taken as prisoners to France informed the Stadaconans that the French were cheating them by exchanging for food wares that were of little value in their own country. As a result, the Stadaconans refused to supply them with food unless higher prices were paid (Biggar 1924:187–8). Huron boys who visited France in the seventeenth century appear to have supplied similar information to their tribesmen.

In general native traders agreed that while the price of goods might increase as they passed along intertribal trading networks, their value should remain constant between the same trading partners and therefore at any one position in the trading network, regardless of short-term fluctuations in availability. Yet at the annual trading ceremonies chiefs did not hesitate to request that Europeans should pay higher than standard exchange rates for the furs as an expression of their friendship. In return, they offered to supply furs of the best quality. Trade was so embedded in the political process as a mechanism for maintaining peace among tribes that Indians refused to haggle over the value of individual items and couched their demands for higher prices not in direct language but in terms of friendship and alliances. This does not, however, mean that Indian traders did not seek to turn a profit on their dealings.

It is clear that where competition existed, native traders were pleased to play rival groups of Europeans against one another. At the beginning of the trading season in 1611, the Montagnais at Tadoussac refused to trade for more than the few items that they required immediately. Instead, they waited for rival French traders to arrive so that competition would increase (in the form of extra goodwill presents?) the amount of European goods they were offered for their furs. Champlain had admired the sagacity with which the Montagnais had handled this situation (Biggar 1922–36, 2:171). The Montagnais and Algonkins were also very angry when the reimposition of a trading monopoly led to an increase in the prices charged for European goods at Quebec and Tadoussac after 1613. Their resentment resulted in personal quarrels between French and Indians. Two Frenchmen were killed at Quebec in 1617; two more in 1627; and another after the return of the French to Quebec in

1633. In 1624 the Montagnais were boasting that if they were to kill all the French who lived at Quebec, other vessels would come and they could buy their goods more cheaply (ibid., 5:124–5). Champlain complained that independent French traders, especially Protestants from La Rochelle, were selling guns to the Montagnais below Tadoussac and encouraging them to use these weapons to attack the French trading post at Quebec (ibid., 3).

In 1634–5, when the Dutch surgeon Harmen Meyndersten van den Bogaert visited the Mohawks and Oneidas, they told him that they wanted the same prices for their furs from the Dutch that the French were offering to the Indians who traded with them. The Oneidas praised the generosity of the French but promised that if the Dutch paid them more for their furs and kept the kinds of goods they wanted in stock at Fort Orange, they would trade exclusively with them (Jameson 1909:139, 151). The implied threat was that the Iroquois would transfer their trade to the French if the Dutch did not increase the amount they paid for furs.

It was observed that when the Indians trading with the Hudson's Bay Company were offered higher prices for their furs they brought in fewer. Such behaviour has been interpreted as evidence that they did not understand the operation of a market economy. Yet, when considered from the natives' point of view, this does not appear to be the case. Both then and in the seventeenth century, the main reason that native people sought higher prices for their furs was not to secure more European goods but to get what they needed with less effort. Rich (1960:53) has suggested that in the late eighteenth century an Indian middleman could satisfy his needs for European goods in return for 70 to 100 beaver skins annually. Even fewer skins appear to have supplied the wants of Indians in eastern Canada in the early seventeenth century. Rough estimates indicate that in the 1620s each Huron trader brought an average of 50 skins to the St Lawrence (Trigger 1976:336–7).

Further restrictions to acquiring large amounts of European goods are evident. Hunter-gatherer bands, such as the Montagnais, that moved from one place to another during the year were limited in the amount of possessions they could carry with them. Hence their failure to accumulate goods can be explained directly in terms of their subsistence patterns rather than attributing it, as Rich (1960:53) has done, to their lack of a sense of property. Although the Hurons and their neighbours represented a vast potential market for European goods, only about 200 Hurons were available each year to trade with the French. This number could manage sixty canoes, each of which was able to transport about 200 pounds of furs or

European goods (Wrong 1939:101; Heidenreich 1971:280). This amount of goods could not begin to satiate the needs and desires of the Hurons and of the many tribes with whom they traded. Therefore, because the supply of European goods was limited, the Hurons and their neighbours did not become totally dependent on these goods during the 1620s, just as the Indians of the central interior of Quebec remained largely self-reliant until trading posts were established in that region in the nineteenth century (Francis and Morantz 1983:61–3). Even in the late 1650s the Siouan-speaking peoples who lived at the western end of Lake Superior still lacked iron weapons (Perrot 1911:159–63), as did the Algonkian-speaking peoples in the lower part of the Ohio Valley (Thwaites 1896–1901, 44:49).

The limited opportunities for many native groups to use or transport European goods explain the absence of any strong desire to maximize the amount of these goods that they could derive from the fur trade. If a fixed number of furs allowed Huron middlemen to purchase all the European goods they could carry home, there was also no economic incentive for them to expand their trading links with other tribes beyond the range they had reached in the early 1620s. The desire to maintain political alliances may explain why the Hurons were so active in the fur trade and why, although they evidently lacked adequate amounts of European goods to satisfy their own needs in the 1620s (Wrong 1939:245), they were willing to pass along large quantities to tribes living still farther inland. Unfortunately, the quantitative data required to explore this problem in greater detail are almost totally lacking for the seventeenth century.

Both chiefs and ordinary native people engaged in foreign trade, one aim of which was to acquire large amounts of exotic goods. Discoverers of new trade routes were theoretically able to regulate their use. We have already seen that this probably meant that the chief of the local clan to which the discoverer belonged acquired this right, which could be shared with other council chiefs. Other traders were allowed to use these routes or to cross tribal lands in return for presents or a share of the goods they obtained, which went to the chief who controlled the route. Ordinary traders probably contributed a portion of the European goods they brought home to the treasury of their local clan, which was controlled by the clan chief and used to conduct diplomacy, subsidize public rituals, and provide the reparations payments needed to prevent blood feuds within the confederacy. Hence, while the acquisition of exotic goods enhanced the reputation of a successful trader, it probably raised the prestige of his clan chief to an even greater degree. At least among the Hurons, the solidarity linking members of local clans explains why rivalries between individual traders did not lead to destabilizing competition for prestige and public office within and among clans, as it appears to have done among some native groups on the west coast (Averkieva 1971). Rather, the power of the hereditary council chiefs seems to have been strengthened. This may also explain why, in the early 1630s, these chiefs were referred to as "big stones" and "stay-at-homes," since they profited from intertribal trade without having to leave home (Thwaites 1896–1901, 10:231–3).

The aim, both of chiefs and of ordinary traders, in accumulating exotic goods was not to retain them but to give most of them away as presents in the varied ceremonial exchanges that characterized native societies. All forms of generosity were publicly noted and acclaimed and were a major source of power and influence. The desire to win prestige therefore provided a major stimulus for economic activities of all kinds. Failure to redistribute was penalized by hostile gossip, denunciations, and in extreme cases accusations of sorcery. Refusal to give a sick person something he had dreamed of or to join in community curing rituals or ceremonies intended to control the weather or avert crop failures threatened the well-being of others; hence it was easy to regard individuals who behaved in this fashion as witches who sought to harm their own people.

In contrasting capitalist with precapitalist economic behaviour, Canadian substantivists, in particular Rotstein, have conflated the economic institutions of societies as different in scale as ancient civilizations, such as Pharaonic Egypt, and hunter-gatherer bands, such as the Montagnais. In smaller tribal societies, institutions tend to be structurally less differentiated than they are in larger, more hierarchical ones. Most of the routine responsibility for the nurture, care, and protection of the individual belongs to the extended family, so that political and economic relations tend to be conceptualized in terms of real or metaphorical extensions of kinship. The native societies of eastern North America were not large enough to produce the anonymous crowds of buyers and sellers that are necessary to make a classical market economy work (Cox 1983). Intertribal trade was embedded in social and political institutions to the extent that trade and peace were virtually synonymous and Indian traders scorned to haggle over the price of individual goods. The personal motive for trade was not for a man or his family to possess an inordinate amount of exotic goods but to be able to acquire prestige by giving them away. These features of native economies accord with a nonmarket model of economic activity. Yet native traders also sought to profit by exchanging goods with other tribes for more than they had paid for them, by playing off foreign trading partners to lower the price of goods, and by asking for more than the standard rate of exchange as evidence of friendship and goodwill. This kind of generalized haggling indicates that intertribal trade was not as embedded in the social and political structure as Rotstein has proposed.

The fact that all these patterns were already present in the seventeenth century suggests that the features of trade that Ray and Freeman regard as transitional had in fact existed in prehistoric times in eastern North America. Profit taking of this sort had probably characterized intertribal exchanges for millennia and seems necessary if trade is to function effectively when various exotic goods are passed from one group to another over long distances, with each group keeping a portion for itself (Renfrew 1975:41–6). It also follows that, with the rise of the fur trade, native people succeeded in imposing their trading conventions on Europeans to a greater extent than Ray and Freeman believe. The uniformity of these intertribal trading patterns over large parts of North America in prehistoric times probably explains the widespread similarities in the conventions of the fur trade, notwithstanding the variations that resulted from differences in terrain and ecology, which make studies of regional variations in the fur trade essential (Francis and Morantz 1983:167).

Finally, it should be noted that the current distinction between a formalist and a substantivist approach obfuscates rather than clarifies an understanding of native behaviour in the fur trade. The substantivists have assumed that the "embeddedness" of precapitalist economies in their political and social organization implies a lack of optimizing behaviour. Yet evidence of native traders seeking to derive substantial profit from their exchanges abounds in the historical literature of the early fur trade. The real question is not whether individual traders sought such profits but why they did so and what they did with their gains. It is clear that they often tried to obtain higher values for their goods not to obtain more of the Europeans' wares but to minimize the effort that had to be expended to satisfy their wants. It is also obvious that the goods obtained were not hoarded by individuals but were redistributed in a traditional fashion as a source of prestige. While there are major differences between the economies of technologically simpler and more complex societies, these differences do not rule out striking a favourable bargain in either type of society (Ekholm and Friedman 1979:41).

## EUROPEAN TRADERS

The most influential of the Europeans who had dealings with the native peoples of the interior prior to 1634 were trading company employees who lived with various groups to encourage them to trade. The majority of these Frenchmen had guns and their presence discouraged Iroquois attacks against the native communities in which they lived. Each summer they travelled with Huron, Nipissing, and Algonkin traders to the French trading stations on the St Lawrence and protected them against Iroquois attacks in the Ottawa Valley. As a result, the Oneidas stopped raiding there in the 1620s as the Mohawks had done along the St Lawrence River a decade earlier (Wrong 1939:261). The presence of Europeans also ensured that the Algonkins did not charge the Hurons and Nipissings extortionately for using the Ottawa River.

The *truchements*, or interpreters, were the most important of these Frenchmen. They were sent, often as teen-agers, to live with Indian groups, learn their languages and customs, and gradually win their trust and respect. Nicolas Marsolet, who dealt with the Montagnais, probably remained most of the time at Quebec, while those responsible for the inland tribes lived with their groups. They encouraged the Indians to collect as many furs as possible and served as interpreters and intermediaries when they traded with the French. The best known of the interpreters were Jean Nicollet de Belleborne, who lived for many years among the Nipissings, and Etienne Brûlé, who remained with the Hurons after 1610. Others however, worked among the Nipissings and Algonkins.

Although Brûlé appears at first to have lived among the Arendahronons, his adult life was spent at Toanché, an important trading centre in the Penetanguishene Peninsula. This move suggests that as trading with the French became more important, the Attignawantans, who were the largest of the Huron tribes, took control of much of it away from the Arendahronons. Brûlé travelled with the Hurons to the French trading stations each year, where he acted as an intermediary for all the Huron tribes. He was also charged to see that the Dutch did not contact the Hurons and persuade them to trade at Fort Orange. This was an easy task, since during the 1620s the Dutch probably did not possess sufficient knowledge of the interior to contact the Hurons, and the Mohawks, who were partly responsible for their ignorance, would not have allowed such trading to take place. Because of the importance that was attached to expanding trade, the trading company paid Brûlé and the other interpreters very highly for their services (Thwaites 1896–1901, 4:209).

The other company employees were paid smaller salaries or none at all, but were allowed to trade for furs with the Indians in return for living amongst them and accompanying them to the St Lawrence. They had, however, to sell these furs to the company at a relatively low fixed price (Sagard 1866:902). Five to twenty Frenchmen stayed among the Hurons each winter. Some of these were boys who were sent to learn the Huron language, but most were adults able to handle guns. Some remained for only one winter; others, for many years.

Gabriel Sagard was one of the first to observe how much more easily European men could adapt to Indian life than Indians could to European ways (1866:166). Most of the French traders quickly adopted items of native dress, accustomed themselves to use canoes and snowshoes, hunted alongside Indian men, and joined them in their ritual steam baths (ibid., 611). All these activities won them the approval of their Indian companions. Most of them also appear to have enjoyed the greater sexual freedom of native life. Because of the uninhibited behaviour of Hurons prior to marriage, young women were easily available. Although the Hurons found beards distasteful (Wrong 1939:137), presents of European goods and the novelty of Frenchmen may have offset this liability. Competition for women did not cause trouble with Huron men, since the Hurons strongly disapproved of overt expressions of sexual jealousy. French traders established their own households, with Huron girls as companions, or married according to native law into Huron extended families (Thwaites 1896–1901, 14:17–19; Wrong 1939:134). If these were influential families, such marriages enhanced the prestige of the French traders. They also enmeshed them in a network of economic commitments to their Huron kinsmen. It did not greatly anger the Hurons when Frenchmen left their wives and children to return to Quebec, since divorce was relatively common and a woman and her children were cared for by her extended family. A departure could be still more amicable if appropriate gifts were made to the woman and her family (Thwaites 1896–1901, 14:19–21). These sexual alliances, both casual and long-lasting, bound the French more closely together to their Huron hosts and enabled them, on an individual basis, to understand the Indians better.

The French occasionally stole from the Indians and shocked the Hurons by the callous and indifferent manner in which they sometimes treated each other (Wrong 1939:141, 194–5). Yet Amantacha, a young Huron who was sent to study in France, was said to have loved Brûlé as if he were his own father (Thwaites 1896–1901, 4:225). These traders provided the Indians with a more intimate and comprehensible view of Europeans than either French priests or government officials did. Moreover, apart from persuading their hosts to collect and trade larger numbers of beaver pelts, they had no motive to challenge or disrupt native life. Hence the two groups got on well together.

Various factors explain the ease with which most traders adapted to Indian life. The majority of them were soldiers, accustomed to a rough life, or lower-class youths in the trading company. Only one, about whom little is known, was identified as a member of the nobility. The young men, in particular, must have had little access to the more substantial comforts of European life and in the normal course of events must have been severely limited in opportunities for advancement. They were often treated scornfully and even brutally by their superiors at Quebec. Among native groups these same men were received as honoured guests by the tribesmen, who regarded all members of a community, including children, as individuals worthy of respect. By demonstrating their skills as hunters or generously distributing European goods, they could also win personal popularity and prestige among the Indians. Many of them found their employment so attractive that they were pleased to work for the English after 1629 rather than abandon it.

Contemporary but clearly hostile sources describe Brûlé as knowing only one brief Christian prayer and as being as credulous and superstitious as any Huron (Wrong 1939:266). On such grounds, later historians have imagined that these early interpreters became deeply integrated into Indian society and adopted a native style of life, as did many of the *coureurs de bois* in the West who founded the Métis nation. It is tempting to believe that young Europeans of low social status would respond warmly to egalitarian native societies and in due course identify with them. Yet this did not happen in early New France. Recent research indicates that Brûlé spent more time in Europe and displayed far more business acumen than traditional biographers have ascribed to him (Campeau 1979:808–9). Other interpreters who outlived him, such as Marsolet and Godefroy de Lintot, became businessmen and landholders of some importance in New France. In the early days, there was considerable opportunity for enhancing one's status in the colony, and work of this sort was a source of income and experience that would allow a young man of humble background to better himself. Being in at least yearly contact with the colony, each of these men remained aware of such possibilities. Hence, whatever passing attractions native life held for them were outweighed by the chances for social advancement within the emerging status-conscious society of New France. These employees of the trading company never came close to identifying their interests with those of the Indians, partly because of European ethnocentricity but mainly because their careers were based on exploiting them. In this respect, their outlook was little different from that of the middle-class traders for whom they worked.

They were nevertheless sufficiently trusted and accepted as members of Huron society that they, like individual Hurons, were allowed to visit and trade with most neighbouring tribes. It is not known whether they could do this freely or whether, like Hurons, they had to share the proceeds of their trade with clan chiefs. Many of them traded with the Neutrals, and Brûlé and a Frenchman named Grenole once travelled as far north as Sault Sainte Marie (Sagard 1866:589). They were not, however, permitted to follow the Huron trade routes into central Quebec because the Hurons feared that if the French became familiar with these routes, they might attempt to trade with the bands who lived there from the St Lawrence (Wrong 1939:87). French traders were also forbidden to spend the winter among neighbouring tribes for fear they would use such an extended visit to encourage these tribes to trade directly with the French (Sagard 1866:809–10). In 1633, when Brûlé was suspected of trying to arrange a trading alliance between the Senecas and the French in order to atone for having worked for the English, he was assassinated on the orders of several chiefs of his own village (Thwaites 1896–1901, 21:211). They did this, however, only after carefully ascertaining that Champlain regarded him as a traitor and after much controversy and dissension among different Huron groups. Guilty fears about this murder were to trouble the Hurons for many years.

Little is known about the organization of trade at Quebec, Tadoussac, and the summer trading stations farther up the St Lawrence. Gravé Du Pont, the chief factor, was skilled in dealing with the Indians but we have no record of his routine activities. He was aided by assistant agents and by the interpreters who accompanied the Indians. Trading appears to have been conducted in native languages or various lingua francas rather than in French (Thwaites 1896–1901, 5:113–15). In intertribal dealings, the Indians normally used the language of the politically or economically more powerful tribe. For example, the Algonkins and Nipissings always spoke Huron when they dealt with the latter. Hence the use of native languages suggests that the Indians did not regard the French with undue respect at this time.

Following the re-establishment of a trading monopoly in 1613, the successive trading companies began to charge the Indians significantly higher prices for European goods. This aroused much bad feeling, especially among the Montagnais, who were more experienced than other tribes in dealing with rival traders and who were still sporadically in contact with clandestine French vessels below Tadoussac. It is not known whether this price rise was initiated by the traders resident at Quebec or was dictated by company officials in France, although the latter seems more likely. Native resentment appears to have been directed against Champlain more than against the local French traders and interpreters.

## FRENCH ADMINISTRATORS

Champlain was the only individual who could be described as a full-time government official at Quebec before the 1630s. Although he appointed Louis Hébert King's Attorney in 1620 and various employees of the trading company to nominal part-time positions, these offices soon languished. Hence it is not surprising that while he represented the viceroy of New France, Champlain never acquired the title of governor, which he coveted. After 1612 he began to view himself as an advocate of colonization, and in 1613 he formally ceased to be the employee of a trading company and was paid his salary as a vice-regal official. After 1620 he devoted himself entirely to the development and administration of New France. These changes brought him into growing conflict with the French traders.

Champlain's relations with the Montagnais also became increasingly acrimonious. He attempted to treat them as subjects of the French crown and as part of his projected colony. He believed that his power as a vice-regal official extended by right over Indian groups inhabiting lands claimed by the French king. He also believed that Montagnais chiefs could control their followers and should be responsible to him for their actions. When resentment over the higher prices being charged for European goods led to Frenchmen being murdered in 1617 and 1627, Champlain, supported by the Recollets, rejected the reparations payments that traditionally settled such offences. In both cases, he sought to arrest and execute the murderers. These actions nearly precipitated full-scale conflicts between the French and the Montagnais. Because the French traders were not prepared to support him in what appeared to be politically and economically disastrous confrontations, he was forced to admit defeat and to let the murderers go unpunished (Trigger 1971b:94–100).

To promote the settlement of New France, Champlain tried to persuade Montagnais families to become farmers, learn to speak French, and convert to Christianity. He was contemptuous of Montagnais culture, believing it to be so insubstantial that it would not take long to make these Indians forget their old ways and learn to think and feel like native-born French people. Yet he also argued that it was necessary to have European colonists present who, when required, would compel the Indians to abandon their "filthy habits, loose morals, and uncivilized ways" (Biggar 1922–36, 4:320–1). Clearly he had no faith in the capacity of the Montagnais to civilize themselves. The French traders opposed such a plan because they wished all the Indians who lived along the St Lawrence River to engage in trapping and feared that French colonists would eventually contest their monopoly. Champlain's plans foundered as a result of the indifference of the Montagnais and the hostility of the trading company.

He also attempted to meddle in Montagnais politics and demanded the right to appoint Montagnais chiefs. He failed completely to understand the consensual nature of native political arrangements. Because he viewed all power as being delegated from above, he did not comprehend that Indian leaders could not decide matters but had to secure individual consent from their followers as each new issue arose. The Indians for their part regarded him only as the spokesman for the French at Quebec. When he was asked to support the investiture of Miristou as chief of the Tadoussac band in 1622, he falsely imagined that the Montagnais were recognizing his right to invest chiefs. He provided a feast at which he presented Miristou and his brother with swords and explained that as his subordinates they were henceforth required to support him with these weapons. The Montagnais probably interpreted this as the sort of feast that was normally given by an ally when a new chief was installed (Biggar 1922–36, 5:60–70).

In 1629 Champlain further insisted that the Montagnais and Algonkin leaders form a council of band chiefs to regulate relations between themselves and the French. He demanded that Chomina, a local Indian who was alcoholic and subservient to him, be recognized as head of this council, while far more distinguished chiefs would be only subordinate members (Biggar 1922–36, 6:7–22). Although the Indians must not have understood clearly what he was doing, his honouring of the despised Chomina clearly angered them.

A controversy also arose with the relatives of two Montagnais girls whom he had been asked to care for during a food shortage in the winter of 1627–8. Failing to understand the temporary nature of his guardianship, he refused to return these girls to their families but intended to take them to France and enrol them in a convent school (Biggar 1922–36, 6:51–124). As a result of their anger with his behaviour, no less than at the high prices being charged by the trading company, the Montagnais aided the Englishman David Kirke and his sons in the attacks that led to the surrender of Quebec in July 1629. They hoped, falsely as it turned out, that with the departure of the French from Quebec free trade would be restored.

Earlier in 1629, Champlain was planning that if no French supply ship reached Quebec that summer, he and his men would seize a Mohawk town and live on its plundered resources over the following winter (Biggar 1922–36, 5:304–5). This scheme shows the total lack of realism in Champlain's thinking about native people at this time. By contrast, over twenty Frenchmen had survived the previous hard-pressed winter in relative comfort by going to the Huron country, where they were welcomed as friends and allies. When Champlain returned to New France in 1633, he was arguing that the French either had to gain control of the English and Dutch colonies to the south or, failing that, to crush the Iroquois. These arguments took on particular force when three French traders were killed that year on the upper St Lawrence by Mohawks who were trying to pillage their vessel. Champlain proposed to lead a force of about 120 French soldiers and several thousand Indian allies armed with iron axes and metal-tipped arrows to conquer the Iroquois (Campeau 1979:381–2). While the trading company probably would have supported his proposal to seize New Netherland, provided that the effort was financed by the crown, they would not have endorsed his second one, since destroying the Iroquois or even the Mohawks, assuming it could have been done, would have opened the way for the Hurons, Algonkins, and Montagnais to trade with the Dutch. In 1634 French agents were trying to promote trade with the Onondagas and Oneidas at the same time that Champlain was planning to attack them (Jameson 1909:148–54).

## MISSIONARIES

The Recollets were able to establish a mission at Quebec in 1615, after Champlain had obtained financial support for them from the

Estates-General of France and the associates of the trading company. While they believed that the populous and sedentary Hurons were their best long-term prospect for conversion and they had missionaries living in the Huron country in 1615 and from 1623 to 1628, lack of funds and personnel forced them to centre most of their activities around Quebec City. There were never more than four Recollet priests working in Canada in this period, and in the winter of 1616–17 their numbers were reduced to one. The missionaries spent considerable time acquiring a rudimentary knowledge of the Montagnais and Huron languages, although they were not well trained for this task and believed that native peoples should be compelled to learn French (Sagard 1866:340). As a result, they were unable to make the meaning of Christianity clear. The Indians seem generally to have regarded them as shamans and to have interpreted baptism as a curing ritual or the token of an alliance with the French rather than a commitment to abandon traditional religious practices (ibid., 478). Like other Franciscan orders, the Recollets firmly believed that before native people could be converted to Christianity, they had to settle amongst Europeans and learn to live like them. They heartily approved of Champlain's plans to encourage French settlement at Quebec and to turn the Montagnais into farmers. They also sought to persuade Huron converts to leave their country and live at Quebec (LeClercq 1691, 1:257).

As missionaries in the Huron country, the Recollets diminished their effectiveness by refusing on moral grounds to live with unconverted Huron families. Instead, they constructed their own cabins on the outskirts of Huron settlements. Because of this, they had to purchase their own food rather than receive it freely as members of Huron families. The Recollets strongly disapproved of the French traders who lived amongst the Indians and blamed their lax moral behaviour, toleration of native customs, and irreverent attitude for hindering their missionary work (Wrong 1939:137). They also tried to demonstrate that they could promote trade more effectively than these company employees. Yet the missionary Joseph de La Roche Daillon's efforts to persuade the Neutrals to trade directly with the French not only were a dismal failure but also angered the Hurons almost to the point of killing him (Sagard 1866:800–7). Daillon's betrayal of his Huron hosts, which contrasted so dramatically with the discreet behaviour of the company employees, may have caused the Hurons to suspect that the shamanistic activities of the priests might extend to malevolent sorcery.

In 1625 Henri de Lévis, duc de Ventadour, the new viceroy of New France, arranged to send to Quebec at his own expense three Jesuit missionaries to assist the Recollets. It was the practice of the Jesuit order, based on its experience in India and China, to alter local customs as little as possible in the course of converting peoples to Christianity. This was a procedure for which there was also considerable warrant in the early history of Christianity (Duignan 1958). Armed with special powers by the viceroy, the Jesuits insisted that the interpreters whom the Recollets claimed were sabotaging their mission work be recalled from the native groups among whom they were living and in some cases be forced to return to France. Brûlé was not allowed to return to the Huron country in 1626, and after being kept at Quebec over the following winter to help the Jesuits learn the Huron language, he was sent back to France (Thwaites 1896–1901, 4:213–15, 225). It is unclear whether he was later given permission to return to Quebec, as Marsolet was (Sagard 1866:522). Nevertheless, like Jacques Michel and some other employees of the trading company, he eventually made his way to England and returned to Quebec with the Kirkes in 1629 (Campeau 1979:809). The Jesuits proposed to replace the interpreters who lived among the Indians with hired men who would work for them and be subject to their close supervision. The implementation of this program meant that some groups, such as the Nipissings, after a long and close association with a resident trader, had no Frenchman living with them for a decade or longer.

Yet the Jesuits, unlike the Recollets, recognized that they were able to live and work among native peoples only because of the trading alliances that these tribes had concluded with the French. They therefore sought to establish an effective working relationship with the trading company and to reconcile the aims of trade and mission work whenever possible. The Jesuits' approach made their work easier for them than it had been for the Recollets. The Recollets regarded European colonization as essential for the work of conversion. The Jesuits, on the contrary, believed that they alone could best instruct the Indians on how to live and act as true Christians and they feared that settlers would provide models of European vices. For this reason, they generally endeavoured to keep their native converts separate from other Europeans and did not encourage them to learn French. They also abandoned efforts to make those Montagnais who were self-sufficient settle down and abandon hunting.

The main focus of the Jesuit mission was in the Huron country. In 1626 Fathers Jean de Brébeuf and Anne de Noué joined Daillon there to study the Huron language. Brébeuf remained among the Hurons until 1629, mastering their language, winning a reputation for his shamanistic skills, especially as a rain-maker, and, as a newcomer, apparently being strongly influenced by the Recollets' day-to-day dealings with the Hurons. Yet he was no more able to undertake an effective mission program than the Recollets were. In 1626 the Jesuits secured guardianship of Amantacha, the teenage son of an Attigneenongnahac trader, and took him to France, where he learned to speak and write French and was baptized in the cathedral at Rouen in 1627. The Jesuits hoped that he could help them with their mission work and would serve as an intermediary between the Hurons and the French. On his way back to Canada in 1628, the ship on which he was travelling was seized by the English and he spent another year in England before he was returned to his people. Amantacha understood both the French and the English and got on well with them but he remained staunchly Huron. He was therefore more valuable to Huron chiefs as a source of information about Europeans than he was helpful to the Jesuits. Whether, because of his youth, the Huron chiefs made full use of his skills remains unknown. Unfortunately, he was killed while participating in a raid against the Senecas in 1636.

## IMPACT ON NATIVE PEOPLES

Written documentation of cultural changes among native peoples between 1600 and 1632 remains extremely fragmentary. We are not told much about alterations in subsistence patterns and material culture even after 1632, which were of relatively little interest to missionaries and government officials. In recent years, however, archaeological research has been helping to fill these gaps. The combination of archaeological and ethnohistorical data has a synergistic effect, permitting conclusions to be drawn that could not be elicited from either source alone. Yet the abundance of ethnohistorical data only partly diminishes the problems that are inherent in interpreting archaeological findings. The synthesis of archaeological and ethnohistorical information, as opposed to the simple use of one type to illustrate the other, requires a thorough knowledge of the potential and limitations of both disciplines.

At present far more is known archaeologically about the Iroquoian peoples in the early seventeenth century than about their Algonkian-speaking neighbours. For the Montagnais who lived around Tadoussac and Quebec, only written data are available. Yet these data are vital for understanding what was happening to native people who lived close to French settlements and who already had intensive contacts with Europeans beginning in the sixteenth century. By 1623 the Montagnais were no longer manufacturing birchbark baskets, clay pots (if indeed they had ever made them), and stone adzes (Sagard 1866:271; Wrong 1939:108). Instead, they were purchasing copper kettles and iron axes. They continued to make canoes but also bought longboats from the French, as the Micmacs had already begun doing several decades earlier, so that they could travel more safely on the lower St Lawrence (Sagard 1866:251). They wore much French clothing, finding woollen garments more convenient than skin ones, especially in wet weather (Thwaites 1896–1901, 5:25; 7:9–11). Like the Mohawks, who after 1612 also lived close to European trading posts, the Montagnais had access to an abundance and wide range of European goods (Jameson 1909:141). As early as 1620 illegal traders from La Rochelle were selling guns and ammunition to the Montagnais, as the English continued to do between 1629 and 1632. In 1634 the Jesuit Paul Le Jeune described some of them as good marksmen (Thwaites 1896–1901, 6:309). Thereafter the sale of guns was halted, and since the Indians did not know how to repair these weapons, the ones they had soon became useless.

The Montagnais purchased large quantities of maize, dried peas, crackers, and sea biscuits from the French (Biggar 1922–36, 5:251, 267). In this too they resembled the Micmacs but differed from the Crees who later traded with the Hudson's Bay Company. Until the nineteenth century the Crees only accepted oatmeal as a gift when they were hungry or visiting English posts (Francis and Morantz 1983:128). It has been suggested that the Montagnais would not have been able to spend so much time trapping and trading without these supplies. Yet Le Jeune's detailed account of the winter that he spent with a Montagnais extended family indicates that they did not keep this food until mid-winter, when big game hunting often failed them. Indeed, they could not easily have carried large amounts of it into the interior with them (Thwaites 1896–1901, 7:67–209). As in the Maritime provinces, this food may have allowed a longer period to be spent trading during the summer, by reducing the amount of time that had to be spent then collecting and preserving food for consumption during the late fall and early winter. It also may have made life easier and the diet more varied during the latter period. There is, however, no evidence that trading with the French adversely affected Montagnais subsistence patterns, since trading and trapping beaver could be done during two brief periods in the summer and spring respectively. The hungry spells reported during various winters probably reflect lack of snow, which made it difficult to bring down large game and was a long-standing cause of starvation in this region. It is possible, however, that the fur trade had gradually depleted the stocks of moose, elk, and beaver, the principal game animals on which the Montagnais depended, along with fish and eels, for food (Gadacz 1975).

Wine and liquors were supplied to the Indians by the independent traders who operated along the lower St Lawrence, although Champlain vigorously opposed their sale at Quebec and other places under his control (Thwaites 1896–1901, 6:251–3). Among the Montagnais, alcoholic beverages were probably initially valued for their hallucinogenic properties and viewed as a way of communicating with the supernatural. Later, as their numbers declined and their economic dependence on the French increased, alcohol also must have become a device for temporarily enhancing self-esteem (Vachon 1960). By the 1630s the Montagnais bands in the Quebec City area were demoralized to the extent that they were convinced that the French intended to exterminate them so they could take possession of their land (Thwaites 1896–1901, 16:93).

Although the Hurons lived far inland, much information was recorded about their culture by Champlain in 1615–16 and Sagard for 1623–4. These early accounts can be compared with the detailed annual records of the Jesuits beginning in 1634. Since the middle of the nineteenth century historical documents have been supplemented by a growing corpus of archaeological data.

By 1615 the Hurons had consolidated their position as the hub of intertribal trade in the upper Great Lakes region. Their central role was based largely on their ability to supply corn as well as European goods on a regular basis to their northern trading partners. Many Nipissing and Algonkin bands spent the winter living in the Huron country, trading furs for cornmeal. In this manner they avoided having to disperse in the forests in a sometimes unsuccessful search for game. Each year the Hurons traded corn for furs with the Nipissings and Algonkins on their way to Quebec and European goods for furs on their way home. Although both the Nipissings and Algonkins traded directly with the French, their desire for Huron corn led them to consolidate their relations with the Hurons by relying on them for part of their European goods as well.

While the Ottawas who lived farther inland appear to have got much of their corn by wintering in or near Petun villages, they obtained all of their European goods from the Hurons. The Hurons also traded corn and European goods with the Algonkian-speaking tribes living around the shores of Georgian Bay and as far west as Sault Sainte Marie and with Algonkin and Montagnais groups living in the interior of southern Quebec. The Nipissings in turn

Huron and Petun settlements, 1615–1649.

traded European goods for furs as far north as James Bay, while the Ottawas carried them westward to the shores of Lake Michigan. The Hurons supplied European goods as well to the Petuns and Neutrals. They did this partly to obtain tobacco and native luxury goods from the south but mainly to acquire furs, since the tribal territories of both groups contained or bordered on large swamps where beavers were plentiful. The Hurons also traded with the far-off Susquehannocks, but only for shell beads and other easily transported native luxuries (Heidenreich 1971:232–80; Trigger 1976:351–8).

The Hurons hunted beavers until these animals became extinct within their tribal territories by about 1630 (Sagard 1866:585; Thwaites 1896–1901, 8:57). Their depletion does not appear to have disrupted the Huron economy or to have reduced the number of furs that they supplied to the French. The Hurons were never able to provide neighbouring tribes with enough European goods to supply all their wants; hence by increasing trade with these tribes they were able to obtain all the furs they needed to trade with the French. Yet, because of their trading commitments, the Hurons were unable to retain as many European goods as they themselves wanted and these goods remained highly valued. As late as 1636 a prestigious Huron shaman offered to heal the French living in the Huron country in return for ten glass beads, plus one extra bead for each patient (Thwaites 1896–1901, 13:103), and in 1640–1, when the Hurons were urging the council of the Neutral confederacy to murder two Jesuit missionaries, nine iron hatchets were considered a suitable diplomatic present (ibid., 21:213; 34:173). Hurons often borrowed tools and kettles from Frenchmen living in their midst and asked them, when they visited the French trading stations, to bring them beads, awls, and other European goods as presents (Wrong 1939:84, 245). They were also prepared to steal such goods from the French if they had not entered into a personal kinship relation with them (ibid., 81).

Some ethnologists see evidence of major changes in social organization as a result of the fur trade in descriptions of Huron life that date from the early seventeenth century. They have argued that increasing trade strengthened the economic importance of males, undermined the traditional matrilocal residence pattern, and eroded the principle of matrilinear succession to public office. W.M. Smith (1970) has claimed that by 1629 the traditional Huron social organization had been radically disrupted by this process. It has also been suggested that growing reliance on trade led unrelated families to establish themselves in the households of successful traders and this, in turn, enabled these traders to challenge the power of hereditary chiefs (Hayden 1977). There is no reliable evidence to support any of these claims in the ethnohistorical sources. Matrilinear principles of social organization are strongly attested in the *Jesuit Relations* for the 1640s (Trigger 1978c), while matrilocal descent groups and residence patterns appear to have survived into the eighteenth century (Clifton n.d.). On more general anthropological grounds, it can be argued that because of the important role that corn played in intertribal trade, an increasing reliance on such trade would have strengthened the position of women in Huron society no less than that of men. Moreover, if more men were absent trading, women would have had to assume greater responsibility for the everyday affairs of their communities and there would have been more reason than ever for matrilinear extended families to live together (Helms 1970). All of this would have reinforced rather than weakened the traditional role of women in Huron society.

I have already suggested that the power of hereditary chiefs appears to have been strengthened rather than threatened by the fur trade because of traditional patterns of redistribution, which continued to operate until the destruction of the Huron confederacy. These required traders to support their local clan chiefs and provide them with goods that could be given away to enhance the prestige of local clan groupings as collective units. Hence, while an ordinary Huron would have gained prestige as a result of his success as a trader, his success would also have bolstered the position of his clan chief.

Despite the rewards and punishments that reinforced redistribution, many traders were no doubt tempted to retain a disproportionate share of metal cutting-tools for themselves and their households. In the 1640s a few traders appear to have converted to Christianity to escape having to participate in traditional rituals involving redistribution (Thwaites 1896–1901, 23:129, 173). In the eyes of the non-Christian natives, such men were self-proclaimed witches. A study of debris found in housepits at the Warminster site, located in the eastern part of the Huron country, which may be contemporary with or slightly later than Champlain's visit, suggests the European goods were not distributed evenly either within or between longhouses (Tyyska 1968). Yet much more research is needed before firm conclusions can be based on such archaeological evidence. In addition to having to learn more about the relationship between material left behind when a settlement was abandoned and wealth actually possessed when it was inhabited, archaeologists must develop criteria for distinguishing between the hoarding of exotic goods for redistribution and their possession on a permanent basis. This will be no easy matter, since the distribution of European goods within a Huron community must have varied considerably at different times of the year and over cycles of ten years or more.

Although there was a growing demand for cornmeal as an item of trade for furs, during the 1620s and 1630s the Hurons were still able to produce surpluses that they stored for their own use in years of crop failure, as they probably had done in prehistoric times. The iron axes that the French sold them were of poor quality by comparison with modern steel ones or even with those used by most Europeans in the seventeenth century (Kidd 1949a:115). Yet they probably speeded forest clearance, which was done by men girdling and later burning trees, and facilitated the collecting and splitting of firewood, which was the work of women. Thus an overall increase in labour equivalent to the increase in corn production was probably not required. Women, however, would have spent considerably more time than they had done previously planting, guarding, and harvesting crops and grinding cornmeal.

Each year during the 1620s the trading company sent two ships to Tadoussac. They were loaded with cargoes of cloaks, blankets, night caps, shirts, sheets, hatchets, iron arrowheads, large needles, swords, ice-picks, knives, kettles, prunes, Indian corn, peas, crackers, sea biscuits, and tobacco, the latter being *Nicotiana tabacum*, introduced into France from Brazil, rather than the stronger *Nicotiana rustica* that was grown by the Hurons and other peoples of eastern North America (Thwaites 1896–1901, 4:207). The food and tobacco were intended mainly for the Montagnais and the Indians of the Maritimes. While the Hurons enjoyed sampling French food and drink given to them when they came to trade or when it was brought to their country by Frenchmen, they did not buy such goods even to eat on their return journey from a trading post. Likewise, while pieces of cloth and items of clothing were given to leading Huron traders as presents and to others in return for services, and the Hurons themselves often requested such presents, they do not appear to have bartered for large amounts of these goods.

Huron traders were primarily interested in obtaining metal cutting-tools. In particular, they wanted iron knives of all sizes, awls, axes, and iron arrowheads. The first three items are found in great abundance on archaeological sites of the historical period (Garrad 1969; Latta 1971). They also sought copper and brass kettles. Besides serving as prestige items, they were useful for travel and when worn out could be cut up to make pendants and other ornaments as well as metal arrowheads. Because they could be reused, the Hurons do not seem to have minded the thinness and short life span of the metal kettles that were sold to them. Huron traders also carried home glass beads, metal bracelets, and other ornaments, as well as occasional novelties such as scissors, magnifying glasses (used to start fires), and keys, the latter probably having been stolen from sailors (Kidd 1953). At least one Huron brought home and planted some peas that he had seen being grown at Quebec (Wrong 1939:91), while the Recollets found that domestic cats were very welcome presents to chiefs (ibid., 118, 270).

Because of the limited amount of goods that the Huron traders could carry home each year, it is not surprising that they emphasized the purchase of metal tools that had cutting edges superior to those of their stone and bone tools. It is also not surprising that the Hurons continued to manufacture pottery vessels as well as bone and stone tools until long after their dispersal in 1649 (Kidd 1950). Nevertheless, there appears to have been a marked decline in the frequency of stone tools on historical Iroquoian sites. M. Latta (1971:130–1) has suggested that women's tools remained largely unchanged either because of the greater conservatism of women or because male traders chose items that were useful to themselves rather than to women. Yet bone and antler tools, which remained common, were manufactured by men, who surely would have sought to replace them with metal counterparts if they had been particularly difficult or time-consuming to produce (for continuity in Neutral bone and antler tools, see Prevec and Noble 1983). Moreover, bone netting needles and stone or bone arrowheads, which are known to have been used by men, remained more common than their metal equivalents. Finally, iron axes were frequently interred with women in Seneca burials (Wray and Schoff 1953:58) as well as at the Neutral Grimsby site (W. Kenyon 1982: graves 3, 31, 42) and were no doubt used by them to cut firewood. This suggests that, given the problems involved in transporting European goods to the Huron country, Huron traders preferred items that replaced native ones that were difficult for men to manufacture or tools used by men that performed markedly better than their Huron counterparts. Iron axes, insofar as they were used by women, may have fallen largely into the former category and iron knives into the latter.

Because so many more Huron traders travelled to the St Lawrence than Frenchmen visited the Huron country, Huron men had more opportunity to evaluate European material culture than Huron women did. This supports K. Deagan's (1982:163) observation that in early contact situations novel information generally reached native societies through males. Yet much detailed analysis of archaeological data is needed if more is to be learned about what kinds of European goods were made available to native men and women. Huron and Petun ossuary burials rarely allow grave goods to be associated with individuals. By contrast, the study of Neutral and Iroquois burials may reveal systematic variations in the European goods that are associated with men, women, and children, and this in turn may provide a more detailed understanding of the relationship between Iroquoian society and the fur trade.

The scanty historical records allow only very limited insights into changes in the gross volume of European goods reaching the Hurons and their neighbours and tell us nothing about fluctuations in individual types. In recent years archaeologists have begun to study this problem by developing a chronology of European material entering southern Ontario in the seventeenth century. In the early 1950s J.N. Emerson and W.D. Bell noted that glass beads differed significantly on Huron sites of different ages. Ian Kenyon and Thomas Kenyon (1982), and following them William Fitzgerald (1982b, 1983), have used glass beads to establish a chronology of historical Iroquoian sites in southern Ontario. The Kenyons' period I, which is characterized by a small number of beads of diverse sizes, shapes, and colours, has already been discussed in chapter 3. Period II is characterized by opaque white and dark blue beads that are either oval or tubular in shape. These beads occur commonly on the Warminster, McMurchy, Graham-Rogers, Ball, and Christianson sites in Ontario, some of which are independently dated to the early decades of the seventeenth century, and on a large number of Iroquois sites in New York State that have long been assigned to the sixteenth century. The Kenyons also observe that there appear to be more beads of these types on sites in Ontario than in New York State. Period III is characterized by round turquoise-coloured and round and tubular red beads. These beads occur on Ontario Iroquoian sites that were occupied in the 1630s and 1640s, such as Teanaostaiaé (St Joseph II), Etharita, and St Louis, and at the Jesuit mission headquarters of Sainte-Marie I and Sainte-Marie II. There is some evidence to suggest that red tubular beads may have increased in frequency during this period. The types and frequencies of beads found on sites in Ontario at this time are no longer matched on sites in New York State.

Precise dates have not been agreed on for the beginnings and ends of these periods. Ontario archaeologists generally reject a sixteenth-century date for period II, which they begin between 1600 and 1615. Ian Kenyon and Thomas Kenyon (1982) suggest that period III began about 1620 on the grounds that it is about then that the increasing availability of goods from Dutch traders on the Hudson River might have differentiated Iroquois sites in New York State from the French-supplied Iroquoian sites in Ontario. Fitzgerald (1983) has tentatively proposed that the transition from period II to period III reflects an abrupt change in European sources of beads after the control of goods reaching New France shifted from Brittany to Paris in 1633. He points to a Jesuit medal said to have been found in association with the period II Shaver Hill Neutral ossuary as evidence that this period could not have ended much earlier than that date. He also contests the validity of the Kenyons' separation of period III into early (IIIa) and late (IIIb) phases in terms of the increasing frequency of red tubular beads; rather, he suggests that period IIIa is an accidental phenomenon found on sites that were occupied during both periods II and III – a conclusion that does not appear to be sustained by Kenyon and Fox's (1982) chronological analysis of glass beads from the Grimsby cemetery. The Warminster site, made up of two apparently contemporary palisaded villages, could have been Cahiagué, which was inhabited in 1615, or the two settlements into which Cahiagué split during a relocation sometime prior to 1623 (Wrong 1939:92); hence this site could indicate that period II lasted into the 1630s. On the other hand, Sagard's assertion that all tribes but the Nipissings preferred red glass beads might mean that period III was already under way by 1623 (ibid., 250).

Much remains to be learned about the precise dates of these changes in glass bead types in southern Ontario prior to 1650. The discrepancy between the dating of sites in Ontario and New York State must also be resolved. Nevertheless a chronological technique is now available that greatly enhances the ability of archaeologists to study cultural change and the impact of the fur trade throughout southern Ontario during the seventeenth century. Ian Kenyon and Thomas Kenyon (1982) do not find evidence that the Hurons were screening out their favourite types of glass beads before passing them along to their trading partners. This suggests that clients, such as the Neutrals, knew what was available and that the Hurons did not dare to withhold new and desirable types of European goods. It also means that similar bead assemblages throughout southern Ontario, and probably until at least 1620 in New York State as well, are of about the same age.

Huron and Petun habitation sites belonging to period II, such as McMurchy, Graham-Rogers, and Warminster, have yielded a richer and more varied selection of European goods than is found on village sites of the sixteenth century. The finds include brass rings, awls, and beads, iron hatchets, and glass beads. Numerous scraps of iron as well as of copper and brass also occur on these sites. This suggests that at the beginning of the historical period more European goods were reaching the Hurons and Petuns. Yet, on the basis of more detailed information about Neutral sites, Fitzgerald (1982a:269–74) has concluded that European goods increased more in variety than in quantity between periods I and II. Only 0.28 per cent of the artifacts found at the Neutral Christianson site (c. 1615) were of European origin compared with 3.7 per cent at the later Neutral Walker and Bogle I sites (c. 1625–40) and 7 to 8 per cent at the still later Hood and Hamilton ones (c. 1630–51). Neutral habitation sites dating from period II are characterized by a paucity of intact iron tools. Many ornaments were made from kettle scraps but there is little evidence of whole kettles, and no metal projectile points. By contrast, burials of this period contain brass and copper pins, bracelets, and ladles as well as much scrap brass; iron axes, knives, awls, and wire (from the rims of brass kettles); and many more glass beads. In period III sites, both Huron and Neutral, European goods become still more common and varied (M. Wright 1981; Lennox 1981, 1984). So many iron axes were ploughed up when northern Simcoe County was cleared for settlement in the last century that scrap-metal dealers found it profitable to visit farms to collect them (Jury and Jury 1954:53). Iron axes are also abundant on late Neutral settlements (Lennox 1981:329). The fact that many iron tools from this period are found intact probably reflects their greater availability.

Archaeologists are currently investigating changes in many aspects of Iroquoian culture during the first half of the seventeenth century. The following observations, without being exhaustive, provide some idea of the variety of work in progress. Most of the problems being studied are very complex and will require much research before definitive answers are obtained. The possibility of firm results also seems to decrease as archaeologists turn from trying to understand prehistoric subsistence patterns and ecology to social organization and religion (Hawkes 1954).

It has been suggested that hunting declined in importance among the Hurons as the fur trade developed. Archaeologists have pointed out that stone artifacts are uncommon in historical Huron sites such as Robitaille (Latta 1971:130), while few of the metal tools appear suitable for hunting. It has also been noted that in late Attignawantan sites dog bones are abundant, while there are relatively few bones of deer or other wild animals (Latta 1971:130; Savage 1971a). We know from historical accounts that Huron hunting parties killed large numbers of deer each spring and autumn in areas located a considerable distance to the south and east of their settlements. They brought home the skins and some of the meat, probably stripped from the bones so that it could be carried more easily (Biggar 1922–36, 3:92–3). This meat would not be represented in the osteoarchaeological record. Yet the *Jesuit Relations* agree that meat was rare in the Huron diet except at festivals in the spring and autumn (Tooker 1964:65). The decline in animal bones in Huron middens probably reflects the depletion of game in nearby areas that resulted from an unprecedented rise in the human population of northern Simcoe County in the historical period rather than less time being spent hunting and more trading. The high percentage of wolf, as opposed to domestic dog at the Maurice site (c. 1570–1620), may indicate a shift in Huron hunting patterns that began with the depletion of local deer stocks, followed by other wild animals. While this made the Hurons different from the Neutrals and Mohawks, who continued to rely more heavily on deer meat, or the Petuns, who seem to have consumed more beavers (Prevec and Noble 1983), hunting was not as important as fishing in any of the northern Iroquoian cultures. Hence this shift was not a difficult or a highly significant one.

Changes in the ratios of the bones of different animal species have also been observed in Neutral sites. The large percentage of beaver bones at the Christianson site (19.1 per cent) compared with later Neutral ones (3.6 per cent or less) suggests that after 1620–35 the Neutrals were trapping fewer beavers close to their settlements; possibly, however, they were obtaining them, as the Hurons were obtaining deer, from farther away (Fitzgerald 1982a:24–5). The large percentage also of raccoon bones at the Hamilton site (16.9 per cent) and (black?) squirrel bones at Walker (10.3 per cent) corresponds with the historical records of the Neutrals trading these fancy furs to the Hurons, who in turn passed them along to their northern Algonkian trading partners (Thwaites 1896–1901, 17:165, 243 n8; 21:197).

There is evidence that after 1620 the Attignawantans were employing larger poles to construct house walls and support sleeping platforms. It has been suggested that the acquisition of iron axes made this possible (Tyyska 1968). Yet the Iroquois used large poles to construct houses and palisades long before iron axes became available (Ritchie and Funk 1973:313–21). Therefore such features should not be attributed automatically to the availability of more effective cutting tools.

In 1969 A.E. Tyyska and W.M. Hurley suggested that a reduction in the length of longhouses at the partially excavated Warminster site indicated the breakdown of the matrilinear extended family as a result of the fur trade. There is corroborating evidence for this trend from more recently excavated Huron historical sites, such as Ball (Knight 1978) and Le Caron (Johnson and Jackson 1980), where average house lengths are shorter than those on protohistoric and late prehistoric ones, such as Benson and Draper, or still earlier ones, such as Nodwell. C.F. Dodd (1984) and Gary Warrick (1984) conclude that the average length of a seventeenth-century long-house in Ontario was about what it had been during the Early Iroquoian period. They also observe, however, that longhouses had attained their maximum length in the Middle Iroquoian period and had been declining since that time. Unfortunately, a scarcity of excavated houses dating from the fifteenth century makes it impossible to determine precisely when this decline began. Reductions in the size of longhouses during the protohistoric period could reflect the demographic consequences of major epidemics on the size of extended families (chapter 5) rather than the impact of the fur trade on family structure. It is also possible that the small size of historical longhouses was the result of changes that had begun in Iroquoian family structure in prehistoric times and hence had nothing to do with European contact. J.A. Tuck (1971:221) suggests that Onondaga longhouses also started to become smaller prior to earliest European contact. At least some large historical Huron settlements had their houses arranged in parallel rows, rather than in aligned or radial clusters, as in earlier periods (Warrick 1984:46). It is unclear what this indicates about clan segments, although the latter are recorded as residence groups in the historical literature (Gendron 1868:19).

There is growing interest in evidence of changes in the trading of native goods that seemingly occurred as a response to the expansion of the fur trade. Ian Kenyon (1972:5) and Fitzgerald (1982a:208–13) detect a vast increase in the amount of marine shell being traded into southern Ontario from the central and southern part of the east coast of the United States between 1600 and 1620. Fitzgerald believes that this increase preceded the major entry of European goods into the Neutral region but was stimulated by economic and ritual activities surrounding the intertribal exchange of European goods in the late sixteenth century.

William Fox (1980) has analysed the distribution of pendants and beads made from red slate or siltstone on historical Iroquoian sites in southern Ontario. This material appears to have been collected on Manitoulin Island or along the north shore of Georgian Bay by the Ottawas, who carried it to the Petuns. There is evidence of the manufacture of slate beads on Petun sites, especially Hamilton-Lougheed, which may be Ehwae, a Petun town abandoned in 1640. The stone was apparently heated to enhance its colour and sawed with nonmetal tools, although the holes may have been drilled with a stiff metal wire. Red slate artifacts first occur on early historical (period II) sites, such as Warminster, Ball, and Christianson, but larger amounts are found on later (period III) sites. It is now suggested that the cylindrical slate beads were manufactured as copies of tubular red glass ones, presumably when the latter were still in limited supply. Previously the opposite view had been entertained: that tubular red glass beads represented a European attempt to copy a traditional native form (Kidd 1953:369). The Neutrals appear to have obtained red slate in a raw as well as a finished state (Fitzgerald 1982a:195–6), although the absence of unworked fragments on some Huron sites has suggested to archaeologists that the Hurons imported only finished objects (Kidd 1952:73; Latta 1971:128–9). A small amount of true catlinite, which comes primarily from western Minnesota, has been found on Ontario sites dating from period III (Kidd 1952). It may have been carried eastward by Ottawa traders.

As early as the sixteenth century the Iroquoians were manufacturing beads, plaques, and pendants from fragments of copper and brass kettles. This activity expanded as metal kettles became more common in the early seventeenth century. Broken iron artifacts were also reworked to manufacture a variety of cutting and piercing implements, and notches were cut into iron knife blades to turn them into harpoons. This work was done by filing, grinding, and hammering, sometimes assisted by heating to make the metal more malleable or to temper cutting edges (Garrad 1969; Bradley 1980). The Indians had used all of these techniques for thousands of years to work native copper and there is no evidence that they acquired any new metal-working skills at this time. For example, they did not learn how to mend metal objects that were broken or worn through and were surprised when French priests and traders, whom they thought would know how to repair them, were unable to do so (Wrong 1939:183). Native metal-working skills were, however, applied on a much vaster scale and were probably practised by more individuals at this time than ever before. There is also evidence

Left: Iroquoian warrior as shown in Champlain's *Voyages* of 1619. Courtesy McGill University Libraries. Right: Warrior with gun and traditional armour from *Novae Franciae Accurata Delineatio*.

that in period II Iroquoians were grinding the blue and white sections off multicoloured beads to reveal the red layer (Kenyon and Kenyon 1982). In period III tubular red beads were similarly ground to give them the more angular appearance of slate ones (ibid.), an activity which suggests that at that time these stone beads may have been esteemed more highly than their glass equivalents.

Early in the seventeenth century, metal arrowheads appear in the archaeological record. Stemmed ones were purchased from Europeans, while the Indians cut lighter triangular ones, resembling Iroquoian stone points, out of metal kettle fragments (Latta 1971:127). At the same time, the Iroquoians continued to manufacture good-quality stone arrowheads (W. Kenyon 1982). From historical accounts we know that the strongest, presumably European-made, metal arrowheads were valued because they could pierce the slatted, wooden body armour that had hitherto protected Iroquoian and Algonkin warriors. As a result, the traditional form of military encounter was quickly discouraged. In it, both sides had lined up in the open and had shot arrows at each other until one side had given way. Even when one or both sides were entrenched in a fortified village or camp, warriors would emerge to fight in this manner. A few losses, in the form of deaths or prisoners being taken, usually signalled the end of such combats (Biggar 1922–36, 2:96–101; 3:66–79). In the 1620s the Hurons and Iroquois preferred to raid each other in scattered groups that could remain hidden in the forests until they were able to surprise small numbers of the enemy and engage them in hand to hand combat. Armour continued to be worn because it was effective against blows in such encounters and against stone-tipped arrows (Otterbein 1964; Trigger 1976:417–18).

There is evidence of a continuing elaboration of ritualism as increasing amounts of European and other exotic goods reached the various Iroquoian tribes. This ritualism was centred on the redistribution of such goods within tribes and communities. It is also possible, though not proved, that because European cutting-tools allowed various utilitarian tasks to be accomplished more quickly, they provided more leisure time that could be devoted to rituals. Burials are unfortunately the only evidence of such activities that is abundantly and unambiguously documented in the archaeological record. As discussed in chapter 3, grave goods appear to have become more common following the earliest substantial trickle of European goods into the Iroquoian area. It appears that, with the growth of the Huron confederacy, ossuary burial ceased to be associated mainly with the western Hurons but was practised by all of the Huron tribes and by their Petun neighbours. Because most historical Huron ossuaries were plundered in the nineteenth century, we are unable to trace regional or chronological variations in their contents. Hence we do not know if grave goods continued to increase in volume as European goods became generally more common or if they reached a peak and began to decline sometime before 1649.

Fortuitously, the best excavated ossuary of the historical period is probably associated with the Feast of the Dead celebrated at Ossossané in 1636, the only one that was described in detail by the French (Kidd 1953). Yet the two or three copper kettles and one complete conch shell from this ossuary fall far short of the twenty-six kettles and sixteen conch shells reported to have come from a single (earlier or later?) plundered one reported in the last century (Bawtree 1848). In the seventeenth century the Feast of the

Dead was a ritual that reinforced solidarity not only within communities and tribes but also between the Hurons and their many trading partners. In addition to the European goods placed in ossuaries, large numbers of beaver skins were used to line and cover them and were given away to honour the chiefs from other tribes who attended these celebrations (Thwaites 1896–1901, 10:279–311).

Neutral burials appear to have made even greater demands on European and native goods than Huron ones did, and more of the evidence is available for study (Fitzgerald 1982b). Much remains, however, to be learned about Neutral burial customs, which involved interring one to over a hundred bodies in varying states of decomposition in a single grave. The graves in the Grimsby cemetery, which was used over a long period of time, indicate that a much wider range of goods was interred in burials during period III than during period II, but also that the number of shell and glass beads per skeleton declined in period III (W. Kenyon 1982; I. Kenyon and Fox 1982). It remains to be seen if this and other patterns can be confirmed in other Neutral cemeteries.

Archaeologists have suggested that the primary function of grave offerings was to perpetuate intertribal trade by taking superfluous European goods out of circulation (Ramsden 1981). Yet European goods were not reaching the Great Lakes region in sufficiently large amounts that such a device would have been needed to maintain demand for them. It seems more likely that European goods were fitted into a pre-existing structure of religious beliefs and that growing access to them stimulated the florescence of a series of mortuary cults throughout the Iroquoian region. The development of these cults may have been encouraged by the fact that in some areas exotic goods served as vehicles for promoting goodwill and hence trade of all sorts between different tribal groups. Yet, in economic terms, the offerings to the dead appear to have been real sacrifices for societies that were not saturated with European goods. These goods were placed in graves probably because they were believed to possess life-giving forces that would benefit the souls of the dead and could not otherwise be obtained by them (Trigger 1982b:254). Among the Neutrals and Iroquois, the burial of exotic goods also appears to have stimulated the routine interment of large numbers of stone arrowheads, bone combs, clay pipes, and ceramic cooking vessels.

Z.P. Mathews (1980) has argued that in historical times in Ontario animal effigy pipes remained the same, while human effigy pipes changed dramatically. She interprets features such as horns on the head, skeletonized bodies, eyes closed in a trancelike condition, head bent back, and hands held to the mouth as being associated with shamanism and the curing of diseases and suggests that these forms represent a response to epidemics of European origin. Yet it is doubtful that interpretations of this sort can be based on archaeological data alone. No specific ethnohistorical information is available concerning the possible meaning of Huron or Iroquois pipe motifs, nor has it been possible for Mathews to relate the designs to masks or other ritual objects of known meaning. Some clues might be obtained from the systematic, comparative study of pipes in later and better documented native cultures, but such studies are only now being undertaken (A. von Gernet, in progress). Mathews's work is also impaired by inadequate chronological control of the data. Human effigy pipes date back to the twelfth century and many sites that she considers to be protohistoric, such as Roebuck and Draper, seem actually to be late prehistoric. Therefore, whatever the significance of human effigy pipes may have been, an elaboration of them had already taken place in prehistoric times. Thus what happened later represented "the florescence of an already dynamic tradition, rather than any radical departure from it" (Trigger 1976:426). It is possible that certain types of pipes were used in specific rituals (Latta 1971:125–6) and that "European" features on some pipes, such as hats or caps, were added as "power symbols" associated with curing. Yet far more detailed studies of the chronologies and distributions of pipes, both within and between sites, will be necessary to lend minimal credence to such interpretations. It should also be remembered that linguistic studies by W.L. Chafe (1964) have indicated that shamanism and curing rites, far from being early historical phenomena, are of great antiquity in Iroquoian culture.

For a long time descriptions of the Hurons between 1615 and 1629 were accepted as those of a pristine Iroquoian culture, largely undisturbed and, where so, generally enriched as a result of European contact. The archaeological evidence for the early seventeenth century documents various changes in Huron culture that are not recorded in the written sources. Yet, in general, it appears to confirm that Huron society was being enriched rather than fundamentally altered at this time. If it were not for the archaeological documentation of the radical changes that had occurred over the sixty years prior to 1615, this view would probably go unchallenged. Yet we can now see early historical Huron culture as the relatively stable product of a former period of stress and major changes. This era of stability was to last for less than thirty years.

## THE HISTORICAL PETUNS AND
## NEUTRALS

The Petuns, and even more so the Neutrals, remain shadowy entities in the historical records of the seventeenth century. Scholars treated these societies as pale reflections of the Hurons instead of taking account of their unique internal features and the complex roles they played in intertribal relations. In recent years extensive archaeological research has begun to redress this balance. There is now, however, a temptation for those studying the Neutrals and Petuns to react against the traditional Huron-centred view by ascribing special characteristics to them that exceed what available evidence can substantiate (Noble 1978; Garrad and Steckley 1984:12). Iroquoian studies will be distorted by such speculations unless new evidence is carefully assessed in relation to all that is known about northern Iroquoian cultures.

Charles Garrad, building on the work of earlier researchers beginning with David Boyle (1889), has carried out extensive archaeological research on the Petuns, about whom he is the foremost authority. He has offered identifications of most of the Petun sites mentioned in the *Jesuit Relations* (Garrad 1980) and has published a number of papers dealing with specific aspects of Petun archaeology, such as pottery (1980) and iron trade knives (1969). Work has also been done on Petun subsistence patterns (Prevec and Noble 1983). Yet, until more research by Garrad and others is published, the Petuns will remain undeservedly obscure in the archaeological literature.

Much more is now known about the historical Neutrals as the result of archaeological research carried out by Frank Ridley (1961) and more recently from McMaster University under the direction of W.C. Noble (1978). The historical Neutrals were long assumed to be a less affluent variant of the Hurons and as dependent on their northern neighbours for European goods. Ethnographers repeated seventeenth-century references to their prowess as hunters, their extravagant ceremonialism, their lack of birchbark canoes (the Iroquois did not have them either), their torture of female as well as male prisoners of war (which turns out to be another pan-Iroquoian trait), and their custom of keeping corpses in their houses for as long as possible prior to burial (Tooker 1964:13–16). Until recently almost nothing was known about their settlement patterns and material culture.

On the basis of erroneous seventeenth-century maps, it was long believed that the historical Neutrals had lived as far west as the

Detroit River. Today the distribution of historical sites reveals that Neutral settlement was confined to an area east of the Grand River. Most sites are found west of Hamilton but they extend through the Niagara Peninsula into New York State. Ian Kenyon (1972) has noted two to four clusters of Neutral sites, each of which may exhibit distinct types of pottery, and Noble (1978) has sought to identify various groups of sites with historically attested but little-known Neutral tribes. Most Neutral sites are under 0.6 hectares in size but at least one site dating from any one time covers between 2 and 6 hectares. The Walker site, which seems to have been an unpalisaded community of about 4 hectares, has been identified as the Neutral "capital," which was visited by the Jesuit missionaries Brébeuf and Pierre Chaumonot in the winter of 1641–2 (M. Wright 1981:137–41). The Donovan site, seven miles northeast of Walker, has been identified as the previous location of this "capital" (then called Ounontisastan), which was visited by Daillon in 1626. The heavily fortified Hamilton site, which covers about 2.5 hectares, was probably the main town of the northern Neutral tribal cluster in the 1640s (Lennox 1981).

Archaeological evidence confirms the historical observation that the Neutrals relied more on hunting than the Hurons did. Deer bones are common in the middens of even the latest Neutral settlements (Lennox 1981:341–3; Prevec and Noble 1983). Neutral houses were more elaborately constructed than Huron ones, with internal divisions partially separating family compartments (Fitzgerald 1982a:43–51; Dodd 1984:290–1). European and other exotic goods occur as abundantly in Neutral village sites as in contemporary Huron ones and grave offerings seem to be considerably more abundant. While the Neutrals, unlike the Hurons, had no direct source of European goods, they did not have to exchange European goods for furs and hence were able to retain more of what they had received. As late as 1626 they were allowing Algonkin visitors to hunt beaver on their lands, presumably in exchange for presents of European goods (Sagard 1866:803). There is archaeological and written evidence that they traded with the Susquehannocks, Senecas, Petuns, Eries, and perhaps with tribes in the Ohio Valley as well. It is also possible that by way of Neutral intermediaries various goods were traded between the Hurons and the Iroquois. In this fashion, European goods supplied only by the French or by the Dutch may have made their way from one intertribal trading network to another to the mutual advantage of the native groups involved. Evidence to determine if this actually happened must be looked for as archaeological knowledge of European trade goods improves. Already, however, it is evident that the Neutrals were not a backwater with respect to intertribal trade but the centre of a major trading network that was markedly different in character from that of the Hurons. The Neutrals appear to have been major suppliers of beaver pelts to the Hurons and possibly also to the Senecas.

There is archaeological evidence of continuing warfare between the Neutrals and the Assistaronons throughout the first half of the seventeenth century. Foreign-style pottery with decorative appliqué strips, strap handles on the neck, and large plat motifs on the exterior rims is common on Neutral sites in the northern Bronte and Spencer Creeks area. Identical pottery has been found at Indian Hills, along with some European goods, and on other sites in northwestern Ohio that are associated with the Fort Meigs culture (Stothers 1981). Historical evidence suggests that the Indian Hills people were ancestral to the Kickapoos, who were one of the Central Algonkian-speaking tribes (Goddard 1972). Similar sorts of pottery occur on late prehistoric Iroquoian sites in the London area, suggesting that warfare between these two groups may have continued as the Neutrals moved westward. Finally, it may have been through female prisoners that the technique of using ground shells to temper pottery was introduced among the Neutrals. This technique, which allowed the manufacture of thinner and lighter vessels, began to be used about AD 800 in the Mississippi Valley. In northern Neutral sites it increased in frequency from 1 to 3 per cent in the late sixteenth century to 15 per cent at Christianson and 64 per cent at Hamilton (Fitzgerald 1982a:94–101).

According to the French sources, the Neutrals had a paramount chief with the hereditary name of Souharissen whose power was unparalleled among other Iroquoian groups. Some archaeologists have therefore argued that the Neutrals had evolved a more unified and hierarchical political organization in the form of a chiefdom, while the Hurons and Iroquois remained at the level of tribal confederacies (Noble 1978; S. Jamieson 1981). If so, the Neutrals should have been politically and militarily stronger than their neighbours. Souharissen lived in Ounontisastan in 1625 and at a centrally located but unnamed town identified with the Walker site in the 1640s. The exceptionally large size of these sites suggests that this community may have had special political importance among the Neutrals. Yet the possibility remains that the French misunderstood the nature of Souharissen's office. Instead of being a paramount chief, he may have been responsible for conducting foreign relations, just as Tsondechaouanouan, an Attignawantan chief, was in charge of dealing with the bands that the Hurons visited along the shores of Lake Huron and whose name was used with all messages sent to these groups. Another example is Atironta, who conducted Huron relations with the French. It is possible that for a similar reason Souharissen appeared more important in the eyes of the French than he was in reality. The restricted distribution of Central Algonkian ceramic features indicates that only the northern Neutrals were waging war against the Assistaronons, and this in turn suggests a typical Iroquoian confederacy rather than a politically more integrated chiefdom (Fitzgerald 1982a:97–101; Lennox 1984:272). Moreover, Souharissen was absent from the Neutral country more often than a paramount chief is likely to have been and he was sometimes lightly obeyed by his supposed subjects (Trigger 1976:401). All this indicates that much more archaeological evidence will have to be produced before it can be established that the Neutrals were other than a confederacy, like their Iroquoian neighbours.

## CREATIVE SYMBIOSIS

The period prior to 1632 was one of nondirected change. The Europeans in eastern Canada were too few, and, what is equally important, lacked the knowledge to control native people, much as Champlain and the missionary orders wished to do this. The basis for all relations between the Indians and the French was the fur trade. Until 1627, this trade also provided the only economic basis for maintaining the meagre and largely transient European settlement in and around Quebec.

At this time the Indians who traded with the French neither feared nor felt inferior to Europeans. They were impressed by the quality of metal cutting-tools. They may also have continued to attribute special supernatural powers to these tools as well as to other European goods such as glass beads, although there is no substantial evidence of this (Martin 1975). Manifestations of supernatural powers were more obviously seen in the ability of some Europeans to read and to write and in their statues and paintings, which were more realistic than any work of art that native people had encountered previously (Thwaites 1896–1901, 5:257; F. Gagnon 1975). At least until they acquired their own guns, as the Montagnais did temporarily in the 1620s, they also attributed magical powers to these weapons, which were equated with lightning and thunder and thought able to control storms (Wrong 1939:183). Yet the Indians probably attributed much of the technological skill of Europeans to the possession of magical powers that were not seen as being different in kind from their own; hence these skills did not imply any inherent superiority in Europeans.

There is no evidence that native groups that had been in contact with Europeans for a long time continued to regard them as supernatural. They ridiculed slowness in learning to speak their languages and to use canoes, snowshoes, or anything else that they regarded as commonplace. When Champlain sought to punish or control the Montagnais, he was repeatedly outmanoeuvred and humiliated by their chiefs. Indians traditionally associated hairiness with a lack of intelligence and pointed to beards as material evidence of the stupidity of Europeans (Wrong 1939:138).

The Indians did not hesitate to criticize Frenchmen for their greed, loquaciousness, and the cruel way they treated one another. They were baffled by the hierarchical nature of European society and were unable to understand how one man could be made to obey another. They greatly offended the French by insisting, contrary to French admonitions, that their chiefs were equivalent in status to the French king (Wrong 1939:149). They also did not understand why European leaders did not make the largest and most complicated trade goods or why an old and experienced man such as Champlain was unable to mend brass kettles (ibid., 183). The Indians believed themselves equal or superior as human beings to the French and remained confident of the criteria by which they judged the world. The most important problem they faced at this time was not how to adjust to Europeans but how to incorporate a larger and more varied supply of European goods into their respective societies.

## CHAPTER FIVE

# Plagues and Preachers, 1632–1663

While popular histories of Canada treat the period from 1603 to 1629 as the era of Champlain, the years 1634 to 1650 are those of the Jesuit mission to the Huron country. Accounts of this period traditionally laud the courage and tenacity of these missionaries, and the deaths of Isaac Jogues, Antoine Daniel, Jean de Brébeuf, and Gabriel Lalemant are celebrated as supreme acts of martyrdom. Even historians such as Parkman, who regarded the Jesuits as fanatical and profoundly misguided in their religious beliefs, have praised them for their tireless efforts to transmit the benefits of civilization to barbarous and often hostile peoples.

The Indians are represented as at best the passive recipients of this bounty. Rarely have historians attempted to ascertain what the Jesuits and their teachings meant to native peoples or what impact they had on native ways of life. Only the development of ethnohistorical techniques has made it possible to study these questions in detail by reassessing the abundant documentation contained in the *Jesuit Relations* and other contemporary sources (Berton 1978:117–45). It has become evident that the development of New France at this time cannot be understood without taking account of the goals and aspirations of native people. Such a perspective not only raises important new issues about what native people themselves were doing but also radically alters our understanding of the actions of Europeans.

## THE JESUITS AND THE NEW ALLIANCE

After the English seized Quebec in 1629, the established trading networks in eastern Canada continued to function for a year but then began to fall into disarray. A record trade at Quebec in 1630 was followed by plummeting figures the next year. As the French presence had weakened along the St Lawrence River in the late 1620s, the Mohawks once more began to raid the valley east of Montreal Island. They destroyed an Algonkin and Montagnais settlement at Trois-Rivières in the summer of 1629 (Thwaites 1896–1901, 8:27–9). This situation grew worse because the English, who were anxious to guard Quebec against a surprise attack by the French, refused to patrol the St Lawrence. At the same time, the Algonkins did all they could to increase Huron mistrust of the English in the hope that they could regain some or all of their earlier role as middlemen between the Hurons and the European traders. It is regrettable that we know so little about this brief but significant episode in Canadian history.

Following the return of the French in 1632, the Algonkins and the Mohawks negotiated a new peace treaty. The Mohawks hoped once again to be able to trade with the French as well as the Dutch, and the Algonkins wanted to obtain European goods from either the Mohawks or the Dutch so that they would be in a stronger position to bargain with the French. The Mohawks, however, were not interested either in trading with the Algonkins or in letting them trade with the Dutch. The peace ended in 1635 when they ambushed and murdered a Kichesipirini chief attempting to trade at Fort Orange (Thwaites 1896–1901, 9:95–7). After this, the Algonkins reluctantly slipped into their former subordinate role in the fur trade, and political and economic relations resumed the same general pattern that they had before 1627.

When the French regained control of Quebec in 1632, the Hurons sought to renew their trading alliance. At the same time, the Jesuits, who were the only religious order allowed to return to Canada, wished to begin a major program to establish missions among these tribes. The Hurons were anxious to have armed French traders again living in their villages and travelling to and from the St Lawrence with their trading convoys, but they were less certain that they wanted the return of the French shamans. In July 1633 a flotilla containing an estimated 500 Hurons arrived at Quebec, the largest number ever to make their way to the St Lawrence in a single year. Over sixty chiefs came with them to renew their alliance with Champlain, who had returned to Quebec two months earlier (Thwaites 1896–1901, 5:239). They must have been surprised when Champlain insisted that they allow the Jesuits to live in their country as a necessary precondition for the renewal of the French-Huron alliance. The Huron chiefs were able to use a quarrel

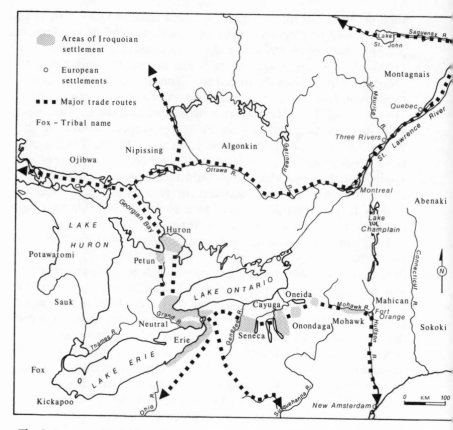

The St Lawrence lowlands, c. 1640.

between the Algonkins and the French as an excuse for not taking any missionaries with them that summer.

The next year, however, ordinary Huron traders were bribed by Charles Du Plessis-Bochart, the head clerk of the trading company, to transport three priests and a few French workmen, led by Jean de Brébeuf, home with them. The Hurons accepted a fait accompli, and the following year the Jesuits' role as their guests was confirmed at another council held at Quebec. There Champlain reiterated that if the Hurons wished to continue trading with the French, they had to treat the priests and their workmen with respect. At the request of Paul Le Jeune, the Jesuit superior, he also informed the Hurons that to preserve their alliance they would have to agree eventually to become Christians and to send a number of Huron boys to Quebec the following year to attend a residential school the Jesuits were establishing there. As well as being important to their mission program, these boys would act as hostages to guarantee the safety of the French living in the Huron country. Champlain suggested as well that eventually many Frenchmen would settle in the Huron country, marry Huron women, and teach the Hurons how to forge iron (Thwaites 1896–1901, 8:49). The latter proposals were his own idea, not Jesuit mission policy. This was the first time that the French traders, as a result of Jesuit insistence, attempted to coerce the Hurons. It is clear, however, that what had transpired was nothing more than a successful bluff. Had the Hurons refused to accept the Jesuits, economic necessity and long-term mission strategy would have dictated that the French would have continued trading with them.

### THE KILLING YEARS

The return of the Jesuits to the Huron country corresponded with the first historically recorded spread of an epidemic disease of European origin throughout this part of the New World. Over the next seven years a series of such epidemics was to devastate the Hurons and their neighbours. The rudimentary state of medical knowledge in the seventeenth century and the lack of sufficiently detailed descriptions of these diseases make the precise identification of most of them impossible. The epidemic of 1634 was probably introduced to the St Lawrence Valley by the ships that had arrived from France in June, although there were also epidemics in New England at this time. When the Hurons visited Trois-Rivières in July, the Montagnais and Algonkins were dying there in large numbers. Before they started for home, the illness had spread up the Ottawa Valley, infecting the Algonkins who lived there. Most of the traders who had been to Trois-Rivières became ill, and the disease spread through all the Huron villages during the late summer and autumn. So many Hurons were stricken that the autumn fishing was seriously curtailed and crops were left rotting in the fields. Among the Indians, the illness began with a high fever, followed by a rash and in some cases blindness or impaired vision that lasted for several days, and then diarrhoea. The rash was described as "a sort of measles or smallpox," a reminder that it was only in the previous century that medical experts in Europe had distinguished the one disease from the other (McNeill 1976:105). It was added that the rash was different from that common in France. While a large number of Hurons became ill, most of them appear to have recovered, although many remained debilitated over the winter.

There has been much debate about the identity of this illness. An epidemic of smallpox, said to have been of English origin, had swept New England in 1633 and is thought by some to be the disease from which the Mohawks suffered in 1634. M.K. Jackes (1983) believes that this same disease either was introduced to the St Lawrence Valley by the English or spread north from the Iroquois and suggests that it was a strain of smallpox that caused relatively few deaths. On the other hand, J. Duffy (1953:165) and H.F. Dobyns (1983:17) have identified it as measles, while still others have suggested that it was influenza (Talbot 1956:131). The fact that some French became ill, apparently of the same disease, but recovered within a few days (Thwaites 1896–1901, 7:221) and that smallpox was immediately identified when it broke out in 1639 indicate that it was more likely one of the latter illnesses.

In August 1636 an outbreak of influenza began to spread from the St Lawrence Valley into the interior, where it caused many deaths, both directly and as a result of starvation, among the hunter-gatherer peoples of that region. It reached the Huron country in early September, and for two weeks the Jesuits and their assistants were confined to their beds with cramps and fever. All of them recovered, however. The disease grew more prevalent as the Hurons settled into their villages for the winter, abated somewhat during the coldest months, and then flared up again the following spring. It took about six weeks to run its course in any one community, but the timing was different from one settlement to another and not all of them were afflicted. It appears that the Attignawantans suffered more than the eastern tribes of the Huron confederacy (Thwaites 1896–1901, 13:131–3, 165). The mortality rate also appears to have been highest in communities that were stricken in the spring, no doubt because food supplies were running low and resistance was weaker then. Ten per cent of the Nipissings who were wintering in the Huron country died of the disease. Even allowing for a lower mortality rate as a result of more food and better housing, a large number of Hurons must have perished.

Soon after the Hurons had departed to trade with the French in 1637, a new outbreak of illness spread through the Huron country. It also reached the Ottawa Valley and the trading post at Trois-Rivières. Many Indians who had contracted this disease died within two days. Yet no French became ill, which suggests that it was probably a European childhood ailment against which most adult Europeans were immune. Scarlet fever has been suggested (Dobyns 1983:22). It seems that this ailment had spread north from the Susquehannocks, who had been stricken by an unidentified malady earlier in the year (Thwaites 1896–1901, 14:9). A large number of Wenros, who lived between the Senecas and the Neutrals and traded with the Susquehannocks, also probably died from it (ibid., 15:159). This epidemic persisted into the autumn and appears to have killed many more people than the two previous ones had.

In the summer of 1639, what was immediately identified as an epidemic of smallpox spread through the St Lawrence Valley, killing many Indians who came to trade. The disease was thought to have been carried from New England by a group of Algonkins returning from a visit to the Abenakis (Thwaites 1896–1901, 16:101). Soon the Algonkins were dying in such large numbers that they could not bury their dead. The Huron traders carried the epidemic home with them, where it persisted over the winter. Many thousands of Hurons died, far more than had perished in the three previous epidemics combined. Only one Frenchman was stricken, while returning from Quebec to the Huron country, but after nearly dying he recovered. The epidemic spread from the Hurons to the Petuns and the Neutrals. In the winter of 1640–1 a serious epidemic, perhaps a continuation of this one, raged among the Senecas (ibid., 21:211).

## DEMOGRAPHIC PROBLEMS

Until now I have generally avoided considering population size and alterations, although it is clear that these are vital for any discussion of ecological adaptation and social change. It is notoriously difficult to estimate the size of aboriginal populations by using historical or archaeological data. Sound archaeological estimates require much systematically collected data about settlement patterns, as well as mortality rates derived from skeletal studies. Detailed statistical information is normally lacking in early historical accounts. The figures that have been recorded are often only fleeting impressions that cannot be subjected to internal verification (Meister 1976).

In recent years Woodrow Borah (1964), H.F. Dobyns (1966, 1983), and others have argued that the population of the New World prior to European contact was many times higher than anthropological estimates made earlier in the twentieth century had indicated and hence that its subsequent decline was more catastrophic than had been previously believed. Diseases that were hitherto unknown in the New World and against which native populations had no opportunity to acquire immunity clearly played the major role in bringing about this decline. These included numerous viral infections, such as measles, influenza, chicken pox, mumps, rubella, and smallpox, the latter being by far the most lethal. Dobyns (1966), on the basis of empirical case studies from Mexico, Peru, California, and elsewhere, has estimated a decline of 95 per cent during the first 130 years (five generations) after initial contact, following which the population slowly began to increase.

Anthropologists now agree that there was a major decline in population after European contact. Yet they do not agree about the overall magnitude of the loss. They are also uncertain about the extent and variability of local declines, the date of the population nadir (lowest point) of different groups, and the population figures at that time. When Dobyns published his original study, he was criticized for accepting the 1930 census figures as representing the nadir of the overall North American Indian population (Kehoe and Kehoe in Dobyns 1966:434). It was argued that if native populations along the east coast of North America had begun to decline in the sixteenth century, Dobyns's theory suggests that recovery should have been under way by the end of the seventeenth century, provided that other factors, such as warfare and population dispersal, did not prevent this. If this recovery had happened, it would tend to inflate projections for that area based on population data from later centuries.

Figures estimated after 1966 for the number of native Americans living north of the Mexican border at the time of European contact vary from H.E. Driver's (1969:63) 3.5 million to Dobyns's 9.8 million, the most recent being D.H. Ubelaker's (1976) 4.4 million, based on tribal estimates of varying reliability submitted for publication in the *Handbook of North American Indians*. All these figures are substantially higher than James Mooney's (1910, 1928)

1.1 million and A.L. Kroeber's (1939) 0.9 million, which were based largely on data from the seventeenth century or later. Many demographers believe that because of the inadequacy of the data, it may never be possible to determine the size of the North American population at the time of European contact. The best that can be done is to fix it within a broad range of variation (Denevan 1976:xvii). Yet, despite these problems, it is now certain that many prehistoric North American societies were significantly larger and more complex than those known in historical times and that the demographic and social changes they experienced following the European discovery of the New World were far greater than anthropologists had previously assumed.

Although the detailed figures collected during the one Jesuit census of the Hurons and Petuns have not been preserved, they recorded a total of approximately 12,000 people for these two groups immediately after the smallpox epidemic of 1639–40 (Thwaites 1896–1901, 19:127). This figure is probably the most reliable population estimate for a native group in eastern North America in the first half of the seventeenth century. C.E. Heidenreich (1971:92) has argued that if the nine Petun villages were proportional in size to the twenty-three Huron ones, the Hurons would have had a population of about 9,000 and the Petuns 3,000. This roughly accords with the round figure of 10,000 that the Jesuits assigned to the Hurons throughout the following decade (Thwaites 1896–1901, 17:221–3; 19:77).

For earlier periods we have Champlain's statement that the Hurons had "two thousand warriors, not counting the common mass, which amounts perhaps to thirty thousand souls," or a population of 32,000 (Biggar 1922–36, 3:122). Although Champlain had visited the entire Huron country in 1615–16, he does not claim this figure as his own estimate but rather as one quoted to him by the Hurons. We do not know how the Hurons estimated their population or if he understood them properly. It is also strange that in a society in which all young and middle-aged men could fight as warriors, the latter should have constituted less than 7 per cent of the population. Sagard set the Huron population between 30,000 and 40,000 in 1623 (Wrong 1939:92). He probably included the Petuns in this count, since he says they were living in twenty-five settlements, not eighteen as Champlain had maintained. The Jesuits continued to state that 30,000 Hurons were living in twenty villages prior to the epidemics, which we may assume was the accepted French estimate for the Hurons at that time (Thwaites 1896–1901, 7:225; 8:115; 10:313).

In 1950 Robert Popham suggested a pre-epidemic Huron population of 45,000 to 50,000, figures that continue to be cited in some
works (Schlesier 1976:137). He believed, on the basis of archaeological distributions of European goods, that prior to 1635 the whole
of Simcoe County had been inhabited, although Champlain and
Sagard had visited and written about only the northern part of it.
Hence their population estimates had to be substantially increased.
We now know that the sites in southern Simcoe County date from
the protohistoric period and that at that time Huron settlements
were less densely concentrated than they were during the first half
of the seventeenth century. Thus there is no factual basis for
Popham's higher figures.

In 1969 I suggested a reduced total of about 18,000 Hurons prior
to the epidemics of the late 1630s (Trigger 1969:11–13). In their
census of 1640 the Jesuits counted among the Hurons and Petuns
32 settlements, 700 longhouses, and 2,000 hearths, which, since
two families normally shared a single hearth, would mean 4,000
families. Thus, after the epidemics, only three people per family
survived. Assuming, however, as seems entirely reasonable given
the proximity of the census to the epidemics, that the hearth count
reflected the situation immediately prior to the smallpox epidemic
and using figures that suggest that in normal times a Huron family
had between five and eight members (Heidenreich 1971:99), we
can calculate a combined Huron and Petun population of between
20,000 and 32,000, the median value of which indicates that 19,500
Hurons were alive in 1639. Allowing for a 20 per cent mortality
rate in the epidemics of 1634 to 1637 would raise this figure to
approximately 23,500 prior to the epidemics. Heidenreich (1971:96–
103) estimated a pre-epidemic Huron population using three separate techniques: a post-epidemic figure of 9,000 and the smallpox
death rates compiled by Dobyns and others; warrior totals; and the
known number and size of Huron settlements. These calculations
produced median estimates running from 16,000 to 22,500 and an
average estimate of 21,000.

As it has become fashionable to propose larger population figures
for native groups in protohistoric and early historical times,
Heidenreich's estimates and my own have been questioned. So far,
these challenges have sought to defend the accuracy of Champlain's
figure of 32,000. Charles Garrad (1980:109) has suggested that the
Hurons and Petuns were perhaps greatly reduced from that figure
by an epidemic that broke out in 1616 as a result of Champlain's
visit. J.A. Dickinson (1980) has argued that because of diseases
brought into the Huron country by Europeans after 1610, its pop-

ulation declined from 25,000 to 30,000 in 1600 to about 20,000 in 1634. It would be unwise to rule out the possibility that major epidemics had occurred in southern Ontario prior to 1634. In the summer of 1611 many Algonkins are reported to have fallen ill with a fever (Biggar 1922–36, 2:207), and during the winter of 1623–4 a large number of the Petite Nation band perished of disease and hunger in the Ottawa Valley (Wrong 1939:263). It is impossible to determine whether these were epidemics of European origin. The ages of skeletons indicate higher than average mortality rates in the Ossossané ossuary, but this interment post-dates the 1634 epidemic (Sullivan 1983). Jackes (1983) has suggested that an apparent case of osteomyelitis variolosa in one adult skeleton from the Grimsby cemetery may offer evidence of an outbreak of smallpox among the Neutrals prior to 1640. While this case is not conclusive, in the future skeletal evidence of this sort may be able to provide significant information about diseases.

The Neutrals, who appear to have had a population of about 12,000 after 1639 (Thwaites 1896–1901, 21:223), had probably suffered a decline proportional to that of the Hurons. Both Champlain and Sagard believed that prior to the 1630s their population had been larger than that of the Hurons (Biggar 1922–36, 3:99; 6:249; Wrong 1939:157). It has long been estimated that the Iroquois had an aboriginal population of 10,000 to 12,000, on the basis of a report which states that they had 2,000 warriors in 1668 (Thwaites 1896–1901, 51:139); however, Mooney reduced this figure to 5,500, apparently because he thought that their population had been increasing prior to then. It is now clear that these figures refer to a time after the Iroquois had experienced a series of epidemics that were at least as severe as those suffered by the Hurons. The Mohawks are recorded to have been stricken by smallpox or some other serious disease (perhaps the same illness that afflicted the Hurons) as early as 1634, while the Senecas suffered from a major epidemic (probably smallpox) in the winter of 1640–1. In 1646 and 1647 the Iroquois were attacked by still more outbreaks of contagious diseases that did not reach the Hurons and another round of smallpox occurred in 1654 (Thwaites 1896–1901, 30:229; 31:121).

On the basis of Bogaert's settlement data for 1634, and assuming a death rate of 50 to 70 per cent, W.A. Starna (1980) has estimated a pre-epidemic population for the Mohawks alone of 10,000 to 17,000. Yet, in making these calculations, he failed to note that insufficient time had elapsed for Mohawk villages to be rebuilt to accommodate a smaller population. Hence the pre-epidemic figures that his data indicate are actually between 6,600 and 8,300. Dean

Snow (1980:34) has estimated a pre-epidemic Mohawk population of 9,000 to 11,300. While his projections would indicate a total Iroquois population close to Dobyns's (1966:402) estimate of 55,000, Starna's reinterpreted data produce a figure closer to 30,000. Much more will be known about Mohawk and Iroquois demography when the systematic site survey and excavations being carried out by Snow and other archaeologists as part of the Mohawk Valley Project are finished. Yet, the seven or more large communities that the Iroquois inhabited before 1650, compared with only six large Huron ones, seem to suggest that, contrary to what was believed until recently, the Five Nations Iroquois were at least as populous as the Hurons prior to the epidemics of the 1630s, and probably somewhat more so (Trigger 1976:98). Even after the epidemics, they may have had several thousand more people, which would have given them an advantage in warfare that has not hitherto been adequately considered. On the other hand, the relative balance of power that was maintained between the two confederacies suggests that prior to 1640 the numerical difference was probably not a great one.

In the past it was generally assumed that the epidemics of the 1630s were the first major ones to reach the interior of northeastern North America and that descriptions of what had happened at that time portrayed the reactions of native people to an unprecedented situation. Today it is acknowledged that the problems of epidemics cannot be restricted to the seventeenth century. European diseases began to slaughter the populations of the New World not long after Europeans had first reached the Caribbean. Smallpox arrived in Hispaniola before 1518 and was carried from Cuba to Mexico by the Spanish expedition that joined Hernando Cortés two years later. Continuing southward, it reached Peru by 1525 or 1526. Throughout these densely populated regions the effect was catastrophic. High mortality continued to be experienced, as recurrent outbreaks of smallpox, measles, influenza, plague, typhus, diphtheria, and mumps swept through Latin America during the sixteenth and seventeenth centuries (McNeill 1976:180–5). Some of these epidemics reached the southeastern United States from Mexico or as a result of European activities in that region (Dobyns 1983). Although it would have been difficult to transmit smallpox across the Atlantic, since the disease ran its course in a period that was shorter than most voyages (Miller 1982:118), once smallpox was established in the West Indies, it was relatively easy for Spanish, French, or English ships coming from that region, or native American contacts, to transmit it to the North American mainland.

It has long been clear that there was a major reduction in the population of the southeastern United States during the sixteenth century. It appears that this reduction played a major role in the disintegration of the more complex cultures that are archaeologically attested there (J.L. Wright 1981). Archaeological settlement data suggest not only massive population declines in the lower Mississippi Valley after 1540, but also possible losses as far north as the middle Missouri region (Ramenofsky 1982). Dobyns (1983) believes that a smallpox pandemic swept almost all of North America between 1520 and 1524. Anthropologists must be careful, however, not to overinterpret the available evidence. For example, major declines in the Chesapeake Bay area are implied by the Jesuit missionary Luis de Quirós's observation that, as a result of six years of famine and death, far fewer people lived there when a short-lived Jesuit mission was established in 1570 than when the Spanish had first explored it in 1561 (Quinn 1979, 2:557). The Jesuit historian F.J. Alegre specifically attributed those losses to a prolonged epidemic, which Dobyns (1983:275–6) has identified with an outbreak of disease that he says spread from Mexico. This interpretation appears to be further corroborated by a claim made by Powhatan in 1609 that during his lifetime he had seen all of his people perish three times (Quinn 1979, 5:330). A more careful reading of the Spanish sources reveals, however, that when the Jesuits had arrived in 1570, much of the population was away from the coast but soon returned in its accustomed numbers (ibid., 2:558–61), while the broader context of Powhatan's speech demonstrates that he was talking about population losses resulting from outbreaks of warfare rather than from disease.

Anthropologists still know very little for certain about the spread of European diseases across most of North America during the sixteenth century. They have not determined how far north and east such illnesses spread from Mexico and the Caribbean. They know almost nothing about the dissemination of diseases from the northeastern tip of the continent which, because of the cod fisheries, was exposed to infections coming directly from Europe. The narrative of Cartier's second voyage reports that there was an epidemic at Stadacona in the winter of 1635–6 during which some fifty Indians (about 10 per cent of the population) died. It has been assumed, although there is no corroborating evidence, that this was an outbreak of some European disease. W.N. Fenton (1940:175) and others have suggested that repeated transmissions of European diseases to this region may have played a major role in the disappearance of the St Lawrence Iroquoians.

In the absence of direct evidence, two alternative positions have been championed concerning European diseases and mortality rates in eastern Canada and New England during the sixteenth century.

Some take it for granted that there must have been massive epidemics throughout this region, which greatly reduced native populations prior to the earliest European records (Martin 1978:42–55). According to this view, the epidemics of the seventeenth century were merely a continuation of previous ones rather than the unprecedented disruption that most European observers have interpreted them to be. On the other hand, Snow (1980) maintains that the massive epidemic, or series of epidemics, that had swept coastal New England between 1616 and 1619 was the first major one to reach that area. Although the identity of this epidemic remains uncertain (Cook [1973a] suggests that it was pneumonic or bubonic plague), it is clear that the loss of life and its impact on native social and political organization were immense. Yet Snow believes that the available records on the population of this region immediately prior to this time constitute a reasonable basis for reconstructing the demography and cultural patterns of the late prehistoric period. Unfortunately, because archaeological data are not yet particularly abundant for the late prehistoric and proto-historic periods in New England, it is impossible to determine whether Snow's assumptions are correct.

The Maritime provinces were more exposed to European contact during the sixteenth century than New England was. In 1616 the Jesuit missionary Pierre Biard pointed out that there had been a marked decline in the population of the Micmacs, which he attributed to their dependence on alcohol and French foodstuffs (Thwaites 1896–1901, 3:105–7). It is unclear, however, how long this decline had been going on. Using Dobyns's formula, Virginia Miller (1982) has estimated a Micmac population of 50,000 in the late prehistoric period. Yet, while she believes that there was intensive contact between the Micmacs and Europeans throughout the sixteenth century (and even earlier), she does not conclude that massive epidemics played a significant role in reducing the population until permanent European settlements were established in this area in the seventeenth century. Instead, she agrees with Biard that the principal causes of Micmac decline were dietary changes that weakened native resistance to endemic diseases and to localized outbreaks of European ones.

At present there are no reliable archaeological or archival data on which to base a discussion of population trends among native groups in the Maritime provinces during the sixteenth century. We do not know when the Micmacs began to decline in numbers or how quickly. Even the date of their nadir is ambiguous (Miller [1982]. Snow (1980:36) has estimated a total of about 12,000 Micmacs prior to their decline instead of Miller's 50,000. His figure was based in part on the assumption that 12.3 persons per 100 square kilometres was a reasonable population density for that region. Until new evidence becomes available, population size, which is crucial for understanding other changes in this region in the sixteenth century, will remain highly controversial. What is perhaps most interesting is that Miller, although arguing in favour of massive depopulation, regards it as unlikely that smallpox would have crossed the Atlantic at this time and does not favour large-scale epidemics that might have spread far inland. Nor does she consider the possibility that major epidemics reached this area from farther south.

It has long been noted that while single burials were the rule among the Senecas and Eries in prehistoric times, two to six individuals in a single grave became common during the protohistoric period. This change has been attributed to the introduction of European diseases after 1550 (Wray 1973:27–8), although the specific dates of protohistoric sites remain controversial. There is also osteological evidence of a high mortality rate among young people in the cemeteries at the Cameron site in New York State, which C.F. Wray and H.L. Schoff (1953:55) dated between 1575 and 1590 (L.P. Saunders, cited by Dobyns 1983:321). Dobyns (1983:313–27) has attempted to identify every Seneca village relocation between 1520 and the 1670s as a response to major epidemics. The earliest of these is the smallpox pandemic of the 1520s, which he assumes reached this far north; followed by severe but unidentified diseases in the 1560s, 1574, and 1586; measles in 1596; and plague between 1615 and 1620. The notion of severe population decline beginning early in the sixteenth century may gain support from the Onondaga settlement sequence. The largest Onondaga site (Barnes), which is about 1.5 hectares, appears to date from late prehistoric or early protohistoric times, while fragmentary data suggest that later sites declined to half that size (Tuck 1971:149, 160; Bradley 1980:113).

On the other hand, while Iroquoian villages are recorded as relocating after epidemics in the seventeenth century, they also did so then and in prehistoric times for other reasons. Moreover, A.F. Ramenofsky (1982), on the basis of settlement counts, estimated settlement size, and estimated areas of houses for twenty-six Iroquois sites dating from Early Owasco times to the end of the seventeenth century, has concluded that the population increased into the sixteenth century and declined during the seventeenth. While these findings contradict Dobyns's belief that the Iroquois population declined throughout most of the sixteenth century, her periodization is not precise enough to indicate whether the decline began during the sixteenth century or sometime after 1600; hence her findings do not help to determine when epidemics of European origin first reached the Iroquois. This study's failure to distinguish among tribal groups may also bias its results to some extent.

Unfortunately, the looting or inadequate excavation of Huron and Petun ossuaries has destroyed much of the best evidence on which a study of changing mortality rates in Ontario could have been based. While a review of late nineteenth- and early twentieth-century records may still yield some valuable information, none of them is likely to supply accurate estimates even of the numbers of skulls that were exhumed. Only a few ossuaries have been excavated systematically and the bones subjected to detailed physical anthropological analysis that provides useful information about age and sex. It is worth noting, however, that a recent study of human bones from the Kleinburg ossuary, a Neutral or Huron interment from around AD 1600 (glass bead period 1), exhibits only a slightly higher mortality rate than that at the Fairty ossuary, which dates from the end of the Middle Iroquoian period. N.C. Sullivan (1983) interprets this to mean that massive depopulation did not occur in Ontario in the late sixteenth century, a conclusion that appears to contradict what has been inferred from burial data in New York State.

Ontario Iroquoian settlement data have been better preserved than data from ossuaries but their interpretation is complicated by the major shifts in population that characterized the Neutrals, Petuns, and Hurons during the protohistoric period. Archaeologists still have not traced specific village movements on a large scale at this time, as has been done in New York State. Yet, if enough regional surveys are executed and special purpose sites are distinguished from regular villages, it still may be possible to estimate changes in the number, size, and population of Iroquoian settlements from prehistoric times into the historical period. Such analyses will be greatly assisted by the relatively large number of sites that have been extensively excavated, since detailed house plans provide the best basis for estimating population size. Eventually, enough data may be available to determine whether there was a decline in population during the protohistoric period. If there had been, it would have been another factor adding to the complexity of the changes that were reshaping the social and political structures of the Iroquoian peoples at this time. Ramenofsky (1982) has suggested that a population decline may have encouraged the formation of the Iroquois confederacy. Yet, until the fact of decline has been established, it is unprofitable to speculate in detail about its social consequences.

Finally, theoretical considerations do not help to resolve when Iroquoian depopulation began. Two prerequisites for applying Dobyns's formula are to determine when the population nadir of a region occurred and what its value was. The population figures contained in the *Handbook of North American Indians* suggest that the Iroquoians reached their nadir around the middle of the eighteenth century (Tooker 1978*b*:421). This would not require a decline to have begun before 1600. A rough estimate indicates that about 8,000 Hurons and Iroquois were alive in the middle of the eighteenth century, including the Iroquois who were living at missions in the St Lawrence Valley. Applying Dobyns's ratio produces an aboriginal population of 160,000. This figure is not of a totally different order from the 110,000 that Norman Clermont (1980) calculated as the total Iroquoian (Ontario Iroquoian, Iroquois, Erie, and Susquehannock) population of northeastern North America around 1600. Since the Five Nations Iroquois later absorbed substantial remnants of the Hurons, Neutrals, Eries, and Susquehannocks, it seems reasonable to regard them, as well as the scattered remnants of the Hurons, as the descendants of all the Iroquoian tribes that lived in that region in early historical times. If all these tribes suffered considerable losses from warfare, the Iroquois, in particular, offset these losses to some degree by incorporating into their society Iroquoian-speaking refugees from farther south, such as the Tuscaroras, and Algonkian female prisoners. One could argue either that these figures are evidence of a relatively modest 30 per cent decline in population prior to 1600 or that a population larger than the one estimated for 1600 is not required to produce the nadir figure. Dobyns has stressed the limitations of his empirical generalization as a means for estimating the prehistoric populations of specific Amerindian groups. He has pointed out the need to consider local variation and to determine the populations of groups individually whenever possible. In his work on the Timucuans of Florida, he himself has taken the lead in doing this (Dobyns 1983). The preceding exercise demonstrates that choices are also involved in deciding what units are being considered in the not uncommon situation where warfare, dispersal, and the incorporation of shattered tribal groupings into stronger surviving ones produced considerable movement and relabelling of populations.

There are few problems relating to the understanding of the protohistoric period that are of greater importance than determining population trends at that time. At present there is no clear proof that the Iroquoian populations of the St Lawrence lowlands were substantially reduced either as a result of European diseases periodically sweeping the whole region or as a result of localized outbreaks of such diseases. On the other hand, substantial population losses cannot be ruled out at this time. What is to be learned about population trends during this period must be elicited from the detailed examination of human skeletal material and settlement patterns. The study of settlements requires the systematic recovery of information about their numbers and distributions, size, and population densities. Above all, more sophisticated chronological controls are needed than have been achieved so far in the study of Iroquoian archaeology.

## THE IMPACT OF EPIDEMICS

According to William McNeill (1976:183–4), in his general study of *Plagues and Peoples*, the great epidemics of the sixteenth century affected the spiritual as well as the material life of the peoples of the New World. He argues that the Indians of Mexico as well as their Spanish conquerors regarded epidemics as manifestations of supernatural power. The nearly total immunity of the Spaniards to diseases that were killing large portions of the native population must have made it seem that the White newcomers enjoyed divine protection. Native deities either supported the Whites or had been rendered powerless by the Christian God. For native people "stunned acquiescence in Spanish superiority was the only possible response" (ibid., 184). Native religious beliefs and the traditional social order that they sanctioned no longer appeared to be valid. In their place came blind obedience to the commands of Spanish officials, entrepreneurs, and tax collectors. The stage was also set for the mass conversions to Christianity that are recorded by European missionaries.

More recently Calvin Martin (1978) has postulated an analogous religious response among the native peoples of North America. In *Keepers of the Game*, he argues that the overexploitation and extinction of fur and game animals after European contact cannot be explained by the growing dependence on European goods. Instead, he suggests that native peoples believed that animal spirits were responsible for the epidemics that began afflicting them, often in advance of actual European contact. This apparent violation of a covenant of mutual respect between humanity and the animal spirits is alleged to have caused the Indians to abandon their former conservation of game animals and to engage in a war of extermination against them. Such a rejection of traditional religious values in turn predisposed native people to accept Christianity as an alternative religious system that offered its adherents protection against epidemics. Martin based his argument on a few enigmatic suggestions of spiritual discord between human beings and animals that had been collected by missionaries among the Micmacs in the seventeenth century and by the surveyor David Thompson and the fur trader Alexander Henry among the Crees and Ojibwas who lived west of Lake Superior about the turn of the nineteenth century. These data are totally insufficient to confirm the theory that has been built on them.

Critics have pointed out that there is no evidence that the Ojibwas, or any other groups that were supposedly caught up in this phenomenon, actually believed that animal spirits would punish violations of taboos by sickness instead of by making game unavailable to hunters. In any case, hunters would blame themselves rather than the animals for contravening the rules governing their relationship (Sturtevant 1981). Moreover, in many areas where beavers were hunted to extinction, traditional beliefs in animal spirits remain strong to the present (Tanner 1979). It is unclear how these beliefs could have survived a major repudiation in the past (Bishop 1981). Often animal spirits did not have an important enough position in the totality of supernatural beings that they would be held accountable for a major transformation of native life (Hudson 1981). A highly specific religious explanation for the widespread overexploitation of game does not take account of the great variation in beliefs about the causes of disease found among native groups in different parts of North America. Martin also fails to consider in detail the sequences in which epidemics, the fur trade, and missionaries reached various areas. Finally, he does not explain why the animals that the Indians sought to destroy were invariably those in demand by the fur trade. Despite these serious inadequacies, the romanticism of his views and the skill with which they were presented have made them attractive to many scholars and the general public. They are of special concern to anthropologists because of what they imply about native American religions. Like McNeill, Martin suggests that these belief systems were not strong enough to cope with the social and psychological disruption brought about by the onslaught of European diseases.

The detailed Jesuit record of how the Hurons coped with the epidemics of 1634 to 1640 provides some of the best documentation of native responses to such a catastrophe that is available for eastern

North America. While the Jesuits did not have the motivation or the knowledge of Huron culture necessary to understand all aspects of what was happening, their observations allow us to trace in some detail the manner in which the Hurons responded physically and psychologically to the illnesses that were assailing them.

As already noted, beavers were reported to be extinct throughout the Huron hunting territories by about 1630. That was well before the epidemics of 1634 to 1640 and possibly before any major epidemics of European origin had reached southern Ontario. On the other hand, if there had been any epidemics in the sixteenth century, the Hurons' revenge on the beavers was slow to materialize. It seems far more likely that as they needed larger numbers of beaver pelts for the fur trade, they found trapping more of these animals to be the cheapest and most direct way to obtain them. In pursuing this short-term strategy to the limit, they knew that when their own beavers had been hunted out, they could continue to obtain pelts either by purchasing the right to trap beavers on neighbouring Algonkian lands or by buying pelts from the Algonkians, Petuns, and Neutrals. The Hurons had been obtaining pelts in increasing numbers from neighbouring tribes throughout the seventeenth century. Such a gradual shift probably made the final extermination of their own beavers of little economic concern to them. Indeed, the purchase of pelts may have encouraged the Hurons to abandon their former policy of conservation. The difficulties involved in policing their hunting territories, most of which lay far to the east and south of their area of settlement, probably made it preferable to hunt these beavers to extermination rather than to let them be poached by neighbouring tribes, especially the Iroquois.

Long before the arrival of the Europeans in North America, the Hurons, like other native peoples, had evolved their own theories of disease and methods for treating illnesses and injuries. The evident antiquity of these practices (Tooker 1960; Chafe 1964) makes it clear that scholars should not succumb to the temptation of believing that in prehistoric times illnesses had not been prevalent or of concern to native peoples. The extraordinary levels of mortality and other misfortunes that followed European contact must have caused them to idealize earlier times as a halcyon age of physical health, economic prosperity, and social harmony, as the New England chief Miantonomi described it in 1642 (Salisbury 1982:13). Yet there is physical anthropological evidence of much chronic illness prior to the sixteenth century (Larocque 1980), and there were probably some outbreaks of indigenous epidemic diseases as well.

The Hurons recognized three major causes of illness: natural ones, the unfulfilled and generally unrecognized desires of a person's soul, and witchcraft. Natural illnesses were ones that could be cured by dieting, sweating, incisions, or herbal remedies. If these treatments did not succeed, the Hurons concluded that the disease was caused either by unfulfilled desires of the soul or by witchcraft. Particular shamans specialized in diagnosing and treating these illnesses. It was believed that diseases caused by desires of the soul could be cured if a shaman could determine the nature of the desire and satisfy it, either by seeing that an appropriate present was given to the sick person or by performing suitable rituals. A.F.C. Wallace (1958), who has analysed this form of treatment in detail, describes it as a sophisticated form of psychotherapy. Illnesses attributed to witchcraft were thought to result from one or more specially prepared charms that someone had caused to enter a person's body. They could be cured if a shaman could discover and extract the charms. The Hurons believed that the principal motivation for witchcraft was jealousy. To avoid arousing it, most Hurons took care to share the proceeds of their hard work and good fortune with their neighbours. Yet an individual could never be certain of not inadvertently arousing jealousy or becoming the victim of someone's irrational hatred. Moreover, people were thought to resort to witchcraft to avenge wrongs and injuries committed by members of other tribes. The source of such disease might therefore be in neighbouring groups, as well as within one's own.

When the Hurons were stricken by epidemics between 1634 and 1640, they attempted to cope with them by traditional means. They assumed, almost from the beginning, that these epidemics were caused by witchcraft, and much effort was directed towards identifying who was responsible and trying to counteract his evil powers. Accusations of witchcraft were levelled against Hurons noted for their lack of generosity and for other forms of antisocial behaviour in the hope this would cause those who were guilty to desist. A few of these individuals were tortured by war chiefs to make them confess, since a confession was believed to destroy the power to practise witchcraft. Other suspected witches were slain in order to halt the epidemic (Thwaites 1896–1901, 13:155–7; 14:37–9; 15:53).

At the same time, curing societies and entire communities performed traditional rituals to repel the illnesses. When these were not successful, shamans began to fast and dream in the hope that supernatural forces would reveal new and more effective rituals to them. Many different rites were performed by stricken communities, which would turn to yet another shaman when the advice

given by his predecessor failed to effect a cure (Thwaites 1896–
1901, 13:227–43). The interest displayed by shamans in monitoring
the effectiveness of their cures indicates that more was involved
in these rituals than the charlatanism ascribed to them by the
Jesuits (ibid., 243). While some of the new rituals may have borrowed elements from Jesuit religious practices (which the Hurons
would have viewed as shamanism), these rituals conformed in their
basic structure and symbolism to native beliefs (Tooker 1964:103
n96). Shamans whose rituals did not work lost personal prestige
as curers, but they were not otherwise penalized by the Hurons.
They were regarded as well-meaning individuals who had tried to
do their best for their countrymen.

The widespread distribution of and high mortality from these
epidemics suggested that some powerful foreign enemy was trying
to injure the entire Huron people. The Nipissings claimed that the
Kichesipirinis were afflicting their neighbours with pestilence
because these tribes had refused to help the Kichesipirinis wage
war against the Iroquois in 1635 (Thwaites 1896–1901, 13:211).
Generally, however, the Hurons believed that the French were
responsible, a view that was encouraged by the Kichesipirinis in
an effort to exculpate themselves and to undermine good relations
between the Hurons and the French. Many Hurons feared that a
sister or uncle of Etienne Brûlé had incited the French to bewitch
them in order to avenge his murder in 1633 (ibid., 14:17). The
Algonkins suggested that before his death in 1635, Champlain had
believed himself bewitched by the Hurons and had ordered the
French to assault them supernaturally in retaliation.

Whatever the motive, it was widely accepted that the Jesuits
were the agents by which the epidemics were being spread. No
other reason could account more plausibly for why the French had
insisted that these priests be allowed to live in the Huron country.
Their celibacy also suggested that they were nurturing great
supernatural power, and their generally sound health and the speed
with which they and their workmen recovered from influenza were
additional proofs that they could control these diseases. While the
Jesuits sought to defeat the Huron shamans by performing religious
rituals that would halt the epidemic of 1636, many Hurons interpreted the failure of the Jesuits' efforts, not as evidence of incom-
petence, but as proof that they were dishonest in their expressions
of friendship for the Hurons.

Indications of the Jesuits' involvement in witchcraft were perceived in many aspects of their behaviour. They were accused of
always talking about death rather than hoping for a sick person's

recovery, as any decent Huron would do (Thwaites 1896–1901, 13:127). Dangerous influences were said to emanate from the paintings and images that they kept in their chapels, as well as from their communion wafers, which were rumoured to be pieces of human flesh that had been brought from France as instruments of sorcery. Their baptismal water and the sugar, food, and drugs that they gave to the sick were thought to be the charms that they were injecting into the bodies of their victims (ibid., 14:51). This fear increased as parental opposition to baptism led the Jesuits to baptize surreptitiously children who were extremely ill. The fact that these children normally died soon after further aroused their fears (ibid., 7–9, 41, 67–9). The Hurons also believed that the Jesuits kept a cloth in their cabin that caused illness, that they bewitched people by stabbing drawings of them with a long needle, and that they caused some to die by tearing their names out of the baptismal register. Rather than being doubted because they contradicted one another, these rumours reinforced the Hurons' conviction that the Jesuits were indeed sorcerers.

As the epidemics became more severe, the Hurons grew more afraid of the Jesuits. They were forbidden to enter many longhouses and even whole villages in the hope that this restriction might deflect their witchcraft. It was said that for a time one Huron settlement stopped using French goods or having anything to do with the French in the hope that this would halt the epidemic (Thwaites 1896–1901, 15:21). On other occasions, presents were offered to persuade them to stop killing Indians. Native fears must have increased when, for various diplomatic reasons, they refused to accept these presents (ibid., 14:101–3; 15:57). Jesuits and their workmen were increasingly harassed and threatened in an effort to compel them to stop practising witchcraft. Huron spirits also were reported to have appeared in visions and warned that all the Hurons would perish if they did not drive the Jesuits from their country (ibid., 20:27–31). On at least two occasions, in 1637 and 1640, general councils met to discuss whether the Jesuits should be slain or at least forced to return to Trois-Rivières.

Yet neither of these things happened. The Hurons had no other source of European goods than from the French and by the 1630s they were convinced that they could no longer do without them (Thwaites 1896–1901, 13:215–17). Because of this, Atironta, in his role as the principal Huron ally of the French, many other chiefs, and the leading Huron traders consistently protected the Jesuits. They warned them when they were in extreme danger and tried to persuade other Hurons, especially the war chiefs who were charged with getting rid of witches, either that it was not clear that the Jesuits were guilty of witchcraft or that their punishment should be delayed until the annual trading was over and the Huron boys studying at Quebec could be brought home.

Each year Achille Bréhaut Delisle, the lieutenant of the governor of New France, lavished presents on the Huron traders who had come to Trois-Rivières to acknowledge the good treatment the Jesuits had received. He also warned them that all trade would be broken off if the Jesuits or their workmen were slain (Thwaites 1896–1901, 12:259). That no Frenchman was murdered as an act of private vengeance by someone whose relatives had died during the epidemics is proof that the vast majority of Hurons felt it necessary, despite apparent provocations, to maintain their trading relations with the French. This in turn is a measure of their increasing dependence on the French. When the Hurons went to trade in 1640, Governor Charles Huault de Montmagny is said to have punished them for acts of violence committed against the Jesuits over the previous winter (ibid., 21:143). Some traders may have been imprisoned for a few days and made to pay fines, or they may have been denied the right to trade until they promised to behave differently in the future. The governor threatened that he would impose more severe penalties if the Jesuits were harmed thereafter. When the Hurons returned home, reparations were offered to the Jesuits to atone for the harassment they had suffered during the smallpox epidemic. Observing the success of this intimidation, which Jérôme Lalemant, the superior of the Huron mission, described as a pious employment of secular power, the Jesuits and the French officials began to feel more confident in bringing still more pressure to bear to direct Huron behaviour.

Yet, if at the end of the epidemics we find a Huron people that for the first time were forced to acknowledge their economic dependence on the French, a similar reliance is not found in the religious sphere. Despite the devastation wrought by a rapid succession of illnesses, the Hurons did not panic. Even at the height of the smallpox epidemic, they remained in their settlements and did what they could to heal the sick and tend the dying. Although many council chiefs had perished, those who had survived continued to guide the affairs of the country and held in check the war chiefs who might have slain the Jesuits as witches. The florescence of ritualism that accompanied the epidemics bears witness to the dynamism and resilience of traditional Huron religious beliefs. The failure of particular rituals to cure the sick did not discredit the Huron religion. Instead, it spurred shamans to communicate more intensively with the spirit world in an effort to discover rituals that would be effective. While many of these were in turn discredited, each epidemic did eventually subside, thereby giving credit to the rituals that were performed at that time and reinforcing the traditional beliefs on which they were based.

Similarly, many Hurons had been baptized in the hope either that it would cure them or that, by making them kinsmen of the French, it would permit them to escape the latter's sorcery altogether. Yet so many of these people died that most Hurons came to associate baptism with sorcery and death. By the time the smallpox epidemic was over, all but the male heads of three or four families, who valued their privileged trading connections with the French, and a few old women, whom the Jesuits appear to have been supporting economically, had publicly renounced any connection with Christianity. The rest had been caught up in the surge of healing cults that had occurred during the winter of 1639–40.

Joseph Chihwatenha, a Huron from Ossossané, who had identified closely with the Jesuits, apparently hoping that he could learn to be as great a sorcerer as they were, was murdered by his fellow villagers in the summer of 1640, although his death was thinly disguised as the work of Seneca raiders. The Hurons obviously loathed him as a sorcerer who had turned against his own people (Thwaites 1896–1901, 19:153; 23:195). The Jesuits believed that a few months earlier Huron shamans had tried to poison Brébeuf, whom they continued to regard as the leader of the missionaries. After he and Chaumonot had spent the following winter among the Neutrals without asking Huron permission, public opinion against him rose to the point that he had to return to Quebec and Trois-Rivières and remain there until 1644. The suggestion that he left the Huron country to receive medical treatment for a broken clavicle (Talbot 1956:241–2) does not make sense. A man with a disabled shoulder would not have abandoned the relative comfort of the Jesuit mission headquarters of Sainte-Marie-among-the-Hurons to undertake an excruciating month-long canoe journey to Quebec. Moreover, it was two years before he disclosed the nature of his injury to a surgeon there. After Brébeuf had returned to the Huron country, he spent his last years working at and near Sainte-Marie rather than in the larger Huron settlements where powerful factions remained hostile to the Jesuits.

It is clear that Huron religious beliefs were sufficiently dynamic to emerge with a sense of victory from the epidemics that during seven years had killed more than half the Huron population as well as that of neighbouring tribes. While the Jesuits appeared to the

Hurons to be dangerous witches, the epidemics had not terrorized them into submission to the European newcomers, as McNeill suggests happened in Mexico. The Hurons may have feared the Jesuits but not to the extent that either their traditional religious beliefs or their morale were broken. Martin clearly underestimated the strength of native American religions to survive major natural catastrophes, just as he seems to have overestimated the capacity of Christianity to offer an attractive alternative during such crises. The possibility must be considered that what held true for the Hurons, who had in their midst during the epidemics missionaries who were actively seeking to undermine their traditional religious system, must apply even more so to native peoples who were not so challenged.

The negative effects of the epidemics were far more serious in the economic and political spheres, and in the conservation of traditional religious knowledge, than they were with respect to religious practices. After the epidemics, the Hurons found themselves living in communities that were half empty. To escape the inconvenience, the disturbing memories, and the unfavourable supernatural connotations of these desolate settlements, they appear to have relocated many of them long before they ordinarily would have done so (Thwaites 1896–1901, 21:159). This imposed a heavy short-term burden on their surviving inhabitants. The Jesuits also noted that many children and old people had died. The loss of the former meant that in the following decade there would be proportionally fewer warriors to defend the Huron country. The sudden demise of so many old people was extremely serious because they included many of the most skilful artisans, both male and female. The Hurons also lost a large number of their most knowledgeable chiefs, including those who had the greatest amount of experience dealing with the French. Traditional religious lore tended to be a prerogative of the elderly, and many must have died before they could transmit what they knew to their heirs. The loss of such a broad spectrum of knowledge must have made the Hurons economically still more reliant on the French and less able at a theological level to resist the attacks of the Jesuits (ibid., 19:127). All of the tribes living throughout the St Lawrence lowlands and to the north had suffered similar losses. Yet at this time only the Hurons were subject to intense European manipulation.

Contrary to what might have been expected, the annual volume of furs supplied to the French did not drop and may even have increased after 1640. Nor was there a decrease in the number of Hurons who came to the St Lawrence to trade each year (Trigger

1976:603–5). Yet there is no evidence that they expanded the total area from which their furs were being collected. As already suggested, only small amounts of European goods had been reaching most of the hunting peoples living in northern Ontario and around the upper Great Lakes prior to this time and any one hunter could have obtained what was available in exchange for only a few pelts. Hence, after the population had declined, little effort was probably required to double or triple the number of skins that each hunter had ready for sale every year and to maintain a constant volume of trade. As a result, many more European goods were accessible to each family than had been previously.

The most arduous burden must have fallen on the Hurons, who had to transport as many or more European goods and furs as before back and forth between the St Lawrence Valley and their own country, as well as to and from their various trading partners, even though their population had been cut in half. A larger percentage of Huron men was evidently engaged in trade after the epidemics than previously. Each Huron also had to work harder to produce the cornmeal, nets, and other manufactured goods that were exchanged with the northern Algonkians for furs. Fewer men therefore were available for war parties, defence, and perhaps for manufacturing goods for their own use, which made them rely more on European tools. In an effort to obtain as many skins as possible, the Hurons appear to have reduced their stocks of surplus corn, which were intended to buffer years of crop failures. This left them more vulnerable when their harvests failed. While the amount of Huron goods on Huron and Neutral sites appears to have been greater than before, for the Hurons this increasing reliance was fraught with danger, both economically and militarily. They probably ran these risks not simply because they wanted more European goods, but because they now saw themselves more dependent than ever on the French and felt obliged to supply them with the accustomed volumes of furs.

## CONVERSIONS AND FACTIONALISM

Prior to 1640 the Jesuits had believed that because the Hurons had no full-time priests or special religious buildings, they held few firm religious beliefs and would be easy to convert. They saw themselves engaged in a battle with Satan himself rather than with the Hurons for the souls of these people. At public meetings the Jesuits tried to instruct them in the basic principles of Christianity. To enhance their reputation as men who possessed extraordinary

supernatural power, they sought to impress the Hurons. To this
end the Jesuits used European technological superiority in terms
of tools and weapons; their ability to predict and therefore apparently to control eclipses and to convey information in written form;
their images and paintings, which the Indians thought to be alive;
and devices such as clocks, magnets, and magnifying glasses. They
also endeavoured to usurp the role of shamans by conducting what
the Hurons viewed as ceremonies to produce rain or cure diseases.
In the long run, these ceremonies were not an unqualified success
and were abandoned.

For a time the Jesuits sought to advance their mission work by
taking a few Huron boys to Quebec where they could instruct them
so that they might later serve as lay preachers. This project was
halted when it became apparent that the Hurons did not pay much
attention to what young men had to say (Thwaites 1896–1901,
16:251). By 1640 the Jesuits had realized that their most stable and
useful converts were older men who played a prominent role in
the fur trade. These men, especially the chiefs, were influential in
Huron society and once they were converted the other members
of their families were likely to seek baptism so that their souls
would be reunited after death (ibid., 15:109; 17:33). The Hurons
believed that the souls of people who died at different stages of
their life or in different ways were separated; hence it was easy for
them to accept the Jesuits' claim that those who had been baptized
went to heaven rather than to the traditional Huron villages of the
dead.

Jérôme Lalemant, who was highly esteemed for his administrative talents, replaced Brébeuf as superior of the Huron mission in
1638. He was charged with preparing for a considerable expansion
of the mission. As part of his program, he insisted upon greater
discipline among the priests and their workmen, the latter having
been accused of laxness in their relations with native women. He
introduced to the mission a new category of lay worker known as
a donné, which had already been experimented with in France.
Donnés were bound by a civil contract to have no personal possessions, to work for the Jesuits without pay, to obey the Jesuit
superior, and to be chaste. In return, the Canadian mission agreed
to provide them with food, clothes, and lodging for the rest of their
lives. In this way, Lalemant hoped to acquire a more disciplined
work force. In 1649 twenty-two donnés worked for the Huron mission compared with only eleven hired men and four boys.

Lalemant's principal innovation was the construction of a permanent mission headquarters where the Jesuits could live and work

View from the Wye River of the modern reconstruction of Sainte-Marie-among-the-Hurons. Courtesy Sainte-Marie-among-the-Hurons.

in stone and timber buildings, much as they did in their colleges in France. The mission of Sainte-Marie-among-the-Hurons was begun in 1639, along the east bank of the Wye River and on land belonging to the Ataronchronons, who were probably an eastern division of the Attignawantans. It grew into a fortified settlement equipped with residences, chapels, and workshops, including a blacksmith's shop. Here Lalemant was able to enforce among the priests a more punctilious and careful observance of daily religious routines than had characterized Brébeuf's fledgling administration. Adjacent to the European compound were a chapel, hospital, residence, and cemetery. In this stockaded area, Christian Indians could remain for some time to perform their religious devotions. There was also a separate area where non-Christians were allowed to come on a daily basis to receive instruction. Adjacent to the settlement, fields were cleared and crops planted. By the late 1640s cattle, pigs, and chickens, all laboriously brought inland from Quebec, were providing the French with some of the more cherished items of a European diet. Sainte-Marie became yet another testimonial to the technological superiority of the French and a powerful symbol of the Jesuits' entrenchment in the heart of the Huron country (Kidd 1949a; Jury and Jury 1954).

From Sainte-Marie, teams of missionaries were sent out to preach in the Huron towns. While making these rounds, they lived with friendly chiefs and later with Christian families. Lalemant had been inspired by accounts of the Jesuit missions in Paraguay to expect that Huron converts might be persuaded to settle at Sainte-Marie and adopt European customs. It soon became apparent, however, that even converts who were prepared to break with their past in other highly significant ways, were too attached to their villages and local clans to leave them and relocate around Sainte-Marie. In 1643 the decision was therefore taken to establish permanent Jesuit residences in the major Huron towns from which the local priests could routinely visit nearby villages. Henceforth, Sainte-Marie served as a mission centre for the neighbouring Ataronchronon villages. The missionaries also visited it for rests and spiritual retreats and assembled there with their followers for special observances at Christmas, Easter, and Pentecost. Most of the missionaries were once again resident in Huron settlements (Thwaites 1896–1901, 27:67; 29:259).

After the epidemics had ceased, the Jesuits adopted a very strict policy concerning baptism. They were anxious to avoid a repetition of what they saw as the apostatizing that had occurred during the smallpox epidemic. As a result of growing familiarity with the Huron language and customs, they also now realized that the Hurons had a complex set of religious beliefs that had to be destroyed or discredited before genuine conversion was possible (Thwaites 1896–1901, 26:213; 30:115). The Jesuits sought to convert married men, especially prominent ones whose opinions were widely respected. To bring about a genuine conversion, the missionaries decided that it was necessary to make such men wish to be baptized, even if initially their motives were not spiritually acceptable. The Jesuits could use this desire to compel potential converts to submit to a long period of instruction and demonstrate their ability to live as Christians. In this manner, they hoped that these Hurons would acquire a working knowledge of Christian doctrines and morality and become accustomed to major changes in their way of life. This probationary period normally lasted for one or two years. At the end of it, those who had stayed the course were sent to Sainte-Marie where they were carefully examined prior to baptism at a major Christian festival (ibid., 23:21–3).

The principal inducements for seeking baptism were economic, political, and military. Christian traders could purchase European goods at Quebec and Trois-Rivières at the same price they were sold to Europeans, which was less than native people were normally charged for these goods. They were also given additional presents by the French traders (Thwaites 1896–1901, 12:257; 16:33). After 1643 the Hurons who came to trade with the French were publicly separated into Christian and non-Christian groups. The Christians were treated with far greater honour by French traders and government officials and assumed the leading role in negotiations with the French. In giving his annual presents to the Hurons, Montmagny began to imply that adherence to Christianity would soon become a prerequisite for continued friendship between Hurons and French traders (ibid., 22:311). There can be no doubt that trading played an important role in encouraging Hurons to seek baptism. In 1648, when less than 15 per cent of the Huron population had been baptized, over half of the 250 traders who came to Trois-Rivières were Christians or were receiving instruction (ibid., 32:179).

After 1641, when the French began to sell guns to the Indians, only those who were baptized were allowed to obtain these weapons. This restrictive policy was adopted in part to protect the Jesuits living in the Huron country from assault by non-Christians. It also provided a strong inducement for young and middle-aged men to request baptism. On military campaigns, warriors sought to learn about Christianity from those who had already been baptized. In 1643 the Jesuits informed the readers of their *Relations* that God had obviously sanctioned the selling of firearms as a way of making Christianity acceptable among the Hurons (Thwaites 1896–1901, 25:27).

Tangible rewards were lavished on converts in the Huron country no less than on those at Trois-Rivières. Blankets were given to elderly Christians and the food that the Jesuits distributed to converts during a famine in 1643 was described as a public testimonial to the close union between French and Huron Christians (Thwaites 1896–1901, 27:65). As they succeeded in converting traders and warriors and then their families and friends, the Jesuits believed that they were starting a process that would lead to the conversion of entire villages and tribes and finally of all the native peoples living in this part of North America. Between 1640 and 1643 they baptized approximately 100 Hurons each year, after which the number increased to about 150 annually. Taking account of those who had died, by 1646 some 500 Hurons were professing to be Christians (Trigger 1976:702). Most of these resided in the larger towns, where the chiefs and traders who had the closest ties with the French lived. Fewer converts were made among the Arendahronons than among the other Huron tribes, probably because the Jesuits began to work there later than elsewhere. It may also be that because they already had a special relationship with the French, most Arendahronons felt less pressured to become Christians. Nevertheless, in 1642, Atironta, the principal Huron ally of the French, was the first of his people to be baptized in good health.

The Jesuits demanded that their converts abandon all of their traditional religious practices, which turned out to be more difficult than the missionaries had imagined. They discovered that Huron religious beliefs permeated every facet of their lives. As among other tribal peoples, religion did not consist of an explicit theology and moral code but was a shared set of beliefs that was often implicit and was expressed in almost every aspect of their daily life. The Jesuits soon observed that it was harder to compel a Huron to remain a Christian than it had been to convert him in the first place (Thwaites 1896–1901, 28:55). Converts were required to destroy their charms, which they had relied on for good luck in every sort of activity, and were forbidden to use dreams as guides to their actions. Because they could no longer consult with shamans about desires of the soul, Christians were deprived of an important means for resolving personal frustrations within the context of a highly conformist society.

Since public feasts and celebrations invariably involved traditional religious rituals, converts were not allowed to participate in them. In effect this meant that they ceased to be an integral part of their community's network of economic reciprocity and redistribution. They were also forbidden to contract ritual friendships with non-Christians and to supply goods that would satisfy the desires of the souls of sick people. To avoid involvement in native rituals, Christian warriors often refused to fight alongside traditionalists or to comply with decisions that were made on the basis of divinations. As a result the effectiveness of Huron resistance to the Iroquois was weakened (Thwaites 1896–1901, 26:175–9). The bodies of Christians could not be reburied at the periodic Feasts of the Dead and in due course separate cemeteries were established where they were buried more or less in conformity with European traditions (ibid., 23:31). Chiefs who converted initially had to give up their public offices, since they would have been obliged to preside over traditional rituals. Later, much to the Jesuits' satisfaction, an agreement was reached whereby Christian chiefs continued to manage public affairs, while an assistant was appointed to take charge of religious matters (ibid., 28:87–9). Despite this important concession by the Huron majority, in their day-to-day life Christians, under Jesuit guidance, became an increasingly isolated minority within their communities. Segregation such as this had never happened before in Huron society.

Most Hurons must have understood the practical motives that were causing a small but prominent minority of their people to embrace Christianity. Yet the refusal of these Christians to participate either in life or after death in the rituals that affirmed the unity of the Huron clans and settlements and that expressed the concern of individuals for one another's welfare would have seemed to their countrymen as something much more serious than a threat to their collective solidarity. According to traditional views, such behaviour was a clear manifestation of witchcraft. The Jesuits themselves had long been regarded as witches. Now a growing number of Hurons were joining them in their nefarious practices. To counteract such accusations, most wealthy converts continued to distribute surplus goods, but in a more informal and clearly nontraditional fashion.

Although the Jesuits encouraged converts to wear rosaries around their necks as a public witness of their faith, until 1645 the Christian minority avoided antagonizing their neighbours by a flamboyant display of their new beliefs and practices. After that time the Christians in at least some of the larger towns, such as Ossossané and Teanaostaiaé, felt numerous and influential enough to abandon such discretion. At the suggestion of the Jesuits, they began to organize public processions, to pray aloud openly, and to carve crosses on trees around their towns. They also asserted their beliefs by reciting stories derived from the Bible in place of Huron myths at public ceremonies and by overtly seeking to baptize Iroquois prisoners before they were slain (Thwaites 1896–1901, 30:53–7). To expiate their sins, Christians would give public feasts at which they would testify to their faith in Christianity and promise henceforth to do nothing contrary to the Jesuits' teaching (ibid., 77–9). They also intensified their efforts to persuade relatives to convert.

The Christian chiefs derived both material and moral support from their close relationship with the French. They had more resources with which to reward their followers than did non-Christian chiefs, and Christians alone had access to guns. Although few in number, the Christians were encouraged to believe that eventually the whole Huron confederacy would be converted and that the traditionalists could not reverse this trend. Hence, they often treated with scorn traditionalists who accused them of witchcraft or who complained about their abandonment of the customs of their forefathers (Thwaites 1896–1901, 26:255; 27:69). While massive epidemics had not subverted the faith of the Hurons in their native religious traditions, their growing economic and technological dependence on the French was causing an increasing number of them to seek baptism in the 1640s.

The Hurons as a whole valued their trade with the French too much to consider killing or even expelling the Jesuits. Yet the majority of Hurons were deeply troubled by the growing success of the Jesuit mission and the threat that it posed to their way of life. Although traditionalists did not feel free to express their hostility towards the Jesuits, they accused Huron converts, both individually and collectively, of witchcraft and threatened them with reprisals for failing to join in rituals to avert crop failures and cure individual illnesses. Wealthy converts also were threatened with death for refusing to participate in major redistributive rituals (Thwaites 1896–1901, 30:19–21). Chiefs who believed that their influence was being undermined by the growing ties between Christian chiefs and the French, leaders of curing societies, and shamans played a leading role in organizing opposition to Christianity. Conversion sometimes resulted in divorce and in the expulsion of Christian men from their wives' or mothers' longhouses. Christians were also ridiculed for being cowards who were afraid of the fires of hell. Especially among children, such taunting led to vigorous exchanges of insults and to fighting. Christian symbols were destroyed and their ceremonies disrupted by violent demonstrations, which led to injuries. Sometimes antagonism became so severe that converts felt obliged to conciliate public opinion (ibid., 26:279–81). In 1645 the Christians in Taenhatentaron offered the chiefs of the town, who were traditionalists, a large bribe not to pressure them to join in customary celebrations. The Jesuits strongly objected to this action because they feared that it would be interpreted as a sign of weakness and might encourage traditionalists elsewhere to demand similar presents (ibid., 29:271).

The traditionalists also sought to undermine the commitment of converts to Christianity by inducing them to ignore or disobey the Jesuits' orders. By means of threats, bribes, and promises that their participation would be concealed from the priests, they were pressured to join in celebrating customary rituals (Thwaites 1896–1901, 26:243–9). Young converts were especially vulnerable to sexual temptations, which traditionalists soon began to exploit to undermine Jesuit control. By 1645 traditionalist chiefs were inciting women to seduce Christian men. The Hurons interpreted the refusal of the staunchest unmarried Christians to engage in sexual activity as further evidence of their involvement in sorcery (ibid., 30:33–9).

Opposition to Christianity also manifested itself on the ideological level. Stories began to circulate that Iouskeha, the god who had refashioned the world for the benefit of mankind, was appearing to people in the forest in the form of a giant holding ears of corn in one hand and fish in the other. He promised that if the Hurons continued to honour him, he would bring them good fortune and they would enjoy a happy life after death in the traditional Huron villages of the dead (Thwaites 1896–1901, 30:27). Another very popular story, which was remembered decades later (ibid., 42:151), claimed that the soul of a Huron woman buried at Sainte-Marie had returned from the dead to warn her countrymen that in the Christian heaven the French tortured the souls of Indians who had become Christians in the same manner that Hurons tortured prisoners of war (ibid., 30:29–31). This story offered a frightening but plausible explanation of why the Jesuits had come to the Huron country and had wanted to baptize them. It also provided a sound reason for resisting conversion. The traditionalists were clearly able to rally their spiritual resources in opposition to the Jesuits. Because of the growing fear of Christianity, many Hurons who had requested baptism decided to postpone it (ibid., 26:301–7).

Nevertheless, Huron society was being increasingly divided between minority Christian and majority traditionalist factions that cut across all of the other community and tribal divisions. By refusing to participate in traditional rituals, Christians were weakening the solidarity of the Hurons and their capacity for effective collective action. The economic and military advantages that Christian chiefs, traders, and warriors derived from their privileged relationship with the French enhanced their prestige in certain respects but also aroused the resentment and hostility of their traditionalist counterparts. The Jesuits' success was thus creating major problems for the Hurons. While the Jesuits may have hoped that the total conversion of the Hurons would reunite the confederacy, it is clear that their own spiritual values led them to place the salvation of individual souls ahead of the collective safety and well-being of the Huron people.

## THE DESTRUCTION OF THE HURONS

At the same time that the growth of a Christian faction was undermining the cohesiveness of the Huron confederacy, the Hurons were having, for the first time at least in the seventeenth century, to face a serious military challenge. The reason for the increasing aggressiveness of the Iroquois after 1640 has been the subject of much debate. It has been suggested that they were waging war to obtain prisoners to replace the population they had lost as a result of the epidemics (Schlesier 1976; Richter 1983). Between 1640 and 1643 the Neutrals also conducted three major military campaigns. They are reported to have destroyed a major Assistaronon settlement and to have carried off over 1,000 prisoners, mainly women and children (Thwaites 1896–1901, 21:195; 27:25–7). They too may have been seeking to recoup population losses. Yet, while the Iroquois successfully incorporated large numbers of prisoners into their society over the next several decades, many of their own warriors were killed in these campaigns. The fact that they incurred many losses and the military strategies that they followed suggest that the search for prisoners was at most a secondary motivation for the conflicts. It is also significant that the Hurons, although culturally very similar to the Neutrals and Iroquois, did not resort to warfare to recover their population losses.

The principal cause of increasing Iroquois and Neutral aggression appears to have been economic. In particular it may have been related to obtaining enough beaver pelts to satisfy their growing demand for European goods. Yet the precise nature of the economic problems that these tribes were facing and of the strategies they used to solve them remains controversial. Until the late 1630s the Iroquois seem to have been able to trap within their own tribal territories all the pelts that they required for trade with the Dutch. In 1634 Bogaert counted 120 beaver skins inside a single Mohawk longhouse and was shown streams where beavers and otters were being taken. It has been suggested, however, that by 1640 the Iroquois had hunted the beaver to extinction, as the Hurons had done about a decade earlier (Hunt 1940:33–5). It is also possible that a widespread wildlife disease, such as tularemia, could have devastated their hunting grounds. Archaeological evidence of a diminished number of beaver bones on late Neutral sites, such as Walker and Hamilton (Fitzgerald 1982a:24), suggests that a similar decline in the beaver supply of that region may have caused the northern Neutrals to disperse the Algonkian-speaking tribes of southeastern Michigan in order to gain control of the rich beaver swamps in the vicinity of Lake St Clair. The large numbers of iron weapons that the Neutrals possessed no doubt gave them an advantage in this warfare, which appears to have resulted in the general abandonment of the area west of Lake Erie by its indigenous population.

Yet it is not until 1671 that a statement can be found to the effect that the Iroquois had "long ago" exhausted the beaver on the south side of Lake Ontario (O'Callaghan and Fernow 1853–87, 9:80). It is therefore possible that in 1640 they still could hunt beaver in New York State but that their demand for European goods had risen to the point where they were driven to seek additional furs outside their tribal territories. C.H. McIlwain (1915:xlii-xlv) and G.T. Hunt (1940:33–5) have argued that after this time they tried to compel the tribes living to the north and west to trade with them rather than with the French. In this way, they would have established themselves as middlemen in a vast network of trade between these northern tribes and the Dutch. There is, however, no evidence that any of the Iroquois tribes sought to do this. Given the logistics of the trading system, they could have usurped the Hurons' role as middlemen to any substantial degree only by settling in large numbers in the Huron country and this they did not do. It also appears that at this time they did not have the experience or entrepreneurial skills required to manage such trade (Boucher 1664:101). The Iroquois were surrounded by tribes that had horticultural economies resembling their own. Hence while they traded luxury goods with these tribes, they did not engage in the routine exchanges of staples that had characterized the relationship between the northern Hurons and the Nipissings already in prehistoric times.

If the Iroquois could not realign traditional trading patterns, they could perhaps achieve their goals by waging war. Warfare between the Iroquois and their neighbours was commonplace and periods of peace with any particular group tended to be short-lived. To be sure, a more enduring peace existed between the Iroquois and the Neutrals, and the Senecas may have obtained some beaver pelts from the Neutrals in exchange for European goods. Most Neutral pelts appear, however, to have been traded to the Petuns and Hurons. Because Neutral trade was directed elsewhere, the Iroquois probably decided to obtain more furs by expanding their hunting territories northward to incorporate the southern perimeter of the Canadian Shield, where beavers were plentiful and of prime quality. This involved expelling or asserting their authority over the hunting peoples who lived there. The Iroquois would also enrich themselves by pillaging furs and European goods from their victims on a larger scale than they had ever done in the past. For the Mohawks and Oneidas this meant attacking the Algonkin tribes in the Ottawa Valley, the Montagnais who lived farther east, and the Abenakis of northern New England. During the 1640s and 1650s Mohawk raiders were to push as far east as Maine and Lac Saint-Jean and as far north as the James Bay watershed. For the western Iroquois tribes the situation was somewhat different. The main fur-rich areas that they sought to exploit were in central Ontario and around the upper Great Lakes. Yet penetrating these regions was dangerous as long as the Hurons were settled astride the main route north. For that reason the Iroquois decided that the Hurons must be dispersed, an activity that would itself yield much booty in the form of furs and European goods.

These operations were made easier as a result of the acquisition of guns by the Iroquois, beginning about 1639. Prior to that time French and Dutch officials had successfully forbidden the sale of guns to the Indians, a measure that both regarded as necessary for the security of their settlements. Around 1639 the Mohawks first purchased guns and ammunition from English traders who were operating in the Connecticut Valley. Fearing that the Mohawks would carry all their furs to the English, the private Dutch traders at Rensselaerswyck defied the law and began selling guns to them. In 1643 the Mohawks owned nearly 300 guns and in 1644 they had enough of them to equip 400 men, while the other Iroquois tribes possessed smaller numbers of them. The Dutch realized that the Iroquois could now more easily raid the tribes living to the north and in this way obtain furs from those groups, which had previously been prevented from trading at Fort Orange by the Mohawks. Dutch officials thus began to condone what had begun as an illicit trade in the hope of acquiring more furs. Guns and ammunition were soon being sold to the Indians by company officials as well as by private traders (Tooker 1963:117–18; Trigger 1976:627–32).

In response, the French began to sell and present guns to their Indian trading partners. Yet, because of Jesuit insistence, it was stipulated that guns be made available only to Indians who had been baptized, thus providing them with another strong inducement to submit to religious instruction. Being shorter and lighter, the guns supplied by the French were inferior to those sold by the Dutch (Thwaites 1896–1901, 32:21). It is agreed that the tribes allied to the French were able to obtain fewer guns than the Iroquois were. In particular, the French were reluctant to supply them to Hurons, whom they did not trust. In 1648 the Hurons probably possessed no more than 120 guns, while the Iroquois had over 500.

Although these guns were clumsy to handle and perhaps not intrinsically superior to the bow and arrow (Given 1981), the thunderous noise they made and their ability to kill by injecting a metal charm into the body, or so the Indians believed, constituted supernatural properties that made them a source of terror to those who did not possess them (F. Jennings 1984:80). They also increased the self-confidence of their owners. In 1633 and 1637 the French had been able to halt Mohawk raids along the St Lawrence River by merely showing the flag. After 1641 the Mohawks were routinely blockading the St Lawrence and robbing Huron and Algonkin traders as they moved to and from Trois-Rivières. In 1643 they separated into smaller bands that stationed themselves at various points along the St Lawrence and Ottawa Rivers. When one band was ready to return home, another one replaced it (Thwaites 1896–1901, 24:273). This system netted a rich harvest of booty.

Throughout the 1640s the Hurons suffered escalating losses as a result of Iroquois attacks, both in their own country and in regions between their home and the St Lawrence. The Mohawks consistently offered to make peace with the French, but except for a short time after a general truce was arranged in 1645 to recover some prisoners, they continued to attack the Indian groups that traded with the French. In the course of these raids, many Huron traders were killed or taken prisoner. Contrary to their former practice, the Mohawks, Oneidas, and some Onondagas began to attack Algonkin and Montagnais family groups after they had dispersed for the winter. Picking them off one by one, the Iroquois were able to seize their furs with little danger to themselves. In addition, they could hunt and trap in these areas. The resulting danger caused many Algonkins to seek refuge on the outskirts of the French settlements. Already, by 1640, Jérôme Lalemant was alarmed by the extent to which Iroquois warriors were marauding throughout the Huron country, killing and capturing women and children who were working in the fields and stealing into Huron houses during the night to rob them. The seizure of furs and European goods appears to have been an important objective of these raids.

In 1642, for the first time, the Iroquois destroyed a small Arendahronon village (Thwaites 1896–1901, 26:175). It is not clear whether it was the Iroquois or the Assistaronons who had devastated the large southern Petun town of Ehwae in the spring of 1640 (Jones 1908:224). The destruction of the Arendahronon village marked the beginning of a policy by which the Iroquois sought to capture one or two settlements at a time, starting along the less densely settled eastern border of the Huron confederacy. By holding out promises of peace, the Iroquois hoped that the Huron tribes would not band together to oppose them, anymore than the Iroquois had come together to combat Champlain's raid in 1615. One may imagine that, as happened in later raids, healthy Huron prisoners were spared and driven south burdened with the furs and other spoils that the victorious Iroquois were carrying off with them. The Iroquois continued to attack Huron hunting and fishing parties, while the Hurons feared further major raids on their settlements. A few Huron families had begun to move north to the Canadian Shield by 1645 in order to escape them (Thwaites 1896–1901, 30:87). By this time also many Hurons were living as captives among the Iroquois. In particular, a large number of Arendahronons were held by the Onondagas.

By 1647 there had developed among the Huron traditionalists who were most strongly opposed to the Jesuits a group that was prepared to terminate the confederacy's trading alliance with the French. In its place they wanted to conclude a lasting peace with the Iroquois that would allow them to obtain their European goods indirectly from the Dutch. These Hurons apparently had come to believe that peace with enemies to whom they were closely aligned in language and culture was preferable to the gradual destruction of their way of life by the Jesuits. They would be able to kill the Jesuits or expel them from their country and thus negate the special influence that the Christian chiefs derived from their association with them. This faction was strongest among the Arendahronons, who hoped that such a peace treaty would lead to the return of tribesmen being held prisoners by the Iroquois. On the other hand, it received relatively little support from the Attignawantans, who remained largely unscathed by warfare (Thwaites 1896–1901, 33:119–21).

Yet, when a leading Onondaga chief named Annenraes was captured, even the Christian Hurons were prepared to release him in the hope of concluding a truce with the Onondagas that would take that tribe at least temporarily out of the war. The Jesuits watched these negotiations with apprehension and wary interest. The embassies that were sent to discuss peace at this time had equal numbers of traditionalists and Christians and were headed by Christian chiefs, even though the Christians constituted only a small fraction of the total Huron population (Thwaites 1896–1901, 33:121, 129). The composition of these delegations indicates both the political importance that was accorded to the split between Christians and traditionalists and the disproportionately important role played by the Christians. The release of Annenraes led to the recall of a very large Iroquois war party that had been on its way to attack the Huron country in the summer of 1647. Fear of this attack had led the Hurons to cancel their annual trip to the St Lawrence. Despite this diplomatic success, the Arendahronons, who lived near Lake Simcoe, decided that their position was no longer tenable and, after the harvest had been gathered, they sought refuge in Taenhatentaron and other Huron villages located farther to the west. Early in 1648 the Huron negotiations with the Onondagas were broken off when a Mohawk war party massacred a Huron embassy on its way to the Onondagas. By this time the Mohawks were diverting their forces from the St Lawrence to join in a final series of attacks on the Huron settlements.

In spite of this, the Hurons who were most violently opposed to the Jesuits and who saw no hope of resisting the Iroquois, decided to take decisive action to convince the Iroquois of their goodwill. In April 1648 six headmen arranged that two Hurons should go to Sainte-Marie and murder the first Frenchman they encountered there. Their victim was a young donné named Jacques Douart. These headmen then publicly demanded that the Jesuits be expelled from the Huron country, together with any Christians who refused to return to traditional Huron ways. The Hurons were thrown into a state of great confusion, and a fierce debate continued for several days at a meeting of the confederacy council. The Jesuits and their followers were accused of destroying the Huron country. The Christian Hurons countered that the chiefs who had planned the murder were being paid by the Iroquois to betray their countrymen to their enemies. It seems likely that the anti-Jesuit faction remained in contact with the Iroquois and that the Senecas and Mohawks were still seeking to divide their victims by encouraging this faction to believe that peace was possible. The majority of traditionalists probably resented the Jesuits as much as this radical faction did, but they feared and mistrusted the Iroquois even more; hence they were unwilling to break off trade with the French. In the end, most of the traditionalists sided with the Christian Hurons in opposing the termination of their alliance with the French. To atone for the murder of Douart, the Jesuits were offered, and accepted, a huge reparations payment by the confederacy (Thwaites 1896–1901, 33:229–49).

The defeat of the anti-Jesuit faction ended organized resistance to the missionaries. The Hurons had been compelled once again to acknowledge publicly their dependence on the French. Overt opposition to the Jesuits declined and many Hurons who had formerly attacked them now listened to their teachings. In an effort to convert whole Huron communities, Paul Ragueneau, who had succeeded Jérôme Lalemant as superior of the Huron mission in 1645, relaxed some of the more stringent requirements for baptism. To this end he also adopted a more tolerant attitude towards a number of traditional practices, which he decided were absurd or unenlightened rather than diabolical and which could be abolished gradually (Thwaites 1896–1901, 33:145–7).

Although the change in the requirements for baptism was rationalized on the grounds that the Jesuits' previous policy had been too severe, its main purpose was to create a new milieu in which Christian conduct could be perfected in an atmosphere from which, as a result of massive conversions, non-Christian norms of conduct had been largely banished. The Jesuits believed that in some of the larger Huron towns they had a large enough number of tested Christians to make this new experiment in mass conversion possible. Because of these more relaxed rules and the deteriorating military situation, by the summer of 1648 about one Huron in five had been baptized and by the following year the figure had risen to one in two (Trigger 1976:739). Yet, instead of being animated by a new faith, many of these converts ceased to try to influence events. Instead, they looked to the Jesuits to use their spiritual and material resources to protect them. The belief that the Jesuits had been responsible for the epidemics also must have left lingering doubts in the minds of many of them. These were reflected in widespread rumours that Montmagny had sent presents to the Mohawks urging them to attack the Huron country rather than the French settlements along the St Lawrence (Thwaites 1896–1901, 35:165–7). Many Hurons who had supported the expulsion of the Jesuits were as prepared to be carried off by the Iroquois as to watch the transformation of their country into a nation of Christians. The Iroquois encouraged this attitude by making it known that they were willing to allow Hurons to join relatives whom they had adopted after capturing them in the past.

Faith in the Jesuits' ability to defend the Hurons was dealt a severe blow in July 1648 when a large Iroquois force attacked and destroyed the two Attigneenongnahac settlements of Teanaostaiaé and Ekhiondastsaan. In the former, which was a mission centre and a strongly fortified town, over 700 Hurons were captured or taken prisoner out of an estimated population of 2,000. During the attack the resident priest Antoine Daniel was slain. Since Isaac Jogues, a Jesuit missionary who had been serving as a French envoy to the Mohawks, and his donné companion Jean de La Lande had already been murdered by the Mohawk faction that favoured war with the French when they had visited the Mohawks in 1646, the death of Father Daniel must have further disillusioned the Hurons about the capacity of the Jesuits living in their midst even to defend themselves. As a result of the dispersal of the Attigneenongnahacs and the general panic that ensued, crop yields were low that autumn. A famine broke out the following winter.

In spite of this, Huron self-confidence continued to decline and growing numbers of them were baptized. Late in 1648 the Christians became a majority in Ossossané. A council was held at which the Christians, instigated by the Jesuits, demanded that the priest who had charge of the mission be recognized as the principal headman of the community and be empowered to reform its ritual and moral life. He was also to be given the right to forbid any practices that contravened Roman Catholic teaching. These demands violated Huron custom. Traditionally decisions were arrived at by means of consensus rather than majority support and no one was bound by a public decision contrary to his or her own will. The Jesuits next sought to use the local council to deny approval for all traditional rituals, including curing ceremonies. When traditionalists came from nearby towns to help perform such ceremonies, the Christians forced them to leave. Thus the traditionalists who lived in Ossossané were given the choice of obeying regulations dictated by the Jesuits or moving elsewhere. By means of these innovations, for the first time a Huron council was trying to impose its will upon an entire community. Although the absence of any concept of obedience in the political sphere made this exercise difficult, Hurons were introduced to the new and more hierarchical society that the Jesuits were seeking to implant in their midst. In Ossossané, the Jesuits, with the compliance of a small majority of Christian followers, were trying to remodel a tribal society and its government along the lines of a European state.

The Jesuits also sought to alter personal behaviour. A Christian woman who lived in Ossossané is reported to have beaten her four-year-old son, a form of behaviour hitherto not reported among the Hurons and one that they would have regarded as disgusting and inhumane. The Jesuits, who believed that the Hurons had to acquire a new sense of discipline in order to be good Christians, heartily approved of her action (Thwaites 1896–1901, 33:177–9).

On 16 March 1649 the Jesuit experiment was brought to an abrupt halt. Without warning, a large Iroquois army entered the town of Taenhatentaron and killed or captured all but 10 of the 400 people who lived there. Taenhatentaron became the base camp from which the Iroquois destroyed neighbouring hamlets in the Sturgeon Valley, as well as the village of St Louis in the Hog Valley, several miles farther west. The missionary Brébeuf and Gabriel Lalemant, a nephew of Jérôme who had arrived in the Huron country the previous year, were taken prisoner and led back to Taenhatentaron

The martyrdom of Brébeuf and Lalemant from *Novae Franciae Accurata Delineatio*. This engraving is probably the earliest known on this theme.

where they were tortured to death. Hurons who had been captured by the Iroquois in recent years and adopted by them played a leading role in killing these priests, whom they regarded as sorcerers responsible for the destruction of their people. Their hatred of Brébeuf was made especially clear in their taunting and abuse of him (Thwaites 1896–1901, 34:27–9, 145). The Iroquois also planned to attack Sainte-Marie but were opposed by a party of 150 Huron warriors, mainly Christians from Ossossané. Although the Iroquois eventually killed all but a handful of this force, their own losses in this engagement were heavy. As a result, they decided to return home with their prisoners and booty.

In the course of this campaign 700 Hurons had been lost, and their remaining settlements had been thrown into another state of panic. The country was already starving, and it seemed clear that the Iroquois would not give the Hurons an opportunity to grow crops that year. The Jesuits had been erecting stone bastions and walls at Sainte-Marie to replace its timber palisades, and extra French soldiers had been sent from the St Lawrence the previous summer to help defend the settlement. The Jesuits had also gathered a good harvest the previous year (Thwaites 1896–1901, 33:259). Yet, despite their impressive resources, they had failed to provide any military support for the Hurons. Because of this, the Hurons became convinced that their position was no longer tenable. Within two weeks, they deserted all of their remaining settlements, which they burned to prevent them from being used by Iroquois raiders.

Most communities split into local clans or even households, which scattered to seek refuge elsewhere. Many Hurons joined their Algonkian, Petun, or Neutral trading partners. Others looked for secluded places where they might live off the land until they could re-establish a viable horticultural economy. Only the Tahontaenrats, who inhabited Scanonaenrat and who had been the last group to join the confederacy, stayed together as a tribe. They moved south to settle among the Neutrals.

Over the next few years a large number of Hurons voluntarily joined the Iroquois. Former Hurons, who had been taken prisoner and adopted by the Iroquois and who accompanied their military expeditions, attempted to rescue as many of their relatives and friends as possible. While some of these Hurons were badly treated and even killed by the Iroquois, most of them made a new life for themselves in the Iroquois country. Extended family households were allowed to join Iroquois villages, and individual Hurons who were adopted into local families eventually were treated as if they had been born Iroquois. The descendants of these Hurons became fully integrated members of the tribes into which they had been adopted, although memories of the origins of at least some of them persisted. For example, the celebrated Mohawk war chief Joseph Brant is reputed to have been descended from Huron prisoners through both his parents (Graymont 1979:416). Given the hard choices that faced the Hurons in the late 1640s, joining the Iroquois was far from the worst solution to their problems, especially for the traditionalists.

Many Hurons who remained in the vicinity of the Huron country continued to look to the Jesuits for support and protection. Yet it was obvious to the Jesuits that Sainte-Marie was no longer an effective mission centre or even a safe place for them to live. They feared that with no Huron villages to plunder, it would be the next target of an Iroquois attack. Even if they were unable to capture the settlement, the Iroquois could besiege it until the French were forced to surrender. After long discussions with Huron chiefs, the Jesuits decided to move to Gahoendoe (now Christian Island) off the west coast of the Penetanguishene Peninsula. There they built a stone fort for themselves to inhabit. They also erected a European-style palisade strengthened with bastions around the native village that was established nearby and helped the Huron refugees to clear land so they might plant crops. The population of the village grew as more Huron groups learned of its existence and made their way there. Eventually it contained over 100 cabins. The Hurons who came to Gahoendoe either were already Christians or agreed to baptism in the hope that their conversion would encourage the Jesuits to care for them.

Prospects for providing for the community, however, were not good. The Hurons had already been suffering from famine in the winter of 1648–9 and no crops had been planted prior to their dispersal. The cleared land on Gahoendoe was inadequate to support the population of the island, and because the crops were planted late, the harvest was extremely poor. The Jesuits had been distributing food to Huron refugees since 1647 and lacked a sufficient surplus to care for more than a small part of the population on the island. This food was distributed daily to those individuals and families whom the priests judged to be most worthy and in need of it. The Jesuits viewed these inadequate supplies less as a means of keeping the Hurons alive than of preparing them for heaven (Thwaites 1896–1901, 35:97, 105). They also regarded the resulting displays of piety as evidence that God, by afflicting the Hurons, had softened their hearts so that large numbers of them might die as true Christians (ibid., 91, 97). The Jesuits and their French workmen did not lack food for themselves. The priests answered their own consciences by viewing their efforts to keep fit as essential so that they could tend to the needs of the dying (ibid., 97).

During the winter of 1649–50 many Hurons perished from hunger and contagious diseases. Some were driven to eating the bodies of the dead. Despite the ritual cannibalism associated with prisoner sacrifice, they regarded eating their own people with even more loathing than the French did. Their sufferings were compounded by a lack of clothing, since many of them had sold their furs either to the French soldiers who had spent the previous winter in the Huron country or to a special force of thirty-four men who had been sent there in June 1649, ostensibly to help resist the Iroquois (Thwaites 1896–1901, 34:53). The situation was worsened by the steady arrival of more bands of Huron refugees who had fled north that summer but who now came to Gahoendoe, hoping that the Jesuits could feed them.

In March, as the snow melted, bands of Hurons began returning to the mainland in search of any available food. They were killed or captured by a large Iroquois force that had been sent to make sure that they did not resettle in their own country. Hurons who had already joined the Iroquois secretly made their way to Gahoendoe to counsel relatives to follow them. Early in June, realizing that their position was once again untenable, the Jesuits abandoned

Gahoendoe and led about 300 Hurons who were judged to be devout Christians to Quebec. An equal number decided to remain on Gahoendoe until the crops ripened. They lived securely in the French fort until the spring of 1651, when they too left for Quebec. Meanwhile the Jesuits, at considerable expense to their order, had established a fortified mission for these Hurons on the Ile d'Orléans.

In order to deprive the Hurons of a base around which they might regroup, the Iroquois decided to disperse the Petuns, who were suffering from hunger as a result of the influx of a large number of Huron refugees. In December 1649 they plundered and burned Etharita, the more southerly of the two large Petun settlements. The following spring the Petuns abandoned their tribal lands and, accompanied by some of the Huron refugees who had joined them the previous year, retreated to the vicinity of Lake Michigan and eventually as far west as Chequemegon Bay, near the west end of Lake Superior. Only about 500 people survived this migration.

During the winter of 1649–50 the Iroquois began to raid and hunt in central and adjacent parts of northern Ontario. The Nipissings were among the first groups to be attacked, but small bands of Iroquois roamed the shores of Georgian Bay into the following summer, looting and killing Hurons and Algonkians alike. As a result, most of the hunting bands in this region fled west, as the Petuns had done. Henceforth central Ontario was the most important hunting territory from which the Iroquois obtained the beaver skins that they traded to the Dutch (see map by Abbé Claude Bernou). The speed with which the Iroquois attacked and dispersed the hunting bands that lived in this area, without trying to negotiate with them, is further evidence that they sought to prey upon these groups and expand their hunting territories rather than to usurp the Hurons' role as middlemen.

The Iroquois' next victims were the Neutrals. The Neutrals possessed no guns and the Huron refugees who had joined them had little or no ammunition for the few they had. Since the Neutrals had considerable supplies of furs and appear to have long traded with the Senecas, the attack on them provides striking additional evidence that at this time the Iroquois were not interested in obtaining furs by means of trade, as the Hurons had done. The Senecas probably coveted the Neutrals' hunting territories around Lake St Clair and also saw their dispersal as opening up a second route, through Michigan, along which their warriors might raid and hunt in the upper Great Lakes region. The three western Iroquois tribes had already attacked and plundered the Neutral tribe

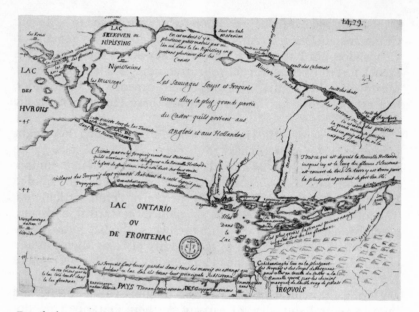

Detail of anonymous map of southeastern Ontario, probably by Claude Bernou, c. 1680. Some of the inscriptions indicate trade relations between the Ottawas and the Iroquois. Courtesy Public Archives of Canada.

that is reported to have been located closest to them during the lull in their fighting with the Hurons in 1647. The excuse that they had given was that these Neutrals had failed to stop Hurons from killing an Iroquois warrior who was crossing their territory (Thwaites 1896–1901, 33:81–3). Their real objective was probably to secure booty in the form of furs and trade goods after they had been compelled to cancel their planned attack against the Hurons that year.

The Iroquois launched their second attack against the Neutrals in the spring of 1650 and the following winter destroyed the town of Teotongniaton. In the course of this campaign many Neutrals were taken prisoner (Thwaites 1896–1901, 36:141–3). The inhabitants of the remaining settlements decided that they were unable to resist the Iroquois and abandoned their homes and clearings. Many fled south and west, but those who survived soon lost their identity so that the Neutrals disappear entirely from the pages of history. Although the Tahontaenrats had won a significant victory over an Iroquois raiding party, at the end of the war these Hurons asked to join the Senecas. The Senecas, who by this time were interested in establishing better relations with the French, welcomed this move and allowed the Tahontaenrats to build a town on Seneca territory where they could retain their own language and customs. Hereafter the two groups lived side by side in peace. Over several generations the Tahontaenrats became indistinguishable from their hosts.

The final Iroquoian group to be dispersed by the Iroquois was the Eries. They too were attacked to eliminate the danger of a Huron revival and to prevent them from opposing the Iroquois, which was being encouraged by Huron refugees. In the summer of 1654 the western Iroquois tribes sent an estimated 1,500 warriors against the Eries and destroyed several important settlements. The war continued on a smaller scale until 1657, with Iroquois war parties capturing many prisoners and much booty. A large number of Eries moved south and established themselves near Chesapeake Bay, possibly under the protection of the Susquehannocks, with whom they had traded (see Bernou map reproduced in Trigger 1976:798). They remained there until about 1680, when some 600 members of this group surrendered to the Iroquois (Thwaites 1896–1901, 62:71). With the Eries dispersed, the Senecas were able to raid and hunt in the Ohio Valley, where they encountered native groups that had no knowledge of European goods (ibid., 44:49).

In 1651 the Dutch encouraged the Mohawks to attack the Susquehannocks. They hoped that if the latter were dispersed, it would cripple the rival trading colony of New Sweden, located on the Delaware River. While some of the Susquehannocks or their allies were overwhelmed, their principal town was well armed by the Swedes and the Mohawks were repelled with heavy losses (Thwaites 1896–1901, 37:97, 111). It was not until after the Dutch had seized New Sweden in 1655 that they were able to persuade the Susquehannocks to make peace with the Mohawks.

## IROQUOIS SUPREMACY

By the early 1650s the Iroquois had dispersed their most populous neighbours and could exploit the lands to the north and west of their tribal territories with relative impunity. They had also shattered the trading network on which New France depended for its economic prosperity, creating despair throughout the colony. Yet military success produced its own problems for the Iroquois. Individuals and groups from many tribes were brought as prisoners to their villages; others joined them of their own volition. Some male prisoners were tortured to death to avenge Iroquois warriors who had been slain but women and children normally were allowed to live. Many Iroquoian men were spared as well because they possessed skills that were prized in a society that was suffering heavy losses as a result of epidemics and warfare. Like other Iroquoian peoples, the Iroquois were adept at using a combination of threats and rewards to make even adult prisoners identify with their adoptive kinsmen. At first such identification was feigned, being motivated by terror, but later it often became genuine. Yet, the capture of so many prisoners and the presence of large numbers of people from the same foreign groups in Iroquois villages inhibited their assimilation. That in turn posed grave problems for Iroquois security (Thwaites 1896–1901, 49:233–5), and compelled the Iroquois to resort to more brutal and repressive measures to keep these prisoners under control. Because men were away from their communities for much longer periods than in the past, hunting and raiding, an increasing responsibility for supervising prisoners and managing village life must have fallen on Iroquois women.

For those who survived the first years of captivity, life appears to have become increasingly congenial and the process of assimilation occurred. One of the Onondaga chiefs who negotiated with the French at Quebec in 1655 was a Huron who had been adopted into an Iroquois lineage and then had been elected to fill a vacant office (Thwaites 1896–1901, 42:57). Iroquois men are claimed to have preferred marrying captive women because these marriages did not oblige them to work for their wives' families. They are also said to have loved these women (Adams 1961:26). In later years a leading Onondaga chief was reported to have been treated severely by two former prisoners that he had adopted to replace his sisters (Thwaites 1896–1901, 62:61–3).

The other penalty of success was increasing factionalism, both within and among the Iroquois tribes. Normally there were significant divisions concerning foreign policy within Iroquoian tribes. Among the Mohawks well-defined factions for and against peace with the French already existed by the mid-1640s. The peace party was associated with the moiety made up of the tortoise and the wolf clans, while the war party embraced the moiety of the bear clan (Thwaites 1896–1901, 8:300; 31:117). From at least the mid-1650s similar pro-French and anti-French factions existed among the Onondagas and the other Iroquois tribes. Bacqueville de La Potherie (1911–12, 2:44) later observed that when it came to foreign affairs, Iroquoian peoples generally developed two opposing factions, especially when they were afraid of their enemies. He noted that instead of weakening them, these alternative positions allowed them to escape humiliating defeats, since the opposing faction could take charge of foreign relations whenever the policies of the prevailing side encountered serious difficulties. This factionalism also made it possible for some leading chiefs to continue informal negotiations with the enemy even in wartime.

After 1650, factional strife among the Iroquois tribes in particular embroiled the three major tribes that made up the "elder brother" moiety of the league (Fenton 1978:310–11). The Senecas, who were the most populous, and the Onondagas, whose principal chief enjoyed ritual precedence in conducting the official business of the confederacy, became increasingly annoyed because of the arrogant conduct of the Mohawk chiefs. The Mohawks possessed more guns than the other tribes did and controlled the routes along which the four western tribes had to travel to trade with the Dutch at Fort Orange. They did not attempt to interfere with this trade, although they denied all non-Iroquois tribes permission to cross their territory and deal with the Dutch. Nevertheless, they regarded the conduct of official negotiations with both the Dutch and the French as their prerogative, since they were the easternmost Iroquois nation. In 1646, when Jogues indicated that the French intended to visit the Onondagas by way of the St Lawrence River and Lake Ontario, the Mohawks informed him that if the French wished to remain on good terms, they would have to continue to conduct their dealings with the other Iroquois tribes through them (Thwaites 1896–1901, 29:57). The Mohawks clearly derived political advantages from their role as intermediaries between the Europeans and the other Iroquois tribes and feared that this position would be lost if the Onondagas established a separate trading alliance with the French. In spite of this, Jogues pursued his efforts to establish direct contact with the Onondagas.

The Mohawks had played an important part in helping the Onondagas, Cayugas, and Senecas to disperse the Hurons. Although they had obtained booty and prisoners, it was the latter tribes that gained in the long run by acquiring new hunting territories. Once the Hurons and Petuns had been dispersed, the Mohawks called on their allies to reciprocate by helping them to attack the French and the Susquehannocks. Their aim was not to drive the French from the St Lawrence Valley but rather to compel them, as they had already forced the Dutch, to stop providing military support to their Algonkian-speaking trading partners. As they had tried to do many times before, the Mohawks sought to persuade the French to remain in their settlements and trade with whatever Indian groups could come to them. That would allow the Mohawks to plunder Algonkin and Montagnais traders and would give them an unhindered crossing of the St Lawrence Valley to rob the campsites of these tribes

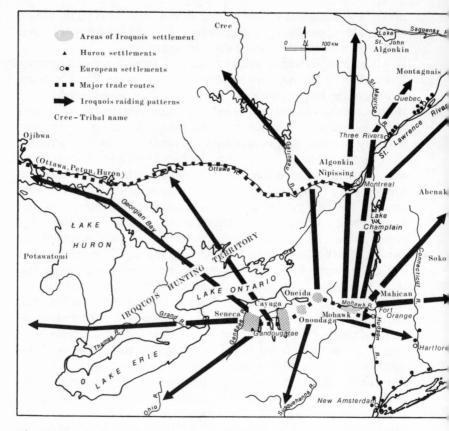

The St Lawrence lowlands, c. 1660.

and trap beavers in the interior of Quebec. This strategy accounts for J.A. Dickinson's (1982) observation that the Iroquois killed only a small number of Frenchmen on their raids against the St Lawrence Valley. Their tactics suggest, however, that at least some Mohawks would have liked to harass the French at Montreal and Trois-Rivières to the point where they withdrew to Quebec, leaving the St Lawrence Valley west of there under Iroquois domination. In August 1653 the Mohawks besieged Trois-Rivières after having failed to overrun it with a surprise attack (Thwaites 1896–1901, 40:97–117).

The Senecas and Onondagas were not prepared to repay their debts to the Mohawks at this time. They were preoccupied with their projected wars against the Neutrals and Eries. They also wished to become less dependent economically on the Mohawks and to curb the growing arrogance of the Mohawk chiefs. In the spring of 1653, no doubt advised and assisted by former Huron chiefs, they began to negotiate a treaty that would allow them to trade with the French. The Onondagas as well hoped to persuade the French to settle in their midst as they had formerly done among the Hurons. French traders could help to defend their towns against enemy attack and a French blacksmith could repair their guns. In addition to making them less dependent on the Mohawks, such an alliance would strengthen them for their projected war against the Eries. The Mohawks were appalled by these negotiations, which threatened to split the confederacy and align most of its member tribes with the French. To prevent this from happening, they decided to conclude at least a temporary peace with the French themselves. All the Iroquois tribes shared another reason for wanting to make peace with the French. An English blockade of the Netherlands had caused the prices of European goods to rise sharply at Fort Orange (Delâge 1981:219). Their usual response to such increases was to threaten a rapprochement with the French.

Probably to their surprise, for the first time the Mohawks and the other Iroquois tribes were able to dictate peace on their own terms. The French knew that the Mohawks would not stop raiding the Algonkins and Montagnais, but the position of the colony had become so precarious, militarily as well as economically, that Governor Jean de Lauson did not require that this peace embrace any of his Indian allies. By concluding their hostilities with the Iroquois on an entirely bilateral basis, the French lapsed into a state of de facto neutrality that left their Indian trading partners and the Huron refugees who had come to the St Lawrence Valley to defend themselves. Thus in 1653 the Mohawks achieved the kind of peace they had long wanted with the French. Dickinson (1982:46) suggests that the main reason the Iroquois concluded this peace was to be free to destroy the tribes that traded with the French so that the French would be forced to trade with them. There is no indication, however, that the Mohawks were primarily interested in trading with the French or that they wished to destroy totally the Algonkins and Montagnais. Their principal objective was to obtain furs that they would continue to trade mainly with the Dutch.

In spite of this peace, the rift between the Mohawks and the other Iroquois tribes continued. The Mohawks were determined to restore their former position within the confederacy by terminating the alliances that had been established between the other Iroquois tribes and the French. A group of Mohawks appears to have murdered three Seneca chiefs who had visited Quebec over the winter of 1655–6 to reaffirm their alliance with the French, and this incident seems to have led to a brief armed confrontation between the two tribes (Thwaites 1896–1901, 43:99–103; 44:149–51). More productively, the Mohawks began to cultivate anti-French sentiment as well as the growing jealousy that was being felt towards the pro-French faction among the Onondagas.

Through the early and middle 1650s, the Iroquois attacked the relatively small number of Huron refugees living in the St Lawrence Valley with great persistence and ferocity. They do not appear to have done this because traditional animosities or "a spirit of vengeance completely incomprehensible to Europeans that was engrained in the Amerindian psyche" made them want to exterminate their enemies (Dickinson 1981:171). On the contrary, Hurons who were captured by the Iroquois were often very well treated by them. Instead, they had two very practical goals. If they could kill the Hurons who were with the French or, better still, have them join them, the thousands of Hurons who were already living among the Iroquois would no longer be tempted to try to rejoin kinsmen living elsewhere. By removing the Hurons from the St Lawrence Valley, the Mohawks would also deprive the French of the assistance of men who were skilled in guerilla warfare and who could thus help the French greatly in any future wars.

Even before the Iroquois had made peace with the French, they began to contact the Hurons at Quebec and to employ a mixture of threats and promises to persuade the Hurons to join them. The Mohawks, Onondagas, and to some degree the Oneidas became locked in bitter competition to gain control of these people. The Hurons who had come to Quebec were totally opposed to joining the Iroquois but dared not formally reject their offers because they knew that the French were unwilling or unable to protect them. Their military position was also weak because the French were apparently not supplying them with guns and ammunition (Thwaites 1896–1901, 44:103–5), either because they believed the Hurons would take these guns with them if they joined the Iroquois or because they feared that the Iroquois would regard it as a breach of the peace if the Hurons used French weapons to attack them. The Hurons' worst fears were confirmed in May 1656 when the Mohawks, tiring of their refusal to leave the Ile d'Orléans, attacked their settlement on the island and killed or carried off about seventy Hurons. Neither at Quebec nor at Trois-Rivières did the French do anything to try to rescue these prisoners. Two of the leading Huron chiefs were tortured to death, but most of the rest were allowed to live (ibid., 43:105–25).

The Jesuits were anxious to establish missions among the Iroquois that could minister to Huron captives and evangelize the Iroquois. They also saw these missions as a way of strengthening the peace between the French and the Iroquois and thus helping to ensure the survival of New France. They therefore proposed that the Hurons join the Iroquois if they could be accompanied by French priests who would continue to live as missionaries among the Iroquois. Under combined pressure from the Iroquois and the French, about 400 Hurons left Quebec in 1656 and 1657, although a small group, including many Attigneenongnahacs, managed to avoid doing so. The Attignawantans chose to go with the Mohawks rather than the western Iroquois tribes, who were their traditional enemies. Most of the Arendahronons preferred to join the Onondagas, among whom many of their fellow tribesmen already lived. In 1657 all but one of the male Arendahronons were slaughtered in cold blood by their Onondaga escort as they were travelling up the St Lawrence, though they were accompanied by Father Ragueneau and a party of French workmen. Ragueneau ordered his workmen, who were outnumbered, not to interfere and they proceeded to join the Onondaga mission (Thwaites 1896–1901, 44:73–7). This massacre apparently avenged the treacherous murder of a group of Onondaga warriors by some of these Hurons while the two groups were parlaying on Gahoendoe in the winter of 1650–1. None of the Hurons alive at that time, whether they lived at Quebec, among the Iroquois, or around the upper Great Lakes, ever forgave this act of treachery by which the French had abandoned so many of their people to the mercy of the Iroquois (Perrot 1911:158, 193).

In 1656 the Jesuits had established the settlement of Sainte-Marie-de-Ganentaa among the Onondagas. It was inhabited by seven priests and about fifty French workmen and was intended as a centre for missionary work among the various Iroquois tribes. By this time, however, many Onondagas were angry because not all of the Quebec Hurons had come to live with them. The Mohawk chiefs were determined that the Onondagas should not have a French colony in their midst; they planned to destroy it as soon as they had won sufficient support for such action among those Onondagas who either feared the Jesuits because of what they had been told about the missionaries' behaviour in the Huron country or suspected them of encouraging Huron prisoners to resist their Iroquois captors.

The Iroquois were also drawn together by the realization that the French were forging a new economic alliance with the tribes of the upper Great Lakes. In 1654, 120 traders came down the Ottawa River seeking to exchange beaver skins for guns, ammunition, and other European goods. Although they were led by a few Hurons, most of these traders were Ottawas, who were visiting the St Lawrence Valley for the first time. Médard Chouart Des Groseilliers and another Frenchman went with them on their return to the interior. Two years later they came back to the St Lawrence accompanied by 250 Indians, mostly Ottawas, and a rich cargo of furs. It has been stated that because the Ottawas were only collectors of furs, rather than horticulturalists adding their own produce to the trading cycle, they were only partially satisfactory as substitutes for the Hurons (Morton 1963:48). Yet, for several decades they were to dominate the trade with the tribes of the upper Great Lakes as the Hurons had done previously. This renewal of trade not only revived the economy of New France but also supplied the Ottawas, Petuns, and Hurons who lived around the upper Great Lakes with arms that made it more difficult for the Senecas and Onondagas to raid and collect furs in that area. These developments made it economically desirable and militarily essential for the Iroquois to attack the Indian fur traders who were using the Ottawa River, even when they were accompanied by Frenchmen. The economic survival of New France contrariwise depended upon the French keeping this trade route open.

In the autumn of 1657, after the French had learned about the murder of the Arendahronons who had agreed to join the Onondagas, Louis d'Ailleboust de Coulonge, who had meanwhile succeeded Lauson as governor, decided to abandon the French policy of appeasement. He declared that hereafter the French must support their Indian allies and prevent the Iroquois from harassing them within sight of French settlements (Thwaites 1896–1901, 44:191–

3). The following August, the new governor, Pierre de Voyer d'Argenson, distributed guns and ammunition to the Algonkins and Montagnais and encouraged them to attack the Iroquois, even before it was clear that the French and Iroquois were again at war. The Iroquois were drawn together by this resistance, and by 1600 the Onondagas were once again fighting alongside the Mohawks and Oneidas.

## THE SAVIOUR OF NEW FRANCE

The most celebrated single incident of this new outbreak of fighting and of the entire Heroic Age was the battle of the Long Sault. In the nineteenth century the historians Jean-Baptiste Ferland and Etienne-Michel Faillon used material contained in the recently rediscovered manuscript of François Dollier de Casson's *Histoire du Montréal* to interpret this encounter as "the most heroic feat of arms in modern times" and as an act of self-sacrifice motivated entirely by religious and patriotic considerations.

According to them, the Iroquois had assembled a great army in the spring of 1660 that intended to destroy all the French people living in Canada. Learning of the approach of this army, Adam Dollard Des Ormeaux, a soldier recently arrived from France, and seventeen companions swore to fight to the death to oppose their advance. Heading north, they encountered at the Long Sault Rapids of the Ottawa River, an advance party of Iroquois who were circling north of Montreal Island. There, deserted by all but a handful of the forty Huron warriors who had accompanied them, they battled the combined forces of the Iroquois from an abandoned Indian fort until their ammunition gave out. Although they were finally overwhelmed, they inflicted such heavy losses on the Iroquois forces that the Iroquois abandoned all hope of seriously injuring the French and returned home. In due course Dollard, as the "Saviour of New France," became the focus of a secular cult that was promoted by Lionel Groulx and other nationalistic historians (Chevalier 1979). As had also happened with Champlain and the Jesuit martyrs, admiration of Dollard's exploits was transmitted to English Canadians by Francis Parkman and widely diffused by the many writers of popular histories who drew inspiration from him.

During the last fifty years, professional historians have detected serious errors in the traditional interpretation of Dollard's actions (Adair 1932; Vachon 1966). From contemporary accounts, it is clear that the Indians did not intend to destroy New France but, as they had done previously, were seeking to capture French and Indians alike in the hope of weakening the French and forcing them to resume their neutrality. It is also evident that neither Dollard nor the Hurons were aware that the Iroquois invasion force was nearby. They did know that each winter the Iroquois raided and hunted for furs in the Ottawa Valley and north of the St Lawrence River. Hence Dollard's force visited the Long Sault hoping to attack and despoil small parties of Iroquois returning from the north heavily laden with furs. They also expected to meet and do business with a large flotilla of Ottawas who were believed to be coming to Montreal to trade that summer. Dollard was unpleasantly surprised when he encountered several hundred Onondaga hunters travelling as a single group from the north. These Onondagas had promised to rendezvous with a large force of Mohawk and Oneida warriors near the mouth of the Richelieu River and help them to attack the French.

The Onondagas laid siege to the French fort and called for the assistance of their Mohawk and Oneida allies, who arrived about a week later. By this time the French and the Hurons were greatly weakened by exposure to bad weather, lack of sleep, hunger, and thirst. Annaotaha, the Huron chief, who was far more experienced in dealing with the Iroquois than Dollard was, proposed that they negotiate with them, using as an intermediary an Oneida who had been adopted by the Hurons. In the course of the talks, some Hurons who had been adopted by the Iroquois persuaded most of the Hurons who had been fighting with Dollard to desert to the Iroquois, promising them good treatment. Alarmed by this turn of events, the French opened fire and the battle resumed.

When the Iroquois penetrated the fort, they found only five French and four Hurons alive. One of the French was immediately tortured to death but the victorious Iroquois decided to return home with the rest of the prisoners. According to Dutch records, fourteen Iroquois had been killed and nineteen wounded in this battle; hence they did not abandon this campaign because of extremely heavy losses. The French prisoners were divided among the three victorious Iroquois tribes and all of them were killed. Although formally treated as prisoners, all of the Hurons were allowed to live. Three escaped and returned to Quebec, but as far as is known the rest remained among the Iroquois. Their separation from their families at Quebec was no doubt partially compensated for by renewed contacts with friends and relatives whom they had not seen for more than a decade.

While historians have generally viewed the Hurons' abandonment of Dollard as a cowardly act, the repeated failure of the French to support the Hurons during the previous decade put the latter under no obligation to die for the French. Moreover, Annaotaha, who did fight to the death alongside the French, is reported to have observed that because the French broke off the negotiations, the only chance for them and the Hurons to extricate themselves from an otherwise hopeless situation had been destroyed (Dickinson 1981). Yet so powerful remains the popular image of Dollard that even a historian such as W.L. Morton (1963:52), who accepted that Dollard and his men were fighting for furs rather than sacrificing their lives to save New France, continued to describe their battle as being as "heroic and necessary as legend has made it, for without furs New France could not live."

### POLITICAL AFTERMATH

From 1599 to 1661 the French government had sought to promote colonization and assist mission work in New France by granting a monopoly of the fur trade to trading companies in return for promises to sponsor these activities. Although the fur trade had flourished, its profits were insufficient to support the large-scale colonization and the development of the diversified economy that Champlain had correctly foreseen were necessary for the expansion of New France. By 1661 it appeared that unless the power of the Iroquois was curbed, the colony would collapse.

In 1663, in response to the pleas of the colonists, Louis xiv and his minister Jean-Baptiste Colbert, who subscribed to the principles of mercantilism, took control of New France and reorganized its administration and economic affairs. Colbert sought to promote immigration to Canada. His aim was to create a population that would be self-sufficient in foodstuffs and large enough to defend the colony, provide a market for French goods, and produce a wide range of commodities wanted in Europe. As a result of Colbert's policies, the population of New France more than tripled over the next twenty years and became reasonably balanced between the sexes. The economy and society of the colony grew more complex and interest groups multiplied. At the same time records became more abundant and diverse. These developments, which transformed New France and what we know about it, brought the Heroic Age to an end, except perhaps in the opposed but equally patriarchal figures of Governor Louis de Buade de Frontenac and Bishop François de Laval. It is nevertheless worth examining in a brief and highly schematic fashion the events of the next half century to put relations with native people during the Heroic Age into perspective.

Although those Iroquois who favoured peace began to make overtures of reconciliation as early as 1661, raids continued and the French government agreed with the colonists that the power of the Five Nations had to be broken. To accomplish this, a local militia began to be trained, and in 1665 the 1,200-man Carignan-Salières regiment was sent to New France under the command of Alexandre de Prouville de Tracy, a veteran of the Spanish and German wars. By 1659 or 1660 the Senecas, Cayugas, and Onondagas had become embroiled in a conflict with the Susquehannocks that was to last until 1675. Its cause was that the Susquehannocks, who also needed furs, were sending warriors north to plunder Seneca and other trading parties as they carried their furs to Fort Orange (Trelease 1960:127). Because of these raids and also because these Iroquois tribes continued to mistrust the Mohawks, they hastened to make peace with the French. So did the more reluctant Oneidas. One condition of this treaty was that they not molest the Ottawas and the other tribes with whom the French traded (Thwaites 1896–1901, 50:281; 51:169; Morton 1963:58).

In January 1666 the first of three campaigns was launched against the recalcitrant Mohawks. Although this effort was not a success, in May the Mohawks sent a delegation to make peace with the French. Francis Jennings (1984:131–2) has accused Tracy of bad faith in ignoring this treaty, but he overlooks the fact that Mohawk war parties continued to attack the French, killing a nephew of Tracy. As a result, a second expedition, in July 1666, was mounted to secure the release of French prisoners. French officials were almost certainly correct when they concluded that a lasting peace with the Mohawks was impossible until the anti-French faction was totally discredited. Although an increasing number of Mohawks favoured peace, the more extreme elements of the anti-French group had worked in the 1650s to destroy the former peace and then to keep the war going despite formidable Iroquois losses and the growing power of their adversary. The following autumn the French burned five Mohawk villages and their winter food stores. The Mohawks saved their lives by fleeing to neighbouring Iroquois groups but they were thoroughly intimidated. In the summer of 1667, with the militant faction finally crushed, the Mohawks made a lasting peace with the French. The indignation and mistrust that Jennings claims Tracy's attack aroused among the Mohawks did not prevent the pro-French faction from welcoming Jesuit missionaries to their settlements and moving in growing numbers to the Jesuit mission of Caughnawaga.

The eighteen peaceful years that followed allowed New France to develop and prosper as never before. Yet the Iroquois continued to manage their affairs as independent nations, and they found the English, who had seized control of New Netherland in 1664, to be powerful allies (Richter 1983:545). Since the 1640s French officials had realized that the Iroquois menace could be definitively removed only if the French were able to buy or seize control of the Hudson Valley. In the late 1680s detailed plans were drawn up for combined land and sea operations to capture New York. Yet successive commitments in Europe and overriding reasons of state prevented these plans from being attempted.

The French and the Iroquois both needed more furs; the French, to ensure the prosperity of their colony, which continued to depend on the fur trade, and the Iroquois, to satisfy their growing requirements for European goods. Because they were committed not to wage war against the Ottawas, the Iroquois began to push west into the Ohio Valley in search of furs and new hunting grounds. By 1678 they had reached the Mississippi Valley, where their first attack upon the Illinois tribes was repelled. As they had traditionally done, young Iroquois men derived considerable prestige by displaying their skill as warriors and they liked to boast of their military exploits. The Iroquois also continued to rationalize their wars as acts of blood revenge. Yet there is no warrant for stating that the Iroquois were seeking power for its own sake at this time (Eccles 1983:343). The capture of prisoners for adoption also appears to have been declining in importance (Richter 1983:543–4). The primary objective of the desperate and often unequal military struggles that the Iroquois waged during the latter part of the seventeenth century was to secure the supplies of furs that were required for trade.

French traders also began to push westward in the 1650s. At first these *coureurs de bois* sought to make alliances with the hunting tribes that had formerly supplied the Hurons and to encourage them to bring their furs to the St Lawrence Valley. In an effort to increase the volume of trade the French gradually began to play an important role in transporting goods back and forth between Montreal and the upper Great Lakes. New and more direct routes were pioneered into the interior, and permanent trading posts were established as far west as the Mississippi Valley. As a result of these activities, the Ottawas were largely bypassed as middlemen and had ceased to travel regularly to the St Lawrence by the 1680s.

In 1679 René-Robert Cavelier de La Salle, who had begun his western explorations ostensibly looking for a route to the Pacific Ocean, established trading posts along the Illinois River and concluded alliances between the French and the Illinois and Miami peoples. The following year the Iroquois refused to obey French orders not to attack the Illinois and began pillaging French canoes. They also resumed attacking tribes who lived in the upper Great Lakes region. In 1684 Governor Joseph-Antoine Le Febvre de La Barre led a large military expedition against the Iroquois towns. In addition to restraining the Iroquois, he appears to have hoped to oblige them to trade with the French rather than the English (La Roque de Roquebrune 1966:444–5). Although many Indians were brought from the upper Great Lakes to join this expedition, it foundered badly as a result of poor planning and illness. The French were forced to conclude a hasty truce with the Iroquois, which involved their promising not to help the Illinois. This caused many of the western tribes to question the wisdom of trusting the French.

After the peace of 1665–6, the Iroquois were able to trade with the French as well as the English. Although Fort Cataraqui was established at the eastern end of Lake Ontario in 1673 to protect the Ottawa Valley from Iroquois incursions and to intercept any furs being carried south to Albany, it also served as a trading post for the Iroquois (Lanctôt 1964:63–4). It is almost universally accepted, on the basis of numerous seventeenth-century claims made by French and English alike, that the English were able to sell goods to the Indians more cheaply than the French could. If so, the commercial benefits of trade with the French were minimal to the Iroquois. W.J. Eccles (1983) has cast doubt on this price disparity and also argues that, with the exception of woollen cloth, French goods were of superior quality to English ones. In particular, he maintains, the Indians preferred French brandy to the poor-quality rum and gin supplied by the British. Nevertheless, the French often observed that guns and other goods they supplied to the Indians were inferior to those obtained in Albany, and their officials repeatedly expressed concern about the higher prices that the English offered for furs (Lanctôt 1964:156). A detailed study of the quality and prices of goods is needed to resolve this controversy.

Yet, however important or unimportant the economic advantages might have been, the opportunity to trade with the French gave the Iroquois significant political and economic leverage. Neither the French nor the English could afford to take their goodwill for granted, nor could they feel free to overcharge for their goods. Already in 1624 the Mohawks had sought to trade with the French so that they could risk the loss of the Dutch trade when they attacked the nearby Mahicans. A decade later the Oneidas noted their ability to trade with the French when they demanded that the Dutch lower their prices and keep in stock a wider and more satisfactory range of goods (Jameson 1909:151). These examples demonstrate that the Iroquois had long understood the value of both forms of leverage.

In the 1670s English buyers persuaded the Iroquois to begin trading with the Ottawas, Nipissings, and Huron-Petuns. These groups had tried to gain control of the rich hunting territories that belonged to Siouan-speaking peoples who lived south and west of Lake Superior. Yet by 1670 they had become embroiled in a war from which they sought to disentangle themselves by moving eastward, following the cessation of Iroquois attacks. In 1685 a party composed of Iroquois and European traders from Albany travelled by way of Lakes Erie and Huron to Michilimackinac, where they attempted to initiate trade with the Huron-Petuns and Ottawas by offering them twice as much as the French did for their furs. The Iroquois and the northern tribes regularly visited each other by way of Lake Simcoe. It has generally been assumed that the Senecas and Cayugas established a string of settlements along the north shore of Lake Ontario in the late 1660s as places of refuge from attacks by the Susquehannocks (see Bernou map). It seems more likely that these settlements were intended to facilitate trade with the Ottawas and for hunting beaver, once these animals had re-established themselves in southern Ontario following the flight of its human inhabitants. That the Iroquois were prepared to trade with the northern hunting peoples also suggests that by now they were looking for alternatives to warfare as a way to obtain furs.

In 1686 the new governor, Jacques-René de Brisay de Denonville, decided that the Iroquois had to be prevented from attacking the western tribes that were allied to the French and helping the English to trade with less remote tribes. To accomplish both goals, he planned to build a series of forts at Toronto, Niagara, and Detroit that would cut the Iroquois off from the territories to the north and west. He also believed that a preventive war with the Iroquois could no longer be avoided. In 1687 the Huron-Petuns, Ottawas, and Potawatomis were with some difficulty persuaded to join some 1,700 French soldiers in an attack. This expedition penetrated the Seneca country, where it burned their towns, destroyed their corn-fields, slaughtered the pigs which they now kept, and looted their graves (Wray 1973:2). A French garrison was established for a short time at Niagara. In the early stages of this expedition, various

Iroquois were seized near Fort Cataraqui, thirty-six of whom were sent to France as galley slaves for the king's Mediterranean fleet.

While peace between the French and the Iroquois was being discussed, James II was expelled from England by his Protestant son-in-law and the Iroquois learned that another war between the French and the English was imminent. Confident that the English would help them, they razed the French settlement at Lachine on 5 August 1689 and sought unsuccessfully to isolate and destroy Montreal. For the next six years they raided and pillaged French settlements along the St Lawrence and Richelieu Rivers. Although blockhouses were constructed, the Iroquois killed large numbers of settlers. They also prevented agricultural activities and forced the French to retreat into urban centres. Near famine prevailed from 1690 to 1693. Cataraqui was partially demolished and abandoned from 1689 to 1695. Frontenac, beginning his second term as governor of New France, offered to make peace with the Iroquois, but they refused, even after Sir William Phips's naval expedition against Quebec failed in 1690.

Yet the Iroquois were suffering very heavy losses from warfare and disease and were increasingly uncertain and divided about what they should do. In February 1693 the French once again destroyed Mohawk settlements, this time capturing 300 men, women, and children. In 1696 another French military expedition burned the abandoned Onondaga and Oneida towns. L.V. Eid (1979; cf. Konrad 1981) has shown that at the same time, the Ojibwas, helped by the Huron-Petuns, took advantage of the Iroquois' preoccupation with the French to defeat and drive the Iroquois out of southern Ontario (Jennings 1984:207). Henceforth these rich hunting grounds were occupied by the Mississaugas. Other Ojibwas occupied the Lower Peninsula of Michigan, where Frontenac had succeeded in stirring up raids against the Iroquois. Over 200 Iroquois warriors were killed in the spring of 1697 alone (Lanctôt 1964:132).

After the war in Europe had been ended in 1697 by the Treaty of Ryswick, it became clear to the Iroquois that the English, who had provided them with no armed assistance during the war, could not be relied on for military aid. Hence in July 1701, following prolonged negotiations, the Iroquois made peace with the French and thirteen western tribes at Montreal. About the same time, they reaffirmed their alliance with the British at Albany. Two months before this treaty was signed, Antoine Laumet, the son of a humble French magistrate who had assumed the noble alias of de Lamothe Cadillac, had left Montreal with fifty soldiers and an equal number of settlers to establish a French colony at Detroit. This colony soon became a major centre of French and Indian settlement and trade in the Midwest. Until this time the French traders had viewed the Iroquois, especially when they were at war, as a valuable buffer that prevented their Indian allies from trading with the English. Now, with their control of the western fur trade seemingly assured and a vast glut of furs threatening New France with financial disaster, the French were prepared to allow some of the northern furs to be traded to the Iroquois in return for their political neutrality.

In June 1700 the Iroquois agreed for the first time to allow various Ottawa bands to cross their territories and trade at Albany in return for presents and hunting privileges in the north (Haan 1980:318). Other Indians and French *coureurs de bois* began to dispose of their surplus furs to the Iroquois. Even during the War of the Spanish Succession, the Iroquois clandestinely routed increasing numbers of furs south from Montreal to Albany in exchange for English goods (Lunn 1939). In this way, while continuing to rely on hunting to obtain many of the furs that they sold to the English, the Iroquois gradually learned to be traders and middlemen rather than pirates. Even so, they still placed more emphasis on hunting rights and less on trade than the Hurons had done prior to 1650.

While French fears of losing their fur trade and their alliances with the northern tribes and Iroquois hopes of regaining their influence in the west continued to threaten the peace treaty, the declining power of the Iroquois compelled them to cling to neutrality as the surest means to protect their interests. For both the British and the French, the principal benefit of Iroquois independence was that it constituted a barrier against the expansionist tendencies of the other colonial power (Haan 1980). Recent studies offer little support for A.F.C. Wallace's (1957) long-accepted view that during the eighteenth century the power of the Iroquois allowed them to play one European group off against the other.

## THE IROQUOIS MISSIONS

Following the dispersal of the Hurons, the Jesuits were anxious to undertake mission work among the Iroquois. They wanted to minister to Christian Hurons who were held captive by the Iroquois, but, more importantly, they sought to establish a new mission field that would win the Iroquois to Christianity and a French alliance. Their missions to the Iroquois began in 1654 when Father Simon Le Moyne visited the Onondagas as a French envoy to discuss peace. Although he was captured by the Mohawks on his way home, they released him and he officially visited that tribe the following year. In 1655 Fathers Chaumonot and Claude Dablon left for the Onondaga country to select a site for the short-lived mission centre of Sainte-Marie-de-Ganentaa. As noted previously, the Jesuits won Iroquois acceptance of their missions by playing a leading role in persuading Huron refugees at Quebec to join the Mohawks and Onondagas. Although increasing hostility compelled the Jesuits to abandon the Iroquois missions in 1658, Le Moyne was invited to return to the Onondagas as early as 1661. By 1668 the Jesuits had missions in all five Iroquois tribes, while the Sulpicians were established among the Cayugas who lived at Kente, on the north shore of Lake Ontario. As relations with the French again became strained, these missions were recalled, until the last one, at Onondaga, was abandoned in 1686. They began again after the peace of 1701 but did not last beyond 1708 when relations with the French temporarily deteriorated.

Many of the Hurons who had been taken prisoner prior to 1649 and the traditionalists who had joined the Iroquois afterward accused the Jesuits of being sorcerers and warned the Iroquois that if the priests were permitted to visit, they would use their spells to ruin crops and spread diseases as they had done in the Huron country (Thwaites 1896–1901, 31:121). These Hurons related in detail the ways in which they believed that the Jesuits, especially Brébeuf, had sought to injure them. Their hatred of the French increased when they saw their countrymen being carried off from Quebec with the acquiescence of the French.

On the other hand, many other Hurons, including ones who had formerly been hostile to the Jesuits, welcomed the priests when they arrived in the Iroquois settlements. They sought out the missionaries, sometimes secretly, to perform their devotions, presented children for baptism, assembled to receive instruction, and attended public worship regularly. The Jesuits credited much of their influence among the Iroquois to the help they had received from them. Some of these Hurons were among the Iroquois who later joined the Hurons at Lorette or other mission settlements in New France (Thwaites 1896–1901, 55:35; 57:75; 60:295). In 1670 the Jesuits reported that the vast majority of Christians in their Iroquois missions were either of Huron descent or other captives (ibid., 54:41–3). Yet the main concern of most Hurons appears to have been to curry favour with their Iroquois hosts or captors. While the Iroquois tribes sought to be on good terms with the French, the majority of Hurons were at least outwardly friendly to the Jesuits, but when relations soured, all but a small number avoided them and anti-Jesuit sentiments were expressed freely. On the whole, there seem to have been few deeply committed believers among the Hurons. While the Jesuits thought that the Tahontaen-rat town of Gandougarae was entirely Christian when they erected a chapel there in 1669 (ibid., 47:113), the mission became ever less promising in later years (ibid., 58:229, 237).

Most Iroquois viewed the Jesuits as a pro-Iroquois faction among the French. Because of this, their presence was valued by the pro-French factions that existed within the various Iroquois tribes. Other Iroquois saw them as useful hostages whose presence ensured the good behaviour of their countrymen. Most of them treated the Jesuits respectfully when they wished to be on good terms with the French but developed an aversion to them and their teachings, which frequently led to overt hostility and persecution, when relations with the French deteriorated. Yet Father Jean de Lamberville, a missionary to the Oneidas, won the confidence of all the Iroquois as a diplomat and a man of honour. It was he who restored peace in the wake of La Barre's disastrous military expedition of 1684. So great was the Oneidas' affection for him that after Denonville had treacherously seized the Iroquois around Cataraqui in 1687, instead of harming him, they conducted him safely to Denonville's camp. The Oneidas also adopted Father Pierre Millet, giving him the role and status of their traditional council chief, Otatchehte.

Some Iroquois, particularly members of the pro-French faction, sought baptism to seal a closer alliance between themselves and the French. The most prominent of these converts was the Onondaga chief Garakontié. He consistently promoted good relations with the French from 1653 until his death in 1677–8. As well he was credited with saving many French from death by torture and warned the Jesuits of the planned attack on Sainte-Marie-de-Ganentaa. After he had been baptized, while on a peace mission to Quebec in 1669, he strongly supported Jesuit missionary activities among the Iroquois.

Yet most Iroquois felt under no pressure to convert. Because they traded with the Dutch and later with the English, it was impossible for the Jesuits to use a system of rewards and punishments to encourage traders, chiefs, and warriors to become Christians, as they had done among the Hurons. While they were recognized as having an important role to play in times of crises, Iroquois chiefs who allied themselves with the French probably derived less credit from doing so than did those who aligned themselves with the English. Jean de Lamberville took account of the problems that the Jesuits were facing when he wrote in 1673 that they could hope to convert only a few Iroquois and even that would require generous presents and force of arms (Thwaites 1896–1901, 57:127–9). The French never acquired the economic control or the military ascendancy that was necessary to achieve the Jesuits' goals.

Because they felt secure, the Iroquois adopted a naturalistic view of the Jesuits. Despite Huron warnings, they did not repeatedly hold them responsible for epidemics and crop failures as the Hurons had done or as the Mohawks had with respect to Jogues in 1646. The Iroquois who remained in New York State regarded them primarily as ambassadors and for a long time their religious teachings made little headway. Towards the end of the seventeenth century, when these Mohawks became more interested in Christianity, the pro-English chiefs requested Protestant missionaries to counterbalance the Canadian Jesuits, who were associated with the pro-French party (Trelease 1960:329, 354). Still earlier, the Jesuits had found that their political influence was more than matched by the kegs of brandy and other presents that the Dutch and later the English sent to the Iroquois as tokens of goodwill.

The Jesuits had markedly more success with the few Hurons who remained at Quebec and the Mohawks and Oneidas who settled after the peace of 1667 at La Prairie south of Montreal. The latter relocated along the south shore of the St Lawrence four times until they reached present-day Caughnawaga in 1716. The Mohawks who settled there and at the Sulpician Mission of the Mountain, founded on Montreal Island in 1676, appear to have come largely from the pro-French faction that had already been associated with the tortoise and wolf clans in the 1640s (Blanchard 1982a:139). The Jesuits and French officials encouraged this settlement because they saw it as weakening long-standing enemies and because they had little hope that converts would continue to live as Christians unless they were separated from their non-Christian countrymen.

What is not clear from the Jesuits' accounts is why so many Mohawks chose to move to the St Lawrence and live under Jesuit supervision. Many adherents of the pro-French faction may not have wished to have their houses and villages burned again for a cause they did not support and therefore believed it wise to move near the French. The same reason may account for the large numbers of Mohawks who moved to Caughnawaga while they and the French were at war during the 1690s (Jennings 1984:205–6). Moreover, since the 1620s, the Mohawks had sought to trade with both the French and the Dutch because this gave them an opportunity to drive harder bargains, obtain a wider selection of goods, and increase their political independence from both European groups.

Native family shown as Christians.
Detail from *Novae Franciae Accurata Delineatio*.

It is possible that these considerations played a significant role in encouraging some Mohawks to move north. The Caughnawaga Mohawks were soon engaged in a clandestine but profitable fur trade between Montreal and Albany. Others no doubt came to join relatives who had already moved. Still others said that they were seeking to escape from the drunkenness that regularly disrupted life in their home towns. In general the Mohawks at Caughnawaga and those who continued to live in their homeland in the Mohawk Valley west of Albany, New York, remained on good terms and their refusal to harm each other was a factor maintaining the peace. The Caughnawaga Mohawks only reluctantly participated in the expeditions that La Barre, Denonville, and Frontenac led against other Iroquois tribes. Finally, in 1693, in the wake of the Lachine massacre and Iroquois attacks directed against them, they took up arms against their countrymen in the Mohawk Valley. Yet, even in the short run, this did not extinguish the powerful bonds of kinship and cooperation that continued to link these two branches of the Mohawk nation (Devine 1922:93–116).

There were considerable disagreements between the Jesuits and French officials about how Indians who settled at missions in the St Lawrence Valley should be treated. The Jesuits maintained their policy of keeping the Indians separate from the French and teaching them in their own language. The Hurons at Quebec and the Mohawks at Montreal also continued to live in bark longhouses and to practise slash and burn agriculture well into the eighteenth century, while their matrilinear social organization appears to have survived as well. In 1667, Colbert, in an effort to augment European settlement, revived the Recollets' idea that Indians should be encouraged to live among the French so they might learn the French language and customs and forget their own (Delanglez 1939:35–65). Louis XIV offered a substantial wedding gift to any Indian girl who married a Frenchman (Lanctôt 1964:38). While the French government was still encouraging the assimilation of the Indians fifteen years later, this policy proved to be a failure, as the Jesuits and Marie de l'Incarnation, the foundress of the Ursuline order in New France, had predicted (Richaudeau 1876, 2:393–4). Gustave Lanctôt (1964:205) has noted that between 1663 and 1700 only nine French colonists married Indian women and one French woman an Indian man (Dickason 1982:9–11). In 1672 Jean de Lamberville renounced the earlier optimistic views of his order when he stated that it was impossible to evangelize Indians and teach them to live like French people because they could not reason properly as do "the Chinese and other civilized nations" (Thwaites 1896–1901, 57:127).

There is no agreement about how much of an accurate understanding of Christianity the Jesuits managed to convey to their early converts, even though they were expert in native languages and possessed highly developed pedagogical skills. At least one modern church historian has claimed that they had succeeded in making its meaning and spirit clear to the Montagnais as early as the 1630s, despite the vast cultural differences that separated them (Campeau 1979:cxxviii–cxxxi); anthropologists, however, are less certain of this. The Iroquoians had been born into egalitarian societies in which one human being did not have the right to command another; even parents could not give orders to their children. Christianity was a creation of hierarchical and coercive societies that were part of the ancient Near East and the Roman Empire and had been nurtured in the monarchies of western Europe prior to being brought to the New World. Obedience to God and to his earthly representatives, within society and the family, was central to the teachings of Christianity. Other theological issues aside, there is no evidence that the Jesuits or any other Christian group in the seventeenth century was able to make Christian doctrines comprehensible to people who lived in a self-sufficient tribal society. This is a problem that missionaries still must resolve if Christianity is to be truly a universal religion. For the Jesuits, despite their limited awareness of cultural relativism, there was no possibility of adapting the Christian message to the needs of an egalitarian society. Instead, they concluded that the implantation of Christianity required that native societies be transformed, as they had begun to do at Sillery and Ossossané, from an egalitarian social order governed by consensus, into a hierarchical one, managed by majority votes or the decrees of acknowledged leaders. Through the Jesuits, such societies would be further rendered subordinate to the French monarchy.

At Quebec and Montreal, the Jesuits acquired some powers to control converts that were never at their disposal in the Iroquois country. Even these powers were limited, however, by the freedom of many Mohawks to return to their settlements in New York State. Yet, both at Lorette and Caughnawaga an increasingly large proportion of the population consisted of women and children who depended upon the Jesuits for charity (Archives des Colonies G[1] art. 461). In return, the Jesuits expected them to attend church and observe Christian religious practices with considerable regularity. In a fashion that anticipates behaviourist psychology, they believed that in time people who could be made to act like Christians would also come to think like them (Trigger 1976:701). To achieve this objective they tried to compel their converts to abandon all native customs that they suspected had non-Christian religious significance, such as face painting (Thwaites 1896–1901, 60:93), and to reinterpret less objectionable ones so that they acquired Christian meaning. One Jesuit missionary stated that had the Hurons remained flourishing, his order could not have acquired so great an ascendancy over them in a century as it had gained over the remnant at Quebec in a few years (ibid., 57:69). They recorded notable displays of piety among these Indians, including painful forms of self-mortification. Yet in 1682, the Intendant Jacques de Meulles noted cynically that one seldom saw the Indians who lived in New France praying (Lanctôt 1964:204). There were also episodes of drunkenness at Caughnawaga, despite the Jesuits' struggle for temperance.

It has been questioned whether converts understood the rituals they performed in Christian terms or continued to view them from a traditional perspective. David Blanchard (1982b) has suggested that the early piety that developed in the Quebec missions was less Christian practice with native colouration than a syncretism in which Jesuit teachings were interpreted within a traditional Iroquoian framework. The evidence for this has yet, however, to be systematically presented. There is also the question of whether the converts only pretended to believe. In the Huron country, the Jesuits had noted that it was hardest to convince the most intelligent Hurons of the validity of Christian teachings (Thwaites 1896–

1901, 23:129). Many converts sought to cultivate the goodwill of the Jesuits; others claimed to be Christians because they feared the supernatural power of the missionaries. In 1671, following his arrest on a charge of kidnapping, a Huron who had been considered a good Christian for more than twenty-five years confessed that he had only feigned to be one in order to gratify the Jesuits; he then requested renewed baptism and continued to live a life of exemplary piety (ibid., 55:291–9). Much more research must be done on the economic and religious life at Caughnawaga and the other missions established within the colony of New France before an understanding will emerge that transcends White stereotypes and the often blatant hagiography of our sources.

It seems highly likely, however, that by the end of the seventeenth century a pervasive sense of political and economic debility by comparison with Europeans was influencing not only the mission Iroquois, but also those who remained in New York State. The Mohawks must have been particularly affected, since their towns had been burned twice by the French and they were the most knowledgeable about affairs in both the English and French colonies. This appears to have produced a loss of self-confidence, which led a growing number of them to turn to Christianity as a source of spiritual renewal. It may also explain why, after decades of neglect, the British authorities believed that it was vital to supply the Mohawks with missionaries to stem the flow of Indians to Caughnawaga. By this time the Indians living at Caughnawaga and other missions were probably familiar enough with hierarchical power that much more of the Christian message was comprehensible to them. This accords with A.W. Trelease's (1960:172) observation that a true conversion of the Indians depended "on their prior submission to the white man, with the attendant disintegration of their own culture." Understanding what Christianity meant to converts clearly requires taking account of decade-by-decade changes in their political and economic situation.

It is also clear that on the basis of their order's experiences in India, China, and Japan, the Jesuits had underestimated the problems involved in making Christianity comprehensible to the tribal societies of North America. Yet, if their attempts to convert native people without unduly altering the way of life of these people were undermined by their lack of flexibility in adapting Christian teaching to the social understanding of an egalitarian society, the Jesuits deserve credit for humane intentions and a respect for cultural differences that are unique in the annals of seventeenth-century missionary endeavours.

## HEROES AND VICTIMS

Even if Europeans and native North Americans had met at approximately the same level of cultural development, the lethal epidemics of European origin that repeatedly afflicted North America in the sixteenth and seventeenth centuries would have created extraordinary social and economic problems for the native peoples of that continent. Yet adequate recognition of this fact must not be permitted to deflect attention from the sufferings and loss that these peoples suffered as a result of the intentional behaviour of Europeans. The encounter of western Europeans and native North Americans was between societies of vastly different scales. They were unequal in terms of their technology, their capacity to mobilize and direct human resources, and their ability to pursue specific goals with great single-mindedness. It was not long before the relations between these societies were marked on the native side by growing economic dependence on European technology, escalating internal competition for the resources required to obtain these goods, decreasing ability to defend themselves as European settlements multiplied, and ultimately varying degrees of demoralization and spiritual dependence. The latter were exacerbated by the blind faith that most Europeans had in their own moral superiority and their increasing disparagement of native cultures.

It is tempting to portray native North Americans in sombre tones as the victims of unremitting European self-interest (Ryerson 1960; Delâge 1981). To some degree this view is a necessary antidote to a long-standing tendency of historians to minimize the moral responsibility of European settlers for the sufferings of native peoples. Yet such a view fails to acknowledge the tenacity with which native peoples, in the face of increasingly unequal odds, continued to defend their lands, customs, and personal dignity, despite a spiralling death rate, growing economic dependence, and unrelenting efforts of Europeans to control every aspect of their lives. This behaviour constitutes a record of continuing resourcefulness and adaptability under conditions of stress that had never been paralleled in North America in prehistoric times or at any time in the history of most other peoples.

## CHAPTER SIX

# Who Founded New France?

Traditionally historians have caricatured European fur traders as mercenary individuals who sought only personal gain at the expense of the general welfare of New France. On the other hand, Champlain, the Recollet and Jesuit missionaries, and those who supported them in France have been praised as the self-sacrificing founders of the colony. Many francophone historians had previously viewed the actions of these two groups as a dichotomy between Protestant acquisitiveness and Roman Catholic altruism. While that interpretation is now realized to be untenable, the image remains, even in recent more economically orientated studies (Trudel 1966a), of traders as opponents of colonization and therefore as a largely negative factor in the early development of New France.

Historians also have treated the events of the sixteenth and first half of the seventeenth centuries as the result of the ambitions and activities of Europeans alone. They have failed to recognize adequately that native peoples constituted an overwhelming majority of North Americans at that time; that they controlled the production and delivery of Canada's major export to European traders; that their cultures, if less advanced technologically than those of Europe, were adapted to local conditions while Europeans were still learning to cope with North American environments; and that in most situations, again despite the limitations of their technologies, native peoples were militarily strong enough to expel the newcomers. If Europeans had gained a toehold in Canada, it was because a substantial number of native peoples wished them to do so. This final chapter will consider the effects of the relations between native groups and Europeans upon colonization in the St Lawrence Valley.

Even historians who are sensitive to variations in goals and interests within native groups tend to restrict their observations to the interactions between native peoples and Whites and the impact that Europeans had on native cultures. They do not treat the expectations and actions of native peoples as factors that may have determined the success or failure of policies pursued by different groups of Europeans and therefore as vital in shaping the development of New France. Such treatment requires defining the major interest groups within New France and considering how each group interacted with native peoples as well as with each other. That, in turn, necessitates abandoning certain traditional explanations of European behaviour.

In chapter 1, I reviewed White stereotypes of native peoples and considered the impediments that they placed in the way of historical interpretation beginning as early as the eighteenth century. The same criticisms apply to the continuing tendency of explaining the behaviour of colonists from various European countries in terms of different national characters. Some of these stereotypes go back to the early days of colonization in the seventeenth century. The Dutch settlers have frequently been portrayed as a commercially orientated people, having little concern for their personal or national honour and willing to tolerate abuse from native peoples so long as they were able to make money. The English are assumed to have been an entrepreneurial and expansionist group, who were quick to exploit and disperse native peoples for their own profit and who were racist in their outlook. Both French and English historians have emphasized the ability of the French to get along with native peoples and their unusual concern for their welfare. Even those historians who are favourably inclined towards the French but who understand that the fur trade required them to cultivate good relations with the Indians out of self-interest have interpreted their behaviour as the manifestation of a special humaneness that has characterized French culture (Campeau 1979:xcvii–c).

National character, as a relic of the racist views of the nineteenth century, provides a highly suspect explanation of human behaviour anywhere. It is especially questionable that it can be applied to settlers coming from northern France, England, and the Netherlands, since these regions constituted the core area of capitalist development in Europe and their populations were therefore experiencing similar economic and political transformations during the sixteenth and seventeenth centuries (Wallerstein 1974, 1980).

This holds true even if, because of its larger size and internal diversity, there was a greater persistence of feudal structures in France than in the other two countries, which inhibited capital accumulation and colonial enterprises during the seventeenth century (Delâge 1981:355).

Before attributing behaviour to national character, historians must compare the activities and attitudes of different social classes, of peoples from regions with differing potentials for economic development, and of various factions struggling for economic and political advantage within each European nation state. Only after the effects of these economic and political factors have been taken into account is it possible to begin to speak about national character. Both in Europe and in the European colonies in North America, these sorts of interests seem to explain much more that is important about human behaviour than do problematical differences in national character.

This chapter will also assess what anthropology can contribute to an understanding of European activities in New France during the sixteenth and seventeenth centuries. The archaeological and ethnohistorical evidence concerning the native peoples of eastern North America at this time remains fragmentary. Because of this, it is generally harder for anthropologists to determine why native peoples behaved as they did than it is for historians to explain the behaviour of Europeans. Yet advances in anthropological research have eliminated major ethnocentric biases and gradually are offering new and more certain insights into the activities of native people. Such knowledge in turn can shed new light on the motives and behaviour of European settlers, as Francis Jennings (1975) has shown in *The Invasion of America*. He demonstrated that major errors in the traditional interpretations of relations among neighbouring colonies in New England had occurred because modern historians had taken at face value the self-serving Puritan distortions of their relations with native peoples. My discussion is directed to the understanding of European activities offered by historians such as Marcel Trudel (1963, 1966a, 1968, 1979), Lucien Campeau (1979), and W.J. Eccles (1973), who generally view early New France as a harmonious society, and by the sociologist Denys Delâge (1981), who adopts a model based on class conflict (Ouellet 1981). There is still no agreement concerning the interpretation of either the broad outlines or the specific detail of the early history of New France, despite long-standing claims that the study of the Heroic Age has been exhausted.

In the case of New France, anthropology does not appear to be able to deliver any single bombshell equivalent to the one Jennings dropped on New England historians. Yet, in both the short and the long run, it may be able to contribute significantly to a better perception of what various groups of Europeans did. What is offered here is not a definitive reinterpretation of the history of New France, but rather an indication of how anthropological findings may help to understand better the internal dynamics of French colonization. It is hoped that as anthropologists and historians learn to use each other's data more effectively, increasing cooperation will enable them not only to approach Canadian history as a study embracing native as well as White activities but also to interpret the behaviour of Europeans with greater accuracy.

### THE NORTHERN EL DORADO

The first stimulus to official French interest in the New World was Francis I's need for wealth to finance his wars with Charles V. News of Magellan's discovery of an ocean passage leading past South America to the riches of the Orient induced him to sponsor and subsidize Verrazzano's North American voyage of exploration in 1524. It was hoped that somewhere north of Florida a navigable strait leading to Cathay might be found or else mines of precious metals that would rival those of Spanish America. The capture of Francis I at the battle of Pavia in 1525, his subsequent imprisonment, and the wars that followed his release inhibited further interest in such ventures for almost a decade.

In 1532 Jean Le Veneur, bishop of Saint-Malo and grand almoner of France, persuaded the king to subsidize explorations by Jacques Cartier. Although Cartier was an experienced navigator and mapmaker, he does not appear to have been adroit or comfortable in his dealings with native people. While the Iroquoian chief Donnacona was anxious to establish a trading relationship with the French, Cartier alienated his two sons on his first voyage to the Gulf of St Lawrence. On his second he offended the Stadaconans by failing to ask their permission before using their land or to make an alliance with them before he visited Hochelaga. After having learned that the St Lawrence was not a navigable route to the Pacific Ocean, Cartier became more interested in Stadaconan accounts of native copper coming from Lake Superior that seem to have been heavily embroidered in the telling. These tales fired visions of another Mexico or Peru, abounding in gold, jewels, and spices, waiting to be discovered in the interior of North America. He kidnapped Donnacona not only to remove what he perceived to be the main source of opposition to French activities along the St Lawrence River but also so that Donnacona could tell the king what he knew about the interior.

Further French wars brought official exploration to a standstill between 1536 and 1538. In the autumn of 1540 Cartier was ordered to establish a settlement on the St Lawrence River that was to be used as a base for finding and conquering the Kingdom of the Saguenay, which was believed to be located west of Hochelaga. The following January, Jean-François de La Rocque, sieur de Roberval, a high-ranking nobleman, soldier, and land developer, was put in charge of the expedition. As lieutenant-general, he was given the right to distribute land in perpetual fief and to control trade through any westward passage that might be discovered. The king invested heavily in this expedition, while Cartier, Roberval, and other associates, many of them nobles in search of seigneuries and commercial advantages, put up money of their own. Profits were to be divided so that the king, Roberval, and the other associates each received a share, although part of Roberval's was to be used to maintain the colony (Trudel 1963:138–9). To compensate for a lack of lower-class volunteers, Roberval was given a mandate to conscript various categories of imprisoned criminals for the voyage.

In 1541 Cartier was ordered to set sail with five ships. They carried several hundred settlers, a supply of provisions adequate for two years, and ample materials to establish a flourishing settlement on the St Lawrence River just west of Quebec. On arriving in Canada, Cartier rejoiced at discovering what he thought were sources of gold and diamonds at the site of his colony, but he made no progress in reaching the Saguenay, which by now he might have realized was a chimera. During the winter, his settlement was besieged by all the Indian groups that lived in the Quebec City region. They were outraged that he had again used their land without permission and that none of their kidnapped compatriots had been returned. The following year he defied Roberval by abandoning the settlement and returning to France, where he hoped to be rewarded for his rich cargo.

Roberval and a new set of colonists remained on the St Lawrence until the spring of 1543 and might have become involved in conflict with the Hochelagans. For him, too, the Kingdom of the Saguenay became a mirage. Over the winter the colony was devastated by scurvy. With no obvious route to the Orient, no gold or diamonds, and no rich kingdoms to exploit, the incentive for European settlement on the St Lawrence evaporated. This was also to be the last instance when the French crown provided financial support for colonization in New France prior to 1663.

## MONOPOLISTS AND FREE TRADERS

Fishing and whaling attracted progressively more Europeans to the east coast of Canada throughout the sixteenth century. The fur trade appears to have developed slowly as a sideline to land-based fishing activities. Relations with native people were variable, and sometimes hostile, but peaceful trade occurred often enough to make hides, fancy furs and increasingly beaver pelts a significant source of extra income for many fishermen.

Although France was wracked by internal conflicts from 1562 to 1594 and finally by an open revolt against the crown, this period also saw a revival of interest in Canada among official circles. By means of royal commissions issued in 1577 and 1578, Troilus de La Roche de Mesgouez, a nobleman, former page at the court of Henri II, and a favourite of the Queen Mother Catherine de' Medici, secured hereditary rights to hold as his domain territories in North America that "he shall conquer and take from the barbarians" (Trudel 1963:217–18). As governor of Morlaix, in western Brittany, he had become aware of the profits to be made on goods brought to France from the coast of North America. Cardinal Charles de Bourbon, archbishop of Rouen, and Anne, duc de Joyeuse and admiral of France, sponsored Etienne Bellenger's trading and abortive colonizing voyage to Nova Scotia and Maine in 1583. La Roche founded a convict settlement on Sable Island in 1598. These colonists engaged in seal hunting until a rebellion brought the venture to an end in 1603 (ibid., 231–5).

Sometime after 1550 Tadoussac became the most important trading centre between European whalers and fishermen and native people in eastern North America. It acquired this role largely because of its location with respect to trade routes leading into the interior, but perhaps also partly because until about 1580 the St Lawrence Iroquoians, still angered by the behaviour of Cartier and Roberval, did not permit Europeans to travel farther upriver. In 1581 the first French ship was sent to the St Lawrence specifically to trade for furs. By 1587 rival trading vessels were battling each other on the river (Biggar 1901:32–3; Quinn 1977:467–9). The following year Jacques Noël, Cartier's nephew and heir, and his partner Etienne Chaton de La Jannaye, a sea captain, obtained a monopoly of mines and furs in Canada and an authorization that would make sixty convicts a year available to them as labourers in return for a promise to settle and fortify the country. This was the first contract with the crown that specifically sought to promote colonization at no cost to the depleted royal treasury. The monopoly was quickly abandoned, however, after protests from the merchants of Saint-Malo and the parliament of Britanny resulted in its being restricted first to new territories that the partners might discover west of Montreal and then to mineral exploitation only (Trudel 1963: 221–6).

Archaeological and historical evidence indicates that by the end of the sixteenth century furs were reaching Tadoussac that had been traded from tribe to tribe from as far away as James Bay and southern Ontario. The desire to obtain European goods also may have been an important factor strengthening (if it did not create) the Iroquois confederacy. It encouraged Mohawk war parties to pillage the tribes that inhabited the St Lawrence Valley and then to try to trade with Europeans, who began venturing upriver after the St Lawrence Iroquoians had vanished from the Quebec City area around 1580. Sometime after 1570 these attacks led to the formation of a defensive alliance among various Algonkin and Montagnais bands. As part of this alliance, the Montagnais at Tadoussac granted certain Algonkin groups limited rights to visit Tadoussac during the summer and to trade directly with the Europeans.

Yet intertribal relations continued to be based on traditional patterns of behaviour. Trade was carried on in a context of political alliances and with the same rituals as it had been in the past. The Iroquois, who had long been compelled to compete with adjacent tribes that had economies similar to their own, were predisposed to resort to warfare to gain access to European goods, whereas the Hurons, whose northern tribes were used to exchanging staples with the hunter-gatherer peoples in central Ontario, easily expanded this trade to acquire European goods after they had become available to the Algonkins. This rapidly changing but still traditional world constituted the economic and political reality to which the French newcomers had to adjust.

There is evidence that at least some of the French who traded at Tadoussac had understood this situation in considerable detail already by the end of the sixteenth century. By 1600 they had realized that a formal alliance with the Montagnais would help to secure their supply of furs against competition from other European traders but that maintaining such an alliance would require them to respect the Montagnais' role as middlemen. They also knew that vast numbers of the best quality beaver pelts could be obtained from north of the St Lawrence River. Yet, if the volume of furs was to be increased significantly, they would have to open the St Lawrence River as an artery of trade and exchange goods directly with native peoples living farther inland. These seemingly incompatible objectives could be achieved only by helping the Montagnais and their allies drive the Mohawk raiders from the St Lawrence Valley. As a first step towards realizing these goals, certain French traders became members of the intertribal alliance against the Mohawks that was led by the Montagnais of Tadoussac. At first they prudently limited their participation to providing metal weapons to the tribes whom the Montagnais allowed to trade at Tadoussac so that they could combat the Iroquois more effectively.

The principal architect of this policy appears to have been François Gravé Du Pont. Born at Saint-Malo around 1554, he had fought in the religious wars that had torn France apart until Henri IV restored royal authority in 1594 and had been a captain in the navy before becoming a merchant. Prior to 1599 he had traded furs on the St Lawrence River and had travelled as far inland as Trois-Rivières. It has been suggested that he contributed the modern place-names that replaced Cartier's toponymy on the map of 1603 by the cartographer G. Levasseur (Trudel 1963:249–52). Despite sickness and advancing age, he was to remain active in the fur trade until 1629, spending several winters at Quebec. During this time, his knowledge of native customs and his ability to inspire confidence and deal effectively with the Indians made him indispensable. Although far less information is available about him, he appears to have played a role in dealing with native peoples that was at least as important as Champlain's during the first three decades of the seventeenth century.

The fur trade required only a few French vessels to visit the St Lawrence Valley each summer. Moreover, because of the role played by the Montagnais in collecting and delivering furs, it was possible to conduct this trade during a brief period each year. Over the winter of 1599–1600 Gravé Du Pont assisted Pierre de Chauvin de Tonnetuit, a wealthy Protestant merchant from Honfleur who had distinguished himself fighting for Henri IV, in obtaining from the king a ten-year monopoly of the fur trade along the St Lawrence River in return for a promise to settle 500 people there at his own expense. The granting of these privileges renewed the battle between monopolists and free traders for the right to do business on the St Lawrence. The opponents of the monopoly, who included Basque whalers as well as merchants from Saint-Malo, Rouen, and La

Rochelle, continued to trade clandestinely with the Indians. More-over, whether Chauvin or the king realized it when the monopoly was granted, the profits of the fur trade, although substantial, were inadequate to support colonization on such a grand scale.

Against the advice of Gravé Du Pont, who found the location too inhospitable, and of his associate Pierre Du Gua de Monts, a Calvinist who had been rewarded for supporting Henri IV with a substantial annual pension and the governorship of Pons in Saintonge, Chauvin decided to protect his monopoly by constructing a trading post at Tadoussac and leaving sixteen men to spend the winter there. Although the Montagnais welcomed this settlement because it offered them additional protection against Iroquois attack, eleven of Chauvin's men died over the winter, and the following year Tadoussac reverted to being a summer trading place. During the winter of 1602–3 the king authorized the merchants of Rouen and Saint-Malo to associate themselves with Chauvin in order to pro-mote colonization more effectively, but those from Saint-Malo re-fused to join any company that required them to share the massive costs that were involved (Trudel 1963:235–44). When Chauvin died, early in 1603, his monopoly passed to Aymar de Chaste, the gov-ernor of Dieppe, who in turn died soon after. The same year de Monts obtained a new ten-year monopoly of the fur trade for the whole of New France in return for undertaking to establish sixty colonists there each year. He formed a trading company with a working capital of 90,000 livres by selling shares to merchants from Rouen, Saint-Malo, La Rochelle, and Saint-Jean-de-Luz. This was the best financed trading company to operate in Canada prior to 1627 (Trudel 1966a:9–15).

Before he died in 1603, de Chaste had invited Gravé Du Pont to inspect the St Lawrence River as far west as Montreal Island, pre-sumably with an eye to locating further settlements. He was accompanied by Samuel de Champlain, a mapmaker and former soldier, who had not previously been connected with Canada or the fur trade. Yet Champlain suggests that he played a significant role in convincing de Monts that his colonizing efforts should be directed towards the Maritimes. According to Champlain, Acadia had a milder climate and more fertile soil than the St Lawrence Valley, seemed rich in mineral deposits, and was possibly close to an easier passage to the Orient than the St Lawrence River appeared to be. Settlement might also make it possible to control the ex-ploitation of the dispersed fur resources of the region. An unstated but more pressing reason for directing settlement towards this area may have been to keep it away from the rich and highly concentrated source of furs at Tadoussac, since from an early date trading companies feared that settlers would seek to usurp their trade. A temporary colony was established at the mouth of the St Croix River in 1604. It was shifted to Port Royal in Nova Scotia the following year, while the search continued for a still more favourable location farther south. De Monts soon discovered that it was impossible to enforce a monopoly along the indented coastline of the Maritime provinces and that the expense of maintaining a colony put him at a great financial disadvantage by comparison with illegal traders.

In 1607 the advocates of free trade, who included many Norman and Breton merchants and the Paris hatters' corporation, succeeded in having de Monts's monopoly cancelled as of the following year, although he obtained a one-year extension in return for a promise to renew his efforts at colonization. Port Royal was abandoned, and in 1608 Champlain was sent, as de Monts's lieutenant, to the St Lawrence Valley to select a site for a new settlement. De Monts hoped that by establishing a trading post he might be able to retain control of trade in that region or at least be better able to cope with rival traders. Already before Champlain had arrived at Tadoussac, Gravé Du Pont had been attacked and disarmed by a Basque captain who was trading there illegally and who apparently carried off most of the furs for that year.

By reminding the Indians at Tadoussac of the benefits they would derive from having Frenchmen live among them, Champlain and Gravé Du Pont secured their permission to found a settlement upriver. At the Narrows of Quebec, a location that allowed the occupants to prevent illicit traders from passing upriver, Champlain had his men erect three two-storey buildings and a warehouse joined by a single external gallery for defence. Outside this wall was a moat and palisade. This settlement was much more carefully fortified than the ones at Sainte-Croix or Port Royal had been, and the defences were clearly intended more against Europeans than against native people. Shortly after he had arrived at Quebec, Champlain put down a mutiny which he claimed was intended to forestall the settlement in hopes of a reward from the Basque traders. The ringleader was executed and his head exposed to public view on a pike, an apparently fratricidal action that must have greatly mystified Montagnais visitors.

It had become evident that if de Monts's company was to cope with rival traders, legal or illegal, it had to forge still closer ties with the Montagnais and at the same time promote trade upriver, where its agents might hope to outrun their rivals. To accomplish these objectives, it was decided that employees of the company would actively help the Montagnais and Algonkins to fight the Iroquois. While Gravé Du Pont may have made this decision, Champlain was called upon to execute it. In 1609 and 1610 he used the terror inspired by French muskets to help these Indians inflict major defeats on Mohawk war parties that were threatening the St Lawrence Valley. He also established new trading places near the mouth of the Richelieu River in 1610 and at Lachine in 1611.

In 1609 the Hurons first visited the St Lawrence and contacted the French. For six years the Kichesipirinis prevented Champlain from visiting the Huron country and concluding a treaty with the Hurons that would weaken the Algonkins' role as middlemen. Then, as a result of increasing warfare between the Algonkins and the Oneidas, Champlain and a number of armed Frenchmen were allowed to travel to the Huron country in 1615 to participate in a joint Huron-Algonkin military campaign against the Oneidas. Although Champlain had not intended to accompany the Hurons that year, Gravé Du Pont insisted that he do so to ensure their continued goodwill and to increase trade (Biggar 1922–36, 3:31–2). Champlain concluded an alliance with each of the Huron council chiefs that permitted the Hurons to trade directly with the French. As armed Frenchmen began to travel more regularly with native groups along the St Lawrence and Ottawa Rivers, the Mohawks and Oneidas ceased to raid these regions. French boys who were employed by the trading company were sent to live with a number of these groups and learn their languages. Many of them eventually won the confidence and respect of these peoples and in later years played a major role in the fur trade.

From 1609 to 1615 de Monts's traders had been extremely successful in expanding trade with native peoples into the interior, thus bypassing the monopolies of Montagnais and Algonkin middlemen. In so doing, they helped to draw the Hurons into the alliance that the Montagnais and Algonkins had already formed against the Mohawks and Oneidas, instead of pitting the Hurons, Montagnais, and Algonkins against one another. They also won the friendship of all three groups for themselves. That these intertribal alliances remained strong after Mohawk and Oneida attacks had declined is a measure of the skill with which Gravé Du Pont had analysed intertribal relations and was able to judge probable native responses to his actions.

It used to be debated whether Cartier with his mass kidnapping in 1536 or Champlain in 1609 had been responsible for starting the warfare between the French and the Iroquois that was to last for the rest of the seventeenth century. Champlain's self-proclaimed defeat by the Oneidas in 1615 has also been seen as a turning point that marked the beginning of the Iroquois' rise to a position of "astonishing supremacy" (Trudel 1966a:223). Today, it is certain that Cartier could not have begun such a war, since the Iroquoian groups that he encountered were not ancestral to the Five Nations. It is also evident that none of the Indians involved regarded the campaign of 1615 as a defeat for Champlain or his allies. The Iroquois killed only four Frenchmen in two isolated incidents prior to 1642 and it appears that even later they did not wish to fight the French. The question that must be asked is why, after the French had played a leading role in killing about 160 Mohawks in 1609 and 1610 and attacking an Oneida settlement in 1615, were these tribes not more vindictive. While they may have been intimidated by the French, that would not have prevented them from seeking blood revenge by harassing small groups of traders.

The rest of the answer is connected with the founding of a rival European colony after Henry Hudson's exploration of the Hudson River in 1609. The following year some Dutch capitalists followed up his discovery by sending a ship to trade for furs, as Breton traders had done on the St Lawrence in 1581. Other small trading companies hastened to take advantage of the situation. In 1614, after a period of free trade, the short-lived United New Netherland Company obtained a trading monopoly for four years and established Fort Nassau on Castle Island, near modern Albany, on the upper Hudson. It was abandoned when the monopoly expired in 1617, but in 1624 the newly founded and much better financed Dutch West India Company, as one of its many projects (Wallerstein 1980:51–2), built Fort Orange, a fortified trading post, on the west bank of the Hudson River, near Castle Island. Mohawk tribal territory did not extend as far east as the Hudson, but they could now hope to obtain European goods either through their Mahican neighbours or directly from the Dutch. With European goods available close at hand, the Mohawks no longer had to face the increasing dangers of raiding the St Lawrence Valley.

The Dutch merchants set about developing trade in the same fashion as their French counterparts. In 1615 three Dutch traders led by a man named Kleynties accompanied a Mohawk raid against the Susquehannocks. The Dutch were apparently seeking to encourage their trading partners by providing them with military assistance just as de Monts's agents had done. Their expedition ended with the Dutch being captured by the Susquehannocks, who ransomed them to Cornelis Hendricksen when he explored and traded on the Delaware River the following year (Murray 1938). The Dutch knew only too well that to the north the French had tapped a source of furs that in quantity and quality was superior to that in New York State. They wished to lure Montagnais and Algonkin traders south to Fort Orange and believed they could because these tribes were accustomed to barter with the Mahicans for shell beads that were manufactured in the Long Island region. The Dutch were able to obtain large quantities of these beads and indeed encouraged their mass production (Fenton 1971; Ceci 1982). Thus they hoped that they could use them to initiate trade with these tribes on their own account. The French were at a disadvantage because they had no supply of wampum and the Montagnais and Algonkins did not consider ivory or glass beads acceptable substitutes. The Mohawks, having already suffered the catastrophic defeats of 1609 and 1610, found themselves threatened by the possibility that their enemies would form a trading alliance with the Dutch as well as the French and once again cut them off from any source of European goods.

In 1624 the Mohawks used an offer to exchange prisoners to make peace with the Montagnais, Algonkins, and French and thus ensured themselves of at least a temporary supply of European goods from that direction. Then they attacked the Mahicans. When the war turned against the Mahicans in 1626, the Dutch traders commissioned the commandant at Fort Orange, Daniel Van Krieckenbeeck, to lead a small party of Dutch musketeers against the Mohawks. This expedition was soundly defeated and some of its members were tortured to death by the victorious Iroquois. Realizing their vulnerable position, the Dutch hastened to re-establish friendly relations with the Iroquois. By 1628 the Mohawks had dispersed the Mahican bands living close to Fort Orange, and had taken control of all the land that provided access to the trading post (Trelease 1960:46–8). Hereafter, although they allowed other Iroquois tribes to trade with the Dutch, they steadfastly refused to allow the Montagnais and Algonkins to visit Fort Orange (Trigger 1971a).

The Dutch were furious that the Mohawks had frustrated their plans to obtain furs from the north. Yet, throughout the period of Dutch rule, too few Europeans lived in the Albany area for them to be able to control the Mohawks. Late in 1626 Isaack de Rasiere, the provincial secretary of the colony of New Netherland, requested permission to lead a stronger force against the Mohawks if they refused to grant the northern tribes a perpetual right-of-way through their territory. This plan was rejected by the Amsterdam directors of the trading company, who were unwilling to become involved in an expensive and uncertain military adventure (Van Laer 1924:212–15). While Dutch traders and officials remained anxious to circumvent the Mohawk boycott, after 1628 rising trade figures reconciled them to the new political situation, at least until they were militarily stronger. For the present, they disengaged themselves from any involvement in intertribal politics and traded only with Indians who were able to reach Fort Orange. In effect, their neutrality meant that the Mohawks determined who might trade with them.

It was not until 1642, after guns had been sold to the Indians, that Arent van Curler concluded the first formal alliance between the Dutch and the Mohawks (Trelease 1960:117). The Dutch refused in later years to send soldiers to help defend the Mohawks, which led the Mohawks to complain in 1659 that the Dutch did not do as much to help them as the French did for their Indian allies (ibid., 125). Later the English, who employed the Iroquois as surrogates and mercenaries in their own wars, also failed to assist them militarily when they were attacked by the French. Yet the alliances between the Dutch and the Mohawks and later between the English and the Iroquois remained strong. In native eyes, trade and nonaggression, rather than military cooperation, constituted the minimal basis of an effective intergroup alliance.

Not without cause, the Mohawks continued to mistrust the Dutch for a long time after 1628, which appears to account for their persistently conciliatory attitude towards the French. The French lived much farther away and for that reason were less desirable trading partners. Yet the Mohawks regarded them as a useful alternative should further troubles arise with the traders at Fort Orange. For the Mohawks, the preferred solution would have been for the French to opt for neutrality as the Dutch had done. To that end they repeatedly offered to form an alliance with the French that excluded the latter's Indian allies. The French traders clearly recognized Mohawk hegemony at Fort Orange to be in their interest, since it ruled out the possibility of the Algonkins and Montagnais trading with the Dutch. Hence, they would not have wished to see the power of the Mohawks substantially reduced unless their Dutch rivals had been eliminated. Thus began what Eccles (1973:45) has observed was a continuing French policy of preserving the Iroquois. On the other hand, while the French traders benefited from chronic, low-level warfare between their Indian allies and the Iroquois, they could not willingly allow these allies to be dispersed or their traders to be severely harassed on the Ottawa and St Lawrence Rivers. Nor could they conclude any formal treaty with the Mohawks that did not involve these allies.

After de Monts's monopoly expired at the end of 1608 and free trade was restored to the St Lawrence Valley, his men succeeded in forming new alliances with native peoples and tried to outrun their French competitors by arranging to trade with these groups farther up the St Lawrence River. The rival French traders quickly followed them. The Montagnais, who had experienced regular free trade prior to 1600 and had continued to do business with illegal traders after that time, took advantage of increased competition to demand more European goods in return for their furs. The Huron and Ottawa Valley Algonkin traders, who were less knowledgeable about dealing with Europeans, felt harassed by the competition for their furs on the upper St Lawrence, although Champlain states that he did all that he could under the circumstances to preserve order among the Europeans. Yet many French who were trading for the first time did not understand the rules and etiquette of native trade as de Monts's agents did. Champlain claimed that robberies and quarrels that occurred during the trading at Montreal Island, especially when he was not there in 1612, angered the Indians and led to a reduction in their participation the following year.

As a consequence of free trade, overall costs to European traders rose and profits fell. More ships were being outfitted for trade but each one returned to France with fewer furs. De Monts's partners lost interest in supporting either the settlement at Quebec or Champlain's explorations, which under the circumstances were benefiting rival traders more than they were themselves. In the autumn of 1611 de Monts had to buy back his partners' shares and he became the sole owner of the habitation at Quebec; being unable to support it by himself, he was forced to cede it to merchants from La Rochelle, who used it as a storage depot (Trudel 1966a:184–5). In 1612 Champlain stayed in France to lobby for the re-establishment of a monopoly of the fur trade. That year he persuaded Charles de Bourbon, comte de Soissons, who was governor of Normandy and a close relative of Louis XIII, to have the king appoint this nobleman lieutenant-general of New France with a twelve-year monopoly of the fur trade from Quebec westward. When Soissons died in November, his nephew and heir, Henri de Bourbon, prince de Condé, who stood second in line to the throne of France, acquired the more imposing title of viceroy of New France and named Champlain his lieutenant. Condé also used violent acts committed by illegal traders as an excuse to have his monopoly extended eastward to include Matane in the Gaspé Peninsula.

In spite of these inducements, Champlain had a difficult time establishing a new trading company. Late in 1613 the Compagnie du Canada was formed. Most of its shareholders were from Saint-Malo and Rouen. The merchants from the independently minded Protestant stronghold of La Rochelle refused to join and continued to trade illegally. The company was granted a monopoly of the fur trade along the St Lawrence River for eleven years in return for presenting the viceroy with a horse worth 3,000 livres each year, paying Champlain's salary and expenses, and undertaking to establish a handful of settlers at Quebec. This was a far lighter burden than had been imposed on previous companies. In March 1615 the directors also agreed to transport six missionaries to New France each year and to support them until they had a seminary (Trudel 1966a:203–8, 211). The latter obligation must have offended Protestant shareholders and been an unwanted expense to many Roman Catholic ones.

According to the new arrangement, Champlain was no longer the employee of a trading company, but a vice-regal official responsible for the government of the colony. He must have been disappointed by the failure of these new agreements to require extensive colonization and even more so when the minimal settlement that was stipulated was not carried out. In 1617 Louis Hébert, who had worked at Port Royal from 1606 to 1613, came to Quebec with his family. He was contracted to work as an apothecary for the trading company for 300 livres yearly but could later take up farming, although he was required to sell all his surplus produce to the company and was forbidden to trade with the Indians (Trudel 1966a:242–5). The trading company was anxious to prevent colonists from challenging its control of the fur trade.

It appears that each year between 1615 and 1629 Canadian furs sold in France for about 150,000 livres, while the expenses of the trading company amounted to less than 50,000 livres (Trudel 1966a: 431–2). Yet, despite these profits, the company had little working capital and each summer's operation depended on the success of the previous year's trade (Eccles 1973:23). A disaster at sea or fewer Indians coming to trade even for a single year could cause severe problems. The company also faced major infringements on its profits as a result of illegal traders. This created a major dilemma for shareholders. They wanted to make as much money as quickly as possible because they feared losing their monopoly prematurely as previous companies had done. Therefore they were anxious to keep expenses to a minimum by maintaining as few workmen at Quebec as possible and by avoiding unnecessary investment in costly facilities (ibid.). They were aware, however, that these tactics were providing the king with grounds for cancelling their monopoly as well as risking that Quebec might be seized by the Dutch or English.

During the period of free trade, the price the French had to pay to the Indians for furs had risen as a result of competition. After the new monopoly had been enforced in 1614, official traders sought to charge the Indians more for European goods. To reduce transportation costs they would also have preferred to have the Hurons and Algonkins come to Quebec to trade. Montagnais demands for tolls, the need for the French to patrol the St Lawrence River to discourage Iroquois raids, and resistance from the Hurons and Algonkins to having to travel so far resulted in a compromise. Lachine was abandoned as a summer trading station, but trading continued at Ile Saint-Ignace and Cap Victoire, near the mouth of the Richelieu River, and at the future site of Trois-Rivières, where the Montagnais and Algonkins established a fortified summer camp.

There is no evidence that the Hurons or the Algonkins from the Ottawa Valley, who had been troubled by European competition for their goods, were greatly upset by the higher prices, although they probably countered by demanding more presents from the French as an expression of friendship. They appear to have placed greater importance on having a stable relationship with European traders and maintaining a formal alliance with them than did the Montagnais. Relations also remained good between these groups and the French interpreters who lived in their midst as agents of the trading company. The Montagnais, however, were very angry as a result of the price increases and did all they could to continue doing business with illegal traders who were operating along the lower St Lawrence. Growing tensions also manifested themselves in the murder of two Frenchmen in 1617 and two more in 1627. Although these incidents resulted from personal disagreements between Frenchmen and Indians, they would not have led to murder if relations between the French and the Montagnais had generally been good. Champlain attributed most of the troubles at Quebec to the greed of the French traders, but we do not know how, or with what public proclamations, the company officials at Quebec actually went about raising prices. It appears that the Montagnais continued to get on well with their interpreter Nicolas Marsolet, Gravé Du Pont, and other traders, while much of their resentment was directed against Champlain.

Analogous monopoly conditions prevailed in New Netherland prior to 1638–9 when, in an effort to stimulate immigration, it was decreed that all persons could trade directly with the Indians and ship goods in and out of the colony on their own account (Trelease 1960:61). In the early 1630s the Mohawks were annoyed by the high prices that the Dutch traders were charging them for European goods. Their anger exploded in 1633, when Hans Hontom, a trader who appears to have kidnapped and murdered a Mohawk council chief, was appointed the new commandant at Fort Orange. The Mohawks attacked the Dutch enclave, burning the trading company's boat and killing most of the cattle at the settlement of Rensselaerswyck. The Dutch realized the weakness of their position and acted quickly to improve their standing with the Mohawks. Hontom soon was killed in a brawl, and while the colonist Kiliaen van Rensselaer still wanted an indemnity for his losses from the Mohawks three years later, it is significant that he asked the governor in New Amsterdam to request it, so that the Mohawks would not hold it against him or the people at Fort Orange (Trelease 1960:51).

Fearing that the Dutch might seek revenge, the Mohawks and Oneidas again made peace with the Algonkins and Montagnais, who at that time were embroiled in a dispute with the French over yet another murder of a Frenchman. The Oneidas reported that in the summer of 1634 six French traders had visited them and offered higher prices for their furs than the Dutch were paying. Alarmed by these reports, the Dutch traders sent the surgeon Bogaert to investigate the situation. The Iroquois told him they were willing to continue trading exclusively with the Dutch but only if the Dutch paid them higher prices for their furs (Jameson 1909:148–54). Neither the Dutch nor the French could be complacent about relations with their native trading partners.

### COLONIZERS AGAINST TRADERS

By 1613 the principle of monopoly had triumphed over free trade in the St Lawrence Valley. Monopolies, however, involved an obligation to promote colonization, which trading companies were loath to carry out even to a modest extent. As a vice-regal official, Champlain became a vociferous advocate of large-scale colonization. No doubt he was partly motivated by a desire to make his own administrative post more secure and illustrious. Yet traders had to agree that without substantial settlement a foreign power could easily seize Quebec and the fur trade at any time. With the development of New England beginning in 1620, the same problem was to confront the Dutch in New Netherland. It was also obvious that if more food were grown locally, Quebec would be less dependent on annual shipments. As matters stood, the failure of the ships to arrive for even a single summer threatened the colony with starvation. Yet the trading company did not have the resources or the will to promote settlement on an extensive scale and the French government was unwilling to invest in doing so. Hence Champlain's insistence on colonization gradually brought him into severe conflict with his former employers. In 1615, however, he was still on sufficiently good terms with Gravé Du Pont that he accepted his advice to travel inland with the Hurons that year.

In 1614 Champlain remained in France to promote colonization. While there he secured donations that enabled three Recollet priests and a lay brother to accompany him to Quebec the following year (Trudel 1966a:210–15). Although only a few Recollets worked in and out of Quebec between 1615 and 1629, the order supported Champlain very effectively in advancing colonization. The Recollets argued that native people had to settle down and learn to live like Europeans in order to convert them and that Indians could be expected to alter their customs only if there were enough European colonists to serve as exemplars and teachers. The Recollets also believed that force would be required to make them abandon aspects of their traditional behaviour. These convictions constituted a powerful argument in favour of colonization, especially in the context of the increasing zeal of the Counter-Reformation that characterized France during the reign of Louis XIII. At the same time that the monarchy was asserting its authority by limiting the power of provincial parliaments and by crushing free cities such as La Rochelle the influence of the clergy was growing at court and throughout the country. Priests dominated the Council of State, Jesuit colleges were educating the upper classes, and enthusiasm for winning Protestants to Roman Catholicism was high (Eccles 1973:24). These conditions permitted Champlain and the Recollets to introduce a new element of confrontation into relations both among the French who were working at Quebec and between them and native peoples.

The attitudes of French traders towards native peoples differed markedly from those of Champlain and the Recollets. They, like their counterparts at Fort Orange, were anxious to make as much profit as possible. Most of them were probably not above cheating native people or trying to intimidate them, but it was in their long-term interest to continue to do business with them. As a result, they had to learn how to deal with the Indians in ways that the latter understood and found acceptable. They also had to learn about the traditional conventions that governed intertribal trade and the conflicts and alliances that prevailed among many native groups in eastern North America. Only when they were armed with this sort of knowledge and an implicit but effective understanding of native behaviour was it possible for traders to pursue their own interests while remaining only a tiny part of the ethnic mosaic of the region. The strength of Gravé Du Pont and the other traders and interpreters was the substantial working knowledge they had acquired of native cultures. Until 1615 this information appears to have allowed Gravé Du Pont to work with Champlain to conclude a series of alliances with the Algonkins and Hurons that greatly benefited French traders.

Champlain on his own and the Recollets did not possess such knowledge or have the motivation to obtain it. Social historians have noted the persistence of feudal ideals in France during the early seventeenth century and the strong tendency of the middle classes to espouse these values (Wallerstein 1974:297). The missionaries who came to New France, whether Recollet or Jesuit, would have shared in this backward-looking tendency. Champlain, the son of a naval captain and a devout Roman Catholic, had fought for Henri IV until 1598. It has been suggested that he was officially elevated to the nobility when he became Condé's lieutenant in 1612 (Trudel 1966d:187); but, if so, like many bourgeois of the period, he made pretensions to this status in the way he styled himself in documents still earlier. Although he had worked for trading companies since 1603, he identified himself as a soldier and administrator and espoused the values of the nobility.

Europeans shared a hierarchical view of society. They believed that everyone occupied a clearly defined station and that superiors had a divinely sanctioned right to give orders to persons of lesser rank. Yet Champlain and the Recollets appear to have subscribed to a far more rigid and exaggerated version of this belief than did the traders. In their view, they had the right to provide leadership not only to the French in Canada but also to native North Americans. Their assumption of natural superiority was accompanied by a paternalistic concern for the welfare of those native people who acknowledged themselves to be in their charge. Yet this same paternalism led them to believe that they inevitably knew all about these people and what was best for them. In 1615 this ethnocentric attitude caused Champlain to conclude that the Hurons were "no warriors" and to assume that they regarded their attack on the Oneida town as a failure, without bothering to determine what the Indians had expected from this campaign (Biggar 1922–36, 3:75). It also led Paul Ragueneau to praise the Jesuits who helped the Hurons in the winter of 1649–50 for performing acts of charity to fellow Christians "however barbarous and lowly they may have been" (Thwaites 1896–1901, 35:95). There was little room for compromises based on an understanding of native cultures in relations that had developed from such premises. Yet many historians have accepted without question the interpretations that Champlain, the Recollets, and the Jesuits have offered of their actions. They have assumed that these "noble" and "disinterested" men had to keep the rapacity of the French traders under control and to protect the Indians from their meanness (Campeau 1979:liv, xcvii–xcviii). Historians have also accepted their claim that the Indians respected only force and that physical compulsion was required to control them for their own good (Trudel 1966a:353; Campeau 1979:lxxxv).

Between 1615 and 1629 Champlain and the Recollets tried to persuade the Montagnais who lived around Quebec City to settle down and become farmers, to recognize the French king as their sovereign and the authority of Champlain as his representative, and, more concretely, to acknowledge Champlain's right to appoint their chiefs. The first demand brought Champlain and the Recollets into conflict with the trading company, whose officials wanted these Indians to continue hunting. When the Recollets, by offering gifts to a few Montagnais families, persuaded them to construct cabins near Quebec, which they could visit periodically, and to plant some corn, the traders warned the priests that if native settlement continued, they would use force to drive the Indians away (Sagard 1866:165). The Recollets further disrupted relations between the Montagnais and the French traders by protesting that to accept traditional native reparations payments for the two Frenchmen murdered in 1617 would be to barter the lives of Christians for beaver skins. The refusal of the French officials to accept these reparations almost resulted in warfare, which was averted only when Gravé Du Pont took the matter in hand and settled it in accordance with native custom. Even so, Champlain continued to feel that French honour had been betrayed (Biggar 1922–36, 5:103–7). By refusing to allow company traders to sell even small amounts of liquor to the Indians, he also undermined the ability of these merchants to compete with independent traders who continued to operate on the lower St Lawrence.

Historians have praised Champlain for understanding the Indians and for knowing how to get along with them. They have also believed that he succeeded in controlling the internal affairs of the Montagnais (Trudel 1966a:358–61), but this would have been impossible because the Montagnais lacked the concept of submission to authority and hence would not even have understood what he was talking about. Champlain also lacked the military force or the knowledge of their culture that would have allowed him to control them. His meddling produced growing hostility between the French and the Montagnais, which eventually drove the Montagnais to help the English to seize Quebec in 1629. Champlain's own frustration was reflected in the fact that by 1624 he was calling them his worst enemies (Biggar 1922–36, 5:124). Such goodwill as remained appears to have been retained by the traders. Because of his long experience in dealing with Indians, the directors of the trading company asked Gravé Du Pont, despite old age and sickness, to return to Quebec from 1627 to 1629 (Trudel 1966e).

After the peace with the Mohawks had collapsed in 1627, Champlain began to view the Iroquois as a hindrance to communications and exploration and as the allies of a colonial power that threatened the existence of New France. He therefore advocated their extermination or subjugation. This policy not only was impossible, even if extensive military forces had been at his disposal, but also ran counter to the French traders' desire to preserve the Mohawks as a buffer that prevented the Montagnais and Algonkins from trading with the Dutch, a role that the Mohawks performed even when they were at peace with these tribes around 1634. It is worth noting that while Champlain was advocating war against the Iroquois, French traders were contacting the Oneidas, Onondagas, and possibly even the Senecas. His behaviour also contrasts with that of Dutch traders and administrators who, once they had adopted a policy of neutrality, were prepared to tolerate a considerable amount of provocative behaviour by the Mohawks, including the killing of some of their livestock each year. The Mohawks, for their part, continued to trade with the Dutch even though occasionally some of them were kidnapped, beaten, and robbed by highly competitive Dutch traders or they were mistreated when they did not have enough furs to sell (Trelease 1960:124–5). Their robust alliance was capable of surviving much interpersonal strain. In 1660 Marie de l'Incarnation observed sarcastically that the desire for beaver skins made the Dutch submit to innumerable indignities "that the French would never be able to endure" (Marshall 1967:255).

It appears more likely that she was speaking of the attitudes of French officials and priests rather than that of French traders. Dutch officials were more sympathetic to the Indian policies of Dutch traders than was the case in New France, since they shared common economic interests and middle-class values.

Another issue that found Champlain and the Recollets in disagreement with the trading company concerned the Frenchmen who were living among the Indians and especially the interpreters, who were valued highly by the company and therefore very well paid for their services. The traders regarded these men as vital for maintaining the alliances on which their business depended. They relied on them to promote trade, keep out the Dutch, and help to keep open the trade routes. On the other hand, Champlain's contempt for these men is evident throughout his writings. Few of Brûlé's accomplishments were adequately credited to him and his personal life was the subject of considerable invective in Champlain's works. In 1634 Champlain officially intervened to reduce the amount of land granted to two former interpreters, Jacques Hertel and Jean Godefroy de Lintot, at Trois-Rivières from 200 to only 50 arpents each (Campeau 1974:76–7). This action was a clear rebuff to the social pretensions of men whose way of life he despised.

The Recollets likewise denounced the interpreters for setting a bad example of Christian life, debauching native women, and ridiculing and contradicting missionaries. They held them responsible for much of their lack of success in converting native people. The interpreters were angered by such accusations and it may have been in retaliation that they refused to help the Recollets to learn native languages. On the other hand, this refusal may have been unofficial company policy. They probably also began to oppose the missionaries consciously in other ways, thus giving further substance to the priests' accusations. The controversy about the interpreters widened the rift between Champlain and the Recollets on the one hand and the trading company and its employees on the other.

In 1616 Champlain and the Recollets began to work in concert to promote their common goals. Champlain and Fathers Denis Jamet and Joseph Le Caron returned together to France to complain to the Compagnie du Canada about the behaviour of its agents and to press generally for more missionaries and expanded settlement. They urged that colonists be encouraged to come to Canada by granting them limited rights to trade with the Indians. The Recollets also argued that the membership of Protestants in the Compagnie du Canada was an obstacle to the spread of Roman Catholicism (Trudel 1966a:233–8). None of these proposals could have been popular with the directors of the company and collectively they must have been seen as posing a significant threat to the company's future operations.

Yet the three had returned to France at a bad time. Condé had become the leader of a league of noblemen and others who opposed the queen regent and her minister Concino Concini. When civil war broke out, Condé was arrested and kept in prison until 1619. In 1617 Louis XIII tried to take power into his own hands, but warfare against his mother and Protestant rebels continued for several years. While Condé was in prison, the Maréchal Pons de Lauzières, marquis de Thémines, became viceroy of New France. Various promises to promote colonization that de Monts had extracted from the Compagnie du Canada fell into abeyance, and in the meanwhile the associates of the company took steps to protect their own interests by trying to demote or dismiss Champlain.

In this period there was much discussion in France about the desirability of colonization in Canada. The Jesuit Pierre Biard, who had worked in Nova Scotia, urged settlement in his *Relation de la Nouvelle France*, published in 1616. Two years later Marc Lescarbot brought out a new edition of his *Histoire de la Nouvelle-France*, while the same year Charles de Biencourt de Saint-Just appealed unsuccessfully to the mayor and aldermen of Paris to assist his efforts at colonization in Nova Scotia. During the winter of 1617–18, Champlain addressed a carefully prepared plan for colonization to the Chamber of Commerce of Paris. He called for the establishment of a colony based on the exploitation and export of fish, timber, minerals, wood ash, plant products, and livestock, as well as furs. He claimed that these activities could yield an annual revenue of 5.4 million livres, of which less than 10 per cent would come from the fur trade. He also referred to the immense profits that could be derived from charging tolls once the St Lawrence River was developed as a route to the Pacific Ocean and the Orient. The colony that he proposed to establish in the valley of the St Charles River at Quebec was to consist of 300 families, an additional 300 soldiers, and 15 priests. It was to be heavily fortified and would flourish as a result of trade and agriculture (Trudel 1966a:250–4).

Champlain's proposal has been greatly admired by modern historians, who have interpreted it as anticipating many of the policies that Louis XIV's minister Colbert was to carry out after 1663. Much of Champlain's reputation as a colonizer rests upon this document. Although he framed his arguments in terms of the mercantilist philosophy that was popular at this period, in promoting colonization in Canada as a financially profitable enterprise he failed to address many serious problems. Hopes of developing the St Lawrence Valley as a trade route to the Orient were no better founded in 1617 than they had been in Cartier's time. He also did not take account of the impact of Canada's short growing season, its lack of ice-free ports that could be used during the winter, and its vast distance from potential markets. Fishing, which was claimed to be the principal asset of New France, was mainly profitable in the Gulf of St Lawrence and off Newfoundland where fish stocks were more abundant and transportation costs lower; but in this area Canadian fishermen later found themselves unable to compete with those who came directly from France each year. Higher labour costs were to make timber from Quebec more expensive in France than that from the Baltic and shipbuilding in Quebec more costly than in Europe. Because of an unfavourable climate, agriculture and cattle breeding did not yield significant exports. In New France only furs could be produced more cheaply than elsewhere; hence they were to remain the chief export of the colony and the principal commodity capable of producing wealth for settlers (Eccles 1973:75–84; Dechêne 1974:481–90).

The demand for furs was, however, considerably more limited in Europe than that for sugar and tobacco, even if proportionally more of these commodities were consumed within France and less was earned through the export of finished products than was the case with beaver pelts (Wallerstein 1980:102). Hence the small French colonies in the West Indies were to grow more rapidly and prosper much more than in Canada. In addition, French colonies as a whole did not expand as rapidly as British ones, partly because France had less need of foreign goods and large external markets than England (ibid.) and partly because capital accumulation was less effective as a result of heavy borrowing by the state and the extensive purchase of estates, offices, and rights to engage in tax-farming by those who were commercially successful (Delâge 1981). Since France was a continental military power, there was also a persistent reluctance to export manpower, while in England enclosures, rising land rents, and crises in cloth production encouraged significant emigration during the seventeenth century. Colbert, who had more resources for gathering information than Champlain did, as well as greater reason for objectivity, also failed to take account of these limitations in his planning for New France. Yet, it remains significant that Champlain, who was personally familiar with Canada, was unwilling to, or dared not, take account of the economic realities of this part of the world in formulating his proposal.

The Chamber of Commerce interviewed Champlain and politely encouraged him to present a memorandum to the king. No financial help was forthcoming from its members or from the crown, although Louis XIII wrote to the shareholders of the Compagnie du Canada confirming Champlain in his command and urging them to support his plan; however, he refrained from imposing any specific conditions forcing them to do so. Late in 1618 Champlain thought that he had persuaded the company to settle eighty colonists at Quebec. Yet, the following spring, in a dramatic move, company officials refused to allow him to embark for Canada despite his commission as lieutenant to the viceroy. Gravé Du Pont was placed in command at Quebec, and Champlain was informed that henceforth he would be employed only as an explorer (Trudel 1966a:260–2). In October Condé was released from prison and resumed his post as viceroy, although he relinquished it almost immediately to his brother-in-law Henri, duc de Montmorency, in return for 30,000 livres. This sale price is an indication that the office was worth more than the nominal 3,000 livres that the company was bound to pay the viceroy each year, although why this is so is unknown. Montmorency confirmed Champlain in his lieutenancy and instructed him to resume his command at Quebec. He returned to Quebec in 1620 and immediately began to renovate the habitation and to build Fort St Louis atop Cape Diamond. Sixty Europeans spent the following winter at Quebec, the largest number recorded there since 1543, but only a few were settlers.

In the autumn of 1620, Montmorency prematurely cancelled the monopoly of the Compagnie du Canada on the grounds that it had failed in its undertaking to promote colonization and granted a new one to a company headed by the de Caëns, a trading family from Rouen. Ezéchiel and his son Emery were Roman Catholics, while Ezéchiel's nephew Guillaume was a Protestant. Gabriel Sagard described Guillaume as a "liberal and understanding man" and at one time it was believed that he might become a Roman Catholic. This suggests the falseness of later efforts by Champlain and the Recollets to portray him as an arch-enemy of Catholicism (Trudel 1966b). The formal obligations that were assumed by the Compagnie de Caën were similar to the not very onerous ones that had been imposed on the previous company. In return for an eleven-year monopoly of the fur trade, later extended to fifteen years, the de Caëns agreed to pay stipends to Montmorency and Champlain, put ten workmen each summer at Champlain's disposal, support six Recollet priests, and settle six families of at least three members each.

In the summer of 1621, a dispute arose at Quebec about whether the old or the new company had the right to trade there, although in May it had been decided in France that both companies could do so for that year only. Champlain and the Recollets took advantage of the crisis to convene an informal "Estates-General" to advise the king about how the colony might be saved from ruin. At this meeting, which was attended only by those who were sympathetic to Champlain and the Recollets, it was recommended that no Protestant should be allowed to live in New France, that more money should be spent to support the clergy, and that Champlain should be given broader powers and more armed strength. The Recollet Georges Le Baillif was chosen to report these deliberations to the king. When he returned to France, Le Baillif published a pamphlet attacking Guillaume de Caën and his associates, and the Recollet superior of the province of Saint-Denis asked Louis XIII to forbid Protestants to live or work in New France. Nevertheless, early in 1622, the Council of State confirmed the monopoly of the Compagnie de Caën although it also made it possible for the shareholders in the old company to acquire a block of shares in the new one (Trudel 1966a:275–93). The de Caëns still had to contend with the activities of illegal traders from La Rochelle and the Basque country, who continued to carry off furs and to make it difficult to enforce monopoly prices.

It is wrong to conclude that the de Caëns sought only to draw profits from the fur trade and that they totally ignored settlement (Campeau 1979:xlix, liv). Their company financed the construction of the fort at Quebec and replaced the wooden habitation with a new stone structure. The new habitation consisted of two wings with defensive turrets at the four corners, while a semi-circular fortification commanded the river and moats surrounded the entire structure (Trudel 1966a:293–4). Louis Hébert was granted possession of farmland as a fief in perpetuity in 1623, and the following year Guillaume de Caën obtained a seigneury at Cap Tourmente, where he established a stock-raising centre to produce meat and milk products for the colony. The company also built a habitation on Miscou Island. While its colonizing activities fell short even of its limited responsibilities, some progress was made. In general, however, the trading company tried to appear to be honouring its obligations, but was reluctant to encourage colonization because it feared that settlement might eventually result in a challenge to its monopolistic control of the fur trade.

## THE JESUIT MISSION COLONY

In 1625 new alliances began to shape the future of New France. Armand-Jean Du Plessis, cardinal de Richelieu, who was now Louis XIII's chief minister, compelled Montmorency to resign his post as viceroy of New France. At this time the Jesuits also became involved in the colony. They had been active in Acadia until Samuel Argall destroyed the French settlements in that region in 1613. While there they had become embroiled in a mutually destructive quarrel with the colonizer Jean de Biencourt de Poutrincourt, who was himself a devout Roman Catholic. Some of these Jesuits wished to return to New France, but instead of seeking an alliance with Champlain as the Recollets had done, they attempted to secure maximum freedom for their mission program by winning the support of the principal officials in France who controlled the destiny of Canada. In 1624 Father Philibert Noyrot became confessor to Henri de Lévis, duc de Ventadour, the nephew of Montmorency. Ventadour and his wife were zealous Roman Catholics. In 1630 he was to found the Compagnie du Saint-Sacrement, a powerful secret association that had as members important laymen and clerics who were dedicated to various projects, including promoting religious reform, undertaking charitable activities, and aiding missionary work, but above all extirpating Protestantism. After his wife died, in 1643, Ventadour became a priest.

In 1625 Noyrot persuaded his patron to purchase the office of viceroy from his uncle for 1 million livres. The same year Ventadour arranged to send three Jesuit missionaries to Quebec at his own expense, to the consternation of many of the Protestants who worked there as well as of Catholics such as Hébert, who had been employed by and was a distant relative of Poutrincourt. The Recollets, aware of the powerful backing that the Jesuits had acquired and knowing that they had many interests in common, welcomed them and offered them temporary accommodation in their mission house. They must, however, have had some misgivings about these uninvited newcomers (Campeau 1979:l).

Ventadour's accession spelled trouble for Guillaume de Caën. In 1626, he was forbidden as a Protestant to travel to New France. Champlain and the Recollets had been seeking to suppress Protestant religious observances in New France since 1621. De Caën's seigneury at Cap Tourmente might have counted as a location where the Protestant cult could be practised legally under the provisions of the Edict of Nantes; hence there were sound religious reasons to ban him (Campeau 1979:101–2). The Jesuits also came armed with the authority to order Brûlé and Marsolet, the two interpreters whose behaviour had been the most offensive to the Recollets, to return to France. These orders greatly angered Emery de Caën, who regarded these men as essential for his trading operation. Nevertheless, they were carried out. This disciplinary action was ultimately to drive these two interpreters and others to defect to the English.

Although they were pursuing common goals at this time, the Jesuits espoused an approach to missionary work that was different in important respects from that of the Recollets. They were more tolerant of cultural differences, provided these were not incompatible with Christian theology or morality, and had a less favourable view of European settlers. They feared that, far from setting an example of Christian life for native peoples, the colonists might teach them new vices and further corrupt them. From their experience in Nova Scotia, they had already concluded that in some aspects of behaviour, such as generosity, native American cultures more nearly realized Christian ideals than European ones did. Large-scale colonization was therefore not essential for the Jesuits' mission program, since they preferred to guide and shape their converts' behaviour themselves. In these programmatic differences lay the potential for later disputes between the two religious orders as well as for some measure of accommodation between the Jesuits and the trading company.

Soon Richelieu decided on major economic reforms affecting New France. In 1625 the Recollet Le Caron, who had been a missionary among the Hurons and a former tutor at court, returned to France where he published two pamphlets charging lack of good faith and efficiency on the part of the private trading companies that had so far managed the affairs of the colony. Noyrot, following a brief visit to Quebec in 1626, had an audience with Richelieu and with the support of Ventadour urged the cancellation of the de Caëns' monopoly and the need for a new company to manage the affairs of the colony. The same year Isaac de Razilly, a knight of the Order of St John of Jerusalem, prepared a memorandum for Richelieu, stressing the importance of overseas colonial development for the prosperity of France. These interventions assisted Richelieu to take control of foreign navigation and commerce and set about founding a larger and more securely financed company to manage the affairs of New France.

This new company, known as the Compagnie des Cent-Associés, or the Compagnie de la Nouvelle-France, was modelled in scale on the English East India Company, established in 1600, and the Dutch United East India Company, chartered in 1602. Yet there were also significant differences. It was to be composed of 100 or more associates, all Roman Catholics, each subscribing 3,000 livres. Limited rights to withdraw profits ensured the stability of the project in its early stages. The company was also bound to establish 4,000 settlers in New France over fifteen years. That meant employing and feeding them for three years and then providing them with seed grain and cleared land. The company also had to support three priests in each settlement for three years. All settlers in New France were to be permitted to trade for furs, provided that they sold them to the company for a fixed price. Indians who became Christians were to be deemed French citizens and to enjoy the same privileges. In return, the company was to control all commerce to and from New France for fifteen years, except the fisheries, and to have a perpetual monopoly of the fur trade (Trudel 1979:7–21).

Historians have been unable to decide whether Richelieu primarily sought to promote overseas trade or whether he was motivated by a *politique de grandeur* and by his anti-Spanish policy (Eccles 1973:26). Campeau (1974:10) with good reasons views the Cent-Associés not as a commercial enterprise but as a philanthropical society whose purpose was to promote colonization and missionary work. The composition of the company and its preoccupation with Canada certainly contrasted sharply with the aggressive and clearly entrepreneurial Dutch West India Company, which had been established in 1621 and which quickly became active throughout West Africa and along the eastern seaboard of North and South America. The Dutch West India Company is also credited with holding the Spanish at bay in the Caribbean and thus providing the naval screen behind which the English and French colonies as well as its own were securely established in North America (Wallerstein 1980:52).

To ensure that fur traders did not control the Compagnie des Cent-Associés, it was stipulated that priests and members of the nobility might invest in it without loss of status. Only twenty-six shareholders were businessmen; the rest came from the upper levels of the civil, judicial, and military administration. As a result, the company was controlled by Parisians rather than by Bretons and Normans, as previous trading companies had been. Noyrot assisted Richelieu in forming the company by persuading Ventadour to resign his vice-regal office.

In 1628 the Compagnie des Cent-Associés invested almost 165,000 livres to send 400 colonists to New France. The king ordered the fleet to sail, although war had broken out with England. All four vessels fell into the hands of the Kirkes, who also destroyed the habitation at Miscou and the buildings at Cap Tourmente. The following year the company lost another investment of 104,000 livres, as well as any profits from the fur trade, when its vessels failed to reach Quebec prior to its surrender.

The quarrelling among the various factions at Quebec reached ludicrous extremes in the early summer of 1629. The colony's food supply was exhausted, and the Jesuits, Recollets, Gravé Du Pont, and Champlain all competed openly with one another for the small amount of cornmeal that the Hurons had brought downriver. In the scramble, Champlain got none at all, and he complained about the lack of concern that the others had for him although he was their commander (Biggar 1922–36, 6:48). This episode reveals not only the extreme weakness of his authority but also the disarray that had resulted from two decades of internecine strife. Hébert's family decided to remain at Quebec after it had been captured, and the English allowed them for the first time to trade with the Indians. At least some French who had been employed by the de Caëns were already working for the Kirkes. Almost all the interpreters remained among or returned to their respective tribes.

When Quebec was returned to France in 1632, the Compagnie des Cent-Associés found itself heavily in debt. The following year, while retaining control of colonization, it transferred its monopoly of the fur trade along the St Lawrence and in the Gaspé Peninsula to a subsidiary commercial company for a period of five years. The Compagnie Cheffault-Rozé was established with a working capital of 100,000 livres of which the Cent-Associés furnished one-third. In return, the Compagnie des Cent-Associés was to receive a fixed payment of 10,000 livres each year and one-third of the profits. Trois-Rivières was founded in 1634 so that Algonkins would not have to proceed farther downriver to trade, since it was feared that if they did, they would continue to contact English vessels still operating illegally below Quebec (Campeau 1979:396). The new settlement was also intended to discourage the Iroquois, who had begun again to attack the Algonkins in the St Lawrence Valley after French control had waned in the late 1620s.

In 1633 the Compagnie des Cent-Associés started sending large numbers of workmen to Quebec, who were indentured to remain there for several years. They were attracted by high wages and by a variety of economic benefits if they chose to stay as colonists (Eccles 1973:50). Yet many of them were repelled by the harsh climate and, after 1640, by the increasing severity of Iroquois attacks. As a result, only a fraction of these workmen remained in New France after their contracts had expired (Campeau 1974:68–70). It cost the company about 1,000 livres to establish each settler, which represented a heavy demand on its resources. To increase immigration, the company granted subfiefs to seigneurs, who were required to settle their estates at their own expense.

Prior to 1663 the society of New France had remained in a formative state. Although much of the population was gathered for protection in or near towns, almost half of the tradesmen had farms and cultivated them. In 1663 the 3.2 per cent of the population who were members of the nobility engaged in commerce, and their ranks included a former sailor (Guillaume Couillard) and domestic (Pierre Boucher). Thus there is evidence of significant social mobility. Another 6.4 per cent of the population were members of the middle class. These included public servants, some military officers, merchants, and master tradesmen. Seven holders of seigneuries were corporate religious institutions; the remaining sixty-two were individuals, fifty-one of whom resided in Canada. While the seigneurs constituted almost 2 per cent of the total population, class and rank strongly influenced the patterns of landholding. Although only thirty-two seigneurs were members of the nobility, they controlled 83 per cent of the land. Significantly, the family of Jean de Lauson, who had been successively director of the Compagnie des Cent-Associés and governor of New France, held more land than anyone else. Twenty-three seigneuries, making up 72 per cent of the ceded land, were held by seven families, four of whom were closely knit together by blood and marriage (Trudel 1973:246–67).

Although long-term profits could be expected from these estates, in the short term the expense of developing them greatly exceeded revenues, even though these costs were reduced significantly as the settlers began to experience considerable natural increase and later as the government transported soldiers and marriageable women to the colony. Most of the money that was generated internally to support colonization came from the fur trade. As major industries failed to develop, the fur trade continued to offer the principal opportunity for colonists at all levels to acquire wealth and achieve social mobility (Eccles 1973:49). Hence, while landholding was valued as a source of prestige and long-term gain, their most important short-term goal was to participate in, and better still to control, those commercial activities from which substantial profits could be made. Lauson provides a spectacular example of this with his efforts to regulate participation in the fur trade in 1654, his seizure of furs valued at 300,000 livres in 1656, and his charging of substantial personal expenses to the trading company (Monet 1966). Ordinary colonists who could not derive some degree of profit from the fur trade were doomed to remain at the bottom of Quebec society.

The French government, which became directly involved in the Thirty Years War from 1635, did not provide any economic assistance to develop New France prior to 1663. Yet by 1663 the number of settlers had risen to about 3,000 as a result of immigration and natural increase. Sixty-five per cent of this population lived around Quebec and most of it was engaged in agriculture (Trudel 1979:407–12). Despite the harsh climate, they seem to have enjoyed a substantially higher standard of living than did peasants in France. Yet, while the power of one group to exploit another remained limited in this frontier situation, the seigneurial system was creating new interest groups and new relationships of dependency that were to be of growing importance within New France.

Although they were periodically attacked by the Iroquois, the French settlers did not experience the tension, growing hostility, and the periodic bouts of warfare with local native peoples that accompanied expanding Dutch settlement around New Amsterdam. French colonization occurred within the context of peaceful relations established by the fur trade and the alliances that were associated with it. Conflict was also minimized because of the low density of native population, their nomadic life, and their lack of cleared land and fixed settlements. Moreover, neither the Montagnais nor the Algonkins had a secure claim to the St Lawrence Valley west of Tadoussac, which had previously belonged to the St Lawrence Iroquoians. These groups welcomed French settlement because it offered them protection against Mohawk raids.

Yet, while the trading companies had at first secured native consent before constructing their buildings, French officials did not acknowledge that native people had any title to land, but claimed ownership as well as sovereignty over it by right of discovery (Dickason 1977b). In this way, they behaved differently from the Dutch and the English. The former recognized native rights of prior ownership, while the latter, although generally denying native rights in theory, were prepared to pay for land "out of Prudence and Christian charity, lest otherwise the Indians might have destroyed the first planters" (Trelease 1960:193). French lack of sensitivity about this issue created bad feelings. During the epidemics of the late 1630s, the Montagnais who lived around Quebec City are said to have been convinced that the French were seeking to exterminate them so that they could take total possession of their land (Thwaites 1896–1901, 16:93). It is fortunate for the French that ownership of land along the St Lawrence River was not as vital an issue to native people at that time as it had been in the sixteenth century.

As a result of clandestine intervention by Jean de Lauson, then director of the Compagnie des Cent-Associés and a firm friend of the Jesuits, the Recollets were prevented from returning to Quebec after 1629. Thus the Jesuits became the only clergy in the St Lawrence Valley. In this and in other ways they demonstrated their great control over the Compagnie des Cent-Associés and through it over New France. They insisted that all the interpreters, including those whose conduct did not offend them and who claimed to have remained loyal to France during the period of British occupation, should settle at Quebec and Trois-Rivières. They were replaced by workmen and later by donnés, who were recruited by the Jesuits and operated among native groups under their close supervision. These workmen, who were armed, travelled with the Hurons, encouraged them to trade with the French, and traded with other tribes as Brûlé and other French residents had done previously. When Champlain died in December 1635, Richelieu had already decided to replace him the following year with Charles Huault de Montmagny, a knight of the Order of Malta and a former pupil of the Jesuits. He was given the title of governor, which Champlain had coveted but had never received. The appointment of Montmagny greatly strengthened the power of the Jesuits at Quebec.

Yet, despite their power, the Jesuits recognized that trade constituted the basis of positive French contacts with native peoples and was the source of whatever influence the French could exert over them. For that reason, they were anxious, whenever it did not conflict with what they saw as their religious duty, to cooperate with the trading company rather than to oppose it. This was a principle that the Recollets had not understood and Champlain in his latter years had been unwilling to acknowledge. In 1637 the Jesuits established a mission at Sillery where the Montagnais from the Quebec City area, who had exhausted the local supplies of beavers and because of their location were unable to obtain more by trading, were encouraged to settle and become farmers. Houses, food, and clothing were provided for them from funds that the Jesuits had collected in France. Because these destitute Indians were becoming a troublesome charge on the company, this first Indian reserve in Canada was enthusiastically welcomed by the French traders. Despite this, the mission had only limited success and the first group of natives who came to live there had abandoned it by 1649. Hereafter, despite initial discouragements, the Jesuits developed "roving missions" that did not interfere with the traditional economies of other groups of Montagnais and Algonkins (Campeau 1979:cxxvii–cxxviii).

The Jesuits also aided the Compagnie des Cent-Associés by promoting colonization. In the course of pursuing their mission program, they developed their own seigneuries and found wealthy donors, who provided the colony with public institutions that vastly exceeded in importance what such a small European population might have been expected to possess. Thus they began a college at Quebec in 1635 and played a major role in bringing the Ursuline and Hospital nuns there in 1639. The former established a school for Indian girls, while the hospital was intended largely for native people. The Jesuits also worked with the Compagnie du Saint-Sacrement to promote the Société Notre-Dame de Montréal, which founded a colony on Montreal Island in 1642 (Trudel 1979:154–8). While the stated purpose of the colony was to convert the Indians, it constituted a western bastion for policing the St Lawrence River as the primary artery of the fur trade. Fort Richelieu, which was built near the mouth of the Richelieu River the same year, was intended to serve the same purpose, but was soon circumvented by Mohawk war parties. Given Montreal's location, it is not surprising that commerce soon overtook religion as the primary overt concern of most of its inhabitants.

Unfortunately it is difficult to penetrate behind the hagiographic accounts of the founding of Montreal and discern the economic motives that led men such as the tax collector Jérôme Le Royer de La Dauversière of La Flèche to invest in it. This would be a significant topic for intensive research. The opposition to the new colony among the inhabitants of Quebec was clearly motivated more by fear that its location would permit it to corner the fur trade than by professed concerns about the dangers involved. Support for the Société Notre-Dame weakened as Iroquois attacks undermined the fur trade, but enough financial backing was secured to send 100 soldier-settlers to Montreal in 1653. Le Royer de La Dauversière died bankrupt in 1659, and four years later the Société, whose associates were diminishing in number, was obliged to abandon its ownership of the Montreal seigneury. Friction between the governor of Montreal and the governor of New France, who was stationed at Quebec, complicated political life, while the Jesuits themselves were later to be hurt by the close ties between Montreal and the Compagnie des Prêtres de Saint-Sulpice. Yet the trouble that the Jesuits took to promote the founding of Montreal was justified, as the settlement was from the beginning a major factor contributing to the military security and economic survival of New France.

The Huron mission, on the other hand, must be judged a liability both to the trading company and to the general well-being of New France. The survival of the Jesuit missionaries among the Hurons, despite the widespread conviction that they were causing major epidemics between 1634 and 1641 by means of witchcraft, indicates the considerable degree to which the Hurons now felt economically dependent upon the French and also the importance of the trading company for the Jesuits' work. After 1640, the Hurons were increasingly attacked by the Iroquois, who were acquiring guns. Their need for more furs to satisfy a growing demand for European goods led them to attack the northern tribes more forcefully than they had done in the past in order to seize more furs and to be able to hunt over a wider area. The Dutch with their slow population growth despaired of ever controlling the Mohawks; hence the traders at Albany saw these raids as the best way to increase the volume of furs reaching the Hudson Valley. Despite prevarications by Dutch officials, which were intended mainly to assuage complaints from neighbouring colonies, they agreed with the traders that the Iroquois should be armed.

At the same time that the Iroquois initiated these new attacks against their neighbours the Jesuits launched their major drive to convert the Hurons. In particular, they manipulated trading privileges and access to guns to convert Huron men. Their efforts not only deprived many Hurons of these weapons but also created major new divisions within Huron society. These did not split the confederacy but they seriously eroded support for it. While the Jesuits had learned enough about Huron social organization and religious customs to know what had to be changed if they were to convert them, it is uncertain whether they understood native customs and beliefs well enough to realize the effects of their actions. By 1644 Huron traders had suffered so badly from Iroquois attacks that they were suggesting that their trade with the French might be broken off, at least on an annual basis. To strengthen the alliance and encourage trade, Montmagny sent twenty-two French soldiers to winter in the Huron country and protect the Huron traders the following year (Thwaites 1896–1901, 26:71).

Despite these energetic efforts to maintain trade, problems were mounting. By 1645 the Compagnie des Cent-Associés had spent 1.2 million livres and was over 400,000 livres in debt. Louis XIII, Richelieu, and Razilly were all dead, and without their encouragement colonization was again lagging. In 1645 there were only 600 Europeans in New France (Trudel 1979:164–5). With Jesuit support, an effort was made to stimulate both immigration and trade by ceding all rights to deal in pelts to the settlers in the colony. These rights were not transferred, however, to individuals but to a company, the Communauté des Habitants, that was bound to pay the salaries of the governor and military officers of the colony, maintain forts, garrisons, and the clergy, and bring twenty persons to New France each year (ibid., 168–72). This arrangement was different from the extension of trading privileges in New Netherland in 1629 to all patroons (seigneurs) who founded a colony with at least fifty settlers who were above the age of fifteen or the establishment of totally free trade in 1638–9 (Trelease 1960:43–4, 61). The Dutch measures were intended to promote colonization, which was seen as necessary to protect a thinly populated colony from being seized by a foreign power. The Estates-General of Holland also sought to diversify the economy of New Netherland by making it a source of grain, fish, and salted beef for the Dutch colonies in South America and the West Indies.

In New France, by contrast, the Communauté des Habitants was controlled by about a dozen leading businessmen of the colony, who in their greed proceeded to forbid the individual trading in furs that had been allowed prior to this time (Trudel 1979:174–8). This ruling was contrary to the interests of most other colonists, including the Jesuits, and by January 1646 the bulk of the population appeared to be about to revolt. One of the leaders of this protest was the former interpreter Nicolas Marsolet, who was now in business on his own. Although Governor Montmagny suppressed this protest, in 1647 in response to these complaints all settlers were once again allowed by royal decree to trade with the Indians, provided that they sold their furs at a fixed price to the Communauté. The following year, another royal edict allowed them to import goods from France for their own use and to export any commodities but furs (ibid., 187–95). Even so, the encouragements for development lagged behind those offered to settlers by the Dutch government.

After a brief general peace with the Mohawks, war had resumed by 1647. The Hurons did not come to trade that year. In 1648 funds were set aside to pay for a *camp volant* of forty armed men to protect the fur trade (Trudel 1979:192–3). That year a few soldiers were sent to the Huron country to defend Sainte-Marie and accompany the Huron traders who would come to Quebec the next summer. While there, they took advantage of their right to trade with the Indians. In the summer of 1649 two expeditions totalling about sixty French travelled to the Huron country where they traded for furs with those Hurons who had not yet fled. Most of these men returned to Quebec the following autumn (Thwaites 1896–1901, 34:83). In the spring of 1650 another twenty-five to thirty or more French were making their way inland, no doubt also hoping to trade with the Hurons (ibid., 35:45, 201–3).

Until 1649 the Jesuits appear to have been able to control which Frenchmen came to the Huron country. It is interesting to speculate what might have happened to the Huron mission had the Hurons realized that accepting the Jesuits was no longer necessary for maintaining their trading relations with the French. Would it have allowed the traditionalists to restore the balance of power and reassert Huron cultural autonomy despite their economic dependence on the fur trade? Before this or anything else could happen, the Hurons and their Algonkian trading partners had been dispersed by the Iroquois.

The dispersal of the Hurons appeared to be a major disaster for the French, and in the short run it disrupted the bulk of the fur trade on which the economic life of the colony depended. Yet the situation would have been far worse for the French if the Huron traditionalists had been able to conclude an alliance with the Iroquois. There is also evidence that the Hurons had reached their maximum capacity for transporting furs to the St Lawrence. It would not have been long before they, like the Montagnais at Tadoussac earlier in the century, would have become a hindrance to the expansion of the fur trade. They eventually might have been bypassed by French traders seeking more furs and thus have been reduced to merely local importance. Almost certainly the Hurons would have resented this infringement on their prerogatives by the French and other Indian groups and would have sought in every way possible to block such expansion.

It is clear that, beginning in 1648, the French were seeking not to have to depend on the Hurons for deliveries of furs, even if initially this amounted to no more than going into the interior to obtain furs that the Hurons had collected. J.A. Dickinson (1982:45–6) believes that the disappearance of the Hurons stimulated French agriculture to produce food that the Hurons had formerly supplied to their trading partners. At first, however, this would have involved provisioning only the Algonkins and neighbouring tribes of south-western Quebec, who were soon dispersed by the Iroquois. Campeau (1974:125–6) argues, on the contrary, that increasing French involvement in the fur trade of the upper Great Lakes region removed manpower that might otherwise have been used to develop the agricultural sector of the Quebec economy.

Throughout the 1640s the Mohawks repeatedly offered to make peace with the French. By this they meant a peace that did not include the Indian tribes that traded with the French. It can be argued that by establishing Trois-Rivières, Fort Richelieu, and Montreal the French forced the Iroquois to fight them as well (Dickinson 1982). Yet the Mohawks must have known that the French had to try to keep their trade routes open and to offer at least minimal protection to their allies when they visited their trading posts. The short-lived peace that was established in 1645 included the tribes that traded with the French, although the Mohawks bargained hard to exclude them. Even after the war faction among the Mohawks ended that peace by killing the Jesuit missionary Isaac Jogues in October 1646, the Mohawks diverted most of their military forces westward until the Hurons, Petuns, and Neutrals were dispersed. Only in 1650 did they begin to attack the French, for the first time killing them and taking prisoners as far east as Quebec City. Yet their aim continued to be to force the French to adopt a neutral stance similar to that of the Dutch. At least some Mohawks also may have hoped that if they could destroy or force the evacuation of Montreal and Trois-Rivières, they would be able to raid and hunt north of the St Lawrence with greater impunity. In the course of these raids, the Ottawa Valley Algonkins and the Attikamegues, who lived in the upper part of the St Maurice Valley, were dispersed, and the Iroquois began to penetrate farther to the east and north.

As a result of the dispersal of so many tribes, the economy of New France collapsed. By 1652, because of the drastically declining delivery of furs, losses at sea, and increasing interest charges, the Communauté des Habitants was unable to honour its debts or to meet the necessary expenses of the colony. In 1653, as an economy measure, the mobile force was disbanded and the garrison withdrawn from Trois-Rivières. Many French were killed or taken prisoner by the Iroquois, and settlers were boarding ships to return to France (Trudel 1979:202–22).

In 1650 the authorities at Quebec had sent Gabriel Druillettes, the Jesuit missionary to the Abenakis, to Boston in the hope of negotiating an alliance with the New England colonies against the Iroquois. Such an alliance seemed possible, since the Iroquois attacks against the Abenakis were also hurting the New England fur trade. The English refused, however, to be drawn into such a doubtful venture. Between 1648 and 1653, during the minority of Louis xiv, France was wracked by the Fronde, another series of civil wars in which the nobility and other privileged groups tried unsuccessfully to regain the powers they had lost to the crown during the reign of Louis xiii. These developments created despair in New France and promoted a fatalistic belief that resistance was useless.

During this period a split had been developing between the Mohawks on the one hand and the Onondagas and Senecas on the other. In 1653 the latter sought to make peace with the French, and the Mohawks, who were also annoyed by the higher prices that the Dutch were again charging for their goods, decided that rather than be isolated, they would make peace as well. The French did not understand why the Iroquois were inclined to conclude a treaty, and Governor Jean de Lauson was widely supported when he agreed to terms dictated by the Mohawks. For the first time, the French in desperation abandoned their native trading partners and negotiated a simple bilateral treaty with the Iroquois. Dickinson (1981:169) says that the French did not understand the terms of the treaty but that can hardly be so, since it was the very agreement that the Mohawks had been calling for in the clearest terms since 1640. Moreover, on Christmas Day, 1653, the Mohawks asked the Dutch at Fort Orange to write on their behalf to the French, reminding them to remain neutral during any further hostilities between themselves and the tribes that traded along the St Lawrence (Trelease 1960:123). This letter clearly reiterated the terms of the treaty. The simple truth was that because they were unable to resist the Mohawks any longer, the French abandoned their allies, as La Barre was to abandon the Illinois tribes in 1684. For the Mohawks and Oneidas, the main advantage of this peace was the freedom it gave them to raid the Algonkins and Montagnais and to exploit the hunting territories of these tribes; for the other Iroquois peoples, it was the enhanced bargaining power that it provided in dealing with the Mohawks.

The Jesuits strongly supported this peace. Their major missionary endeavour of the previous twenty years had been shattered, six priests had been killed, and eight more had to return to France in 1650 because there was no longer any useful employment for them in Canada (Trudel 1979:212). They wished above all to establish a mission to the Iroquois so they could continue to minister to large numbers of Huron Christians who were living there and begin to make new converts among the Iroquois. Therefore they were prepared to support the Iroquois' demands that the Huron refugees living at Quebec join them, provided that the Iroquois would in turn allow the Jesuits to come with them. The Iroquois saw the Jesuits as a French peace faction and as hostages guaranteeing that the French would respect the terms of their treaty.

Trade from the west resumed in 1654 despite Iroquois attacks on the Ottawa Valley. Yet while trade prospered, the Communauté des Habitants suffered disastrous financial reverses from major losses at sea in 1653 and 1655 (Trudel 1979:228, 234–5). The Iroquois continued to harass the tribes allied with the French. The Mohawks, in particular, humiliated the French with their attack on the Huron settlement on the Ile d'Orléans in 1656; and the Onondagas outraged them when they murdered Huron captives in the company of Father Ragueneau in 1657. Raoul Naroll (1969) and Dickinson (1982:46) have both documented the slow slide into yet another Iroquois war. They wrongly conclude, however, that the Iroquois sincerely tried to keep the peace but that it was shattered because of the pride of French officials, the undue harshness with which they treated Iroquois prisoners, and their failure to understand the consensual nature of Iroquois social organization, which resulted in minor infractions of any peace.

French officials were often arrogant and insensitive. It is evident, however, that a high degree of discipline could be maintained among Iroquoians when public opinion strongly favoured a particular line of action. The survival of the Jesuits among the Hurons during the epidemics is proof of this. Some Iroquois clearly did try to maintain the peace of 1653, but many others had not welcomed it from the beginning. Although the Mohawks had obtained the kind of treaty they had long wanted, most of them began immediately to encourage anti-French factions among the other Iroquois tribes. They hoped that renewed warfare would sever relations between these tribes and the French and restore the political prestige that they had derived from being the only link between the confederacy and the European traders at Fort Orange. The increasingly provocative treatment of the French mirrored the growing strength of the anti-peace factions among the various Iroquois tribes. At a still more fundamental level, the Iroquois must have realized that their attacks on the Ottawas would eventually force the French to provide the latter with military aid for economic reasons. The growing importance of the furs being supplied by the Ottawas made this inevitable, even if the desperate fear that the Montagnais and

Algonkins, who were now badly depleted by diseases, had of the Iroquois caused these tribes not to turn against the French for having abandoned them. The Iroquois must have expected that the French would attack them as soon as they felt strong enough to do so, just as the Mohawks had mistrusted the Dutch after they had been forced into a position of de facto neutrality in 1628.

As French traders and settlers became increasingly exasperated by Iroquois provocations and what they saw as attacks against their prosperity, they turned against Lauson and the Jesuits, who had been the chief architects of the peace. The pre-eminence of the Jesuits was first challenged in 1656 when Paul de Chomedey de Maisonneuve, the governor of Montreal, persuaded Jean-Jacques Olier, founder of the Compagnie des Prêtres de Saint-Sulpice, to send priests of his order to Montreal. It was politely claimed that the Jesuits were too occupied with their missions to attend to the affairs of the colony. The arrival of the Sulpician priests the following year ended the religious monopoly that the Jesuits had enjoyed since their return to New France in 1632. In France conditions were no longer propitious for the Jesuits' retaining control of New France. The piety born of the Counter-Reformation that had characterized previous decades was on the wane, and the young Louis xiv was turning against the dévots who had hitherto played such an important role in French politics (Campeau 1974:149). Lauson, finding his power to control the fur trade being challenged, returned to France in 1656, and his son Charles, who had been left to administer the colony, followed him the next year.

The new acting governor, Louis d'Ailleboust de Coulonge, who had come to Montreal in 1643, issued the welcome order that hereafter the French should fight to prevent the Iroquois from harassing their Indian allies within sight of French settlements (Thwaites 1896–1901, 44:191–3). This marked the beginning of a new war in which the Mohawks and their Iroquois allies sought to compel the French to resume their neutrality. Yet, despite continuing economic problems, the population of New France had increased rapidly during the fragile peace that had prevailed since 1653. Hence, while the losses of life from Mohawk attacks, in particular between 1660 and 1661, were much higher than between 1650 and 1653, the threat that they posed to the colony's continued existence was far less serious (Dickinson 1982:44). Nevertheless, the colony appeared to be on the brink of economic and military ruin, and fears that New France might not be able to survive suggested an urgent need for reforms in the way that it was administered. In 1663 the

French crown was at last compelled to accept responsibility for the affairs of the colony.

Historical judgments about the relative accomplishments of the Compagnie des Cent-Associés and the royal regime have varied. Eccles (1973:56) has concluded that administration by a private company, accompanied by a measure of self-government, had proved a failure, but that when the crown accepted full responsibility for security, finance, administration, and economic development, significant progress was forthcoming. Campeau (1974:155) suggests that, in terms of promoting immigration, Colbert failed to do as much for New France as the Cent-Associés had done. Yet it is clear that the new administration was able to provide a level of financial and military security for New France that exceeded what had been available from the Cent-Associés or any of the smaller companies. Through investments in various economic activities, even when they were not successful, and increasingly through military spending, the French government helped to promote the development of a colony whose principal export remained furs. These new sources of income also provided capital that allowed the expansion of the seigneurial system.

By the early 1660s the Iroquois were becoming weary of a war that was not achieving their objectives. They were also suffering badly from epidemics. The decisive episode for the Mohawks, though it did not involve significant loss of life, was the destruction of their villages by the Carignan-Salières regiment. After this, the Iroquois felt obliged to make peace on terms that were less favourable to them than the treaty of 1653 had been, since a new one once again included the Indian groups that were allied with the French. Although the Iroquois retained their hunting grounds in southern and central Ontario, this treaty curtailed their raiding and hunting in Quebec and around the upper Great Lakes and therefore forced them to push westward into the Ohio Valley to obtain furs. Their conflicts with the native peoples of that region do not appear to have been motivated by a desire for domination but by a need for furs.

While the Iroquois continued to suffer losses of manpower from war and disease, New France enjoyed almost two decades during which it was free to develop in peace. Yet during these years the Iroquois maintained their political independence, despite British and French assertions of sovereignty over their lands. They also managed, despite their increasing reliance on European technology, to retain far more economic independence than the Hurons had done prior to 1650. The Jesuits, while highly successful as French envoys, made little progress in converting the Iroquois in their own country. It has often been observed that their mission to the Iroquois lacked the zeal and self-confidence that had characterized the Huron program. That absence reflected, in part, their inability to manipulate the Iroquois politically and economically in order to pursue their religious goals as they had done the Hurons. It also reflected their declining prestige in official circles in France and Quebec and a more secular trend in French society generally, especially as the power of the nobility declined and after 1630 they abandoned Protestantism, which for many had symbolized their resistance to royal authority (Wallerstein 1980:286–7).

## FINAL OBSERVATIONS

There has been a serious imbalance in the traditional interpretations of early Euro-Canadian history. Too much attention has been paid to the activities of priests and officials; too little, to those of traders and their employees. Despite limited documentation, it is clear that traders played a major role in forging productive working relations between Europeans and native people. The French traders were almost certainly no more altruistic or benevolent than their Dutch counterparts in upper New York State. Yet their desire for profitable trade led them to study Indian ways and made them willing to adopt native conventions and become involved in native alliances when it was in their economic interest to do so. Furthermore, the traders who were the most willing to do these things were the most successful in the long run.

Although de Monts's employees have been accused of starting the later wars between the French and the Iroquois because of their supposedly injudicious alliances with the Montagnais and Algonkins, there is no evidence to support this argument. What is clear is that the ties these traders forged with their native trading partners provided the basis for later cooperation between other groups of Frenchmen and the indigenous inhabitants of the St Lawrence Valley. This situation contrasts sharply with the failure of Cartier and Roberval to establish effective working relations with the St Lawrence Iroquoians, which contributed to the failure of their enterprise. As well, after 1615, Champlain and the Recollets undermined relations between the French and the Montagnais by their high-handed, ethnocentric treatment of native peoples. As a result, the Montagnais helped the English to capture Quebec in 1629.

The Jesuits recognized the trading alliance between the Hurons and the French as the essential basis on which their mission work depended, and they exploited the increasing economic dependence of the Hurons in order to convert large numbers of them. Hence, although they sought to control the fur traders, they also realized that it was necessary to cooperate with them. Only in the late 1650s did the Jesuits' commitment to peace with the Iroquois bring them into serious conflict with French traders, whose economic activities were being undermined by Iroquois attacks.

In general the Dutch traders at Albany, while severely constrained by the Mohawks after 1628, dealt with problems in the same fashion as did their French counterparts along the St Lawrence. The significant differences between the two colonies reflect social and economic, rather than ethnic and cultural, variations between their mother countries. While various conflicting economic interests existed with respect to New Netherland, Dutch traders and government officials in America and the Netherlands alike sought to promote the fur trade and to realize a profit from it. In New France, Champlain's desire to promote settlement and the missionaries' zeal to pursue religious goals frequently created conflicts of interest with the traders, and in these situations the traders, as members of a less influential social class, were at a serious disadvantage. In both colonies the main long-term problem was the lack of any inherent incentive for traders, who were of necessity concerned with short-term profits, to promote colonization on a large scale. Nor prior to 1663 was either government prepared to invest in such activities. Without settlement, the ability of each colony to withstand attack by other European powers was threatened. Yet, even as New France became more populous, neither the Indians nor the French traders became less important to the welfare of the colony, although the traders' activities continued to be condemned as detrimental to its agricultural and industrial development. Even when New France was glutted with furs, the fur trade remained vital for maintaining a system of alliances with native peoples on which the French government relied to ensure its military position in North America.

If a historical perspective in which the activities of French traders, their employees, and native people are duly emphasized alongside those of Champlain, the Recollets, and Jesuits makes the Heroic Age seem less heroic, it also shows it to have been a time when two major groups of peoples, with radically different cultures, were attempting to solve mutual problems of coexistence. Examining the activities of native peoples at this time reveals the constructive role that European traders and their employees played in laying the basis for successful European colonization in the St Lawrence Valley. In chapter 4 it was noted that methodologically the history of native peoples has much in common with that of those classes in Western society lacking abundant written documentation of their activities. In the case of early Canadian history, the French traders, although they were not illiterate, as well as their European employees, would also fall into this category. It is perhaps no accident that an approach that attempts to minimize ethnic stereotypes also draws attention to the distortions caused by seventeenth-century class biases. Such an approach helps to make the early history of Canada less a chronicle of the pursuits of a chosen few and more the study of the activities of all native Canadians and European newcomers.

# Notes on Sources

The sources on which specific statements are based are cited in the text. This section provides a general guide to the most important literature relevant to each chapter. Ephemeral works, as well as ones that are clearly antiquated or have been superseded by more recent publications by the same author, have been omitted.

## CHAPTER ONE

A comprehensive treatment of Canadian historiography is provided for writings in English by Berger (1976) and for works in French by S. Gagnon (1982), supplemented by Gagnon (1978) and Ouellet (1982). For a critical guide to Canadian historical writing on the pre-Confederation period, see Muise (1982). The classic discussion of the role assigned to Indians in English-Canadian historical writing is Walker (1971). This theme is also examined by essays in Muise (1977) and more recently by Walker (1983). D. Smith (1974) deals in detail with the treatment of native peoples in French-Canadian historical writing. My own interpretations of the views of Charlevoix, Dainville, and Garneau differ substantially from those of Smith, and his conclusions about later historians should be checked against the more recent and painstaking research of Gagnon (1982).

The unsatisfactory treatment of native peoples in American textbooks is discussed by Henry (1970) and Bowker (1972); Canadian textbooks are surveyed by Price (1979) and Ontario ones by McDiarmid and Pratt (1971). Vincent and Arcand (1979) analyse in detail stereotypes in textbooks written in French. There is a spirited discussion of that subject in an exchange between Vincent (1978a, 1978b) and Vaugeois (1978). The treatment of Indians in Canadian popular literature was first examined by Maclean (1896:456–540). Atwood (1972:87–106) has written a perceptive essay on the subject, and Monkman (1981) has provided a comprehensive survey of English-Canadian literature. Keiser (1933) offers a similar study of stereotypes of native people in American literature, and Price (1973), of stereotypes in motion pictures. It is worthwhile to compare these works with Street's (1975) examination of the representation of Africans by English novelists between 1858 and 1920. Bissell (1925) discusses the American Indian in eighteenth-century English literature.

The most comprehensive ethnographic survey of Canadian Indian tribes remains Jenness (1960). More detailed and up-to-date coverage is provided by the relevant volumes of the Smithsonian Institution's *Handbook of North American Indians*, a series edited by W.C. Sturtevant. The volumes published to date concerning Canada cover the *Northeast* (Trigger 1978a), *Subarctic* (Helm 1981), and *Arctic* (Damas 1985). Major ethnographic bibliographies of the native peoples of northeastern North America are found in Murdock and O'Leary (1975), especially volumes 1 and 4, and Tooker (1978a). The only comprehensive treatment of the history of the native peoples of Canada since European contact is E. Patterson (1972). For additional bibliography relating to native people in Canada, see Allen (1984).

There is a voluminous and rapidly growing literature dealing with the history of the attitudes and policies of European settlers towards Indians in the United States. General works include Jones (1964), Pearce (1965), Honour (1975), Chiappelli (1976), Berkhofer (1978), and Vaughan (1982). Fairchild (1928) discusses the concept of the noble savage. Among books dealing with the period of English settlement in Virginia and New England are Jennings (1975) (a powerful and fundamental study), Porter (1979), Vaughan (1979), Kupperman (1980), and Sheehan (1980). Later periods are covered by Prucha (1962), Horsman (1967, 1975, 1981), Sheehan (1973), and Drinnon (1980). A review by Axtell (1982a) provides a useful framework for evaluating this literature. For parallels between English policy towards the Irish and the Indians, see Quinn (1966). Early Spanish views of native Americans are surveyed by Hanke (1959), Keen (1971), Pagden (1982), and Todorov (1982). For similar treatments of New France, see Kennedy (1950), Jaenen (1976, 1978, 1980), Dickason (1977a, 1979, 1984a), and F.-M. Gagnon (1984). Billington (1981) discusses European opinions of the American Indians. Wade (1942), Doughty (1962), Jennings (1963), and Shulman (1971) are useful for understanding Parkman's views of them. Levin (1959) examines the relationship between Parkman's work and that of other historians.

The most comprehensive and informed discussion of the scope and history of anthropology, with the main emphasis on ethnology or social anthropology, is Harris (1968). Voget (1975) and Honigmann (1976) provide alternative versions. Hodgen (1964) examines the development of anthropology prior to 1800, and Darnell (1971), the professionalization of American anthropology. Stocking's (1982) essays survey important themes relating to the general development of anthropology. The growth of American anthropology during the nineteenth century is examined by Gruber (1967), and by Hinsley's (1981) history of the Smithsonian Institution, Resek's (1960) biography of L.H. Morgan, and Stocking's (1974) edition of the early writings of Franz Boas. The most comprehensive history of American archaeology is Willey and Sabloff (1980). Much of the same material is presented in a more popular form by Fagan (1977). Other important studies of the development of American archaeology are Haven (1856), Silverberg (1968) on the Moundbuilders, and Fitting (1973) on regional trends. The development of physical anthropology and of racial views concerning North American Indians has been studied by Glass et al. (1959), Stanton (1960), Glacken (1967), Jordan (1968), and Horsman (1975).

Cole (1973) discusses the early history of Canadian anthropology. The history of Canadian archaeology is examined by Jenness (1932), Noble (1972), and Trigger (1981a). Connolly (1977) surveys the development of archaeology in the Maritimes; Martijn (1978) does the same for Quebec; Kidd (1952), Killan (1980, 1983), and Noble (1982) cover Ontario. Biographical studies of Daniel Wilson have been written by Hale (1893), Simpson (1963), McIlwraith (1964), Trigger (1966a), McCardle (1980), and Ash (1981); of J.W. Dawson by Trigger (1966b) and O'Brien (1971); and of Horatio Hale by Gruber (1967) and Fenton in the Introduction to Hale (1963). David Boyle is the subject of an outstanding biography by Killan (1983).

An important discussion of the bias inherent in the interpretation of Indian-White relations in western Canada is provided by Tobias (1983).

CHAPTER TWO

My comments on the study of Iroquoian prehistory draw heavily on three previous papers: a thematic history of Iroquoian archaeology (Trigger 1978d); a review of the archaeological study of social and political organization in the Iroquoian area (Trigger 1981b); and a consideration of archaeology as native history (Trigger 1983). The historical section of this chapter covers generally the same ground as did chapter 3 of The Children of Aataentsic (Trigger 1976), but the treatment is modified to take account of almost a decade of major archaeological discoveries and significant reinterpretations of Iroquoian prehistory.

The classic survey of nonarchaeological methods for investigating prehistory is Sapir (1916), which was written while he was in charge of anthropological research at the National Museum of Canada. In recent decades, the most important works of this sort have come mainly from the study of African prehistory. The more comprehensive include Murdock (1959), McCall (1964), Tardits (1981), and the theoretically oriented chapters in volume 1 of the UNESCO General History of Africa (Ki-Zerbo 1981).

Recent work in this tradition relating to Canada has been done by Dyen and Aberle (1974) and Perry (1983). Vansina (1965) has made an important statement about oral traditions, and Ehret and Posnansky (1982) have examined the relevance of linguistic data with reference to Africa.

The early development of archaeology in Europe is chronicled by Daniel (1975). Modern archaeological goals and methods are discussed in textbooks by Hole and Heizer (1973), Knudson (1978), and D. Thomas (1979). Among the most important works defining the goals of modern archaeology are those by Clarke (1968), Binford (1972, 1983a, 1983b), and Schiffer (1976). The major serial publication giving recent developments in archaeological research methods is *Advances in Archaeological Method and Theory*, edited annually since 1978 by M.B. Schiffer. Important articles are included in the *Annual Review of Anthropology*, edited by B.J. Siegel. Innovative studies appear as volumes in the Studies in Archaeology Series, published by Academic Press.

Clark (1977), Fagan (1980), and Wenke (1980) provide up-to-date surveys of world prehistory. Willey (1966) and Jennings (1978) offer major surveys of the prehistory of North America, as do Farb (1969) and Snow (1976a) in a more popular form. Moeller (1977) gives the most extensive bibliography covering the archaeology and prehistory of eastern North America. For major syntheses of the prehistory of different regions of eastern North America, see Tuck (1976) for Newfoundland and Labrador; Chapdelaine (1978) and J.V. Wright (1979) for Quebec; Snow (1980) and Haviland and Power (1981) for New England; Ritchie (1965), Tuck (1971), and Ritchie and Funk (1973) for New York State; J.V. Wright (1966, 1967, 1972) for Ontario; Fitting (1970) for Michigan; and R. Mason (1981) for the western Great Lakes. The special problems encountered by researchers in this region are discussed in a set of papers edited by Snow (1981). The calibration of radiocarbon dates is explained in Watkins (1975), and Timmins (1984) evaluates Iroquoian dates.

Major recent works dealing with Iroquoian physical anthropology are Molto (1983) and D. Patterson (1984).

It is a challenge to keep abreast of developments in Iroquoian archaeology. Much important research done in Ontario and Quebec in recent years has been published as volumes in the Archaeological Survey of Canada, Mercury Series. Other findings are reported in journals. Among the most important of these are *Ontario Archaeology* and *Arch Notes* (both published by the Ontario Archaeological Society), *Canadian Journal of Archaeology*, *Archaeology of Eastern North America*, *Mid-Continental Journal of Archaeology*, *New York State Archaeological Association Researches and Transactions*, *Pennsylvania Archaeologist*, *Michigan Archaeologist*, and *Wisconsin Archaeologist*. Significant articles also appear occasionally in *American Antiquity*, *Anthropologica*, *Ethnohistory*,

*Journal of Field Archaeology, Man in the Northeast,* and *Recherches Amérindiennes au Québec.*

Iroquoian prisoner sacrifice and ritual cannibalism are discussed in a hemispheric perspective by Knowles (1940) and Rands and Riley (1958). Arens (1979) has suggested that there is no direct evidence that the Iroquoians practised cannibalism as part of his broader argument that European claims of cannibalism among so-called primitive peoples were invented to justify their colonial activities. While there is no doubt considerable truth in Arens's general position, his specific claims with respect to the Iroquoians have been decisively refuted by Abler (1980) and J.B. Jamieson (1983). On the role of warfare in promoting the development of bounded tribes, see Haas (1982:9–10); the theoretical basis of his arguments is presented by Bradley and Hodder (1979).

## CHAPTER THREE

The sixteenth century presents problems of exceptional difficulty for understanding both what Europeans in eastern North America were doing and what was happening to native peoples. The historical documentation is sparse and uneven. Most Europeans who visited North America left no record of their activities, either because they were illiterate or had no reason to do so or because they were behaving illegally. Other Europeans, such as André Thevet, claimed they made visits that they obviously had not, while still more assertions fall into a dubious category. The nature of the evidence tempts modern scholars to maintain that events had occurred that their personal theories and predilections suggest should have happened. It is abundantly clear that much of what remains to be learned about both native and European activities will be discovered from archaeological data. In that respect, the historiography of sixteenth-century North America is different from that of prehistoric times, when written records are lacking, and from the seventeenth century onward, when such records are abundant. As yet, however, archaeological research on this period remains in its infancy (Witthoft 1966). Because of this, the main emphasis of this chapter is placed less on chronicling the events in eastern Canada during the sixteenth century than on understanding the limitations of existing data and assessing current interpretative controversies.

The most important written sources concerning eastern Canada in the sixteenth century have been edited by Biggar (1911, 1924, 1930). Quinn (1979) has published an extremely valuable five-volume compendium of documents concerning the whole of North America prior to 1612. For matters not directly relating to the St Lawrence Valley, I have generally cited that work rather than the numerous publications and archives from which its material has been drawn. The social and economic background of European exploration in the fifteenth and sixteenth centuries is discussed by Parry (1966, 1981), Wallerstein (1974), and Quinn (1977:71–107). For the development of French trade with the Amerindians of Brazil, see Dickason (1984b). Early studies of European activities in eastern North America, based primarily on written documents, by Biggar (1901), Ganong (reprinted 1964), and Innis (1930, 1940) have been superseded on specific topics by Morison's (1971) critical account of European exploration, Sauer's (1971) examination of the ecological aspects of early contact between Indians and Europeans, and Quinn's (1977) comprehensive but sometimes controversial analysis of European activities. The latter work also provides an extensive annotated bibliography to which should be added only some recent studies of Basque activities in the Gulf of St Lawrence by Barkham (1980, 1982), Tuck (1982), and Turgeon (1982). Much of the ethnographic material recorded by early explorers for northeastern North America has been collected and commented on by Quinn (1981). Reid (1979) and Upton (1980) provide useful discussions of early Indian-White contact in the Maritimes.

Some idea of the extent of recent changes in interpretations of what happened to the native people of eastern Canada and adjacent parts of the United States during the sixteenth century can be gained by comparing chapter 4 of *The Children of Aataentsic* with the present one. Papers marking the transition between the two include Trigger (1978e, 1979, 1982a, 1984). The most important published work involving a reassessment of sixteenth-century Ontario is Ramsden (1977). A useful bibliography of recent protohistoric research in southern Ontario is given by Noble (1982:180). Significant unpublished studies include Ceci (1977) on coastal New York, Bradley (1979) on the Iroquois of New York State, and J.B. Jamieson (1982) on the St Lawrence Iroquoians.

Before further progress can be made, a more precise chronological correlation must be achieved between Iroquoian sites in Pennsylvania, New York State, and southern Ontario. While small quantities of European goods may have been reaching these areas throughout the sixteenth century, the comparative study of glass beads and other European artifacts by Kenyon and Kenyon (1982) and by Fitzgerald (1982a, 1982b, 1983) seems to be strengthening the long-standing contention of Ontario archaeologists that their American colleagues have been dating many protohistoric sites in upper New York State, and by extrapolation in neighbouring regions, approximately twenty-five years too early. It remains to be seen, however, if this position can be sustained. The chronology of European goods, as it is emerging at present, tends to negate some of the more radical reinterpretations of Iroquoian prehistory that have been put forward in recent years.

A major advance in understanding the significance of European goods within the context of protohistoric native cultures has been provided by the extensive ethnographic research of Hamell (1980, 1982) and to a lesser extent by that of Hall (1979). Both work within an interpretative tradition already successfully employed by Vastokas and Vastokas (1973) in their study of Algonkian rock art. By identifying the religious significance of various natural substances among the native peoples of northeastern North America, Hamell allows us for the first time to understand why "trading in exotic goods ... was out of all proportion to its utilitarian significance" (Trigger 1976:245).

Arguments, as of 1970, concerning the disappearance of the St Lawrence Iroquoians are summarized in Trigger (1972). Since then, the controversies have continued without satisfactory resolution. For recent claims by archaeologists that the Hurons dispersed them, see Ramsden (1977), J.V. Wright (1979:71–5), and Pendergast (1982b). Pendergast's (1982a) study of Iroquoian material from Jefferson County, New York, has cast a totally different light on this problem. His conclusions underlie the new "compromise" solution proposed in chapters 2 and 3.

Pendergast (1983) has shown that McIlwain's (1915:xxxii) claim that a coastal trade in deerskins between Virginia and the Maritimes existed during the sixteenth century was based on Parkman's misreading of Menéndez de Avilés's letters. He is currently working on a major study entitled "The Introduction of European Goods on the Atlantic Coast and the Iroquoian Protohistoric Era."

## CHAPTER FOUR

The primary sources of ethnohistorical information concerning the native peoples of eastern and central Canada during the first half of the seventeenth century are the writings of Samuel de Champlain (Biggar 1922–36), Marc Lescarbot (1907–14), and Gabriel Sagard (1866; Wrong 1939); the annual *Relations* and other documents of the Jesuits reproduced in Thwaites (1896–1901), Chaumonot (1869), and Campeau (1967, 1979); documents found in Le Clercq (1691); and the work of Denys (1908). On the authorship of Le Clercq, see Hamilton (1976). Minor sources are Boucher (1664) and Gendron (1868). Gendron's work must be used with caution because it surreptitiously includes material excerpted from the *Jesuit Relations*, which raises doubts about the origin and authenticity of the rest of this document. Other sources relevant to the Iroquois are found in O'Callaghan and Fernow (1853–87), Jameson (1909), and Radisson (Adams 1961). Later primary sources on native people that are of major importance are Perrot (1911), Bacqueville de La Potherie (1911–12), and Lafitau (Fenton and Moore 1974–7); while early secondary sources include Du Creux (1951–2) and Charlevoix (1866–72). Much of the best of the Iroquois material in Bacqueville de La Potherie is in volumes 3 and 4, which Blair did not translate. Ethnographic sketches of the Indians of eastern Canada appear in Jenness (1960) and Kinietz (1940); and more detailed studies of the Hurons, in Tooker (1964), Trigger (1969), and Heidenreich (1971). The Iroquois are covered in Morgan (1851) and in various articles in Trigger (1978a:296–546). For the Indians of the southeastern United States, see Hudson (1976).

The nature of ethnohistory has been discussed in many articles, but no extensive treatment of the discipline or its methodology is available. For basic statements concerning its aims, techniques, and use, see Fenton (1952, 1957, 1962, 1966), Dorson (1961), Lurie (1961), Hudson (1966, 1973), Sturtevant (1966), Cohn (1968), Hickerson (1970), Carmack (1971, 1972), Dobyns (1972, 1978), Euler (1972), Pearce (1974), Trigger (1975; 1976:1–26), Schwerin (1976), Helms (1978), and Martin (1978). Specific discussions of the relationship between history and ethnohistory are provided by Washburn (1961, 1971), Berkhofer (1971), Axtell (1979, 1983), and Cohn (1980, 1981), while the relationship between archaeology and ethnohistory is examined by Baerreis (1961) and Trigger (1978e). The principal ethnohistorical journal *Ethnohistory* has been published since 1953, first by the American Indian Ethnohistoric Conference and later by the American Society for Ethnohistory. A bibliography of ethnohistory prior to 1969 is provided by Olien (1969). In Australia, there is a closer relationship between archaeology and ethnohistory than in America. For discussions of Australian ethnohistory, see Corris (1969), McBryde (1979), and articles appearing in the journal *Aboriginal History*.

A minority of anthropologists define ethnohistory not as the study of the past of nonliterate peoples using written documents and oral traditions, but as the examination of how these peoples perceive their own history. For statements of this view, see Gubser (1965:29–60), Dening (1966), and Blanchard (1982a).

The substantivist position in economics was developed by Karl Polanyi. It is outlined most succinctly in Polanyi (1957). For more detailed expositions of his ideas, see Polanyi (1944, 1966), as well as his essays reprinted in Dalton (1968). A good discussion of his work is provided by Humphreys (1969). Theoretical expositions in the substantivist tradition are found in Polanyi et al. (1957) and Dalton (1961, 1969, 1977, 1981), while various case studies are reprinted in Dalton (1967). Formalist rejoinders are provided by Burling (1962), LeClair (1962), Cancian (1966), and S. Cook (1966). Both positions are represented in the articles reprinted in LeClair and Schneider (1968). The substantivist/formalist dichotomy is called into question by Salisbury (1968) and Ekholm and Friedman (1979).

Discussions of the early Canadian fur trade that are of theoretical interest include Innis (1930, 1956), Rich (1960), Rotstein (1967, 1970, 1972), Ray (1974), Ray and Freeman (1978), essays in Judd and Ray (1980), Cox (1983), and Francis and Morantz (1983). For recent criticism of Innis's work, see Eccles (1979) and a reply by Grant (1981). An extended critical discussion of Martin's (1978) view of native participation in the fur trade is provided by Krech (1981). Possible evidence of trading between the French and the Mohawks as early as 1612 has been published by Burnham (1983).

The biographies of Champlain, even recent ones, are for the most part works of hagiography: Dionne (1891–1906), Bishop (1948), Trudel (1966d), and Morison (1972). For background on the Jesuits, see Kennedy (1950) and Broderick (1967). Seventeenth-century Jesuit missionary activities in China are discussed by Rowbotham (1966); in Japan by Boxer (1951); and in Paraguay by Mörner (1953) and McNaspy (1982). The best comparisons of Jesuit and Franciscan mission work in North America are found in Spicer (1961, 1962) and Bowden (1981); see also Pagden (1982:78).

Archaeological work on historical Amerindian sites in southern Ontario prior to 1948 is summarized in Kidd (1952). Surveys of these sites began in the last century with Boyle's research on the Petuns and Hunter's systematic work in Simcoe County. Their findings were taken account of by Jones (1908) in his efforts to identify Jesuit missions. There was also sporadic interest in Huron, Petun, and Neutral burial sites. It was not until after World War II that Ridley (1947) and Kidd (1949b) continued survey work in the Huron country. This period also saw scientific excavations being carried out at the Ossossané ossuary (Kidd 1953), the Orr Lake site (Kidd 1950), the Huron village identified as St Louis (Jury and Jury 1955), and the beginning of work at the Warminster site (McIlwraith 1946; Emerson 1961). Ridley (1961) published an important monograph on historical Neutral archaeology.

After a brief period devoted almost exclusively to prehistoric Iroquoian archaeology, the study of historical sites resumed as part of the Penetang Project (Hurley and Heidenreich 1969, 1971). Since then the volume of research has expanded rapidly, although most of the results are reported only in provisional form in archaeological journals. The historical Neutrals have been intensively studied since the early 1970s (Noble 1978). Monographs published to date include reports on the Walker (M. Wright 1981), Hamilton (Lennox 1981), Christianson (Fitzgerald 1982a), Hood, Bogle I, and Bogle II (Lennox 1984) habitation sites as well as on the Grimsby cemetery (W. Kenyon 1982; I. Kenyon and Fox 1982). While the Petun Studies Group founded by Charles Garrad has undertaken various analyses and fresh excavations, published reports are limited to brief articles and notes. Works on historical Huron sites include Heidenreich's (1971) geographical analysis and Latta's (1977) study of cultural change. Other research has been carried out at the Ball (Knight 1978), Le Caron (Johnston and Jackson 1980), and Warminster sites.

Monographs on the archaeological investigation of the Jesuit mission of Sainte-Marie I have been published by Kidd (1949a) and Jury and Jury (1954); however, no scientific report has been presented on the work carried out by W. Jury, although it was the basis for the physical reconstruction of the mission. For a discussion of this reconstruction, see Trigger (1976:668–81). Sainte-Marie II, on Christian Island, has been less intensively investigated, but reports can be found in Boyle (1898) and Saunders et al. (1974). Kidd and Kidd (1970) have provided the standard classification of European glass beads found on sites of this period. Important studies of the chronology of the historical period based mainly on European goods have been published by Wray and Schoff (1953), Wray (1973), Fitzgerald (1982a, 1982b, 1983), and Kenyon and Kenyon (1982).

## CHAPTER FIVE

There is no problem more important for understanding the history and social organization of native American peoples than determining the magnitude of the demographic collapse following the European rediscovery of the New World in the fifteenth century. The best general introduction to the subject of epidemic diseases is McNeill (1976). Older discussions of demographic decline in the New World include Stearn and Stearn (1945), Ashburn (1947), and Duffy (1951, 1953). Another general study is Crosby (1972). Estimates of population loss in Mexico are provided by Borah and Cook (1960, 1963) – but for disagreement see Sanders (1970) – and for Peru by N. Cook (1981). The most important effort to measure the general extent of the collapse is Dobyns (1966). Ramenofsky (1982) has attempted to use archaeological evidence to demonstrate significant demographic decline in North America during the sixteenth century. For a critical review of current estimates of loss, see Denevan (1976) and Ubelaker (1976). Other general discussions of this problem have been published by Jacobs (1974), Crosby (1976), and Dobyns (1976b). Dobyns (1976a) provides a critical bibliography of studies of native American historical demography into the mid-1970s.

The most extensive discussion of demographic loss in eastern North America during the sixteenth century is Dobyns (1983), who attempts to correlate outbreaks of disease in that region with those in Mexico and the Caribbean. Many of his conclusions are of necessity based on limited evidence and therefore far from certain. This work should be supplemented by Miller's (1976, 1982) examination of the possible demographic consequences of direct contact between Europeans and native Americans in Atlantic Canada during the sixteenth century. Early demographic trends in New England are discussed by S.F. Cook (1973a, 1973b), for the southeastern United States by Milner (1980), and for the Iroquoians by Dobyns (1983:313–27), Jackes (1983), and Sullivan (1983).

A general study of missions to native North Americans can be found in Berkhofer (1965), Bowden (1981), J. Grant (1984), and Axtell's forthcoming *The Invasion Within*. See also Axtell (1982b) for a valuable discussion of ethnohistorical studies of missions. Ronda and Axtell (1978) provide an extensive critical bibliography of works dealing with Indian missions to the mid-1970s. Studies relating specifically to northeastern North America have been published by Talbot (1935, 1956), Delanglez (1939), Kennedy (1950), Stanley (1950), Gray and Gray (1956), Jennings (1971), N. Salisbury (1974, 1975), Axtell (1975, 1981), Jaenen (1976), Ronda (1977, 1981), and Moore (1982). Blanchard (1982b) offers an interesting preliminary view of native cognitive responses to early missionary instruction at Caughnawaga, but his arguments require more substantiation to be fully convincing. On efforts at francization by missionaries, see Stanley (1949) and Jaenen (1968).

Lafitau provides the best description of the Iroquois at Caughnawaga where he lived from 1712 to 1717 (Fenton and Moore 1974–7). The only comprehensive history of Caughnawaga is Devine (1922). It is written from a Christian religious perspective and does not deal to any significant degree with economic and social aspects of the mission or with native beliefs and aspirations. Béchard (1945) contains additional information for the period 1900 to 1945. Blanchard's (1982a) doctoral dissertation provides little insight into the history of Caughnawaga during the seventeenth century because he does not employ sound historiographic principles. Nor is much new found in Béchard (1976). D. Smith (1974:124–6) gives additional references to studies of social and cultural life at Caughnawaga over the years.

## CHAPTER SIX

For discussions of stereotypes, see Lippmann (1922) and Harding (1968). Most histories of New France that have condemned French traders judge historical events in terms of modern values or aspirations rather than explain them in relationship to the conditions and attitudes that prevailed at the time they happened. Presentism of this sort has long been condemned as unprofessional by historians in general (Fischer 1970:135–40) as well as by those studying New France (McIlwain 1915:ix; Eccles 1973:viii).

Some historians have argued that because the Heroic Age was an "embryonic" stage when "institutions were scarcely in place," that period is of little importance for understanding the later development of New France (Jaenen 1982b:44). Such a view cannot be sustained. While it is true that important new factors shaped New France after 1663, the relationships that had developed prior to this time, including those between Indians and Whites, continued to influence life in the colony to a significant degree.

Because they do not pertain directly to relations between European colonists and native people, I have not examined economic and political interactions between France and the Netherlands as these may have influenced the colonization of New France. For provisional studies of this very important subject by Th. J. Kupp, see "Quelques aspects de la dissolution de la Compagnie de M. de Monts, 1607," *Revue d'Histoire de l'Amérique française* 24 (1970): 357–74, and "Le développement de l'intérêt hollandais dans la pêcherie de la morue de Terre-Neuve – L'influence hollandaise sur les pêcheries de Terre-Neuve au dix-septième siècle," *Revue d'Histoire de l'Amérique française* 27 (1974): 565–9.

Elisabeth Tooker has published a major reassessment of relations between the Iroquois and the Susquehannocks, "The Demise of the Susquehannocks: A 17th Century Mystery," *Pennsylvania Archaeologist* 54(3–4) (1984): 1–10.

# References

## ABBREVIATIONS

| | |
|---|---|
| *AA* | *American Anthropologist* |
| AAA,M | American Anthropological Association, Memoir |
| *AARO* | *Annual Archaeological Report, Appendix to the Report of the Minister of Education, Ontario* |
| *Am.Ant.* | *American Antiquity* |
| *AN* | *Arch Notes*, Newsletter of the Ontario Archaeological Society |
| *Anth.* | *Anthropologica* |
| ASC,MS | National Museum of Man, Archaeological Survey of Canada, Mercury Series |
| *BAE,AR* | *Bureau of American Ethnology, Annual Report* |
| BAE,B | Bureau of American Ethnology, Bulletin |
| *CA* | *Current Anthropology* |
| CES,MS | National Museum of Man, Canadian Ethnology Service, Mercury Series |
| *CHR* | *Canadian Historical Review* |
| *CJA* | *Canadian Journal of Archaeology* |
| *DCB* | *Dictionary of Canadian Biography* (Toronto: University of Toronto Press) |
| *Eth.* | *Ethnohistory* |
| *Kewa* | *Kewa*, Newsletter of the London Chapter, Ontario Archaeological Society |
| NMC,B | National Museum of Canada, Bulletin |
| *OA* | *Ontario Archaeology* |
| *OH* | *Ontario History* |
| *PA* | *Pennsylvania Archaeologist* |
| *PAPS* | *Proceedings of the American Philosophical Society* |
| *RAQ* | *Recherches Amérindiennes au Québec* |

RHAF    Revue d'Histoire de l'Amérique française
TRSC    Transactions of the Royal Society of Canada
WMQ     The William and Mary Quarterly


Abler, T.S. 1980. "Iroquois Cannibalism: Fact Not Fiction." Eth. 27: 309–16.

Adair, E.R. 1932. "Dollard Des Ormeaux and the Fight at the Long Sault: A Re-interpretation of Dollard's Exploit." CHR 13: 121–38.

Adams, A.T. 1961. The Explorations of Pierre Esprit Radisson. Minneapolis: Ross and Haines.

Allen, R.S. 1984. Native Studies in Canada: A Research Guide. 2nd ed. Ottawa: Research Branch, Indian and Northern Affairs.

Anderson, J.E. 1963. "Osteology of the Donaldson Site." NMC,B 184: 93–113. Ottawa.

Arber, Edward, ed. 1910. Travels and Works of Captain John Smith. Edinburgh: John Grant.

Arens, W. 1979. The Man-Eating Myth: Anthropology and Anthropophagy. New York: Oxford University Press.

Ash, Marinell. 1981. " 'A Fine, Genial, Hearty Band': David Laing, Daniel Wilson and Scottish Archaeology." In The Scottish Antiquarian Tradition, edited by A.S. Bell, 86–113. Edinburgh: John Donald.

Ashburn, P.M. 1947. The Ranks of Death: A Medical History of the Conquest of America. New York: Coward-McCann.

Ashe, G., ed. 1971. The Quest for America. London: Pall Mall.

Atwater, Caleb. 1820. "Description of the Antiquities Discovered in the State of Ohio and Other Western States." Archaeologia Americana: Transactions and Collections of the American Antiquarian Society 1: 105–267.

Atwood, Margaret. 1972. Survival: A Thematic Guide to Canadian Literature. Toronto: Anansi.

Averkieva, J. 1971. "The Tlingit Indians." In Leacock and Lurie, 317–42.

Axtell, James. 1975. "The European Failure to Convert the Indians: An Autopsy," In Cowan, 274–90.

– 1979. "Ethnohistory: An Historian's Viewpoint." Eth. 26: 1–13.

– 1981. The European and the Indian: Essays in the Ethnohistory of Colonial North America. New York: Oxford University Press.

– 1982a. "Bronze Men and Golden Ages: The Intellectual History of Indian-White Relations in Colonial America." Journal of Interdisciplinary History 12: 663–75.

– 1982b. "Some Thoughts on the Ethnohistory of Missions." Eth. 29: 35–41.

– 1983. "A Moral History of Indian-White Relations Revisited." *The History Teacher* 16: 169–90.

– n.d. *The Invasion Within: The Contest of Cultures in Colonial North America.* Forthcoming.

Bacqueville de La Potherie, Claude Charles Le Roy, sieur de. 1911–12. "History of the Savage Peoples Who Are Allies of New France." In Blair, 1: 273–372; 2: 13–136.

Baerreis, D.A. 1961. "The Ethnohistoric Approach and Archaeology." *Eth.* 8: 49–77.

Bailey, A.G. 1933. "The Significance of the Identity and Disappearance of the Laurentian Iroquois." *TRSC*, 3rd series, 27, ii: 97–108. Ottawa.

– 1937. *The Conflict of European and Eastern Algonkian Cultures, 1504–1700: A Study in Canadian Civilization.* St John: New Brunswick Museum (reprinted by University of Toronto Press, 1969).

– 1977. "Retrospective Thoughts of an Ethnohistorian." *Canadian Historical Association, Historical Papers* 1977: 15–29.

Barbour, P.L. 1964. *The Three Worlds of Captain John Smith.* Boston: Houghton Mifflin.

Barkham, Selma. 1980. "A Note on the Strait of Belle Isle during the Period of Basque Contact with Indians and Inuit." *Inuit Studies* 4: 51–8.

– 1982. "The Documentary Evidence for Basque Whaling Ships in the Strait of Belle Isle." In Story, 53–65.

Bawtree, E.W. 1848. "A Brief Description of Some Sepulchral Pits, of Indian Origin, Lately Discovered near Penetanqueshene." *The Edinburgh New Philosophical Journal* 45: 86–101.

Beardsley, R.K., et al. 1956. "Functional and Evolutionary Implications of Community Patterning." *Society for American Archaeology, Memoir* 11: 129–57.

Beauchamp, W.M. 1901. "Wampum and Shell Articles Used by the New York Indians." *New York State Museum, Bulletin* 41: 319–480. Albany.

Beaugrand-Champagne, A. 1948. "Les origines de Montréal." *Les Cahiers des Dix* 13: 39–62.

Béchard, Henri. 1945. *J'ai cent ans: L'église Saint-François-Xavier de Caughnawaga.* Montreal: Messager Canadien.

– 1976. *The Original Caughnawaga Indians.* Montreal: International Publishers' Representatives.

Benedict, Ruth. 1934. *Patterns of Culture.* Boston: Houghton Mifflin.

Berger, Carl. 1970. *The Sense of Power: Studies in the Ideas of Canadian Imperialism, 1867–1914.* Toronto: University of Toronto Press.

– 1976. *The Writing of Canadian History: Aspects of English-Canadian Historical Writing, 1900–1970.* Toronto: Oxford University Press.

Berkhofer, R.F., Jr. 1965. *Salvation and the Savage: An Analysis of Prot-*

*estant Missions and American Indian Response, 1787–1862.* Lexington: University of Kentucky Press.

– 1971. "The Political Context of a New Indian History." *Pacific Historical Review* 40: 357–82.

– 1978. *The White Man's Indian: Images of the American Indian from Columbus to the Present.* New York: Knopf.

Berton, Pierre. 1978. *The Wild Frontier.* Toronto: McClelland and Stewart.

Bibaud, Maximilien. 1848. *Biographie des Sagamos illustres de l'Amérique septentrionale* ... Montreal: Lovell et Gibson.

– 1855. "Discours préliminaire sur les origines américaines." *Les institutions de l'histoire du Canada ou Annales canadiennes jusqu'à l'an 1819,* 5–64. Montreal: Senécal et Daniel.

Bibaud, Michel. 1837. *Histoire du Canada, sous la domination française.* Montreal: Jones.

Bieder, R.E. 1975. "Albert Gallatin and the Survival of Enlightenment Thought in Nineteenth-Century American Anthropology." In *Toward a Science of Man: Essays in the History of Anthropology,* edited by T.H. Thoresen, 91–8. The Hague: Mouton.

Biggar, H.P. 1901. *The Early Trading Companies of New France.* University of Toronto Studies in History.

– ed. 1911. *The Precursors of Jacques Cartier, 1497–1534.* Publications of the Canadian Archives 5. Ottawa.

– ed. 1922–36. *The Works of Samuel de Champlain.* 6 vols. Toronto: The Champlain Society.

– ed. 1924. *The Voyages of Jacques Cartier: Published from the Originals with Translations, Notes and Appendices.* Publications of the Public Archives of Canada 11. Ottawa.

– ed. 1930. *A Collection of Documents Relating to Jacques Cartier and the Sieur de Roberval.* Publications of the Public Archives of Canada 14. Ottawa.

Billington, R.A. 1981. *Land of Savagery, Land of Promise: The European Image of the American Frontier in the Nineteenth Century.* New York: Norton.

Binford, L.R. 1972. *An Archaeological Perspective.* New York: Seminar Press.

– 1980. "Willow Smoke and Dogs' Tails: Hunter-Gatherer Settlement Systems and Archaeological Site Formation." *Am.Ant.* 45: 4–20.

– 1983a. *In Pursuit of the Past.* London: Thames and Hudson.

– 1983b. *Working at Archaeology.* New York: Academic Press.

Binford, L.R., and W.J. Chasko, Jr. 1976. "Nunamiut Demographic History: A Provocative Case." In *Demographic Anthropology,* edited by E.B.W. Zubrow, 63–143. Albuquerque: University of New Mexico Press.

Bishop, C.A. 1981. "Northeastern Indian Concepts of Conservation and the Fur Trade: A Critique of Calvin Martin's Thesis." In Krech, 39–58.

Bishop, Morris. 1948. *Champlain: The Life of Fortitude*. New York: Knopf.

Bissell, Benjamin. 1925. *The American Indian in English Literature of the Eighteenth Century*. New Haven: Yale University Press.

Blair, E.H., ed. 1911–12. *The Indian Tribes of the Upper Mississippi Valley and Region of the Great Lakes*. 2 vols. Cleveland: Clark.

Blanchard, D.S. 1982a. "Patterns of Tradition and Change: The Re-creation of Iroquois Culture at Kahnawake." PH D diss., Department of Anthropology, University of Chicago.

– 1982b. "… To the Other Side of the Sky: Catholicism at Kahnawake, 1667–1700." *Anth*. 24: 77–102.

Blau, Harold. 1966. "Function and the False Faces: A Classification of Onondaga Masked Rituals and Themes." *Journal of American Folklore* 79: 564–80.

Borah, Woodrow. 1964. "America as Model: The Demographic Impact of European Expansion upon the Non-European World." *Actas y memorias, xxxv Congreso Internacional de Americanistas, Mexico, 1962*, 3: 379–87.

Borah, W., and S.F. Cook. 1960. *The Population of Central Mexico in 1548*. Berkeley and Los Angeles: University of California Press.

– 1963. *The Aboriginal Population of Central Mexico on the Eve of the Spanish Conquest*. Berkeley and Los Angeles: University of California Press.

Boucher, Pierre. 1664. *Histoire véritable et naturelle des moeurs et productions du pays de la Nouvelle-France, vulgairement dite le Canada*. Paris: Lambert (photographic reprint with notes by Société historique de Boucherville, 1964).

Bowden, H.W. 1981. *American Indians and Christian Missions: Studies in Cultural Conflict*. Chicago: University of Chicago Press.

Bowen, Jonathan. 1980. "The Sandusky Tradition: People of the Southwestern Lake Erie Drainage." *Toledo Area Aboriginal Research Bulletin* 9: 39–59.

Bowker, L.H. 1972. "Red and Black in Contemporary American History Texts." In *Native Americans Today: Sociological Perspectives*, edited by H.M. Bahr et al., 101–10. New York: Harper and Row.

Boxer, C.R. 1951. *The Christian Century in Japan, 1549–1650*. Berkeley and Los Angeles: University of California Press.

Boyle, David. 1889. "The Land of Souls." *AARO* 1889: 4–15.

– 1898. "Ahoendoé Ossuary." *AARO* 1897–8: 40–2.

Bradley, J.W. 1979. "The Onondaga Iroquois, 1500–1665: A Study in Acculturative Change and Its Consequences." PH D diss., Department of Anthropology, Syracuse University, Syracuse, NY.

– 1980. "Ironwork in Onondaga, 1550–1650." In *Studies on Iroquoian Culture*, edited by Nancy Bonvillain, 109–18. Occasional Publications in Northeastern Anthropology 6. Rindge, NH.

– 1982. "Blue Crystals and Other Trinkets: Glass Beads from 16th and Early 17th Century New England." Rochester Museum and Science Center, Conference on Glass Trade Beads. Manuscript.

Bradley, R., and I. Hodder. 1979. "British Prehistory: An Integrated View." *Man* 14: 93–104.

Brasser, T.J.C. 1971. "Group Identification along a Moving Frontier." *Verhandlungen des xxxviii Internationalen Amerikanistenkongresses*, 2: 261–5. Munich.

Briant, Pierre. 1982. *Etat et pasteurs au Moyen-Orient ancien*. Cambridge: Cambridge University Press.

Broderick, J.F. 1967. "Jesuits." *New Catholic Encyclopedia* 7: 898–909. New York: McGraw-Hill.

Brose, D.S. 1970. *The Summer Island Site: A Study of Prehistoric Cultural Ecology and Social Organization in the Northern Lake Michigan Area*. Case Western Reserve University Studies in Anthropology 1. Cleveland.

Brose, D.S., and N. Greber, eds. 1979. *Hopewell Archaeology: The Chillicothe Conference*. Kent: Kent State University Press.

Brown, I.W. 1979. "Functional Group Changes and Acculturation: A Case Study of the French and the Indian in the Lower Mississippi Valley." *Mid-Continental Journal of Archaeology* 4: 147–66.

Buell, N.S. 1979. "The Proto-Iroquoian Homeland." MA thesis, Department of Anthropology, State University of New York at Albany.

Burley, D.V. 1981. "Proto-historic Ecological Effects of the Fur Trade on Micmac Culture in Northeastern New Brunswick." *Eth.* 28: 203–16.

Burling, Robbins. 1962. "Maximization Theories and the Study of Economic Anthropology." *AA* 64: 802–21.

Burnham, K.D. 1983. "Notes Regarding the First White Fur Traders on Lake Champlain." *The Bulletin of the Fort Ticonderoga Museum* 14: 197–202.

Byers, D.S. 1961. "Second Comment on William A. Ritchie's 'Iroquois Archeology and Settlement Patterns.' " BAE,B 180: 47–50. Washington.

Caldwell, J.R. 1958. *Trend and Tradition in the Prehistory of the Eastern United States*. AAA,M 88. Menasha.

– 1959. "The New American Archeology." *Science* 129: 303–7.

Campeau, Lucien. 1967. *La première mission d'Acadie (1602–1616)*. Quebec: Les Presses de l'Université Laval.

– 1974. *Les Cent-Associés et le peuplement de la Nouvelle-France (1633–1663)*. Montreal: Bellarmin.

– 1979. *Etablissement à Québec (1616–1634)*. Quebec: Les Presses de l'Université Laval.

*Canadian Journal* [Anonymous]. 1852. Plan to Collect Information Concerning Indian Remains. *Canadian Journal* 1: 25.

Cancian, Frank. 1966. "Maximization as Norm, Strategy, and Theory: A

Comment on Programmatic Statements in Economic Anthropology."
*AA* 68: 465–70.

Carmack, R.M. 1971. "Ethnography and Ethnohistory: Their Application
in Middle American Studies." *Eth.* 18: 127–45.

– 1972. "Ethnohistory: A Review of Its Development, Definitions, Methods, and Aims." In *Annual Review of Anthropology* 1: 227–46. Palo
Alto: Annual Reviews Inc.

Ceci, Lynn. 1977. "The Effect of European Contact and Trade on the
Settlement Pattern of Indians in Coastal New York, 1524–1665." PH D
diss., The City University of New York.

– 1982. "The Value of Wampum among the New York Iroquois: A Case
Study in Artifact Analysis." *Journal of Anthropological Research*
38: 97–107.

Chafe, W.L. 1964. "Linguistic Evidence for the Relative Age of Iroquois
Religious Practices." *Southwestern Journal of Anthropology* 20: 278–
85.

Chapdelaine, Claude, ed. 1978. *Images de la préhistoire du Québec*. Montreal: Recherches Amérindiennes au Québec.

– 1980. "L'ascendance culturelle des Iroquoiens du Saint-Laurent." *RAQ*
10: 145–52.

Chapman, Robert, Ian Kinnes, and Klavs Randsborg. 1981. *The Archaeology of Death*. Cambridge: Cambridge University Press.

Charlevoix, P.F.X. de. 1866–72. *History and General Description of New
France*. Edited by J.G. Shea. 6 vols. New York: J.G. Shea.

Chaumonot, P.J.M. 1869. *Le Père Pierre Chaumonot de la Compagnie de
Jésus: autobiographie et pièces inédites*. Edited by A. Carayon. Poitiers:
Oudin.

Chevalier, Jacques. 1979. "Myth and Ideology in 'Traditional' French Canada:
Dollard, the Martyred Warrior." *Anth.* 21: 143–75.

Chiappelli, Fredi. 1976. *First Images of America: The Impact of the New
World on the Old*. Berkeley and Los Angeles: University of California
Press.

Childe, V.G. 1956. *Society and Knowledge*. New York: Harper.

Clark, Grahame. 1977. *World Prehistory in New Perspective*. Cambridge:
Cambridge University Press.

Clarke, David. 1968. *Analytical Archaeology*. London: Methuen.

Clarke, P.D. 1870. *Origin and Traditional History of the Wyandotts*.
Toronto: Hunter, Rose.

Cleland, C.E. 1982. "The Inland Shore Fishery of the Northern Great Lakes:
Its Development and Importance in Prehistory." *Am.Ant.* 47: 761–84.

Clermont, Norman. 1980. "L'augmentation de la population chez les Iroquoiens préhistoriques." *RAQ* 10: 159–63.

Clermont, Norman, and Claude Chapdelaine. 1982. *Pointe-du-Buisson 4:*

*Quarante siècles d'archives oubliées.* Montreal: Recherches Amérindiennes au Québec.

– 1983. *Le site iroquoien de Lanoraie: témoignage d'une maison-longue.* Montreal: Recherches Amérindiennes au Québec.

Clifton, J.A. n.d. "Northern Iroquoian Sociopolitical Organization: An Analysis of Four Wyandot Villages in 1747." Manuscript deposited with National Museum of Man, Canadian Ethnology Service, Ottawa.

Cohn, B.S. 1968. "Ethnohistory." In Sills, 6: 440–8.

– 1980. "History and Anthropology: The State of Play." *Comparative Studies in Society and History* 22: 198–221.

– 1981. "Anthropology and History in the 1980s: Toward a Rapprochement." *Journal of Interdisciplinary History* 12: 227–52.

Cole, Douglas. 1973. "The Origins of Canadian Anthropology, 1850–1910." *Journal of Canadian Studies* 8: 33–45.

– 1982. "Tricks of the Trade: Northwest Coast Artifact Collecting, 1875–1925." *CHR* 63: 439–60.

Collingwood, R.G. 1946. *The Idea of History.* Oxford: Oxford University Press.

Connolly, John. 1977. "Archeology in Nova Scotia and New Brunswick between 1863 and 1914 ..." *Man in the Northeast* 13: 3–34.

Cook, N.D. 1981. *Demographic Collapse: Indian Peru, 1520–1620.* Cambridge: Cambridge University Press.

Cook, Scott. 1966. "The Obsolete 'Anti-Market' Mentality: A Critique of the Substantive Approach to Economic Anthropology." *AA* 68: 323–45.

Cook, S.F. 1973a. "The Significance of Disease in the Extinction of the New England Indians." *Human Biology* 45: 485–508.

– 1973b. "Interracial Warfare and Population Decline among the New England Indians." *Eth.* 20: 1–24.

Cooper, J.F. 1826. *The Last of the Mohicans: A Narrative of 1757.* Philadelphia: Carey and Lea.

Copway, G. 1850. *The Traditional History and Characteristic Sketches of the Ojibway Nation.* London: Gilpin.

Corris, Peter. 1969. "Ethnohistory in Australia." *Eth.* 16: 201–10.

Cowan, W., ed. 1975. *Papers of the Sixth Algonquian Conference, 1974.* CES,MS 23. Ottawa.

Cox, Bruce. 1983. *The French Run Away with Our Trade: Another Look at Early Fur-Trade Statistics.* Carleton University, Department of Sociology and Anthropology, Departmental Working Paper 83–2.

Crean, J.F. 1962. "Hats and the Fur Trade." *Canadian Journal of Economics and Political Science* 28: 373–86.

Crosby, A.W., Jr. 1972. *The Columbian Exchange: Biological and Cultural Consequences of 1492.* Westport, Conn.: Greenwood.

– 1976. "Virgin Soil Epidemics as a Factor in the Aboriginal Depopulation in America." *WMQ* 33: 289–99.

Dainville, D. 1821. *Beautés de l'histoire du Canada* ... Paris: Bossange Frères.

Dalton, George. 1961. "Economic Theory and Primitive Society." *AA* 63: 1–25.

– ed. 1967. *Tribal and Peasant Economies: Readings in Economic Anthropology*. Garden City: Natural History Press.

– ed. 1968. *Primitive, Archaic, and Modern Economies: Essays of Karl Polanyi*. Garden City: Anchor Books.

– 1969. "Theoretical Issues in Economic Anthropology." *CA* 10: 63–102.

– 1977. "Aboriginal Economies in Stateless Societies." In *Exchange Systems in Prehistory*, edited by T.K. Earle and J. Ericson, 191–212. New York: Academic Press.

– 1981. "Anthropological Models in Archaeological Perspective." In *Pattern of the Past*, edited by I. Hodder, G. Isaac, and N. Hammond, 17–48. Cambridge: Cambridge University Press.

Damas, David, vol. ed. 1985. *Handbook of North American Indians*. Vol. 5, *Arctic*. Washington: Smithsonian Institution.

Daniel, Glyn. 1975. *A Hundred and Fifty Years of Archaeology*. London: Duckworth.

Darnell, Regna. 1971. "The Professionalization of American Anthropology." *Social Science Information* 10: 83–103.

Davies, Arthur. 1984. "Prince Madoc and the Discovery of America in 1477." *Geographical Journal* 150: 363–72.

Dawson, J.W. 1880. *Fossil Men and Their Modern Representatives: An Attempt to Illustrate the Characters and Condition of Prehistoric Men in Europe by Those of the American Races*. Montreal: Dawson (3rd ed., 1888).

Day, G.M. 1972. "Oral Tradition as Complement." *Eth.* 19: 99–108.

Deagan, K. 1982. "Avenues of Inquiry in Historical Archaeology." *Advances in Archaeological Method and Theory* 5: 151–77.

Dechêne, Louise. 1974. *Habitants et marchands de Montréal au XVIIᵉ siècle*. Paris: Plon.

Delâge, Denys. 1981. "Amérindiens et Européens en Amérique du Nord-est, 1600–1664." Doctoral diss., Ecole des Hautes Etudes en Sciences Sociales, Paris.

Delanglez, Jean. 1939. *Frontenac and the Jesuits*. Chicago: Institute of Jesuit History.

Denevan, W.M., ed. 1976. *The Native Population of the Americas in 1492*. Madison: University of Wisconsin Press.

Dening, Gregory. 1966. "Ethnohistory in Polynesia: The Value of Ethnohistorical Evidence." *Journal of Pacific History* 1: 23–42.

Denys, Nicolas. 1908. *The Description and Natural History of the Coasts of North America*. Edited by W.F. Ganong. Toronto: The Champlain Society.

De Poli, Oscar. 1894. "Samuel de Champlain, notes et documents." *Annuaire du Conseil Héraldique de France* 7: 31–55.

Desrosiers, Léo-Paul. 1947. *Iroquoisie*. Vol. 1. Montreal: Institut d'Histoire de l'Amérique française.

Devine, E.J. 1922. *Historic Caughnawaga*. Montreal: Messenger Press.

Dewdney, Selwyn, and K.E. Kidd. 1967. *Indian Rock Paintings of the Great Lakes*. 2nd ed. Toronto: University of Toronto Press.

Dickason, O.P. 1977a. "The Concept of *l'homme sauvage* and Early French Colonialism in the Americas." *Revue française d'Histoire d'Outre-Mer* 64: 5–32.

– 1977b. "Renaissance Europe's View of Amerindian Sovereignty and Territoriality." *Plural Societies* 8(3–4): 97–107.

– 1979. "Europeans and Amerindians: Some Comparative Aspects of Early Contact." *Canadian Historical Association, Historical Papers* 1979: 182–202.

– 1982. "From 'One Nation' in the Northeast to 'New Nation' in the Northwest: A Look at the Emergence of the Métis." *American Indian Culture and Research Journal* 6(2): 1–21.

– 1984a. *The Myth of the Savage and the Beginnings of French Colonialism in the Americas*. Edmonton: University of Alberta Press.

– 1984b. "The Brazilian Connection: A Look at the Origin of French Techniques for Trading with the Amerindians." In *Rendezvous: Selected Papers of the Fourth North American Fur Trade Conference, 1981*, edited by T.C. Buckley, 27–42. St Paul: Minnesota Historical Society.

Dickinson, J.A. 1980. "The Pre-Contact Huron Population: A Reappraisal." *OH* 72: 173–9.

– 1981. "Annaotaha et Dollard vus de l'autre côté de la palissade." *RHAF* 35: 163–78.

– 1982. "La guerre iroquoise et la mortalité en Nouvelle-France, 1608–1666." *RHAF* 36: 31–54.

Diebold, A.R., Jr. 1960. "Determining the Centers of Dispersal of Language Groups." *International Journal of American Linguistics* 26: 1–10.

Dionne, N.-E. 1891–1906. *Samuel Champlain*. 2 vols. Quebec: Côté.

Dobyns, H.F. 1966. "Estimating Aboriginal American Population: An Appraisal of Techniques with a New Hemispheric Estimate." *CA* 7: 395–416, 425–45.

– 1972. "Ethnohistory and Contemporary United States Social Problems." *Eth.* 19: 1–12.

– 1976a. *Native American Historical Demography: A Critical Bibliography*. Bloomington: Indiana University Press.

– 1976b. "Brief Perspective on a Scholarly Transformation: Widowing the 'Virgin' Land." *Eth.* 23: 95–104.

– 1978. "Ethnohistory and Human Resource Development." *Eth.* 25: 103–20.

– 1983. *Their Number Become Thinned: Native American Population Dynamics in Eastern North America*. Knoxville: University of Tennessee Press.

Dodd, C.F. 1984. *Ontario Iroquois Tradition Longhouses*. ASC,MS 124: 181–437. Ottawa.

Dorson, R.M. 1961. "Ethnohistory and Ethnic Folklore." *Eth.* 8: 12–30.

Doughty, Howard. 1962. *Francis Parkman*. New York: Macmillan.

Drinnon, Richard. 1980. *Facing West: The Metaphysics of Indian-Hating and Empire Building*. Minneapolis: University of Minnesota Press.

Driver, H.E. 1969. *Indians of North America*. 2nd ed. Chicago: University of Chicago Press.

Driver, H.E., and W.C. Massey. 1957. "Comparative Studies of North American Indians." *Transactions of the American Philosophical Society* 47: 165–456.

Du Creux, François. 1951–2. *The History of Canada, or New France*. Edited by J. Conacher. 2 vols. Toronto: The Champlain Society.

Duffy, John. 1951. "Smallpox and the Indians in the American Colonies." *Bulletin of the History of Medicine* 25: 324–41.

– 1953. *Epidemics in Colonial America*. Baton Rouge: Louisiana State University Press.

Duignan, P. 1958. "Early Jesuit Missionaries: A Suggestion for Further Study." *AA* 60: 725–32.

Dyen, Isidore. 1956. "Language Distribution and Migration Theory." *Language* 32: 611–26.

Dyen, I., and D.F. Aberle. 1974. *Lexical Reconstruction: The Case of the Proto-Athapaskan Kinship System*. Cambridge: Cambridge University Press.

Eccles, W.J. 1973. *France in America*. Vancouver: Fitzhenry and Whiteside.

– 1979. "A Belated Review of Harold Adams Innis, *The Fur Trade in Canada*." *CHR* 60: 419–41.

– 1983. "The Fur Trade and Eighteenth Century Imperialism." *WMQ* 40: 341–62.

Edmonson, M.S. 1961. "Neolithic Diffusion Rates." *CA* 2: 71–102.

Eggan, F.R. 1966. *The American Indian*. London: Weidenfeld and Nicolson.

Ehret, Christopher, and Merrick Posnansky. 1982. *The Archaeological and Linguistic Reconstruction of African History*. Berkeley and Los Angeles: University of California Press.

Eid, L.V. 1979. "The Ojibwa-Iroquois War: The War the Five Nations Did Not Win." *Eth.* 26: 297–324.

Ekholm, K., and J. Friedman. 1979. " 'Capital', Imperialism and Exploitation in Ancient World Systems." In *Power and Propaganda*, edited by M.T. Larsen, 41–58. Copenhagen: Akademisk Forlag.

Ember, M. 1973. "An Archaeological Indicator of Matrilocal versus Patrilocal Residence." *Am.Ant.* 38: 177–82.

Emerson, J.N., ed. 1961. *Cahiague, 1961*. Orillia: Archaeological Field School, University of Toronto.

Engelbrecht, W.E. 1974. "The Iroquois: Archaeological Patterning on the Tribal Level." *World Archaeology* 6: 52–65.

Engelbrecht, W.E., and D.K. Grayson, eds. 1978. *Essays in Northeastern Anthropology in Memory of Marian E. White*. Occasional Publications in Northeastern Anthropology 5. Rindge, NH.

Euler, R.C. 1972. "Ethnohistory in the United States." *Eth.* 19: 201–7.

Fagan, Brian. 1977. *Elusive Treasure: The Story of Early Archaeologists in the Americas*. New York: Charles Scribner's.

– 1980. *People of the Earth: An Introduction to World Prehistory*. 3rd ed. Boston: Little, Brown and Company.

Fagan, B.M., and J.B. Carlson. 1982. "Advances in New World Archeology in 1981." *Early Man* 4(2): 6–15.

Faillon, Etienne-Michel. 1865–6. *Histoire de la colonie française en Canada*. 3 vols. Bibliothèque Paroissiale.

Fairchild, H.N. 1928. *The Noble Savage: A Study in Romantic Naturalism*. New York: Columbia University Press.

Farb, Peter. 1969. *Man's Rise to Civilization as Shown by the Indians of North America from Primeval Times to the Coming of the Industrial State*. New York: Avon.

Feit, Harvey. 1973. "The Ethno-ecology of the Waswanipi Cree; or How Hunters Can Manage their Resources." In *Cultural Ecology*, edited by Bruce Cox, 115–25. Toronto: McClelland and Stewart.

Fell, Barry. 1982. *Bronze Age America*. Boston: Little, Brown and Company.

Fenton, W.N. 1940. "Problems Arising from the Historic Northeastern Position of the Iroquois." *Smithsonian Miscellaneous Collections* 100: 159–252.

– 1949. "Seth Newhouse's Traditional History and Constitution of the Iroquois Confederacy." *PAPS* 93(2): 141–58.

– 1952. "The Training of Historical Ethnologists in America." *AA* 54: 328–39.

– 1953. *The Iroquois Eagle Dance: An Offshoot of the Calumet Dance*. With an "Analysis of the Iroquois Eagle Dance and Songs" by Gertrude P. Kurath. BAE,B 156. Washington.

– 1957. "Indian and White Relations in Eastern North America: A Common Ground for History and Ethnology." In *American Indian and White Relations to 1830*, by W.N. Fenton et al., 3–27. Chapel Hill: University of North Carolina Press.

– 1962. "Ethnohistory and Its Problems." *Eth.* 9: 1–23.

– 1966. "Field Work, Museum Studies, and Ethnohistorical Research." *Eth.* 13: 71–85.

– 1969. "J.-F. Lafitau (1681–1746), Precursor of Scientific Anthropology." *Southwestern Journal of Anthropology* 25: 173–87.

– 1971. "The New York State Wampum Collection: The Case for the Integrity of Cultural Treasures." *PAPS* 115(6): 437–61.

– 1978. "Northern Iroquoian Culture Patterns." In Trigger 1978a, 296–321.

Fenton, W.N., and E.L. Moore, eds. 1974–7. *Customs of the American Indians Compared with the Customs of Primitive Times*, by Father Joseph François Lafitau. Toronto: The Champlain Society.

Ferland, J.-B.-A. 1882. *Cours d'histoire du Canada*. Vol. 1, *1534–1663*. Quebec: Hardy.

Finlayson, W.D. 1977. *The Saugeen Culture: A Middle Woodland Manifestation in Southwestern Ontario*. ASC,MS 61. Ottawa.

Finlayson, W.D., and R.H. Pihl. 1980. "Some Implications for the Attribute Analysis of Rim Sherds from the Draper Site, Pickering, Ontario." In Hayes, 113–31.

Fischer, D.H. 1970. *Historians' Fallacies: Toward a Logic of Historical Thought*. London: Routledge and Kegan Paul.

Fisher, Robin. 1977. *Contact and Conflict: Indian-European Relations in British Columbia, 1774–1890*. Vancouver: University of British Columbia Press.

Fitting, J.E. 1970. *The Archaeology of Michigan*. Garden City: Natural History Press.

– ed. 1973. *The Development of North American Archaeology*. Garden City: Anchor Books.

– 1978. "Prehistory: Introduction." In Trigger 1978a, 14–15.

Fitting, J.E., and C.E. Cleland. 1969. "Late Prehistoric Settlement Patterns in the Upper Great Lakes." *Eth.* 16: 289–302.

Fitzgerald, W.R. 1982a. *Lest the Beaver Run Loose: The Early 17th Century Christianson Site and Trends in Historic Neutral Archaeology*. ASC,MS 111. Ottawa.

– 1982b. "A Refinement of Historic Neutral Chronologies: Evidence from Shaver Hill, Christianson and Dwyer." *OA* 38: 31–46.

– 1983. "Further Comments on the Neutral Glass Bead Sequence." *AN* 83(1): 17–25.

Ford, C.S., ed. 1967. *Cross-Cultural Approaches: Reading in Comparative Research*. New Haven: HRAF Press.

Fox, W.A. 1980. "Miskwo Sinnee Munnidominug." *Archaeology of Eastern North America* 8: 88–98.

– 1982. "The Princess Point Concept." *AN* 82(2): 17–26.

Francis, D., and T. Morantz. 1983. *Partners in Furs: A History of the Fur Trade in Eastern James Bay, 1600–1870*. Kingston and Montreal: McGill-Queen's University Press.

Friederici, Georg. 1907. "Scalping in America." Smithsonian Institution, *Annual Report, 1906*: 423–38.

Gadacz, R.R. 1975. "Montagnais Hunting Dynamics in Historicoecological Perspective." *Anth.* 17: 149–67.

– 1982. "The Language of Ethnohistory." *Anth.* 24: 147–65.

Gaffarel, Paul, ed. 1878. *Les singularitez de la France antarctique*, by André Thevet. Paris: Maisonneuve.

Gagnon, C.A.N. 1894. *Etudes archéologiques et variétés*. Levis: Mercier.

Gagnon, François-Marc. 1975. *La conversion par l'image*. Montreal: Bellarmin.

– 1984. *Ces hommes dits sauvages*. Montreal: Libre Expression.

Gagnon, Serge. 1978. "The Historiography of New France, 1960–1974: Jean Hamelin to Louise Dechêne." *Journal of Canadian Studies* 13(1): 80–99.

– 1982. *Quebec and Its Historians, 1840 to 1920*. Montreal: Harvest House.

Ganong, W.F. 1964. *Crucial Maps in the Early Cartography and Place-nomenclature of the Atlantic Coast of Canada*. Toronto: University of Toronto Press.

Garneau, F.-X. 1882–3. *Histoire du Canada depuis sa découverte jusqu'à nos jours*. 4th ed. 4 vols. Montreal: Beauchemin et Valois (1st ed., 1845–8).

Garrad, Charles. 1969. "Iron Trade Knives on Historic Petun Sites." *OA* 13: 3–15.

– 1980. "Petun Pottery." In Hayes, 105–11.

Garrad, Charles, and John Steckley. 1984. Review of *The Re-emergent Wyandot*, by J.A. Clifton. *Kewa* 84(7): 10–14.

Gaumond, Michel. 1979. "La presence euscarienne dans le bas Saint-Laurent aux XVIᵉ et XVIIᵉ siècles." Ministère des Affaires Culturelles, Quebec. Mimeographed.

Gellner, Ernest. 1982. "What is Structuralisme?" In *Theory and Explanation in Archaeology: The Southampton Conference*, edited by C. Renfrew, M.J. Rowlands, and B.A. Segraves, 97–123. New York: Academic Press.

Gendron, François. 1868. *Quelques particularitez du pays des Hurons* ... Albany: J.G. Shea.

Gimbutas, Marija. 1963. "The Indo-Europeans: Archeological Problems." *AA* 65: 815–36.

Given, B.J. 1981. "The Iroquois Wars and Native Firearms." In *Canadian Ethnology Society, Papers from the Sixth Annual Congress, 1979*, edited by M.-F. Guédon and D.G. Hatt, 84–94. CES,MS 78. Ottawa.

Glacken, C.J. 1967. *Traces on the Rhodian Shore: Nature and Culture in Western Thought From Ancient Times to the End of the Eighteenth Century*. Berkeley and Los Angeles: University of California Press.

Glass, H.B., O. Temkin, and W.L. Straus, Jr., eds. 1959. *Forerunners of Darwin, 1745–1859*. Baltimore: Johns Hopkins Press.

Goddard, Ives. 1972. "Historical and Philological Evidence Regarding the Identification of the Mascouten." *Eth.* 19: 123–34.

Goldschmidt, Walter, ed. 1959. *The Anthropology of Franz Boas: Essays on the Centennial of His Birth*. AAA,M 89. Menasha.

Gramly, R.M. 1977. "Deerskins and Hunting Territories: Competition for a Scarce Resource of the Northeastern Woodlands." *Am.Ant.* 42: 601–5.

Grant, H.M. 1981. "One Step Forward, Two Steps Back: Innis, Eccles, and the Canadian Fur Trade." *CHR* 62: 304–22.

Grant, J.W. 1984. *Moon of Wintertime: Missionaries and the Indians of Canada in Encounter since 1534*. Toronto: University of Toronto Press.

Gray, E.E., and L.R. Gray. 1956. *Wilderness Christians: The Moravian Mission to the Delaware Indians*. Ithaca: Cornell University Press.

Graymont, Barbara. 1979. "Koñwatsi?tsiaiéñni." *DCB* 4: 416–18.

Griffin, J.B. 1944. "The Iroquois in American Prehistory." *Papers of the Michigan Academy of Science, Arts and Letters* 29: 357–74.

Groulx, Lionel-Adolphe. 1919. *La naissance d'une race*. Montreal: Bibliothèque de l'Action française.

Gruber, J.W. 1967. "Horatio Hale and the Development of American Anthropology." *PAPS* 111: 5–37.

Gubser, N.J. 1965. *The Nunamiut Eskimos: Hunters of Caribou*. New Haven: Yale University Press.

Guemple, Lee. 1972. "Eskimo Band Organization and the 'D P Camp' Hypothesis." *Arctic Anthropology* 9(2): 80–112.

Haan, Richard. 1980. "The Problem of Iroquois Neutrality: Suggestions for Revision." *Eth.* 27: 317–30.

Haas, Jonathan. 1982. *The Evolution of the Prehistoric State*. New York: Columbia University Press.

Hakluyt, Richard. 1589. *The Principall Navigations Voiages and Discoveries of the English Nation*. Facsimile edited by D.B. Quinn and R.A. Skelton. Cambridge: Cambridge University Press 1965.

Hale, Horatio. 1883a. *The Iroquois Book of Rites*. Philadelphia: Brinton (reprinted with an Introduction by W.N. Fenton, Toronto: University of Toronto Press 1963).

–1883b. "Indian Migrations, as Evidenced by Language." *American Antiquarian* 5: 18–28, 108–24.

– 1893. "Sketch of Sir Daniel Wilson." *Popular Science Monthly* 44: 256–65.

Hall, R.L. 1979. "In Search of the Ideology of the Adena-Hopewell Climax." In Brose and Greber, 258–65.

Hamell, George. 1980. "Sun Serpents, Tawiskaron and Quartz Crystals." Rochester Museum and Science Center. Mimeographed.

– 1982. "Trading in Metaphors: The Magic of Beads." New York State Museum, Albany. Mimeographed.

Hamilton, R.N. 1976. "Who Wrote *Premier Etablissement de la Foy dans la Nouvelle France?" CHR* 57: 265–88.

Hanke, Lewis. 1959. *Aristotle and the American Indians.* Chicago: Regnery.

Harding, John. 1968. "Stereotypes." In Sills, 15: 259–62.

Harris, Marvin. 1968. *The Rise of Anthropological Theory: A History of Theories of Culture.* New York: Crowell.

Haven, Samuel. 1856. *Archaeology of the United States.* Smithsonian Contributions to Knowledge 8(2). Washington.

Haviland, W.A., and M. Power. 1981. *The Original Vermonters: Native Inhabitants, Past and Present.* Hanover, NH: University Press of New England.

Hawkes, C.F.C. 1954. "Archeological Theory and Method: Some Suggestions from the Old World." *AA* 56: 155–68.

Hayden, Brian. 1977. "Corporate Groups and the Late Ontario Iroquoian Longhouse." *OA* 28: 3–16.

– 1978. "Bigger is Better? Factors Determining Ontario Iroquois Site Sizes." *CJA* 2: 107–16.

– ed. 1979. *Settlement Patterns of the Draper and White Sites: 1973 Excavations.* Simon Fraser University, Department of Archaeology, Publication 6. Burnaby.

Hayes, C.F., III, ed. 1980. *Proceedings of the 1979 Iroquois Pottery Conference.* Rochester Museum and Science Center, Research Records 13.

Heckewelder, John. 1841. "Indian Tradition of the First Arrival of the Dutch at Manhattan Island, now New-York." *Collections of the New-York Historical Society,* 2nd series, 1: 69–74.

Heidenreich, C.E. 1967. "The Indian Occupance of Huronia, 1600–1650." In *Canada's Changing Geography,* edited by R.L. Gentilcore, 15–29. Scarborough: Prentice-Hall.

– 1971. *Huronia: A History and Geography of the Huron Indians, 1600–1650.* Toronto: McClelland and Stewart.

Helm, June, vol. ed. 1981. *Handbook of North American Indians.* Vol. 6, *Subarctic.* Washington: Smithsonian Institution.

Helms, Mary. 1970. "Matrilocality, Social Solidarity, and Culture Contact: Three Case Histories." *Southwestern Journal of Anthropology* 26: 197–212.

– 1978. "Time, History, and the Future of Anthropology: Observations on Some Unresolved Issues." *Eth.* 25: 1–13.

Henry, Jeanette. 1970. *Textbooks and the American Indian.* San Francisco: Indian Historian Press.

Heriot, George. 1804. *The History of Canada, from Its First Discovery ...* London: Longman and Rees.

Herskovits, M.J. 1953. *Franz Boas: The Science of Man in the Making.* New York: Scribner's.

Hickerson, Harold. 1970. *The Chippewa and Their Neighbors: A Study in Ethnohistory.* New York: Holt, Rinehart and Winston.

Hinsley, C.M., Jr. 1981. *Savages and Scientists: The Smithsonian Institution and the Development of American Anthropology, 1846–1910.* Washington: Smithsonian Institution Press.

Hodder, Ian. 1982*a*. *Symbols in Action: Ethnoarchaeological Studies of Material Culture.* Cambridge: Cambridge University Press.

– ed. 1982*b*. *Symbolic and Structural Archaeology.* Cambridge: Cambridge University Press.

– 1982*c*. *The Present Past: An Introduction to Anthropology for Archaeologists.* London: Batsford.

Hodgen, M.T. 1964. *Early Anthropology in the Sixteenth and Seventeenth Centuries.* Philadelphia: University of Pennsylvania Press.

Hoebel, E.A. 1960. "William Robertson: An 18th Century Anthropologist-Historian." *AA* 62: 648–55.

Hoffman, B.G. 1961. *Cabot to Cartier: Sources for a Historical Ethnography of Northeastern North America, 1497–1550.* Toronto: University of Toronto Press.

Hole, Frank, and R.F. Heizer. 1973. *An Introduction to Prehistoric Archeology.* 3rd ed. New York: Holt, Rinehart and Winston.

Holmes, W.H. 1903. "Aboriginal Pottery of the Eastern United States." *BAE,AR* 20: 1–237.

– 1914. "Areas of American Culture Characterization Tentatively Outlined as an Aid in the Study of the Antiquities." *AA* 16: 413–46.

Homans, G.C. 1962. *Sentiments and Activities: Essays in Social Science.* Glencoe: The Free Press.

Honigmann, J.J. 1976. *The Development of Anthropological Ideas.* Homewood, Ill.: Dorsey.

Honour, Hugh. 1975. *The New Golden Land: European Images of America from the Discoveries to the Present Time.* New York: Pantheon Books.

Hopkins, J.C. 1901. *The Story of the Dominion: Four Hundred Years in the Annals of Half a Continent.* Toronto: Winston.

Horsman, Reginald. 1967. *Expansion and American Indian Policy, 1783–1812.* East Lansing: Michigan State University Press.

– 1975. "Scientific Racism and the American Indian in the Mid-Nineteenth Century." *American Quarterly* 27: 152–68.

– 1981. *Race and Manifest Destiny: The Origins of American Racial Anglo-Saxonism.* Cambridge: Harvard University Press.

Hudson, Charles. 1966. "Folk History and Ethnohistory." *Eth.* 13: 52–70.

– 1973. "The Historical Approach in Anthropology." In *Handbook of Social and Cultural Anthropology*, edited by J.J. Honigmann, 111–41. Chicago: Rand McNally.

– 1976. *The Southeastern Indians*. Knoxville: University of Tennessee Press.

– 1981. "Why the Southeastern Indians Slaughtered Deer." In Krech, 155–76.

Humphreys, C.S. 1969. "History, Economics, and Anthropology: The Work of Karl Polanyi." *History and Theory* 8: 165–212.

Hunt, G.T. 1940. *The Wars of the Iroquois: A Study in Intertribal Trade Relations*. Madison: University of Wisconsin Press.

Hunter, W.A. 1959. "The Historic Role of the Susquehannocks." In Witthoft and Kinsey, 8–18.

Hurley, W.M., and C.E. Heidenreich, eds. 1969. *Palaeoecology and Ontario Prehistory*. University of Toronto, Department of Anthropology, Research Report 1.

– eds. 1971. *Palaeoecology and Ontario Prehistory II*. University of Toronto, Department of Anthropology, Research Report 2.

Huston, James, ed. 1893. *Le répertoire national ou recueil de littérature canadienne*. Vol. 2. Montreal: Valois.

Hymes, D.H. 1960. "Lexicostatistics So Far." *CA* 1: 3–44.

Ingstad, Helge. 1971. "Norse Sites at L'Anse aux Meadows." In Ashe, 175–96.

Innis, Harold. 1930. *The Fur Trade in Canada*. New Haven: Yale University Press.

– 1940. *The Cod Fisheries: The History of an International Economy*. New Haven: Yale University Press.

– 1956. *The Fur Trade in Canada: An Introduction to Canadian Economic History*. 2nd ed. Toronto: University of Toronto Press.

Jackes, M.K. 1983. "Osteological Evidence for Smallpox: A Possible Case from Seventeenth Century Ontario." *American Journal of Physical Anthropology* 60: 75–81.

Jackson, L.J. 1983. "Early Maize in South-Central Ontario." *AN* 83(3): 9–11.

Jacobs, W.R. 1974. "The Tip of an Iceberg: Pre-Columbian Indian Demography and Some Implications for Revisionism." *WMQ* 31: 123–32.

Jaenen, Cornelius. 1968. "The Frenchification and Evangelization of the Amerindians in the Seventeenth Century New France." *Canadian Catholic Historical Association, Study Sessions* 35: 57–71.

– 1976. *Friend and Foe: Aspects of French-Amerindian Cultural Contact in the Sixteenth and Seventeenth Centuries*. Toronto: McClelland and Stewart.

– 1978. "Conceptual Frameworks for French Views of America and Amerindians." *French Colonial Studies* 2: 1–22.

– 1980. "French Attitudes towards Native Society." In Judd and Ray, 59–72.

– 1982*a*. "Canada during the French Régime." In Muise, 3–44.

– 1982*b*. " 'Les Sauvages Amériquains': Persistence into the 18th Century of Traditional French Concepts and Constructs for Comprehending Amerindians." *Eth.* 29: 43–56.

Jameson, J.F., ed. 1909. *Narratives of New Netherland, 1609–1664.* New York: Scribner's.

Jamieson, J.B. 1982. "The Steward Site: A Study in St. Lawrence Iroquoian Chronology." MA thesis, Department of Anthropology, McGill University.

– 1983. "An Examination of Prisoner-Sacrifice and Cannibalism at the St. Lawrence Iroquoian Roebuck Site." *CJA* 7: 159–75.

Jamieson, S.M. 1981. "Economics and Ontario Iroquoian Social Organization." *CJA* 5: 19–30.

Jenness, Diamond. 1932. "Fifty Years of Archaeology in Canada." *Royal Society of Canada, Fifty Years Retrospect, Anniversary Volume, 1882–1932*: 71–6. Toronto: Ryerson Press.

– 1960. *The Indians of Canada.* 5th ed. NMC,B 65. Ottawa.

Jennings, Francis. 1963. "A Vanishing Indian: Francis Parkman versus His Sources." *Pennsylvania Magazine of History and Biography* 87: 306–23.

– 1971. "Goals and Functions of Puritan Missions to the Indians." *Eth.* 18: 197–212.

– 1975. *The Invasion of America: Indians, Colonialism, and the Cant of Conquest.* Chapel Hill: University of North Carolina Press.

– 1984. *The Ambiguous Iroquois Empire.* New York: Norton.

Jennings, J.D., ed. 1978. *Ancient Native Americans.* San Francisco: Freeman.

Johnson, G.A. 1981. "Monitoring Complex System Integration and Boundary Phenomena with Settlement Size Data." In *Archaeological Approaches to the Study of Complexity*, edited by S.E. van der Leeuw, 143–88. Amsterdam: Van Giffen Instituut.

Johnston, R.B. 1968*a*. *Archaeology of Rice Lake, Ontario.* National Museum of Canada, Anthropology Papers 19. Ottawa.

– 1968*b*. *The Archaeology of the Serpent Mounds Site.* Royal Ontario Museum, Occasional Paper 10. Toronto.

Johnston, R.B., and L.J. Jackson. 1980. "Settlement Pattern at the Le Caron Site, a 17th Century Huron Village." *Journal of Field Archaeology* 7: 173–99.

Jones, A.E. 1908. *"8endake Ehen"* or *Old Huronia.* Fifth Report of the Bureau of Archives for the Province of Ontario. Toronto.

Jones, H.M. 1964. *O Strange New World: American Culture: The Formative Years.* New York: Viking Press.

Jordan, W.D. 1968. *White over Black: American Attitudes toward the Negro, 1550–1812*. Chapel Hill: University of North Carolina Press.

Jouve, O.-M. 1914. "Une page inédite d'histoire canadienne." *La Nouvelle-France* 13: 433–44.

Judd, C.M., and A.J. Ray, eds. 1980. *Old Trails and New Directions: Papers of the Third North American Fur Trade Conference*. Toronto: University of Toronto Press.

Jury, W., and E.M. Jury. 1954. *Sainte-Marie Among the Hurons*. Toronto: Oxford University Press.

– 1955. *Saint Louis: Huron Indian Village and Jesuit Mission Site*. University of Western Ontario, Museum of Indian Archaeology, Bulletin 10.

Kapches, M.C. 1981. "The Middleport Pattern in Ontario Iroquoian Prehistory." PH D diss., Department of Anthropology, University of Toronto.

Kaplan, L. 1967. "Archaeological Phaseolus from Tehuacan." In *The Prehistory of the Tehuacan Valley*, vol. 1, edited by D.S. Byers, 201–11. Austin: University of Texas Press.

Keen, Benjamin. 1971. *The Aztec Image in Western Thought*. New Brunswick, NJ: Rutgers University Press.

Keene, A.S. 1981. *Prehistoric Foraging in a Temperate Forest: A Linear Programming Model*. New York: Academic Press.

Keiser, Albert. 1933. *The Indian in American Literature*. New York: Oxford University Press.

Kendrick, T.D. 1950. *British Antiquity*. London: Methuen.

Kennedy, Brenda. 1981. *Marriage Patterns in an Archaic Population: A Study of Skeletal Remains from Port au Choix, Newfoundland*. ASC,MS 104. Ottawa.

Kennedy, J.H. 1950. *Jesuit and Savage in New France*. New Haven: Yale University Press.

Kenyon, Ian. 1972. "The Neutral Sequence in the Hamilton Area." Paper presented at the fifth annual meeting of the Canadian Archaeological Association, St John's.

Kenyon, Ian, and Thomas Kenyon. 1982. "Comments on 17th Century Glass Trade Beads from Ontario." Rochester Museum and Science Center, Conference on Glass Trade Beads. Mimeographed.

Kenyon, Ian, and W. Fox. 1982. "The Grimsby Cemetery – A Second Look." *Kewa* 82(9): 3–16.

Kenyon, W.A. 1968. *The Miller Site*. Royal Ontario Museum, Occasional Paper 14. Toronto.

– 1982. *The Grimsby Site: A Historic Neutral Cemetery*. Toronto: Royal Ontario Museum.

Kidd, K.E. 1949a. *The Excavation of Ste. Marie I*. Toronto: University of Toronto Press.

– 1949b. "The Identification of French Mission Sites in the Huron Country: A Study in Procedure." *OH* 41: 89–94.

– 1950. "Orr Lake Pottery." *Transactions of the Royal Canadian Institute* 28(2): 165–85. Toronto.

– 1952. "Sixty Years of Ontario Archeology." In *Archeology of Eastern United States*, edited by J.B. Griffin, 71–82. Chicago: University of Chicago Press.

– 1953. "The Excavation and Historical Identification of a Huron Ossuary." *Am.Ant.* 18: 359–79.

– 1981. "A Radiocarbon Date on a Midewiwin Scroll from Burntside Lake, Ontario." *OA* 35: 41–3.

Kidd, K.E., and M.A. Kidd. 1970. "A Classification System for Glass Beads for the Use of Field Archaeologists." *Canadian Historic Sites, Occasional Papers in Archaeology and History* 1: 45–89.

Kidder, A.V. 1962. *An Introduction to the Study of Southwestern Archaeology*. With an Introduction, "Southwestern Archaeology Today," by Irving Rouse. Yale: Yale University Press (Kidder section originally published 1924).

Killan, Gerald. 1980. "The Canadian Institute and the Origins of the Ontario Archaeological Tradition, 1851–1884." *OA* 34: 3–16.

– 1983. *David Boyle: From Artisan to Archaeologist*. Toronto: University of Toronto Press.

Kingsford, William. 1887–98. *The History of Canada*. 10 vols. Toronto: Rowsell and Hutchison.

Kinietz, W.V. 1940. *The Indians of the Western Great Lakes, 1615–1760.* Ann Arbor: University of Michigan Press.

Ki-Zerbo, J., ed. 1981. *General History of Africa*. Vol. 1, *Methodology and African Prehistory*. Berkeley and Los Angeles: University of California Press.

Knight, Dean. 1978. "The Ball Site: A Preliminary Statement." *OA* 29: 53–63.

Knowles, Nathaniel. 1940. "The Torture of Captives by the Indians of Eastern North America." *PAPS* 82: 151–225.

Knudson, S.J. 1978. *Culture in Retrospect: An Introduction to Archaeology*. Chicago: Rand McNally.

Kohn, H. 1960. *The Mind of Germany*. New York: Scribner's.

Konrad, Victor. 1981. "An Iroquois Frontier: The North Shore of Lake Ontario during the Late Seventeenth Century." *Journal of Historical Geography* 7: 129–44.

Krech, Shepard, III, ed. 1981. *Indians, Animals, and the Fur Trade*. Athens: University of Georgia Press.

Kroeber, A.L. 1909. "The Archaeology of California." In *Putnam Anniversary Volume*, 1–42. New York: Stechert.

– 1939. *Cultural and Natural Areas of Native North America*. Berkeley: University of California Press.

Kroeber, A.L., et al., eds. 1943. *Franz Boas, 1858–1942*. AAA,M 61. Washington.

Kupperman, K.O. 1980. *Settling with the Indians: The Meeting of English and Indian Cultures in America, 1580–1640*. Totowa, NJ: Rowman and Littlefield.

Lanctôt, Gustave. 1946. *Garneau: historien national*. Montreal: Fides.

– 1963. *A History of Canada*. Vol. 1, *From Its Origins to the Royal Régime, 1663*. Toronto: Clarke, Irwin.

– 1964. *A History of Canada*. Vol. 2, *From the Royal Régime to the Treaty of Utrecht, 1663–1713*. Toronto: Clarke, Irwin.

– 1967. *Canada and the American Revolution, 1774–1783*. Toronto: Clarke, Irwin.

Larocque, Robert. 1980. "Les maladies chez les Iroquoiens préhistoriques." *RAQ* 10: 165–80.

La Roque de Roquebrune, R. 1966. "Le Febvre de La Barre, Joseph-Antoine." *DCB* 1: 442–6.

Latta, M.A. 1971. "Archaeology of the Penetang Peninsula." In Hurley and Heidenreich, 116–36.

– 1977. "The Iroquoian Cultures of Huronia: A Study of Acculturation through Archaeology." PH D diss., Department of Anthropology, University of Toronto.

Leacock, E.B., and N.O. Lurie, eds. 1971. *North American Indians in Historical Perspective*. New York: Random House.

Leacock, Stephen. 1941. *Canada: The Foundations of Its Future*. Montreal: Gazette.

Le Blant, R. 1972. "Le commerce compliqué des fourrures canadiennes au début du XVII$^e$ siècle." *RHAF* 26: 53–66.

Le Blant, R., and R. Baudry. 1967. *Nouveaux documents sur Champlain et son époque*. Vol. 1, (1560–1622). Publications of the Public Archives of Canada 15. Ottawa.

LeClair, E.E., Jr. 1962. "Economic Theory and Economic Anthropology." *AA* 64: 1179–1203.

LeClair, E.E., Jr., and H.K. Schneider, eds. 1968. *Economic Anthropology*. New York: Holt, Rinehart and Winston.

Le Clercq, Chrestien. 1691. *Premier établissement de la foy dans la Nouvelle France*. 2 vols. Paris: Auroy.

Lee, R.B., and I. DeVore. 1968. "Problems in the Study of Hunters and Gatherers." In Lee and DeVore, 3–12.

Lee, R.B., and I. DeVore, eds. 1968. *Man the Hunter*. Chicago: Aldine.

Lefebvre, Jean-Jacques, ed. 1945. *Centenaire de l'"Histoire du Canada" de François-Xavier Garneau*. Montreal: Société Historique de Montréal.

Legendre, Napoléon. 1884. "Les races indigènes de l'Amérique devant l'histoire." *TRSC*, 1st series, 2, i: 25–30. Ottawa.

Lenig, Donald. 1977. "Of Dutchmen, Beaver Hats and Iroquois." In *Current Perspectives in Northeastern Archaeology*, edited by R.E. Funk and C.F. Hayes, III, 71–84. Researches and Transactions of the New York State Archaeological Association 17(1). Buffalo.

Lennox, P.A. 1981. *The Hamilton Site: A Late Historic Neutral Town*. ASC,MS 103: 211–403. Ottawa.

– 1984. *The Hood Site: A Historic Neutral Town of 1640 A.D./The Bogle I and Bogle II Sites: Historic Neutral Hamlets of the Northern Tier*. ASC,MS 121. Ottawa.

Lescarbot, Marc. 1907–14. *The History of New France*. Translated by W.L. Grant. 3 vols. Toronto: The Champlain Society.

Levin, David. 1959. *History as Romantic Art: Bancroft, Prescott, Motley, and Parkman*. Stanford: Stanford University Press.

Lévi-Strauss, Claude. 1981. *The Naked Man*. Translated by J. and D. Weightman. New York: Harper and Row.

Lighthall, W.D. 1899. "Hochelagans and Mohawks; A Link in Iroquois History." *TRSC*, 2nd series, 5, ii: 199–211. Ottawa.

Linton, Ralph, ed. 1940. *Acculturation in Seven American Indian Tribes*. New York: Appleton-Century.

– 1944. "North American Cooking Pots." *Am.Ant.* 9: 369–80.

Lippmann, Walter. 1922. *Public Opinion*. New York: Macmillan.

Lloyd, H.M., ed. 1901. *League of the Ho-dé-no-sau-nee or Iroquois*, by L.H. Morgan. 2 vols. New York: Dodd, Mead.

Longley, W.H., and J.B. Moyle. 1963. *The Beaver in Minnesota*. Minnesota Department of Conservation, Technical Bulletin 6.

Lounsbury, F.G. 1978. "Iroquoian Languages." In Trigger 1978a, 334–43.

Lubbock, John (Lord Avebury). 1865. *Pre-historic Times, as Illustrated by Ancient Remains, and the Manners and Customs of Modern Savages*. London: Williams and Norgate.

– 1882. *The Origin of Civilisation and the Primitive Condition of Man*. 4th ed. London: Longmans, Green.

Lunn, Jean. 1939. "The Illegal Fur Trade out of New France, 1713–60." Canadian Historical Association, *Annual Report*, 61–76.

Lurie, N.O. 1961. "Ethnohistory: An Ethnological Point of View." *Eth.* 8: 78–92.

McBryde, Isabel. 1979. "Ethnohistory in an Australian Context: Independent Discipline or Convenient Data Quarry?" *Aboriginal History* 3: 128–51.

McCall, D.F. 1964. *Africa in Time-Perspective: A Discussion of Historical Reconstruction from Unwritten Sources*. Boston: Boston University Press.

McCardle, B.E. 1980. "The Life and Anthropological Works of Daniel Wilson (1816–1892)." MA thesis, Department of Anthropology, University of Toronto.

McDiarmid, Garnet, and David Pratt. 1971. *Teaching Prejudice*. Toronto: Ontario Institute for Studies in Education.

McGhee, Robert. 1982a. "Possible Norse-Eskimo Contacts in the Eastern Arctic." In Story, 31–40.

– 1982b. "Beneath the Streets of Montreal: Where is the Legendary City of Hochelaga?" Canadian Heritage (February): 19–21.

– 1984. "Contact between Native North Americans and the Medieval Norse: A Review of the Evidence." Am.Ant. 49: 4–26.

McGuire, J.D. 1899. "Pipes and Smoking Customs of the American Aborigines, Based on Material in the U.S. National Museum." Washington: United States National Museum, Annual Report, 1897, pt. 1: 351–645.

McIlwain, C.H., ed. 1915. An Abridgement of the Indian Affairs ... Transacted in the Colony of New York, from the Year 1678 to the Year 1751, by Peter Wraxall. Harvard Historical Studies 21. Cambridge.

McIlwraith, T.F. 1946. "Archaeological Work in Huronia, 1946: Excavations near Warminster." CHR 27: 394–401.

– 1948. The Bella Coola Indians. 2 vols. Toronto: University of Toronto Press.

– 1964. "Sir Daniel Wilson: A Canadian Anthropologist of One Hundred Years Ago." TRSC, 4th series, 2, ii: 129–36. Ottawa.

McKusick, M., and E. Wahlgren. 1980. "Vikings in America – Fact and Fiction." Early Man 2(4): 7–11.

Maclean, John. 1889. The Indians – Their Manners and Customs. Toronto: Briggs (2nd ed., 1907; reprinted by Coles Canadiana Collection, 1970).

– 1896. Canadian Savage Folk: The Native Tribes of Canada. Toronto: Briggs (reprinted by Coles Canadiana Collection, 1971).

McMullen, J.M. 1855. The History of Canada from Its First Discovery to the Present Time. Brockville: McMullen.

McNaspy, C.J. 1982. Lost Cities of Paraguay: Art and Architecture of the Jesuit Reductions, 1607–1767. Chicago: Loyola University Press.

McNeill, W.H. 1976. Plagues and Peoples. Garden City: Anchor Books.

MacNeish, R.S. 1952. Iroquois Pottery Types: A Technique for the Study of Iroquois Prehistory. NMC,B 124. Ottawa.

– 1972. "Comments on the Archaeology of the Dawson Site." In Pendergast and Trigger, 297–308.

McPherron, Alan. 1967. "On the Sociology of Ceramics: Pottery Style Clustering, Marital Residence, and Cultural Adaptations of an Algonkian-Iroquoian Border." In Tooker, 101–7.

Marshall, Joyce. 1967. Word from New France: The Selected Letters of Marie de l'Incarnation. Toronto: Oxford University Press.

Martijn, Charles. 1978. "Historique de la recherche archéologique au Québec." In Chapdelaine, 11–18.

Martin, Calvin. 1975. "The Four Lives of a Micmac Copper Pot." Eth. 22: 111–33.

– 1978. *Keepers of the Game: Indian-Animal Relationships and the Fur Trade.* Berkeley and Los Angeles: University of California Press.

– 1979. "The Metaphysics of Writing Indian-White History." *Eth.* 26: 153–9.

Mason, O.T. 1896. "Influence of Environment upon Human Industries or Arts." Smithsonian Institution, *Annual Report, 1895:* 639–65.

Mason, R.J. 1981. *Great Lakes Archaeology.* New York: Academic Press.

Mathews, Z.P. 1980. "Of Man and Beast: The Chronology of Effigy Pipes among Ontario Iroquoians." *Eth.* 27: 295–307.

Matthew, G.F. 1884. "Discoveries at a Village of the Stone Age at Bocabec, N.B." *Bulletin of the Natural History Society of New Brunswick* 3: 6–29.

Maurault, J.-P.-A. 1866. *Histoire des Abenakis depuis 1605 jusqu'à nos jours.* Sorel: Gazette.

Meister, C.W. 1976. "Demographic Consequences of Euro-American Contact on Selected American Indian Populations and Their Relationship to the Demographic Transition." *Eth.* 23: 161–72.

Meltzer, D.J. 1983. "The Antiquity of Man and the Development of American Archaeology." *Advances in Archaeological Method and Theory* 6: 1–51.

Miller, V.P. 1976. "Aboriginal Micmac Population: A Review of the Evidence." *Eth.* 23: 117–27.

– 1982. "The Decline of Nova Scotia Micmac Population, A.D. 1600–1850." *Culture* 2(3): 107–20.

Milner, G.R. 1980."Epidemic Disease in the Postcontact Southeast: A Reappraisal." *Mid-Continental Journal of Archaeology* 5(1): 39–56.

Mithun, Marianne. 1984. "The Proto-Iroquoians: Cultural Reconstruction from Lexical Materials." In *Extending the Rafters: Interdisciplinary Approaches to Iroquoian Studies,* edited by M.K. Foster, J. Campisi, and M. Mithun, 259–81. Albany: State University of New York Press.

Moeller, R.W., ed. 1977. *Archaeological Bibliography for Eastern North America.* Washington, Conn.: Eastern States Archaeological Federation and American Indian Archaeological Institute.

Molto, J.E. 1979. *Saugeen Osteology: The Evidence of the Second Cemetery at the Donaldson Site.* Museum of Indian Archaeology, Bulletin 14. London.

– 1983. *Biological Relationships of Southern Ontario Woodland Peoples: The Evidence of Discontinuous Cranial Morphology.* ASC,MS 117. Ottawa.

Monet, J. 1966. "Lauson, Jean de, senior." *DCB* 1: 427–9.

Monkman, Leslie. 1981. *A Native Heritage: Images of the Indian in English-Canadian Literature.* Toronto: University of Toronto Press.

Mooney, James. 1910. "Population." In *Handbook of American Indians North of Mexico,* edited by F.W. Hodge, 2: 286–7. BAE,B 30. Washington.

– 1928. *The Aboriginal Population of America North of Mexico*, edited by J.R. Swanton. Smithsonian Miscellaneous Collections 80(7).

Moore, F.W., ed. 1961. *Readings in Cross-Cultural Methodology*. New Haven: HRAF Press.

Moore, J.T. 1982. *Indian and Jesuit: A Seventeenth-Century Encounter*. Chicago: Loyola University Press.

Moorehead, W.K. 1910. *The Stone Age in North America*. 2 vols. Boston: Houghton Mifflin.

Morgan, L.H. 1851. *League of the Ho-dé-no-sau-nee, or Iroquois*. Rochester: Sage (reprinted as *League of the Iroquois*, New York: Corinth, 1962).

Morison, S.E. 1971. *The European Discovery of America: The Northern Voyages, A.D. 500–1600*. New York: Oxford University Press.

– 1972. *Samuel de Champlain: Father of New France*. Boston: Little, Brown and Company.

Morlot, A. 1861. "General Views on Archaeology." Smithsonian Institution, *Annual Report, 1860*: 284–343.

Mörner, M. 1953. *The Political and Economic Activities of the Jesuits in the La Plata Region – the Hapsburg Era*. Stockholm: Library and Institute of Ibero-American Studies.

Morton, W.L. 1957. *Manitoba: A History*. Toronto: University of Toronto Press.

– 1963. *The Kingdom of Canada*. Toronto: McClelland and Stewart.

Muise, D.A., ed. 1977. *Approaches to Native History in Canada: Papers of a Conference Held at the National Museum of Man, October, 1975*. National Museum of Man, History Division, Mercury Series, Paper 25. Ottawa.

– ed. 1982. *A Reader's Guide to Canadian History*. Vol. 1, *Beginnings to Confederation*. Toronto: University of Toronto Press.

Murdock, G.P. 1949. *Social Structure*. New York: Macmillan.

– 1959. *Africa, Its Peoples and Their Culture History*. New York: McGraw-Hill.

Murdock, G.P., and T.J. O'Leary. 1975. *Ethnographic Bibliography of North America*. 5 vols. New Haven: HRAF Press.

Murray, J.E. 1938. "The Early Fur Trade in New France and New Netherland." *CHR* 19: 365–77.

Naroll, Raoul. 1969. "The Causes of the Fourth Iroquois War." *Eth.* 16: 51–81.

Neumann, G.K. 1952. "Archeology and Race in the American Indian." In *Archeology of Eastern United States*, edited by J.B. Griffin, 13–34. Chicago: University of Chicago Press.

Noble, W.C. 1969. "Some Social Implications of the Iroquois 'In Situ' Theory." *OA* 13: 16–28.

– 1971. "The Sopher Celt: An Indicator of Early Protohistoric Trade in Huronia." *OA* 16: 42–7.

– 1972. "One Hundred and Twenty-five Years of Archaeology in the Canadian Provinces." *Bulletin of the Canadian Archaeological Association* 4: 1–78.

– 1978. "The Neutral Indians." In Engelbrecht and Grayson, 152–64.

– 1982. "Potsherds, Potlids, and Politics: An Overview of Ontario Archaeology during the 1970's." *CJA* 6: 167–94.

O'Brien, C.F. 1971. *Sir William Dawson: A Life in Science and Religion.* Philadelphia: The American Philosophical Society.

O'Callaghan, E.B., and B. Fernow, eds. 1853–87. *Documents Relating to the Colonial History of the State of New-York.* 15 vols. Albany: Weed, Parsons.

Olien, M.D. 1969. *Ethnohistory: A Bibliography.* Athens: University of Georgia, Department of Anthropology.

Orme, Bryony. 1981. *Anthropology for Archaeologists: An Introduction.* London: Duckworth.

Otterbein, K.F. 1964. "Why the Iroquois Won: An Analysis of Iroquois Military Tactics." *Eth.* 11: 56–63.

Ouellet, Fernand. 1981. "La formation d'une société dans la vallée du Saint-Laurent: d'une société sans classes à une société de classes." *CHR* 62: 407–50.

– 1982. "Quebec, 1760–1867." In Muise, 45–77.

Pagden, A. 1982. *The Fall of Natural Man.* Cambridge: Cambridge University Press.

Parker, A.C. 1907. *Excavations in an Erie Indian Village and Burial Site at Ripley, Chautauqua County, New York.* New York State Museum, Bulletin 117. Albany.

– 1916. "The Origin of the Iroquois as Suggested by Their Archaeology." *AA* 18: 479–507.

– 1920. *The Archaeological History of New York.* New York State Museum, Bulletin nos. 235–8. Albany.

Parkman, Francis. 1899. *The Conspiracy of Pontiac and the Indian War after the Conquest of Canada.* Toronto: George Morang (originally published 1851).

– 1927. *The Jesuits in North America in the Seventeenth Century.* Boston: Little, Brown and Company (originally published 1867).

Parry, J.H. 1966. *The Establishment of the European Hegemony, 1415–1715: Trade and Exploration in the Age of the Renaissance.* 3rd ed. New York: Harper Torchbooks.

– 1981. *The Discovery of the Sea.* Berkeley and Los Angeles: University of California Press.

Patterson, D.N., Jr. 1984. *A Diachronic Study of Dental Palaeopathology and Attritional Status of Prehistoric Ontario Pre-Iroquois and Iroquois Populations.* ASC,MS 122. Ottawa.

Patterson, E.P., II. 1972. *The Canadian Indian: A History since 1500.* Don Mills: Collier-Macmillan.

Pearce, R.H. 1965. *Savagism and Civilization: A Study of the Indian and the American Mind.* Baltimore: Johns Hopkins University Press.

– 1974. "From the History of Ideas to Ethnohistory." *Journal of Ethnic Studies* 2: 86–92.

Pearce, R.J. 1984. "Mapping Middleport: A Case Study in Societal Archaeology." PH D diss., Department of Anthropology, McGill University.

Pendergast, J.F. 1975. "An In-situ Hypothesis to Explain the Origin of the St. Lawrence Iroquoians." *OA* 25: 47–55.

– 1982a. "The Significance of a Huron Archaeological Presence in Jefferson County, New York." Paper read at McMaster University, 20 February 1982.

– 1982b. "The History of the St. Lawrence Iroquois and Some Recent Research." *AN* 82(1): 2–4.

– 1983. "Proto-Historic European Trade Routes into Iroquoia with Particular Emphasis on Ontario." Paper read to the Ontario Archaeological Society, tenth annual symposium, Toronto, 29 October.

Pendergast, J.F., and B.G. Trigger. 1972. *Cartier's Hochelaga and the Dawson Site.* Montreal: McGill-Queen's University Press.

Perrault, Joseph-François. 1832–6. *Abrégé de l'histoire du Canada.* 5 vols. Quebec: Ruthven.

Perrot, Nicolas. 1911. "Memoir on the Manners, Customs, and Religion of the Savages of North America." In Blair, 1: 23–272.

Perry, R.J. 1983. "Proto-Athapascan Culture: The Use of Ethnographic Reconstruction." *American Ethnologist* 10: 715–33.

Polanyi, Karl. 1944. *The Great Transformation.* New York: Farrar and Rinehart.

– 1957. "The Economy as Instituted Process." In Polanyi, Arensberg, and Pearson, 243–70.

– 1966. *Dahomey and the Slave Trade: An Analysis of an Archaic Economy.* Seattle: University of Washington Press.

Polanyi, K., C.M. Arensberg, and H.W. Pearson. 1957. *Trade and Market in the Early Empires.* Glencoe: The Free Press.

Popham, R.E. 1950. "Late Huron Occupations of Ontario: An Archaeological Survey of Innisfil Township." *OH* 42: 81–90.

Porter, H.C. 1979. *The Inconstant Savage: England and the North American Indian, 1500–1660.* London: Duckworth.

Poulton, D.R. 1980. *A Preliminary Report on the 1980 Archaeological Survey of the Catfish Creek Drainage, East Elgin County, Ontario.* Museum of Indian Archaeology, Research Report 11. London.

Powell, J.W. 1891. "Indian Linguistic Families of America North of Mexico."
    *BAE,AR* 7: 1–142.
Pratt, P.P. 1976. *Archaeology of the Oneida Iroquois*. Vol. 1. Occasional
    Publications in Northeastern Anthropology 1. Rindge, NH.
Prescott, W.H. 1909. *The Conquest of Mexico*. 2 vols. New York: Dutton
    (originally published 1843).
Prevec, R., and W.C. Noble. 1983. "Historic Neutral Iroquois Faunal
    Utilization." *OA* 39: 41–56.
Price, J.A. 1973. "The Stereotyping of North American Indians in Motion
    Pictures." *Eth.* 20: 153–71.
– 1978. *Native Studies: American and Canadian Indians*. Toronto: McGraw-
    Hill, Ryerson.
– 1979. *Indians of Canada: Cultural Dynamics*. Scarborough: Prentice-
    Hall.
Prichard, J.C. 1843. *The Natural History of Man; Comprising Inquiries
    into the Modifying Influence of Physical and Moral Agencies on the
    Different Tribes of the Human Family*. London: Bailliere.
Prucha, F.P. 1962. *American Indian Policy in the Formative Years: The
    Indian Trade and Intercourse Acts, 1790–1834*. Cambridge: Harvard
    University Press.
Quinn, D.B. 1966. *The Elizabethans and the Irish*. Ithaca: Cornell Uni-
    versity Press.
– 1977. *North America from Earliest Discovery to First Settlements: The
    Norse Voyages to 1612*. New York: Harper and Row.
– ed. 1979. *New American World: A Documentary History of North America
    to 1612*. 5 vols. New York: Arno and Bye.
– 1981. *Sources for the Ethnography of Northeastern North America to
    1611*. CES,MS 76. Ottawa.
Quinn, D.B., and A.M. Quinn. 1983. *The English New England Voyages,
    1602–1608*. London: The Hakluyt Society, 2nd series, vol. 161.
Ramenofsky, A.F. 1982. "The Archaeology of Population Collapse: Native
    American Response to the Introduction of Infectious Disease." PH D
    diss., Department of Anthropology, University of Washington, Seattle.
Ramsden, P.G. 1977. *A Refinement of Some Aspects of Huron Ceramic
    Analysis*. ASC,MS 63. Ottawa.
– 1978. "An Hypothesis Concerning the Effects of Early European Trade
    among some Ontario Iroquois." *CJA* 2: 101–5.
– 1981. "Rich Man, Poor Man, Dead Man, Thief: The Dispersal of Wealth
    in 17th Century Huron Society." *OA* 35: 35–40.
Rand, S.T. 1894. *Legends of the Micmacs*. New York: Longmans, Green.
Rands, R.L., and C.L. Riley. 1958. "Diffusion and Discontinuous Distri-
    bution." *AA* 60: 274–97.

Rawls, J.J. 1984. *Indians of California: The Changing Image*. Norman: University of Oklahoma Press.

Ray, A.J. 1974. *Indians in the Fur Trade*. Toronto: University of Toronto Press.

Ray, A.J., and D.B. Freeman. 1978. *"Give Us Good Measure."* Toronto: University of Toronto Press.

Raynal, Guillaume-Thomas. 1795. *Histoire philosophique et politique des établissemens et du commerce des Européens dans les deux Indes*. Vol. 8. Paris: Berry.

Redfield, R., R. Linton, and M.J. Herskovits. 1936. "Outline for the Study of Acculturation." *AA* 38: 149–52.

Reid, J.G. 1979. "The Significance of the Sixteenth Century for Atlantic Regional Historians." *Acadiensis* 8(2): 107–18.

Renfrew, A.C. 1975. "Trade as Action at a Distance: Questions of Integration and Communication." In *Ancient Civilization and Trade*, edited by J.A. Sabloff and C.C. Lamberg-Karlovsky, 3–59. Albuquerque: University of New Mexico Press.

– 1982. *Towards an Archaeology of Mind*. Cambridge: Cambridge University Press.

Resek, Carl. 1960. *Lewis Henry Morgan: American Scholar*. Chicago: University of Chicago Press.

Rich, E.E. 1960. "Trade Habits and Economic Motivation among the Indians of North America." *Canadian Journal of Economics and Political Science* 26: 35–53.

Richards, Cara. 1967. "Huron and Iroquois Residence Patterns, 1600–1650." In Tooker, 51–6.

Richaudeau, P.F. 1876. *Lettres de la révérende mère Marie de l'Incarnation (née Guyard)*. Paris: Casterman.

Richter, D.K. 1983. "War and Culture: The Iroquois Experience." *WMQ* 40: 528–59.

Ridley, F. 1947. "A Search for Ossossané and Its Environs." *OH* 39: 7–14.

– 1954. "The Frank Bay Site, Lake Nipissing, Ontario." *Am.Ant.* 20: 40–50.

– 1961. *Archaeology of the Neutral Indians*. Etobicoke: Etobicoke Historical Society.

Ringuet (Philippe Panneton). 1943. *Un monde était leur empire*. Montreal: Editions Variétés.

Ritchie, W.A. 1944. *The Pre-Iroquoian Occupations of New York State*. Rochester Museum of Arts and Sciences, Memoir 1.

– 1965. *The Archaeology of New York State*. Garden City: Natural History Press.

Ritchie, W.A., and R.E. Funk. 1973. *Aboriginal Settlement Patterns in the Northeast*. New York State Museum and Science Service, Memoir 20. Albany.

Rohner, R.P. 1966. "Franz Boas: Ethnographer on the Northwest Coast." In *Pioneers of American Anthropology*, edited by June Helm, 149–222. Seattle: University of Washington Press.

Ronda, J.P. 1977. " 'We Are Well as We Are': An Indian Critique of Seventeenth-Century Christian Missions." *WMQ* 34: 66–82.

– 1981. "Generations of Faith: The Christian Indians of Martha's Vineyard." *WMQ* 38: 369–94.

Ronda, J.P., and James Axtell. 1978. *Indian Missions: A Critical Bibliography*. Bloomington: Indiana University Press.

Roosa, W.B., and D.B. Deller. 1982. "The Parkhill Complex and Eastern Great Lakes Paleo Indian." *OA* 37: 3–15.

Rotstein, Abraham. 1967. "Fur Trade and Empire: An Institutional Analysis." PH D diss., Department of Political Economy, University of Toronto.

– 1970. "Karl Polanyi's Concept of Non-Market Trade." *Journal of Economic History* 30: 117–30.

– 1972. "Trade and Politics: An Institutional Approach." *Western Canadian Journal of Anthropology* 3(1): 1–28.

Rousseau, Jacques. 1945. *L'hérédité et l'homme*. Montreal: Les Editions de l'Arbre.

Rowbotham, A.H. 1966. *Missionary and Mandarin: The Jesuits at the Court of China*. New York: Russell and Russell.

Rowe, F.W. 1977. *Extinction: The Beothuks of Newfoundland*. Toronto: McGraw-Hill.

Ryerson, Stanley. 1960. *The Founding of Canada: Beginnings to 1815*. Toronto: Progress Books.

Sagard, Gabriel. 1866. *Histoire du Canada* ... 4 vols. Paris: Tross.

Salisbury, Neal. 1974. "Red Puritans: The 'Praying Indians' of Massachusetts Bay and John Eliot." *WMQ* 31: 27–54.

– 1975. "Prospero in New England: The Puritan Missionary as Colonist." In Cowan, 253–73.

– 1982. *Manitou and Providence: Indians, Europeans, and the Making of New England, 1500–1643*. New York: Oxford University Press.

Salisbury, R.F. 1968. "Anthropology and Economics." In LeClair and Schneider, 477–85.

Salwen, Bert. 1978. "Indians of Southern New England and Long Island: Early Period." In Trigger 1978a, 160–76.

Sanders, W.T. 1970. "The Population of the Teotihuacan Valley, the Basin of Mexico, and the Central Mexican Symbiotic Region in the Sixteenth Century." In *The Teotihuacan Valley Project, Final Report*, edited by W.T. Sanders, 1: 385–487. University Park: Pennsylvania State University.

Sapir, Edward. 1916. *Time Perspective in Aboriginal American Culture*. Canada Department of Mines, Memoir 90. Ottawa.

Sartre, Jean-Paul. 1963. *Search for a Method*. New York: Knopf.

Sauer, C.O. 1971. *Sixteenth Century North America: The Land and the People as Seen by the Europeans*. Berkeley and Los Angeles: University of California Press.

Saunders, S.R., D. Knight, and M. Gates. 1974. "Christian Island: A Comparative Analysis of Osteological and Archaeological Evidence." *Bulletin of the Canadian Archaeological Association* 6: 121–62.

Savage, H.G. 1971a. "Faunal Analysis of the Robitaille Site (BeHa-3) – Interim Report." In Hurley and Heidenreich, 166–72.

– 1971b. "Faunal Analysis of the Maurice Site (BeHa-2)." In Hurley and Heidenreich, 173–8.

Schäfer, Heinrich. 1974. *Principles of Egyptian Art*. Translated by John Baines. Oxford: Oxford University Press.

Schiffer, M.B. 1976. *Behavioral Archeology*. New York: Academic Press.

– ed. 1978–. *Advances in Archaeological Method and Theory* (issued annually). New York: Academic Press.

Schindler, D.L., G.J. Armelagos, and M.P. Bumsted. 1981. "Biocultural Adaptation: New Directions in Northeastern Anthropology." In Snow, 229–59.

Schlesier, K.H. 1976. "Epidemics and Indian Middlemen: Rethinking the Wars of the Iroquois, 1609–1653." *Eth.* 23: 129–45.

Schmalz, P.S. 1977. *The History of the Saugeen Indians*. Ontario Historical Society, Research Publication 5. Toronto.

Schwerin, K.H. 1976. "The Future of Ethnohistory." *Eth.* 23: 323–41.

Sheehan, B.W. 1973. *Seeds of Extinction: Jeffersonian Philanthropy and the American Indian*. Chapel Hill: University of North Carolina Press.

– 1980. *Savagism and Civility: Indians and Englishmen in Colonial Virginia*. New York: Cambridge University Press.

Shulman, Robert. 1971. "Parkman's Indians and American Violence." *Massachusetts Review* 12: 221–39.

Siebert, F.T., Jr. 1967. "The Original Home of the Proto-Algonquian People." NMC,B 214: 13–47. Ottawa.

Siegel, B.J., ed. 1972–. *Annual Review of Anthropology* (issued annually). Palo Alto: Annual Reviews Inc.

Sills, D.L., ed. 1968. *International Encyclopedia of the Social Sciences*. 17 vols. New York: Macmillan.

Silverberg, Robert. 1968. *Mound Builders of Ancient America: The Archaeology of a Myth*. Greenwich: New York Graphic Society.

Simpson, W.D. 1963. "Sir Daniel Wilson and the *Prehistoric Annals of Scotland*: A Centenary Study." *Proceedings of the Society of Antiquaries of Scotland* 96: 1–8. Edinburgh.

Skinner, Alanson. 1921. "Notes on Iroquois Archeology." Museum of the American Indian, Heye Foundation, *Indian Notes and Monographs* 18: 5–216. New York.

Smith, D.B. 1974. *Le Sauvage: The Native People in Quebec Historical Writing on the Heroic Period (1534–1663) of New France*. National Museum of Man, History Division, Mercury Series, Paper 6. Ottawa.

– 1981. "The Dispossession of the Mississauga Indians: A Missing Chapter in the Early History of Upper Canada." *OH* 73: 67–87.

Smith, H.I. 1910. "The Prehistoric Ethnology of a Kentucky Site." *Anthropological Papers of the American Museum of Natural History* 6, pt. 2: 173–241. New York.

Smith, P.E.L. 1972. "Land-use, Settlement Patterns and Subsistence Agriculture: A Demographic Perspective." In *Man, Settlement and Urbanism*, edited by P.J. Ucko, R. Tringham, and G.W. Dimbleby, 409–25. London: Duckworth.

Smith, W.M. 1970. "A Re-appraisal of the Huron Kinship System." *Anth.* 12: 191–206.

Smith, William. 1815. *History of Canada; From Its First Discovery, to the Peace of 1763*. Quebec: Neilson.

Snow, D.R. 1976a. *The Archaeology of North America: American Indians and Their Origins*. London: Thames and Hudson.

– 1976b. "The Ethnohistoric Baseline of the Eastern Abenaki." *Eth.* 23: 291–306.

– 1977. "Archaeology and Ethnohistory in Eastern New York." *Researches and Transactions of the New York State Archaeological Association* 17(1): 107–12. Buffalo.

– 1980. *The Archaeology of New England*. New York: Academic Press.

– ed. 1981. *Foundations of Northeast Archaeology*. New York: Academic Press.

Spence, M.W. 1982. "The Social Context of Production and Exchange." In *Contexts for Prehistoric Exchange*, edited by J. Ericson and T. Earle, 173–97. New York: Academic Press.

Spence, M.W., W.D. Finlayson, and R.H. Pihl. 1979. "Hopewellian Influences on Middle Woodland Cultures in Southern Ontario." In Brose and Greber, 115–21.

Spicer, E.H., ed. 1961. *Perspectives in American Indian Culture Change*. Chicago: University of Chicago Press.

– 1962. *Cycles of Conquest*. Tucson: University of Arizona Press.

Squier, E.G. 1849. *Aboriginal Monuments of the State of New York*. Smithsonian Contributions to Knowledge 2(9). Washington.

Squier, E.G., and E.H. Davis. 1848. *Ancient Monuments of the Mississippi Valley*. Smithsonian Contributions to Knowledge 1. Washington.

Stanley, G.F.G. 1949. "The Policy of 'Francisation' as Applied to the Indians during the Ancien Régime." *RHAF* 3: 333–48.

– 1950. "The First Indian 'Reserves' in Canada." *RHAF* 4: 178–210.

– 1960. *The Birth of Western Canada: A History of the Riel Rebellions.* Toronto: University of Toronto Press.

Stanton, William. 1960. *The Leopard's Spots: Scientific Attitudes toward Race in America, 1815–59.* Chicago: University of Chicago Press.

Starna, W.A. 1980. "Mohawk Iroquois Populations: A Revision." *Eth.* 27: 371–82.

Starna, W.A., G.R. Hamell, and W.L. Butts. 1984. "Northern Iroquoian Horticulture and Insect Infestation: A Cause for Village Removal." *Eth.* 31: 197–207.

Starr, F. 1892. "Anthropological Work in America." *Popular Science Monthly* 41: 289–307.

Stearn, E.A., and A.E. Stearn. 1945. *The Effect of Smallpox on the Destiny of the Amerindian.* Boston: Bruce Humphries.

Steckley, John. 1982. "The Clans and Phratries of the Huron." *OA* 37: 29–34.

Stephens, J.L. 1841. *Incidents of Travel in Central America, Chiapas, and Yucatan.* New York: Harper and Brothers.

Stern, B.J. 1933. "The Letters of Asher Wright to Lewis Henry Morgan." *AA* 35: 138–45.

Stocking, G.W., Jr. 1968. *Race, Culture, and Evolution: Essays in the History of Anthropology.* New York: Free Press.

– 1974. *A Franz Boas Reader: The Shaping of American Anthropology, 1883–1911.* New York: Basic Books.

– 1982. *Race, Culture, and Evolution: Essays in the History of Anthropology* (with a new preface). Chicago: University of Chicago Press.

Storck, P.L. 1984. "Research into the Paleo-Indian Occupations of Ontario: A Review." *OA* 41: 3–28.

Story, G.M., ed. 1982. *Early European Settlement and Exploitation in Atlantic Canada.* St John's: Memorial University of Newfoundland.

Stothers, D.M. 1977. *The Princess Point Complex.* ASC,MS 58. Ottawa.

– 1981. "Indian Hills (33Wo4): A Protohistoric Assistaeronon Village in the Maumee River Valley of Northwestern Ohio." *OA* 36: 47–56.

Stothers, D.M., and J.R. Graves. 1982. "Cultural Continuity and Change: The Western Basin, Ontario Iroquois, and Sandusky Traditions – A 1982 Perspective." Mimeographed.

Street, B.V. 1975. *The Savage in Literature: Representations of "Primitive" Society in English Fiction, 1858–1920.* London: Routledge and Kegan Paul.

Strong, W.D. 1940. "From History to Prehistory in the Northern Great Plains." *Smithsonian Miscellaneous Collections* 100: 353–94.

Sturtevant, W.C. 1966. "Anthropology, History, and Ethnohistory." *Eth.* 13: 1–51.

– 1981. "Animals and Disease in Indian Belief." In Krech, 177–88.

Sullivan, N.C. 1983. "Some Comments on John A. Dickinson's 'The Pre-Contact Huron Population: A Reappraisal.'" OH 75: 187–90.

Sulte, Benjamin. 1882–4. Histoire des Canadiens-français, 1608–1880. Montreal: Wilson.

Sutherland, G.E. 1980. "The Transition between the Early and Middle Ontario Iroquois Stages." AN 80(6): 13–37.

Swadesh, Morris. 1960. "On Interhemisphere Linguistic Connections." In Culture in History, edited by Stanley Diamond, 894–924. New York: Columbia University Press.

Sykes, C.M. 1980. "Swidden Horticulture and Iroquoian Settlement." Archaeology of Eastern North America 8: 45–52.

– 1981. "Northern Iroquoian Maize Remains." OA 35: 23–33.

Talbot, Francis. 1935. Saint among Savages: The Life of Isaac Jogues. New York: Harper and Brothers.

– 1956. Saint among the Hurons: The Life of Jean de Brébeuf. Garden City: Image Books.

Tanner, Adrian. 1979. Bringing Home Animals: Religious Ideology and Mode of Production of the Mistassini Cree Hunters. Institute of Social and Economic Research, Social and Economic Studies 23. St John's.

Tardits, Claude, ed. 1981. Contribution de la recherche ethnologique à l'histoire des civilisations du Cameroun. 2 vols. Paris: Editions du CNRS.

Taylor, W.W. 1948. A Study of Archeology. AAA,M 69. Menasha.

Thieme, Paul. 1964. "The Comparative Method for Reconstruction in Linguistics." In Language in Culture and Society, edited by Dell Hymes, 585–98. New York: Harper and Row.

Thomas, Cyrus. 1894. "Report on the Mound Explorations of the Bureau of Ethnology." BAE,AR 12: 3–742.

– 1898. Introduction to the Study of North American Archaeology. Cincinnati: Clarke.

Thomas, D.H. 1979. Archaeology. New York: Holt, Rinehart and Winston.

Thwaites, R.G. 1896–1901. The Jesuit Relations and Allied Documents. 73 vols. Cleveland: Burrows Brothers.

Timmins, Peter. 1984. "The Analysis and Interpretation of Radiocarbon Dates in Iroquoian Archaeology." MA thesis, Department of Anthropology, McGill University.

Tobias, J.L. 1983. "Canada's Subjugation of the Plains Cree, 1879–1885." CHR 64: 519–48.

Todorov, T. 1982. La conquête de l'Amérique: la question de l'autre. Paris: Seuil.

Tooker, Elisabeth. 1960. "Three Aspects of Northern Iroquoian Culture Change." PA 30(2): 65–71.

– 1963. "The Iroquois Defeat of the Huron: A Review of Causes." PA 33(1–2): 115–23.

– 1964. *An Ethnography of the Huron Indians, 1615–1649.* BAE,B 190. Washington.

– ed. 1967. *Iroquois Culture, History, and Prehistory.* Albany: The University of the State of New York.

– 1971. "Clans and Moieties in North America." *CA* 12: 357–76.

– 1978*a*. *The Indians of the Northeast: A Critical Bibliography.* Bloomington: Indiana University Press.

– 1978*b*. "The League of the Iroquois: Its History, Politics, and Ritual." In Trigger 1978*a*, 418–41.

Toulmin, S.E., and J. Goodfield. 1966. *The Discovery of Time.* New York: Harper and Row.

Trelease, A.W. 1960. *Indian Affairs in Colonial New York: The Seventeenth Century.* Ithaca: Cornell University Press.

Trevor-Roper, H.R. 1966. *The Rise of Christian Europe.* 2nd ed. London: Thames and Hudson.

Trigger, B.G. 1960. "The Destruction of Huronia: A Study in Economic and Cultural Change, 1609–1650." *Transactions of the Royal Canadian Institute* 33(1): 14–45. Toronto.

– 1962. "The Historic Location of the Hurons." *OH* 54: 137–48.

– 1963. "Settlement as an Aspect of Iroquoian Adaptation at the Time of Contact." *AA* 65: 86–101.

– 1966*a*. "Sir Daniel Wilson: Canada's First Anthropologist." *Anth.* 8: 3–28.

– 1966*b*. "Sir John William Dawson: A Faithful Anthropologist." *Anth.* 8: 351–9.

– 1968. "Archaeological and Other Evidence: A Fresh Look at the 'Laurentian Iroquois'." *Am.Ant.* 33: 429–40.

– 1969. *The Huron: Farmers of the North.* New York: Holt, Rinehart and Winston.

– 1971*a*. "The Mohawk-Mahican War (1624–28): The Establishment of a Pattern." *CHR* 52: 276–86.

– 1971*b*. "Champlain Judged by His Indian Policy: A Different View of Early Canadian History." *Anth.* 13: 85–114.

– 1972. "Hochelaga: History and Ethnohistory." In Pendergast and Trigger, 1–93.

– 1975. "Brecht and Ethnohistory." *Eth.* 22: 51–6.

– 1976. *The Children of Aataentsic: A History of the Huron People to 1660.* 2 vols. Montreal: McGill-Queen's University Press.

– vol. ed. 1978*a*. *Handbook of North American Indians.* Vol. 15, *Northeast.* Washington: Smithsonian Institution.

– 1978*b*. "William J. Wintemberg: Iroquoian Archaeologist." In Engelbrecht and Grayson, 5–21.

– 1978*c*. "Iroquoian Matriliny." *PA* 48(1–2): 55–65.

– 1978*d*. "The Strategy of Iroquoian Prehistory." In *Archaeological Essays* *in Honor of Irving B. Rouse,* edited by R.C. Dunnell and E.S. Hall, Jr., 275–310. The Hague: Mouton.

– 1978e. "Ethnohistory and Archaeology." *OA* 30: 17–24.

– 1979. "Sixteenth Century Ontario: History, Ethnohistory, and Archaeology." *OH* 71: 205–23.

– 1980. "Archaeology and the Image of the American Indian." *Am.Ant.* 45: 662–76.

– 1981a. "Giants and Pygmies: The Professionalization of Canadian Archaeology." In *Towards a History of Archaeology,* edited by Glyn Daniel, 69–84. London: Thames and Hudson.

– 1981b. "Prehistoric Social and Political Organization: An Iroquoian Case Study." In Snow, 1–50.

– 1982a. "Response of Native Peoples to European Contact." In Story, 139–55.

– 1982b. "Indians and Ontario's History." *OH* 74: 246–57.

– 1982c. "Ethnohistory: Problems and Prospects." *Eth.* 29: 1–19.

– 1983. "American Archaeology as Native History: A Review Essay." *WMQ* 40: 413–52.

– 1984. "The Road to Affluence: A Reassessment of Early Huron Responses to European Contact." In *Affluence and Cultural Survival,* edited by R.F. Salisbury and Elisabeth Tooker, 12–25. Washington: American Ethnological Society.

Trigger, B.G., L. Yaffe, et al. 1980. "Trace-Element Analysis of Iroquoian Pottery." *CJA* 4: 119–45.

Trudel, Marcel. 1963. *Histoire de la Nouvelle-France.* Vol. 1, *Les vaines tentatives, 1524–1603.* Montreal: Fides.

– 1966a. *Histoire de la Nouvelle-France.* Vol. 2, *Le comptoir, 1604–1627.* Montreal: Fides.

– 1966b. "Caën, Guillaume de." *DCB* 1: 159–62.

– 1966c. "Cartier, Jacques." *DCB* 1: 165–72.

– 1966d. "Champlain, Samuel de." *DCB* 1: 186–99.

– 1966e. "Gravé Du Pont, François." *DCB* 1: 345–6.

– 1968. *Initiation à la Nouvelle-France.* Montreal: Holt, Rinehart and Winston.

– 1973. *The Beginnings of New France, 1524–1663.* Toronto: McClelland and Stewart.

– 1979. *Histoire de la Nouvelle-France.* Vol. 3, *La seigneurie des Cent-Associés, 1627–1663, I: Les événements.* Montreal: Fides.

Tuck, J.A. 1971. *Onondaga Iroquois Prehistory: A Study in Settlement Archaeology.* Syracuse: Syracuse University Press.

– 1976. *Newfoundland and Labrador Prehistory.* Ottawa: National Museum of Man.

– 1977. "A Look at Laurentian." *Researches and Transactions of the New York State Archaeological Association* 17(1): 31–40. Buffalo.

– 1982. "A Sixteenth Century Whaling Station at Red Bay, Labrador." In Story, 41–52.

Turgeon, L. 1982. "Pêcheurs basques et Indiens des côtes du Saint-Laurent au XVIᵉ siècle." *Canadian Studies* 13: 9–14.

Turnbull, C.M. 1968. "The Importance of Flux in Two Hunting Societies." In Lee and DeVore, 132–7.

Tyyska, A.E. 1968. "Settlement Patterns at Cahiague." Report submitted to the Archaeological and Historic Sites Board of the Province of Ontario. Toronto.

Tyyska, A.E., and W.M. Hurley. 1969. "Maurice Village and the Huron Bear." Paper presented at the second annual meeting of the Canadian Archaeological Association, Toronto.

Ubelaker, D.H. 1976. "Prehistoric New World Population Size: Historical Review and Current Appraisal of North American Estimates." *American Journal of Physical Anthropology* 45: 661–5.

Upton, L.F.S. 1979. *Micmacs and Colonists: White-Indian Relations in the Maritimes, 1713–1867.* Vancouver: University of British Columbia Press.

– 1980. "Contact and Conflict on the Atlantic and Pacific Coasts of Canada." *Acadiensis* 9(2): 3–13.

Vachon, André. 1960. "L'eau-de-vie dans la société indienne." Canadian Historical Association, *Annual Report*, 23–32.

– 1966. "Dollard Des Ormeaux, Adam." *DCB* 1: 266–75.

van der Merwe, N., and J.C. Vogel. 1978. "13C Content of Human Collagen as a Measure of Prehistoric Diet in Woodland North America." *Nature* 276: 815–16.

Van Laer, A.J.F., ed. 1924. *Documents Relating to New Netherland, 1624–1626, in the Henry E. Huntington Library.* San Marino, Calif.: Huntington Library.

Vansina, Jan. 1965. *Oral Tradition: A Study in Historical Methodology.* Chicago: Aldine.

Vastokas, J.M., and R.K. Vastokas. 1973. *Sacred Art of the Algonkians: A Study of the Peterborough Petroglyphs.* Peterborough: Mansard Press.

Vaugeois, Denis. 1978. "Réponse au texte de Sylvie Vincent." *Bulletin de la Société des Professeurs d'Histoire du Québec* 14(2): 29–30.

Vaughan, A.T. 1979. *New England Frontier: Puritans and Indians, 1620–1675.* 2nd ed. New York: Norton.

– 1982. "From White Man to Red Skin: Changing Anglo-American Perceptions of the American Indian." *American Historical Review* 87: 917–53.

Vincent, Sylvie. 1978a. "Les manuels d'histoire, sont-ils porteurs de stéréotypes sur les Amérindiens? ou que sont devenus le 'bon Huron' et le 'méchant Iroquois'? " *Bulletin de la Société des Professeurs d'Histoire du Québec* 14(2): 26–9.

– 1978b. "Réponse à une critique de Denis Vaugeois: et si on se bricolait un autre mythe national?" *Bulletin de la Société des Professeurs d'Histoire du Québec* 16(4): 33–6.

Vincent, Sylvie, and Bernard Arcand. 1979. *L'image de l'Amérindien dans les manuels scolaires du Québec.* Montreal: Hurtubise.

Vogel, J.C., and N. van der Merwe. 1977. "Isotopic Evidence for Early Maize Cultivation in New York State." *Am.Ant.* 42: 238–42.

Voget, F.W. 1975. *A History of Ethnology.* New York: Holt, Rinehart and Winston.

von Gernet, Alexander. 1982. "Analysis of Intrasite Artifact Spatial Distributions: The Draper Site Smoking Pipes." MA thesis, Department of Anthropology, McGill University.

Wade, Mason. 1942. *Francis Parkman: Heroic Historian.* New York: Viking Press.

– 1956. *The French Canadians: 1760–1945.* Toronto: Macmillan.

Walker, J.W. St G. 1971. "The Indian in Canadian Historical Writing." *Canadian Historical Association, Historical Papers* 1971: 21–47.

– 1983. "The Indian in Canadian Historical Writing, 1972–1982." In *As Long as the Sun Shines and Water Flows: A Reader in Canadian Native Studies,* edited by I.A.L. Getty and A.S. Lussier, 340–57. Vancouver: University of British Columbia Press.

Wallace, A.F.C. 1957. "The Origins of Iroquois Neutrality: The Grand Settlement of 1701." *Pennsylvania History* 24: 223–35.

– 1958. "Dreams and the Wishes of the Soul: A Type of Psychoanalytic Theory among the Seventeenth Century Iroquois." *AA* 60: 234–48.

Wallace, P.A.W. 1946. *The White Roots of Peace.* Port Washington, NY: Kennikat Press.

Wallerstein, Immanuel. 1974. *The Modern World-System.* Vol. 1. New York: Academic Press.

– 1980. *The Modern World-System.* Vol. 2. New York: Academic Press.

Warrick, Gary. 1984. *Reconstructing Ontario Iroquoian Village Organization.* ASC,MS 124: 1–180. Ottawa.

Washburn, W.E. 1961. "Ethnohistory: History 'In the Round.' " *Eth.* 8: 31–48.

– 1971. "The Writing of American Indian History: A Status Report." *Pacific Historical Review* 40: 261–81.

Watkins, Trevor, ed. 1975. *Radiocarbon: Calibration and Prehistory.* Edinburgh: University of Edinburgh Press.

Wedel, W.R. 1936. *An Introduction to Pawnee Archeology.* BAE,B 112. Washington.

Wenke, R.J. 1980. *Patterns in Prehistory*. New York: Oxford University Press.

Whallon, Robert, Jr. 1968. "Investigations of Late Prehistoric Social Organization in New York State." In *New Perspectives in Archeology*, edited by S.R. Binford and L.R. Binford, 223–44. Chicago: Aldine.

White, M.E. 1971. Review of *The Bennett Site*. *Am.Ant.* 36: 222–3.

Wilcox, D.R., and W.B. Masse, eds. 1981. *The Protohistoric Period in the North American Southwest, AD 1450–1700*. Arizona State University, Anthropological Research Papers 24.

Willey, G.R. 1966. *An Introduction to American Archaeology*. Vol. 1, *North and Middle America*. Englewood Cliffs: Prentice-Hall.

Willey, G.R., and J.A. Sabloff. 1980. *A History of American Archaeology*. 2nd ed. San Francisco: Freeman.

Williamson, R.F. 1983a. *The Robin Hood Site: A Study of Functional Variability in Late Iroquoian Settlement Patterns*. Ontario Archaeological Society, Monographs in Ontario Archaeology 1. Peterborough.

– 1983b. "The Mill Stream Cluster: The Other Side of the Coin." *Kewa* 83(1): 3–12.

Wilson, Daniel. 1851. *The Archaeology and Prehistoric Annals of Scotland*. Edinburgh: Sutherland and Knox (2nd ed., 1863).

– 1862. *Prehistoric Man: Researches into the Origin of Civilization in the Old and the New World*. London: Macmillan (3rd ed., 1876).

– 1884. "The Huron-Iroquois of Canada, A Typical Race of American Aborigines." *TRSC*, 1st series, 2, ii: 55–106. Ottawa.

Wintemberg, W.J. 1931. "Distinguishing Characteristics of Algonkian and Iroquoian Cultures." NMC,B 67: 65–125. Ottawa.

– 1939. *Lawson Prehistoric Village Site, Middlesex County, Ontario*. NMC,B 94. Ottawa.

Wissler, Clark. 1914. "Material Cultures of the North American Indians." *AA* 16: 447–505.

– 1943. "The American Indian and the American Philosophical Society." *PAPS* 86(1): 189–204.

Witthoft, John. 1959. "Ancestry of the Susquehannocks." In Witthoft and Kinsey, 19–60.

– 1966. "Archaeology as a Key to the Colonial Fur Trade." *Minnesota History* 40: 203–9.

Witthoft, John, and W.F. Kinsey, III, eds. 1959. *Susquehannock Miscellany*. Harrisburg: Pennsylvania Historical and Museum Commission.

Wood, William. 1634. *New Englands Prospect. A True, Lively and Experimentall Description of that Part of America, Commonly Called New England*. London: Thomas Cotes.

Wray, C.F. 1973. *Manual for Seneca Iroquois Archeology*. Honeoye Falls, NY: Cultures Primitive.

Wray, C.F., and H.L. Schoff. 1953. "A Preliminary Report on the Seneca Sequence in Western New York, 1550–1687." *PA* 23(2): 53–63.

Wright, J.L., Jr. 1981. *The Only Land They Knew: The Tragic Story of the American Indians in the Old South*. New York: Free Press.

Wright, J.V. 1966. *The Ontario Iroquois Tradition*. NMC,B 210. Ottawa.

– 1967. *The Laurel Tradition and the Middle Woodland Period*. NMC,B 217. Ottawa.

– 1972. *Ontario Prehistory: An Eleven-Thousand-Year Archaeological Outline*. Ottawa: National Museums of Canada.

– 1974. *The Nodwell Site*. ASC,MS 22. Ottawa.

– 1979. *Quebec Prehistory*. Toronto: Van Nostrand Reinhold.

– 1984. "The Cultural Continuity of the Northern Iroquoian-Speaking Peoples." In *Extending the Rafters: Interdisciplinary Approaches to Iroquoian Studies*, edited by M.K. Foster, J. Campisi, and M. Mithun, 283–99. Albany: State University of New York Press.

Wright, M.J. 1981. *The Walker Site*. ASC,MS 103: 1–210. Ottawa.

Wrong, G.M., ed. 1939. *The Long Journey to the Country of the Hurons*. Toronto: The Champlain Society.

Yarnell, R.A. 1964. *Aboriginal Relationships between Culture and Plant Life in the Upper Great Lakes Region*. University of Michigan, Anthropological Papers 23.

# Index